Forensic Gait Analysis

Forensic Gait Analysis

Haydn D. Kelly

CRC Press
Taylor & Francis Group
Boca Raton London New York

CRC Press is an imprint of the
Taylor & Francis Group, an **informa** business

First edition published 2020
by CRC Press
6000 Broken Sound Parkway NW, Suite 300, Boca Raton, FL 33487-2742
and by CRC Press
2 Park Square, Milton Park, Abingdon, Oxon, OX14 4RN

ISBN: 978-1-4665-0414-1 (hbk)
ISBN: 978-1-315-37455-0 (ebk)

Typeset in Palatino
by Deanta Global Publishing Services, Chennai, India
Deanta Global Publishing Services, Dublin, Ireland

CONTENTS

FOREWORD BY PETER JAMES

It is a truism that we owe so much of our modern technology and medicine to warfare, where rapid advances take place out of necessity. The fight against crime, too, results in constantly advancing law enforcement technology, in particular, in the forensic sciences, and these have been complemented by advances in other fields which I try hard to keep abreast of, and which will undoubtedly continue to expand in the age of a digital revolution and beyond.

For the past twenty-five years, in the course of research for my crime thrillers, I've spent a great deal of time with both investigators and, sometimes, villains too. Two of the most significant things I have observed are that, firstly the criminal status quo is constantly changing, and secondly, there is a constant game of catch-up going on between law enforcement and felons, which creates a real dynamic, in trying to keep us safe.

I was attending a 0900 hours daily briefing meeting in Brighton Police Station, one Monday morning, around fifteen years ago, when the Divisional Commander turned to me and said, 'Peter you've come on a historic day. This is the first time since records began that there has not been an overnight domestic burglary in the city.'

'Congratulations!' I replied. 'So you've won the war on crime!'

He laughed, and said that the old school style of *creeper* burglar – the kind who shins up your drainpipe in the middle of the night and steals your silverware and jewellery – was becoming a dinosaur. He could make much more money out of drug dealing, or the very latest area of crime, internet fraud, and with a less severe sentence if caught.

It wasn't so long ago that some police officers' kit comprised a whistle and a truncheon, together with special police phone booths, just like Dr Who's tardis, that they could run too in order to make an emergency call or to report their whereabouts. Now GPS trackers tells the Control Room exactly where every officer is; and he or she has Captor spray and many carry a taser and other modern equipment. In some areas they patrol on a Segway. And the high-tech and cybercrime units are the fastest growing areas in many police departments but that's not all that is evolving!

Technology has always interested me and having co-founded an internet service provider in the early 1990s I realised right back then that alongside its potential to become the Information Superhighway, the internet was also likely to open up a whole new area of violations needing to be countered.

In 1994 in addition to the usual print formats, Penguin published my science thriller, *Host*, on two floppy discs, billing it as the world's first electronic novel – and I'm very proud there is a copy of it in the Science Museum, London.

The creation of new things and the development of science never cease to amaze me and I feel it is vital always to be on the cutting edge for my books to feel current – and that means being abreast of the advances in law enforcement.

Occasionally in the course of my research I strike gold, and I consider the day I met Haydn Kelly to be just that. We were introduced at a dinner by a mutual friend in the security business, and from the moment I discovered that Haydn was a pioneering specialist in Forensic Podiatry – something I had not heard about – I pestered him with questions for the rest of the evening around the remarkable area of forensics he had created and which was first introduced as admissible evidence in criminal law in 2000, at the Old Bailey Central Criminal Court in London – Forensic Gait Analysis. To introduce a new form of identification to the forensic toolbox, and for that to be utilised in legal systems around the world, is a considerable undertaking and a rare achievement. I found it not only fascinating, but saw an opportunity to write about an area of expertise in the battle against crime that no author had yet used. Haydn has subsequently appeared in nine of my most recent Detective Superintendent Roy Grace novels as himself (right down to the details of the clothes he wears!) and forensic podiatry has become a major weapon in Grace's armoury for solving homicide cases.

I've had comments from many police officers around the world, who had not previously heard of this developing field, so quite apart from now being a good friendship, it is a great symbiotic relationship that Haydn and I have – he's brought me the ability to write innovative aspects that are deployed in homicide investigations, that have never before appeared in fiction, and I hope through my novels and works to have brought this invaluable new tool in the fight against crime – of all kinds – to a wider law enforcement audience.

Peter James
www.peterjames.com

FOREWORD BY
DR WILLIAM A. WOOD

The involvement of healthcare professionals in forensic sciences has expanded the tools available in the examination of crime scene evidence. Podiatrists bring to the table a bedrock understanding of human biomechanics and ambulation. Which not only has an essential role in the clinical diagnosis and treatment of many conditions, but also qualifying and quantifying individual human gait patterns observed at crime scenes and related environments.

Traditionally, forensic evidence in connection with the foot has involved aspects such as the evaluation of static findings and physical evidence associated with a crime scene. Generally, these have included footprints and footwear impressions with various techniques for capturing imprints, which also reveal elements such as foot angulation, step and stride lengths. Numerous methods have evolved to categorise incriminating or exclusionary evidence to a class level of findings, or ideally, to a specific individual's characteristics and probabilistic evidential value. Review of medical records are also useful when considering the presence of any underlying pathology, injury or surgery that can affect an individual's style or manner of walking or running gait – that is, movement of the whole body from the head to feet; where permutations of variability can have effects at micro and macro levels.

Forensic gait analysis engages a person's gait or features of their gait as physical evidence in the form of CCTV material and other video footage associated with a crime scene. The widening prevalence of CCTV and other video footage is indispensable in assisting the identification of an individual, including where disguises occur. Evaluation of the gait displayed on CCTV footage of an unknown individual and comparison to those of a suspect/s is the essence of forensic gait analysis.

With increased processing power and storage capacity of computers, and the incorporation of sophisticated software technology, it would not be unexpected to realise the facility to identify an individual by their gait remotely.

This publication is a definitive text on forensic gait analysis. We are grateful for the insights into this forensic specialty which this book has given us.

William A. Wood, DPM, MPH
Diplomate, American Board of Foot and Ankle Surgery (ABFAS)
Fellow, American College of Foot and Ankle Surgeons (ACFAS)

PREFACE

Is anything truly new or are innovations formed from what is already in existence? The genesis of forensic gait analysis included a combination of factors which helped shape the inception. The first use and admissibility of forensic gait analysis as expert evidence in criminal law was in July 2000, [R v Saunders], at the Old Bailey Central Criminal Court, London. During the writing and compiling of this first book and introduction to the subject of forensic gait analysis, one has remained innately aware of the need to try and help those engaged with the use of this forensic tool, whether for evidential, investigative, educational or other purposes. In three decades of providing expert evidence for use in the civil and criminal justice systems and in different jurisdictions, one sees the need for experts to have comprehension on what is required of them by the various legal structures, including expert witness training. When absent, the tasks are so much more challenging all around. Recognising the same is also helpful and well understood by those who engage in reflective practice and a long tenet of the medical professions.

Whether reading here for general interest or for more particular purposes on the subject of forensic gait analysis, the aim of this treatise is geared to be of broad assistance including healthcare professionals, lawyers, counsel, investigators, forensic practitioners, and students wishing to know more on the subject.

An 'expert' in any area has two roles: as a specialist in their chosen field and as an expert witness. Many an expert has been undone in the courtroom not necessarily because they do not know their subject, but because they do not understand the arena in which they are in. It is so very, very true and often avoidable with proper expert witness training that sits alongside the requisite specialist knowledge an expert has in their area of expertise. This is vital and includes report writing, cross-examination, courtroom skills and law and procedure, insofar as they relate to the duties and responsibilities of an expert, and as per the relevant court rules and jurisdiction. Without such skills, it could perhaps be more gently described as akin to one's turn to go to the bar for a round of drinks, only to forget the order on arrival.

The role, duty and responsibilities of an expert do not usually vary widely between jurisdictions. But the appreciation of the subtlety and learned use of lucid communication in the legal systems, and the effects thereof, can be more so. With such knowledge comes the delivery of clear and concise material in the form of expert's opinions, reports, and oral evidence, and avoiding the overuse of technical language becomes much less enduring. It also significantly contributes to narrowing the issues. Whilst solid knowledge in the subject area should be a given, without education and training in the skills required to properly deliver that information into the legal arena as an 'expert', the effects can at one end be testing and at the other potentially devastating. Simply because one may have expertise in one area, it does not follow that they do so in another. To know is one thing and to realise is another.

Any area of science and practice is about acknowledging what we can and cannot reliably say. Having a balanced approach is a must and is required of all experts providing evidence, and being aware of limitations is important in any area of practice. We should remember that all forms of identification are based on probability. Bearing in mind that whilst one may not be aware of technical information or material, it does not follow that it does not exist. As the math area of calculus shows us, there is more than one solution to a problem. Or, put another way on a lighter note, as illustrated by the words of Inspector Harry Callaghan (Clint Eastwood) when declaring to his superior Lieutenant Briggs in the film *Magnum Force*, 'A good man always knows his limitations' ('man' being gender neutral).

Gait analysis is a longstanding component of the diagnostic and therapeutic toolset of medical disciplines, although the knowledge of 'gait' goes back much further. It is also the subject of laboratory analysis and has attracted the interest of technology engineers and others. The appreciation and utilisation of forensic gait analysis is but one of many instruments in the forensic toolbox and the jigsaw of evidence. How forensic gait analysis is accomplished and deployed is what determines its usefulness and there are a number of aspects to consider in forensic gait analysis which are inextricably linked. The chapters herein begin with: Gait Analysis – A Historical Overview; followed by Observational Gait Analysis – Progression and Application; Neurological Disorders Affecting Gait; Emotions and Gait; Video Image Analysis; Gait Analysis in Identification; Height Estimation Using the Foot or Lower Limb as a Dimension; Photogrammetry; Interpreting and Communicating Forensic Statistics; Reports and Report Writing; Expert Evidence in Court; and The Expert in Court – The Expert's Perspective.

Having been asked whether there are any principally entertaining aspects that have come to my attention with forensic gait analysis, there are several. In brief, an occasion in cross-examination when counsel presented a particularly convoluted question to the expert. Having paused to consider the question and needing to refer to their report which took a little time before answering, the expert cordially requested whether counsel could kindly repeat the question. Along with a bemused look came the reply, 'we will come back to that.' An instance where counsel being late in attendance at court one morning with the explanation, 'apologies your honour, my wet cat walked all over my notes on the kitchen table.' Of course, such situations are not rehearsed and merely illustrate the serious business and exchanges of the courtroom can result in unintentional quips.

The intention of this introductory text is to assist in the knowledge and understanding of forensic gait analysis and to encourage further learning and development.

Haydn D. Kelly

ACKNOWLEDGEMENTS

There is much that goes into the writing, compiling and production of a book and may I take this opportunity to express my gratitude to all involved.

A very special thanks to those who have contributed to the chapters.

Mrs Sue Hardiman: Gait Analysis – A Historical Overview.

Dr Emma Cowley: Observational Gait Analysis – Progression and Application.

Dr Stephen J. Wroe: Neurological Disorders Affecting Gait.

Dr Orlando Trujillo Bueno: Emotions and Gait.

Mr Jon Walklin and Mr Clive Evans: Video Image Analysis.

Dr J. Gordon Burrow: Height Estimation Using the Lower Limb or Foot as a Dimension.

Prof. Niels Lynnerup and Dr Peter Kastmand Larsen: Photogrammetry.

Prof. Atholl Johnston: Interpreting and Communicating Forensic Statistics.

Mr Mark Solon: Reports and Report Writing.

Mr Barry E. Francis: The Expert in Court – The Expert's Perspective.

Also, to Mr Barry E. Francis and Dr J. Gordon Burrow for reviewing the chapter on Gait Analysis in Identification. Dr Mike Curran for reviewing the section on footwear too.

Counsel and advocates for sharing and suggestions in relation to the chapter on Expert Evidence in Court. Thank you. Special thanks also to Brian Rust for the brilliant illustrations. Jens Vedel for several graphics in the chapter on Photogrammetry. Dominic Hardiman for providing additional information to the chapter on Gait Analysis – A Historical Overview.

In the early years, David Randle (lawyer) for suggesting all those years ago to engage in medico-legal matters with expert witness work. Geoff Oxlee (formerly of Kalagate Imagery). Control Risks Group. Ian Evett (formerly of the forensic science service) for a steer on statistical aspects at the outset of forensic gait analysis. Kate Horne (former CEO and head of policy development at the Council for the Registration of Forensic Practitioners) and my role as a lead assessor in forensic podiatry.

Thanks also along the way to Prof. Alon Wolf. Also, to Yongseok Choi. To Jo for her administration assistance in more years than I can remember.

Colleagues and friends in the USA and their inspiring vista. For the support of colleagues as the founding Chair of the Forensic Podiatry Group (UK). Bond Solon Expert Witness Training. The Expert Witness Institute. The Faculty of Podiatric Surgery (UK) for backing and activity in my term as Dean, in promoting and furthering advancement and development of podiatric surgery skills for the benefit and health of the public, all of which whilst this book was in progress.

I must single out all those involved at CRC Press/Taylor & Francis and Deanta Global for their invaluable succour. Also, Becky Masterman (author and formerly of CRC Press), who first helped initiate bringing this book to life whilst at CRC Press.

Peter James, crime thriller author, for broadening the education and audience of forensic gait analysis and forensic podiatry, from a specialist area in the forensic arena to the wider public domain in an informative, enjoyable and entertaining way. And not forgetting his wonderful wit!

Finally, to my endearing friends and family. As with any book there are so many who add in one way or another, so thank you. Forgive me, if I have missed anyone. Ardour to you all and I hope you enjoy reading.

Haydn Kelly
2020

AUTHOR

In July 2000, Haydn Kelly made legal history with 'forensic gait analysis' which he created and was first admissible as expert evidence in criminal law [R v Saunders] at the Old Bailey in London. This was widely reported in the media and elsewhere at the time, and verified in Guinness World Records. He is a University accredited expert witness by Cardiff University and Bond Solon training and has provided expert evidence in numerous medico-legal matters and in different jurisdictions; has a degree in Podiatric Medicine, Fellowships in Podiatric Surgery (London) and a Fellow of the Faculty of Podiatric Medicine of the Royal College of Physicians and Surgeons of Glasgow. Former Elected Dean, Faculty of Podiatric Surgery (London) and during his tenure secured access to government resources for the further development of podiatric surgery and podiatry. Haydn Kelly has published in journals, periodicals, book chapters, and given presentations at international scientific conferences, with lectures on forensic gait analysis, biomechanics of foot and lower limb injuries, foot pathology, and podiatric surgery. He has also contributed to news items with television appearances. Having treated over 100,000 patients, and a clinical career in London's Harley Street over three decades. He continues internationally extending the uses of gait analysis and the application of innovative medical IT and processing capabilities.

CONTRIBUTORS

J. Gordon Burrow
Forensic Podiatrist, Chartered Scientist,
Chartered Safety & Health Practitioner,
Former Senior Lecturer
Glasgow Caledonian University
Glasgow
Scotland

Dr Burrow is former lecturer and senior lecturer at Glasgow Caledonian University, School of Podiatry, for thirty-eight years, where he was also the programme lead for the MSc Theory of Podiatric Surgery and MSc Podiatric Medicine. He is a contributor and an editor of Neale's Disorders of the Foot (6ᵗʰ- 9ᵗʰ editions); a peer reviewer of a number of international forensic, medical and health journals and a member of the editorial board for Journal of Forensic Identification. His Professional Doctorate was awarded for his research into bare footprints and also has MSc, MPhil and BA degrees; has a number of Fellowships including in Podiatric Medicine; former elected Chair of the Forensic Podiatry Special Advisory Group (UK); Accredited Expert Witness and Forensic Podiatrist. He has a number of Health and Safety responsibilities.

Emma Cowley
Senior Teaching Fellow in Podiatry.
University of Southampton
Southampton, UK

Dr Cowley is a Senior Research Fellow in Podiatry at the University of Southampton. A Chartered Scientist, and former lecturer in Podiatry at the University of Plymouth for many years, with over twenty years' experience in clinical observational gait analysis and laboratory video gait analysis in musculoskeletal practice, research and teaching. In addition to her PhD, Emma has Master's and Bachelor degrees; Fellowships in Podiatric Medicine at the College of Podiatry, London; Faculty of Podiatric Medicine of the Royal College of Physicians and Surgeons of Glasgow;

and is a Fellow of the Higher Education Academy (UK). Specialist areas of interest include problem solving pain and pathology of the lower limb that has its origins in mechanical tissue stress as a result of gait patterns in walking and running.

Michael J. Curran
Associate Professor (Podiatry)
Faculty of Health, Education & Society
University of Northampton
Northampton, UK

Dr Curran initially qualified in Podiatry at the University of Salford, and later gained a BSc (Hons) in Health Science and an MPhil in Computer Coding Systems at the University of Leicester. This was followed by a PhD in Computer Expert Systems at the University of Northampton. He was also awarded an MBA with Distinction at the University of Northampton. His interests include research in forensic science including footwear and gait analysis. In addition to this and publications he supervises research students. He is also on the SATRA advisory board and Chair's a group of footwear companies who compose the healthy footwear guide. He has also worked in the National Health Service. He is currently an Associate Professor at the Faculty of Health & Society, University of Northampton, UK.

Clive Evans
Director, Videnda Imagery Analysis Ltd.
Cambridgeshire, UK

Director of Videnda Imagery Analysis Ltd. Formerly lead imagery investigator at Eurofins Forensic Services; LGC Forensics, and having served for over twenty years in a military career as an imagery analyst in the Royal Air Force (RAF), including as an instructor at the UK Imagery Analysis School. As a senior instructor, he was the Infrared and Radar imagery analysis specialist for the UK's Ministry of Defence. Whilst in RAF service, he was approached by a London based forensic company and transitioned to the field of forensic imagery analysis. Clive Evans has provided imagery analysis support to several hundred cases for both the prosecution and defence, and given expert witness evidence at courts throughout the United Kingdom.

Barry E. Francis
Consultant Podiatric Surgeon & Forensic Podiatrist
London, UK

Consultant Podiatric Surgeon and Forensic Podiatrist, with extensive clinical and surgical experience including four decades of carrying out clinical and video gait analysis in the diagnosis and treatment of conditions. He has Fellowships in Podiatric Surgery (England) and is a Fellow of the Faculty of Podiatric Medicine at the Royal College of Physicians and Surgeons of Glasgow (Scotland). A former tutor in podiatric surgery, examiner, and ex-council member for podiatry. His duties and responsibilities have included podiatrist to the British Medical Team at the 1984 Olympics in Los Angeles, USA; 1988 in Seoul, South Korea and 1986 Commonwealth Games in Edinburgh, Scotland. He is a former adviser to the Lawn Tennis Association (UK) and the Health Ombudsman and spent many years working in NHS practice. He has acted as an expert witness to healthcare regulatory bodies in the United Kingdom and Australia and provides gait analysis reports and oral evidence for the civil and criminal justice systems in the UK and overseas. He has lectured on podiatric surgery; sports injuries; clinical podiatry and practice; medico-legal matters and forensic podiatry. He is in independent practice in London, UK.

Sue Hardiman
Author and Historian
Bristol, UK

Sue Hardiman has an MA in History with a particular interest in medical history and is the author of the book entitled 'The 1832 Cholera Epidemic and its Impact on the City of Bristol' (BBHA, 2005). She also contributed a chapter to an academic publication entitled, 'Cholera and Conflict: 19th Century Cholera and its Social Consequences' (Thackray Museum Press, 2009). With a background in library and information services she is currently curating the archives for the College of Podiatry (UK), and is a regular feature writer.

Atholl Johnston
Professor of Clinical Pharmacology, Chartered Scientist & Clinical Scientist
Barts & The London School of Medicine and Dentistry
Queen Mary University of London.

Visiting Professor of Forensic Pharmacology & Toxicology
St George's, University of London.
Science Director, Analytical Services International
UK

Professor Atholl Johnston, Fellowships include the Faculty of Pharmaceutical Medicine; British Pharmacological Society, Royal College of Pathologists, Royal Society of Medicine, and Royal Statistical Society. He is registered as a Chartered Scientist and Clinical Scientist. In addition to a PhD in Pharmacology, he holds an MSc in Applied Statistics; BSc, Biochemistry (Toxicology); BA, Mathematics and Statistics, along with over forty years of experience in the measurement of drugs as a guide to therapy and toxicity and has published over three hundred articles in peer-reviewed journals. He maintains interest and practice in Forensic Toxicology and is a frequent speaker including on statistical data analysis, and an accomplished expert witness giving evidence for many years including high profile trials.

Haydn D. Kelly
Former Elected Dean of Podiatric Surgery
Forensic Podiatrist
University Accredited Expert Witness
London, UK

Former elected Dean of the Faculty of Podiatric Surgery, London; a Cardiff University Accredited Expert Witness; has a degree in Podiatric Medicine; Fellowships in Podiatric Surgery (London) and is a Fellow of the Faculty of Podiatric Medicine, Royal College of Physicians and Surgeons of Glasgow. Former lead assessor in forensic podiatry at the Council for Registration of Forensic Practitioners (CRFP); over ten years as a lecturer and examiner for the Faculty of Forensic and Legal Medicine at the Royal College of Physicians, London; and prior to that five years at the Society of Apothecaries, London. He has also given counsel to the Health Ombudsman (UK); and is the founding Chair of the Forensic Podiatry Special Interest Group (UK). Haydn Kelly has extensive clinical experience in a podiatry career of over thirty years, including professional sport, and as an expert witness having given expert testimony in many medico-legal matters and encompassing high-profile cases.

Peter K. Larsen
Department of Forensic Medicine
University of Copenhagen
Copenhagen
Denmark

Peter K. Larsen is forensic anthropologist at the Forensic Anthropology section of Forensic Medicine at the Faculty of Health Sciences, University of Copenhagen, where he has been engaged since 2004. He has an MSc in Sport Science from the University of Copenhagen, and his Master's thesis related to the reproducibility of biomechanical gait analysis. He subsequently obtained a PhD at the Forensic Anthropology department, University of Copenhagen and has published articles relating to forensic gait analysis and forensic photogrammetric measurements. Alongside teaching assignments at the University of Copenhagen, he presents lectures to law enforcement officers and lawyers on identification of the living based on CCTV material.

Niels Lynnerup
Professor, Head of Department
Department of Forensic Medicine
University of Copenhagen
Copenhagen
Denmark

Niels Lynnerup is a Professor at the section of Forensic Medicine, Faculty of Health Sciences, University of Copenhagen, where he has worked since 1990. He is a Doctor of Medicine from the University of Copenhagen. Since his PhD, he has worked with Forensic Anthropology becoming Head of the Unit of Forensic Anthropology at the Section of Forensic Medicine. Aside from working with human remains, the unit also works with identification of the living, based on CCTV material, for example, matching perpetrators as seen on CCTV with suspects. This work also includes the application of photogrammetric methods. Niels is author and co-author of more than two hundred journal articles and book chapters, focusing both on forensic anthropology and biological anthropology. Since 2012 he is the editor-in-chief of the Scandinavian Journal of Forensic Science and lectures internationally.

Mark Solon
Chairman
Wilmington Legal
Wilmington plc
London

UK lawyer and US Attorney at law
London, UK

Mark Solon is a UK lawyer and a US Attorney at law. He trained at Clyde & Co, London and was the founding partner of Young & Solon Solicitors in Greenwich, London. He also founded the well-known and highly regarded Bond Solon Training that has become a leading legal training consultancy delivering a range of specialist face to face and web learning training courses and qualifications targeted specifically at non-lawyers who are involved in the legal system and especially around the generating of legally compliant evidence in many forms. He was also involved in forming the Expert Witness Institute. Mark is Chairman of Wilmington Legal, the public limited company that owns Solicitors Journal. Wilmington Legal has become a centre of excellence for professionals, providing trusted and valued legal education, insight and networking services.

Orlando Trujillo Bueno
Specialty Doctor in Forensic Psychiatry
Oxford Health NHS Foundation Trust
Oxford, UK

Qualified as a medical doctor in Colombia before specialising in clinical forensic medicine and later moved to the UK to further his interest in clinical and forensic psychiatry practice where he is a specialty doctor. He also has an MSc in Neuroscience from the Institute of Psychiatry, University of London and a post-graduate diploma in cognitive behavioural therapy from University of Oxford. In addition to clinical, forensic duties and responsibilities, he has also been an academic tutor to medical students on rotation in clinical psychiatry at the department of psychiatry, University of Oxford.

Jon Walklin
Imagery Analyst
Partner, Diligence International LLC
London, UK

Jon Walklin is a partner at Diligence International LLC, London. He has over twenty-five years of working in imagery analysis & enhancement, digital, audio and cell site analysis for both the civil and criminal justice systems on matters involving serious crime, corporate fraud, personal injury claims, professional sport and air accidents, including giving expert evidence in the courts, including many high-profile cases. He is a founder member of the Forensic Imagery Analysis Group (FIAG) and sat on the British Standards technical working group to establish the code of practice (BS7958) for the management and operation of CCTV systems. He has given considerable expert witness testimony in the UK courts and presents to various courses and audiences, including lecturing widely on detectives training courses.

Stephen J. Wroe
Consultant Neurologist
Essex Centre for Neurosciences
Queen's Hospital
London, UK

Dr Wroe is a Doctor of Medicine and Fellow of the Royal College of Physicians (FRCP), London; a Consultant Neurologist to the Essex Centre for Neurosciences, Queen's Hospital, London. He qualified in medicine from the University of Liverpool before post-graduate appointments in neurology and clinical pharmacology in Liverpool; Cardiff; Edinburgh; The National Hospital for Neurology and Neurosurgery, Queen Square, London; and as Medical Research Council (MRC) Senior Scientist at the Institute of Neurology, London. He has extensive experience in all areas of clinical neurology and particular expertise in neurodegenerative disease and cognitive impairment; epilepsy and episodes of altered consciousness; head injury; stroke; neurorehabilitation and medico-legal practice. The main focus of his academic activity has been the development of new therapies for neurological disease. Contributions in the field of epilepsy include design and implementation of trials for the more recently introduced anti-epileptic drugs. Other therapeutic areas of interest have included interferons for multiple sclerosis and treatments for neuro-degenerative disease. A former secretary to the Association of British Neurologists, he has represented the organisation on a number of committees advising the Department of Health, particularly regarding implementation of government policy for long-term conditions and on the National Service Framework for neurological disorders. He is also a member of the American Academy of Neurology, American Epilepsy Society and International League Against Epilepsy.

1

Gait Analysis
A Historical Overview

Contents

A MOVE TO UNDERSTANDING: THE CLASSICAL PERIOD

It was during the period of classical antiquity that fundamental changes in mankind's world view were codified and transcribed. These societies formulated a basic understanding of mathematical and mechanical principles and were subsequently able to separate cultural myth from human reality. Additionally, this period witnessed a new thinking in medicine with an emphasis on empiricism and experimentation. One of the first to make a significant contribution to this field was Plato (c. 427–347 BCE), who as a student of Socrates was quoted as observing that 'the best tool for the pursuit of knowledge is through maths'. In particular, he used the science of geometry and applied it to solving issues in the world around him. One of his most influential works was the *Timaeus*,[1] in which Plato linked the make-up of the human body to transcendental geometric shapes.[2] In this treatise, he explained the reasoning that the Gods bestowed mankind with 'four limbs – extended and flexible' for means of locomotion:

> Such was the origin of legs and hands, which for this reason were attached to every man; and the gods, deeming the front part of man to be more honourable and more fit to command than the hinder part, made us to move mostly in a forward direction.[3]

Plato's student Aristotle (384–322 BCE) was the son of a royal physician and later became tutor to Alexander the Great. He was considered to be the natural successor to his mentor's philosophy, but it was found that their ideologies differed in several key respects. Aristotle was an empiricist and believed that knowledge came after experience and experimentation. He was a true polymath but considered himself foremost to be one who studied living things and an observer of nature who contributed and expanded the knowledge of anatomy and locomotion in animals. This was enshrined in a key text entitled *On the Movements of Animals*.[4] It was based on observations describing the muscular action and movement of animals. It was also the first scientific analysis of human and animal locomotion, gait and muscular action. The mechanical comparisons illustrated a deeper understanding of the functions of bones and muscles. Aristotle explained ground reaction forces and discussed the use of levers. He likened animal movements to those of puppets. He expressed such movements through the use of mathematics and physics and observed:

> For as the pusher pushes so is the pushed, and with equal force. But the prime mover moves that which is to begin with at rest, so that the power it exerts is greater, rather than equal and like to the power which produces absence of motion in that which is moved.[5]

He then went on to explain that, 'when movement arises out from a joint, one of the extreme points must remain at rest, and the other be moved (for as we explained above the mover must support itself against a point of rest)'[6]

Working in Syracuse, Sicily, Archimedes (287–212 BCE) produced his treatise *Equilibrium of Planes*, and his application of Euclidian methodology to mechanics provided the basis of rational mechanics. Archimedes' thinking was occupied with movement as he solved the problem of how to transfer a given weight by a given force, and his works dominated until the times of Simon Stevin (1548–1620) and Galileo.[7]

In general, these important observations by classical scholars could be considered as the birth of 'kinematics' – that is 'the branch of mechanics concerned with the motion of objects without reference to the forces which cause the motion' – derived from the Greek 'kinema' (to move).[8] This is also linked to 'kinetics', which is the energy an object creates during motion.

Somewhat later, the first significant study of biomechanics was created by the leading authority in ancient Roman medicine, Galen (c.130–c.210 AD). Biomechanics is defined as 'the study of biological systems, particularly their structure and function, using methods derived from mechanics, which is concerned with the effects that forces have on the motion of bodies'.[9] Although a Greek, Galen had experience as a medical consultant to gladiatorial combatants in Asia Minor (comprising most of what is now modern day Turkey). Galen was appointed as physician to the College of Gladiators at the age of 28 and probably became the first 'sports physician' and 'team doctor' as we know the terms. He practised surgery and dietetics for four years and in doing so gained considerable knowledge of the human body and human motion. His talents were recognised by the highest authorities, and later he was to hold a position as physician to the Roman Emperor Marcus Aurelius, where he remained for 20 years.[10] Of particular note was his discourse *De Motu Musculorum* (On the Movement of Muscles), which concerned motion and motility and which embodied his eternal passion for the mechanism of movement.[11] He made huge advances in the understanding of muscles and, in so doing, establishing of the science of myology. The emphasis that he placed on structure showed 'innervation that makes muscle substance into a muscle proper'.[12] *De Usu Partium* (On the Use of Parts) gave Galen inimitable influence on the medical sciences at the time. His observations were based on numerous animal dissections, particularly those of dogs, pigs and apes as human dissection was discouraged during the Roman period. He described tonus and paid specific attention to the differences which he distinguished between agonist and antagonistic muscles, motor and sensory nerves and the functions of the nervous system in aiding motion. However, Galen was alive to the deficiency that presented to him by the unavailability of human dissection and encouraged students to travel to Alexandria for such experience. His work in this field and his other seminal texts on medical theory became the standard throughout the medieval period and beyond.

THE REBIRTH OF SCIENTIFIC THOUGHT

There was little in the way of advances in this field throughout the medieval period. It was not until what is known as 'the Renaissance' that there was not only a rebirth of classical art but correspondingly a renewed interest in the medical and scientific knowledge of the ancient world. Perhaps the most famous example of a 'Renaissance man' was Leonardo da Vinci (1452–1519), who was not only an accomplished artist but indeed a dedicated and talented scientist and anatomist, with an astonishing talent for conveying motion through his drawings. He saw the human body as that of a machine, and his copious illustrations of human anatomy were depicted in a similar manner to those of his mechanical inventions. Da Vinci's anatomical studies joined art and science which emphasised the significance of perspective in producing pictures of actuality. The quality and clarity of these anatomical drawings showed that he must have had access to cadavers for dissection.

Some have dubbed da Vinci the 'father of biomechanics', and indeed his innovative vision of the body as a machine supports this view, as depicted in Figure 1.1.[13]

On the mechanics of gait, he wrote:

> The gait of man is always after the manner of the universal gait of four-footed animals; seeing that as these move their feet crosswise, as a horse does when it trots, so a man moves his four limbs cross-wise, that is he thrusts the right foot forward as he walks he thrusts the left arm forward with it, and so it always continues.[14]

Furthermore, da Vinci's anatomical sketches include several of the leg, foot and ankle, and are but some of his many illustrations that help make knowledge visible. His accompanying notes (written in his trademark mirror writing) described the anatomy and working of the lower limb in great detail. In fact, da Vinci is famously quoted as saying, 'the foot is the most marvellous of machines'.[15]

Andreas Vesalius (1514–1564) was born in the latter years of da Vinci's life; he continued this work and went on to build further on the studies of both Galen and da Vinci. Trained as a physician, Vesalius used a critical eye when comparing his dissections of the human body with the anatomical observations of Galen and realised that the latter was based solely on animal physiology. In order to undertake the dissection of a human body, Vesalius was able to procure the cadavers of felons for this express purpose. In 1539, Judge Marcantonio Contarini had become intrigued by Vesalius' anatomical studies, encouraging him in further detailed

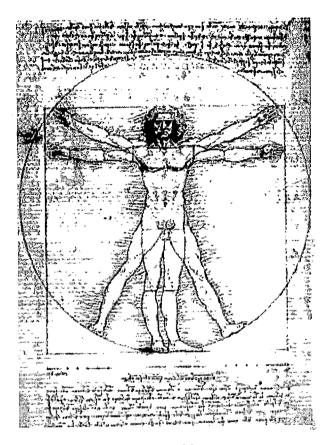

Figure 1.1   Leonardo da Vinci – Vitruvian Man.

investigation by making available the bodies of executed felons. The observations of Vesalius resulted in a ground-breaking text entitled *De Humani Corporis Fabrica Libri Septem* (On the Fabric of the Human Body).[16] This revolutionised human anatomy by challenging Galen's view that had dominated for 1,300 years. In this, he dedicated books one and two to bones and muscles, respectively. The book was lavishly illustrated and was a pioneering text in the field of anatomy and consequently of great importance to those studying human movement and locomotion.[17] A typical example can be found as per Figure 1.2.[18]

Vesalius' observations influenced the work of Fallopius (1523–1562), who was fervently interested in the connection of fibrous tissue in

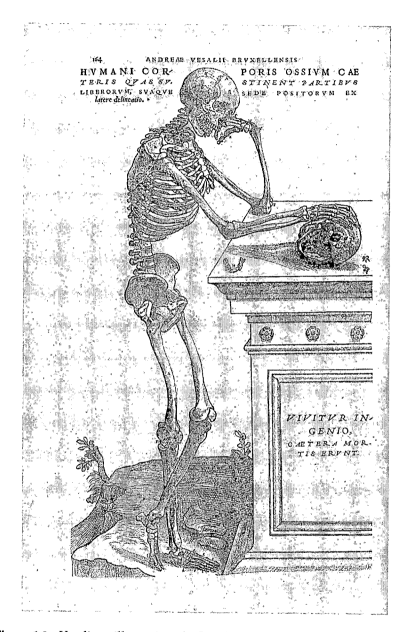

164   ANDREAE VESALII BRVXELLENSIS

HVMANI COR-   PORIS OSSIVM CAE
TERIS QVAS SV.   STINENT PARTIBVS
LIBERORVM, SVAQVE   SEDE POSITORVM EX
latere delineatio.

VIVITVR IN-
GENIO,
CAETERA MOR-
TIS ERVNT.

Figure 1.2   Vesalius – illustration of a flexed human skeleton.

movement. Fallopius stated, 'motion requires a fibrous nature in the actual body that is moved; since whatever moves itself does so by contraction or extension'.[19]

THE EMERGENCE OF MODERN SCIENTIFIC THOUGHT

The emergence of what is now deemed 'modern science' began during the early modern period and ran until the eighteenth-century Enlightenment. The period embraced such giants of scientific thought as Galileo and Isaac Newton. It is often dubbed 'The Age of Scientific Revolution'.

Santorio Santori, also known as Sanctorius (1561–1636), was a contemporary and colleague of Galileo. He was the first scientist to apply mechanics and quantifiable methods to medicine. He was the author of a medical treatise entitled *De Statica Medicina*.[20]

Galileo Galilei (1564–1642) is perhaps better known for his work in the field of mathematics and astronomy. However, he made important contributions to the field of biomechanics by his application of the theory of levers to the human skeleton. In particular, he made the connection regarding the scale of bones in relation to the size, known as allometry.[21] Furthermore, he was one of the pioneers of the 'scientific method', having been ejected from many of the most prestigious learning academies of the day for insisting that every factual statement taught should be accompanied by scientific proof.[22] The publication of *Letters on Sunspots* (1613), in which Galileo initially gave a public commitment to the Copernican theory, resulted in positive support from the church, and Cardinals Borromeo and Barberini (future Pope Urban VIII) wrote to Galileo with admiration. In 1624, under the restraint of the 1616 decree, Galileo met with Pope Urban VIII to obtain permission to publish his analysis of the Copernican system. Urban, who was an admirer of Galileo, suggested a way to publish the analysis which avoided theological arguments. Galileo's approach sealed his fate as he then placed the Pope's arguments in the mouth of a simpleton in his *Dialogue* (1631). Consequently, he was commanded to appear before the Inquisition in 1633. Despite earlier Papal support, Galileo was accused of heresy and forced to recant his theories. His punishment was to endure house arrest for the remainder of his life; this he did in the hills outside Florence.[23] Somewhat later, Galileo provided the bedrock for Newton's three laws. Interestingly, Galileo Galilei (1564–1642) and William Shakespeare (1564–1616) were born in the same year.

Shakespeare makes numerous references to gait.[24]

In Shakespeare's plays:

All's Well That Ends Well
Act 2 Scene 1: There do muster true gait

A Midsummer Night's Dream
Act 2 Scene 1: Which she, with pretty and with swimming gait
Act 5 Scene 1: The heavy gait of night
Act 5 Scene 1: Every fairy take his gait

Antony & Cleopatra
Act 3 Scene 3: What majesty is in her gait? Remember,
                       If e'er thou look'dst on majesty.
                       She creeps:
                       Her motion and her station are as one.
                       She shows a body rather than a life,
                       A statue than a breather.
                       Is this certain?
                       Or I have no observance

Hamlet
Act 1 Scene 2: His further gait herein

Henry IV, Part 1
Act 3 Scene 1: 'Tis like the forced gait of a shuffling nag

Henry IV, Part 2
Act 2 Scene 3: He had no legs that practised not his gait
Act 2 Scene 3: To seem like him: so that in speech, in gait

Henry V
Act 2 Scene 2: Should with his lion gait walk the whole world

Henry VI, Part 2
Act 3 Scene 1: In face, in gait, in speech, he doth resemble

Henry VIII
Act 3 Scene 2: Springs out into fast gait, then stops again

Julius Caesar
Act 1 Scene 3: Tis Cinna, I do know him by his gait

King Lear
Act 4 Scene 5: Good gentlemen, go your gait, and let poor volk pass
Act 5 Scene 3: Methought thy very gait did prophesy

Love's Labour's Lost
Act 4 Scene 3: When shall you hear that I
                  Will praise a hand, a foot, a face, an eye,
                  A gait, a state, a brow, a breast, a waist,
                  A leg, a limb–
Act 5 Scene 1: His humour is lofty, his discourse peremptory,
                  his tongue filed, his eye ambitious, his gait majestical,
                  and his general behaviour vain, ridiculous and
                  thrasonical.
                  He is too picked, too spruce, too affected, too odd,
                  as it were, too peregrinate, as I may call it

Merry Wives of Windsor
Act 1 Scene 4: O, I should remember him: does he not hold up his
                  head, as it were, and strut in his gait
Act 3 Scene 3: The firm fixture of thy foot would give an excellent
                  motion to thy gait
                  in a semi-circled farthingale

Othello
Act 5, Scene 1: I know his gait, 'tis he.—Villain, thou diest!

The Taming of the Shrew
Induction Scene 1: Voice, gait and action of a gentlewoman
Act 2 Scene1: As Kate this chamber with her princely gait?
Act 3 Scene 4: In gait and countenance surely like a father

The Tempest
Act 4 Scene 1: Highest queen of state,
                  Great Juno, comes: I know her by her gait

The Winter's Tale
Act 4 Scene 4: Hath not my gait in it the measure of the court

Timon of Athens
Act 5 Scene 4: But pass and stay not here thy gait

Troilus and Cressida
Act 1 Scene 1: Her eyes, her hair, her cheek, her gait, her voice[25]
Act 4 Scene 5: Tis he, I ken the manner of his gait

Twelfth Night
Act 1 Scene 4: Therefore, good youth, address thy gait unto her
Act 2 Scene 3: By the colour of his beard, the shape of his leg, the manner of his
gait, the expressure of his eye, forehead, and complexion, he
shall find himself most feelingly personated

Act 3 Scene 1: I will answer you with gait and entrance

Two Noble Kinsman
Act 1 Scene 2: Affect another's gait, which is not catching

In Shakespeare's poems:

Venus and Adonis
Look, the world's comforter with weary gait.

The Rape of Lucrece
And solemn night with slow, sad gait descended
An humble gait.

In Shakespeare's Sonnets, 128:
O'er whom thy fingers walk with gentle gait.

René Descartes (1596–1650), a French philosopher, mathematician and scientist, was exposed to the mechanical observations of Galileo. Descartes was one of the originators of mechanical philosophy and heavily influenced physiology with a mechanical approach in their investigations as per his treatise *L'homme* (1664), which applied mechanical principles to the human body. This work emphasised the role of the nervous system in coordinating movement. Descartes is perhaps also well known for his statement *Cogito ergo sum* (I think, therefore I am).[26]

Giovanni Alfonso Borelli (1608–1679) was a physiologist and mathematician, who has likewise been considered as 'the father of biomechanics'. His text *De Motu Animalium* was published in 1680.[27] He followed on from the work of Galileo and described the movement of animals and humans using mathematics and mechanics, then relating them to muscle function. He analysed the role of limbs and how they related to movements such as running and swimming. He collaborated in this field with his contemporary Marcello Malpighi (1628–1694), who contributed a thorough knowledge of anatomy, particularly that on a microscopic level.[28] The work of Borelli can be further demonstrated by the illustration of joints and their movement (Figure 1.3).[29]

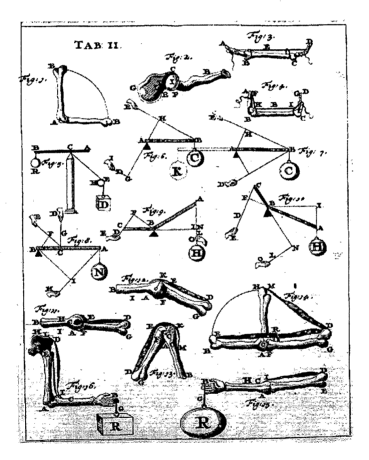

Figure 1.3   Giovanni Borelli – limb joints as depicted in De Motu Animalium.

The American Society of Biomechanics continues to honour him with the annual presentation of the Giovanni Borelli Award in recognition of 'exemplary research in the field'.[30]

Isaac Newton (1642–1727) was born in the same year that Galileo died. Newton clearly had great respect for those scientific masters who came before him, famously saying, 'Plato is my friend – Aristotle is my friend – but my greatest friend is truth'.[31] He studied at Cambridge and made ground-breaking strides in mathematics and the science of optics, and followed this with the discovery of gravity, famously coming after an epiphany at the sight of a falling apple. It was, however, Newton's application of the laws of mechanics to human movement that led to major advances in the study of gait. His seminal work, commonly known as *Principia*, was first published in 1687. Newton's *Principia* fell upon European intellectual circles like a bombshell. The first edition was written in Latin, and after annotating and correcting his personal copy of the first edition, Newton also published two further editions, in 1713 and 1726. After Newton's death in 1727, an English translation occurred in 1728.[32] Newton outlined three laws with regard to motion as applied to a body.

The first is the law of inertia, first hypothesised by Galileo, which declared that if an object or body is in motion, it will continue to do so unless acted on by an outside force. This has been applied to the analysis of gait, in particular to the arrangement of muscles in the human leg and foot to counteract inertia.[33]

The second law states that the force needed to move an object is in direct proportion to its mass. Newton expressed this in the formula $F = ma$. This can be applied biomechanically to calculate the forces acting on muscles, tendons and so on.

The third law states that for each action there is an equal and opposite reaction.[34] This particularly applies to the analysis of gait and foot strike.

Jacob Leupold (1674–1727), a German contemporary of Newton, penned an influential text concerning the theory of machines entitled *Theatri Machinarum Supplementum*.[35] In the supplement to his work on mechanics, he included what is probably the first description of a pedometer. A posthumous addition to his larger work showed a pedometer and its potential use for the study of not only human gait but also that of horses.

ADVANCES IN THE AGE OF ENLIGHTENMENT

Enlightenment scholars used Newtonian physics and applied mathematics as a basis for further examination of the science of human movement.

The application of force on the human body was more clearly understood as was the structure and function of muscles. One such scholar was Charles-Francois Dufay (1698–1739), a scientist and curator of the Jardin des Plantes in Paris. He spent time studying electricity and its effects and believed that all living bodies had electrical properties. He experimented with the conductivity of the human body, even using himself as an electrical conductor![36]

A pioneering treatise in the study of human biomechanics was entitled *L'Orthopedie*, published in 1741 by Nicolas Andry (1658–1742).[37] The frontispiece is shown in Figure 1.4[38]

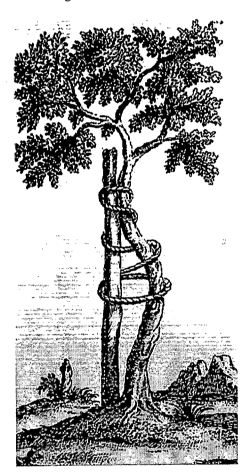

Figure 1.4   Nicolas Andry – frontispiece to L'Orthopedie.

Andry coined the term 'orthopaedics' and believed that muscular imbalances were responsible for producing skeletal deformities. In this seminal work, Andry outlined treatments for 'correcting and preventing deformities in children' covering conditions such as club-foot and rickets'. Andry's use of the 'crooked tree' motif as the frontispiece of this work is still reflected in modern medicine. He also proposed that exercise during childhood could prevent musculoskeletal deformities in adulthood.

Another contributor to this field was Jean le Rond d'Alembert (1717–1783). He was co-editor of *Encyclopédie* with Denis Diderot and embraced a wide range of disciplines, including mathematics, philosophy and music. In 1743 he published *Traité de Dynamique*. Contained therein was 'd'Alembert's principle' 'that Newton's third law of motion holds not only for fixed bodies but also for those free to move'.[39]

However, it was his work in the field of mechanics which is directly applicable to gait analysis, in particular, the use of a revised version of Newton's second law, subsequently named 'd'Alembert's principle'. This principle stated that the 'reaction due to the inertia of an accelerated body is equal and opposite of the force causing the acceleration and results in a condition of kinetic equilibrium'.[40] Furthermore, the mathematical theories of Joseph Louis Lagrange (1736–1813) added to the understanding of mechanical forces, which was to be encapsulated in his treatise on analytical mechanics.[41]

Other important contributors include Jean Jallabert (1712–1768), a professor from Geneva, who investigated the effects of electrical discharge and was the first to re-educate paralysed muscles with electricity. In 1747, he used electricity to attempt to cure paralysis in the arm of a locksmith, which resulted in significant progress. This is considered the beginning in the application of electrotherapy.[42]

Furthermore, Robert Whytt (1714–1766), one-time President of the Royal College of Physicians in Edinburgh, was a pioneer in the field of neuroscience. He was particularly interested in reflex actions and concluded that the spinal cord could produce involuntary movements.[43] In 1751, he published *The Vital and Other Involuntary Motions of Animals*, in which his observations on involuntary movements were recorded.[44] John Hunter (1728–1793), also a Scottish medic, created a descriptive analysis of muscle functions, stating, 'muscle was fitted for self-motion and was the only part of the body so fitted'. Hunter believed that muscle function should be studied with live persons and not cadavers.[45] Subsequently, the late eighteenth century saw further development in sporting and leisure activities, which stimulated a renewed scientific interest in human locomotion.

1800–1900: THE GAIT CENTURY

The nineteenth century has been dubbed 'The Gait Century' as there were a number of critical breakthroughs during this time, characterised by the development of instruments and experimental methods to increase the knowledge of how humans move. This was the period when the field of study moved on from observation to direct experimentation. Whilst the study of locomotion had commenced as an observational science, photography took things to another level in revolutionising the examination of the movements of humans and animals.

Two brothers from Germany, Eduard Weber (1806–1871) and William Weber (1804–1891), established an agenda for research into human gait. They co-published a text entitled *The Mechanics of Walking in Humans*, which is considered the first book of its type on the subject.[46] This treatise contained almost 150 hypotheses on human gait obtained by the Weber brothers via observations and/or theoretical considerations. In particular, they devised tools with which to measure elements of gait such as stance and foot swing. Amongst their primary observations were the differences between running and walking. Their work is considered to have laid the foundation for further experimentation and research into this field of study. As proposed by Cavanagh (1990) the primary importance of Webers' hypotheses lay not in the accuracy and suitability of their statements, but rather in establishing an agenda for further research on human gait.[47] Indeed, it was followed by a collaborative work between anatomist Christian Wilhelm Braune (1831–1892) and physiologist Otto Fischer (1861–1917). Their seminal text on the subject was entitled *The Human Gait*. They pioneered the first tri-dimensional study of gait to establish the methodology for the calculation of the mechanical parameters of walking.[48] They created a formula for determining the net forces acting on the relevant part of the leg and foot whilst the body is in the act of walking. Furthermore, they highlighted the importance of the body's musculature during such an act. However, their work went on to contradict that previously outlined by Weber and Weber.[49]

In 1806, Duchenne (1806–1875) published *Physiologie des Mouvements*, which described the muscle action of each important superficial muscle. He was the first to use abnormal muscle function to analyse normal function.[50]

Although George Gilles de la Tourette (1857–1904) is now more commonly known for the neurological disorder named after him, his doctoral thesis is dedicated to 'Gait in diseases of the nervous system, studied by the method of imprints'. His work with Albert Londe (1858–1917) described and defined many gait disorders and made use of coloured powders applied to the soles of the feet to map an individual's gait pattern.[51] This influential work is not as well known as others in this area, and this could have been due to Tourette's research being overshadowed by the contemporary work of Etienne-Jules Marey (1830–1904). However, it was almost certainly the case that Tourette's important contribution to gait analysis was eclipsed by his work on the syndrome that now bears his name.[52]

Marey developed probably the most extensive facility ever dedicated exclusively to examining human gait. This was built on what is presently Roland Garros Tennis Courts in the Parc de Princes in Paris. The Station Physiologique had a 500 m circular running track with monitoring equipment. This was the place where Marey comprehensively analysed movements of adults and children both during sport and work. He also assessed the movements of animals, including horses, birds, fish, insects and jellyfish. The locomotion studies which Marey embarked upon were limitless, and he was the first to combine and synchronise kinematic and force measurement. Marey's contribution to this field was the use of high-speed photography to capture movement, and he pioneered the use of a chronophotographic gun in order to record locomotion frame by frame (this was done with a disc containing 12 frames). Marey also introduced a system wherein the subject was clothed entirely in black with white lines outlining the various limbs. The progression of movement was then captured on film, and this was effectively the first use of 'motion capture photography'; an example is shown in Figure 1.5.[53] In yet another contribution to cinematography, Marey invented the darkroom on rails, which was able to run parallel with the subject who ran against a black screen.[54]

Marey also pioneered the recording of the duration of foot contact to the ground whilst walking. This was made possible with the use of air chambers built into shoes complete with specialised recording devices.[55] Marey was an inspiration with the variety and abundance of his data collection methods, from which others adapted and formed implements.

Marey's work was followed by the work of Eadweard Muybridge (1830–1904), who was a contemporary of Marey. His birth name was Edward Muggeridge, and he was an English photographer renowned for his pioneering work in the studies of motion and early work in motion picture projection. He acquired experience as a photographer in landscapes and as a war photographer in the United States. Additionally, he was the pioneer of motion capture using multiple cameras. With serial photography he was able to record the movement of animals, chiefly that

Figure 1.5 Man walking – as captured by Etienne-Jules Marey.

of horses and birds. Muybridge became well known as a result of his studies of motion, which commenced in 1872 when attempting to capture a galloping horse in photographic pictures. In 1877 he expanded his experiment by placing multiple cameras in series so that a running horse could be recorded in all phases of its motion. With the pictures secured next to one another, they were viewed through a zoetrope, and for the first time photographs became moving pictures.[56] Muybridge used a similar apparatus that he himself conceived (zoopraxiscope) to project his images onto a screen, for which he is considered as a pioneer in cinematography. Muybridge's beginnings in the analysis of locomotion stemmed from Leland Stanford, former governor of California and later a US senator, who was an avid horse racing fan. While owning and training many of his horses, he developed an interest in their anatomy and movements. Stanford was of the view that during a horse's motion, there was a period in which all four hooves were off the ground. This had been shown earlier by Marey with his pneumatic device at slower gaits, but not at faster

17

speeds. Muybridge was commissioned by Stanford to verify his belief that a horse has unsupported transit at faster speeds. The experiment was successful and showed the assertion to be true, much to the chagrin of many in the horse racing industry who had laid large bets to the contrary. Therein commenced a lifetime of work on recording the motion of humans and animals (Figure 1.6).[57]

The contribution made by Muybridge to the study of human locomotion was the enormous amount of pictures (20,000 images) he produced in documenting movement. Muybridge's pictures were evidence on the significance of photography as a new language of science. The site on which Muybridge conducted much of his work was what is now the site of Stanford University, California.

Muybridge started his work with the human figure in 1879, and this eventually led to the publication of *The Human Figure in Motion: An Electro-Photographic Investigation of Consecutive Phases of Muscular Actions* in 1901. Prefaced with an introduction and a statistical breakdown, his work depicted both men and women in a series of athletic and more sedentary

Figure 1.6 Muybridge – horse in motion.

18

positions. He even included images of those with disabilities, including a child with no legs getting on and off a chair. In his introduction he explained the value of his images:

> Consists, not as individual photographs ... but as seriates of phases, demonstrating the various changes which take place in the disposition of the limbs and body during the evolution of some act of motion from its inception to its completion.[58]

Marey's acknowledgement of the Muybridge–Stanford study accorded it the status of scientific research. In their time Marey and Muybridge collaborated in their fascination of locomotion and teamed up in Paris to document the flight of birds. Marey was interested in Muybridge's methods. Marey adopted photography as an instrument in the study of locomotion. In addition to his books *Animal Locomotion* and *The Human Figure in Motion*, Muybridge invented the zoöpraxiscope – a mechanical device for projecting motion pictures onto a screen (and pre-dated the flexible perforated film strip used in cinematography) – which he used to animate the still sequences from his motion studies. This was the forerunner of a cinema projector.[59]

THE TWENTIETH CENTURY AND BEYOND

Further and wider interest in human motion proliferated in the course of the twentieth century. Winner of the Nobel Prize for Physiology and Medicine, Archibald Vivian Hill, also known as A.V. Hill (1886–1977), an English physiologist, carried out considerable research on muscle structure and function. He, along with his co-workers, also studied human locomotion, giving insights to running and sports medicine. The period since 1900 has also witnessed the development of 'biomechanics' as a component in the approach to the study of the human body. Biomechanics is defined by Nigg as 'the science that examines forces acting upon and within a biological structure and effects produced by such forces'.[60]

Nikolai Bernstein (1896–1966), a Russian neurophysiologist and pioneer in the area of motor control and learning, performed a range of experiments involving human movement, including effects of age and gait, and individuals with brain damage. He examined human walking initially to assist with the engineering of pedestrian bridges. His publications include the text *The Co-ordination and Regulation of Movements*.[61]

Verne Thompson Inman (1905–1980), a surgeon and an anatomist in the United States of America, along with his colleagues advanced the comprehension and application of human gait, including contributions on muscle activity, prostheses design and normal and pathological gait, considering gait efficiency and features in patterns of locomotion with vertical and horizontal displacements of the body's centre of gravity.[62] *Human Walking* published in 1981 and shortly after Inman's passing continues to have utility.[63]

The fascination and examination of human gait also attracted the attention of Alberto Giacometti (1901–1966), a Swiss born and Paris based artist, draughtsman and printmaker from a family of designers (which included his father, post-impressionist painter, Giovanni Giacometti). Alberto is probably most famous for his remarkable career as a sculptor and particularly his figurative work of skeletal bronzes. One of his most famous sculptures is the six-foot-tall bronze that depicts a wiry man in mid-stride, his right foot jutting forward, his head erect and his arms hanging at his side. This is Alberto Giacometti's 1960 sculpture, *Walking Man I*. Perhaps there is something of significance depicted by the way he walks? Alberto Giacometti's *The Four Women on a Base* and *Four Figurines on a Stand* materialise two visions involving four standing women as seen from a distance and in different circumstances. With *Three Men Walking*, Giacometti tried to grasp in sculpture the fleeting sight of figures in motion. In 1921 and 1946, Giacometti witnessed two deaths which left him with an indelible memory. He had been fascinated since his early days by the human gaze and the impression that life lies in the eyes. On talking about those years, he declared:

> I cannot simultaneously see the eyes, the hands, and the feet of a person standing two or three yards in front of me, but the only part that I do look at entails a sensation of the existence of everything.[64]

In 1965, the year preceding his death, Giacometti was awarded the French national Grand Prize for the Arts. He is said to have uttered these words close to his death:

> The more you fail, the more you succeed. It is only when everything is lost and – instead of giving up – you go on, that you experience the momentary prospect of some slight progress. Suddenly you have the feeling – be it an illusion or not – that something new has opened up.

GAIT ANALYSIS AND PODIATRY

Gait analysis was part of William Scholl's 1915 text regarding the human foot, which included chapters on comparative anatomy and physiology. In particular, a chapter covered the 'Mechanical Consideration of the Human

Foot'. In this, he described the action of walking and how that could lead to various foot dysfunctions. Furthermore, Scholl (1882–1968) considered the impact of footwear on walking.[65] Similarly, *Practical Podiatry*, published in 1918 by Joseph, Burnett & Gross, included a chapter entitled 'Locomotion as an Aid in Diagnosis'.[66] In this, two methods of diagnoses in gait analysis were discussed: the observation method and the ichnogram method (the latter using powder or ink on the soles of the feet to leave a trace of footprints on paper). The remainder of that chapter is dedicated to the classification of gait under three basic types: paretic, ataxic and choreic. Interestingly, there is a note at the end of the chapter stating, 'the first compilation of its kind ever published and should prove as valuable aid to both practitioners of medicine and podiatry'.[67]

Later on came Dr Merton Root, DPM (1922–2002), a podiatrist in California and a pioneer of lower limb and foot biomechanics. Root, along with podiatrist colleagues Dr William Orien and Dr John Weed, developed a number of techniques and the field of 'podiatric biomechanics' came to be seen as standards within this area. Their text *Biomechanical Examination of the Foot*[68] was published in 1971, and landmark developments were further enshrined in the 1977 treatise entitled *Normal and Abnormal Function of the Foot*. Root's primary theory was the 'Subtalar Joint Neutral Approach'. He suggested that there was an ideal functional point where 'the position of the rear foot neither pronated, nor supinated'.[69] Frontal, sagittal and transverse plane abnormalities of different skeletal segments were recounted and how these affected the functioning of the foot. A systematic method for performing biomechanical examinations evolved and from which foot orthoses (corrective shoe inserts) could be prescribed to correct deviations from this ideal. In the textbook *Clinical Biomechanics of the Lower Extremities*, by US podiatrist Ronald L. Valmassy, the foreword to that book is by Merton L. Root, Professor Emeritus, which opens with:

> Biomechanics is a necessary basic science for the field of Podiatry. No specialty in the field of medicine is more intimately involved, on an everyday basis, with the clinical application of biomechanics. The understanding of basic mechanics and biomechanics of the lower extremity can provide the Podiatrist with an invaluable diagnostic ability that cannot be otherwise matched.[70]

A seminal piece of work in 2001 on *Podiatric Biomechanics*, undertaken by podiatrist William Eric Lee, details the development of Root's clinical system of approach towards the treatment of mechanically induced foot ailments (referred to as the Root model) and alternative models.[71] Whilst the 'Root' approach has been widely adopted in practice, it has also received challenges and eclipsed by other models such as Dananberg's Sagittal Plane Facilitation-of-Motion model[72,73] (also known as Sagittal Plane Blockade), which recognises the significance on gait of the foot and more proximal structures, including the 'spinal engine'[74]; Kirby's SALRE theory (Subtalar Joint Axis Location and Rotational Equilibrium)[75] and Glaser's MASS (Maximal Arch Subtalar Stabilisation) Position theory.[76]

Further applications, study and deployment of gait analysis were later taken into the twenty-first century by Haydn Kelly, a podiatrist, podiatric surgeon and elected Dean of the Faculty of Podiatric Surgery, UK (2014–2017), with his innovative work in forensic gait analysis.

Forensic gait analysis was first defined by Kelly in 2000:

> The identification of a person or persons by their gait or features of their gait, usually from closed circuit television (CCTV) footage and comparison to footage of a known individual.[77]

To put it simply, Kelly states, 'Forensic Gait Analysis is the application of gait analysis knowledge to legal matters/problems'.[78,79]

Kelly's work in the recognition of individuals using gait was a landmark in 2000 when his expert evidence was admissible in a trial at the Old Bailey Central Criminal Court, London.[80] This made legal history, being the first occasion gait analysis was admissible as expert evidence in criminal law.[81] This was widely reported in the media and elsewhere at the time, including front page newspaper coverage describing the robber wearing a mask, gloves and two pairs of trousers to aid disguise but could not alter his peculiar gait, caught on CCTV.[82]

In addition to providing expert evidence in legal systems internationally, giving presentations at international scientific conferences and to general audiences, articles, publications and television appearances by Kelly in relation to forensic gait analysis[83–86] have pioneered and broadened the awareness and understanding of the subject and which has encouraged others to become occupied. Kelly also supported a podiatry promotion event at Plymouth University in 2015, 'Walk This Way',[87] Careers in Podiatry: Forensic Podiatry and Crime Fiction, along with bestseller crime thriller writer Peter James, and attended as a panel guest the 2016 Theakston's Crime Writing Festival, Harrogate, England.[88,89] In addition to his other commitments, Kelly was elected by his peers as Dean of Podiatric Surgery (2014–2017), a pinnacle of responsibility and leadership in a career spanning over three decades with the diagnosis and treatment of gait related musculoskeletal conditions and foot surgery, including in professional sport. During his tenure as Dean, he initiated and took lead on securing national resources for podiatric surgery and podiatry in the UK which had not previously been achieved.

The use of CCTV to capture activity provides a means to analyse an individual's gait pattern and features of their gait, which contributes information to the identification process that supports or negates two individuals being the same. This involves observing not only the lower limbs and feet but also the movement of the whole body.

Gait analysis has also been used to great effect in palaeoanthropology in helping determine the anatomy and development of Early Man. Fascinating discoveries such as the foot bones and debate around bipedalism of 'Ardi'[90-92] (Ethiopia), the relative completeness of perhaps the most well-known skeleton of 'Lucy'[93,94] (Ethiopia), fossil footprints on the African continent at Laetoli[95-98] (Tanzania), Koobi Fora[99] (Kenya), Happisburgh[100] (England) and the findings of Homo Naledi[101] (South Africa) have also provided material for further work to those interested in the development of walking and locomotor behaviours in proto-humans.[102,103] Neanderthal children's footprints in Normandy[104] [France], and footprints of ancient humans alongside mammals in New Mexico[105] [USA] have also been unearthed.

The travel of humans via spacecraft into deep space led to the first human steps on a lunar surface when, on 20 July 1969, American astronauts Neil Armstrong followed by Edwin 'Buzz' Aldrin walked on the surface of the earth's moon. Their moonwalk and the imprints in the 'Moon dust' from the treads of their boots as they carried out tasks were captured on camera and the images relayed back to planet earth.[106]

Gait analysis has also attracted the attention of filmmakers, which, in addition to being educational, and part of the entertainment industry, has widened the audience and general understanding on 'gait'. For example, *The Usual Suspects* (1995), *American Sniper* (2014), *Mission Impossible – Rogue Nation* (2015) and *Going in Style* (2017) are films in which gait is specifically featured. In the literary world, crime thriller writer Peter James and his fictional Detective Roy Grace series deploys the skills and expertise of a forensic podiatrist 'Haydn Kelly', in the novels *Not Dead Yet* (2012); *Dead Man's Time* (2013); *Want You Dead* (2014); *You Are Dead* (2015); *Love You Dead* (2016); *Need You Dead* (2017); *Dead If You Don't* (2018); *Dead At First Sight* (2019) and *Find Them Dead* (2020).[107] The media has also promulgated coverage involving gait, for example, where passers-by thwarted disguised robbers in recognising them as not being women by the way they walk.[108]

PODIATRY EDUCATION AND TRAINING
IN RELATION TO GAIT ANALYSIS

The following section is a general overview aimed in the main for those who may not be familiar with the profession of podiatry. Knowledge and tuition in gait analysis are fundamentally provided during undergraduate podiatry education. Biomechanics is a component of gait analysis, and the understanding of gait analysis assists the clinician in the diagnosis and treatment of a multitude of conditions, as well as in comprehending the impact of systematic disease on gait. While podiatrists need to have a sound understanding of clinical biomechanics and gait analysis to underpin the diagnosis, treatment and management of patients, some podiatrists will specialise further through a wide range of postgraduate options. Of course, there are areas where clinical skills are less utilised as with any of the medical and healthcare professions, such as management posts which can be largely administrative in their requirements. Some areas of podiatry practice require a higher level of knowledge in gait and biomechanics, including the area of forensic gait analysis.

- Podiatric Surgery – biomechanics and gait analysis are utilised as part of the diagnosis of structural and functional problems, and which helps in determining whether podiatric surgery is indicated. A comprehension of biomechanics and gait analysis enables the podiatric surgeon to be able to recognise the cause and effect relationship and thereby aid in planning which procedures are likely to be suitable and help to maximise a patient's ability to recover and rehabilitate. This also includes diagnostic and interpretive radiology, including the 'charting' of imaging in the planning of surgical procedures. Podiatric surgery training in England commences at postgraduate level, spanning a period of around seven to eight years.
- Musculoskeletal (MSK) – individuals present to podiatrists seeking diagnosis and treatment with a variety of musculoskeletal injuries, including foot, ankle, leg, knee, hip and low back pain, related to biomechanical problems affecting their stance and gait. These can be multifactorial in both the aetiology (cause) and the presenting symptoms, which requires not only understanding of human anatomy, biomechanics and gait, but also the presentation and effects of any underlying or co-existing medical conditions.

24

- Sports Podiatry – in-depth knowledge of the different impacts from the wide range of sporting activities on the musculoskeletal system and the effects of different sports and footwear, both as a cause of injury and as an aid in recovery, including flexibility (stretching) and strengthening programmes, biomechanics and gait. These build into recognising the potential causative factors of an injury and therefore a diagnosis, and thereby to be able to tailor treatment programmes such as the provision of foot or ankle orthoses for the sports participant's specific needs.
- Podopaediatrics – understanding of the growth and development from birth to adulthood, including recognition of underlying conditions, normal and abnormal gait and features displayed for an age group, and the management thereof.
- Diabetes – to understand the impact of glycosylation of nerve, muscle and blood vessels; consideration of neurological, vascular and other systemic or local conditions; the consequences of mechanical overloading on the foot and its associated structures; imaging; and the management of those conditions affecting the foot, including recognising the crucial role of preventative care, and to avoid escalating foot problems, including the potential development of foot ulcers, amputation and sequelae. Maintaining patient mobility is a key part of the podiatrist's toolbox and as part of the multi-disciplinary team.
- Rheumatology – to link the disease process of arthropathies and inflammatory disorders with their impact on mobility and gait, and the treatment of related and unrelated conditions affecting the foot.
- Peripheral Vascular Disease (PVD) – patients present to general and specialist podiatry clinics with undiagnosed vascular disease and who can have other co-existing and underlying conditions. Screening techniques, including investigations and imaging techniques, are therefore paramount for early detection to enable lifestyle changes and thereby allow for an improved outcome, quality of life and life expectancy.
- Dermatology – dermatology of the foot is part of the core of podiatry care and which in turn is important in maintaining the integrity of the foot. The presence or absence of calluses and other lesions can give an indication of pathology and where the larger forces are acting on the foot. Dermatology of the foot has a role not only in the treatment of skin conditions and infections

25

but also in screening patients for the presence of underlying pathology manifesting itself in the foot and thereby helping to prevent the development, or mitigate the risk, of more serious and complex conditions from occurring.

• Forensic Podiatry – utilises podiatry based knowledge and training which can be deployed in the civil and criminal justice systems, health and care adjudication services, tribunals and elsewhere, in order to help address legal matters. The main areas of forensic podiatry for deployment in the justice systems include: forensic gait analysis, bare footprints/shoe prints, footwear and treatment records. These tools can be utilised in the process of identification of individuals, which is determined on a case by case basis of various jurisdictions on behalf of the prosecution and the defence. In the civil justice systems, podiatrists are also regularly called upon to provide expertise on such matters as personal injury and clinical negligence, where their specialist knowledge, training and experience are of value in providing opinion for the Courts and in helping to narrow the issues. Podiatrists may also be instructed as 'single joint experts' where both parties agree to instruct one expert in a particular area of expertise.

Whilst an experienced podiatrist can determine a great deal from observing a patient's gait in the consulting room or other facilities (including outdoors where appropriate, for example with sports), they may also carry out such assessments with the use of a treadmill, recognising that walking[109-112] and running[113] on a treadmill can alter results compared to that of overground. Whether those undergoing examination are familiar in utilising such equipment can also have effects. That said, the use of a treadmill can be helpful to ensure the patient's cadence is controlled and is a 'space saver'.

Clinical examinations in podiatry are supported by the use of video or photography that allow the podiatrist to review and analyse the gait of the patient in normal time, in slow motion or by advancing frame by frame to determine small abnormalities. This is a particularly useful tool during training and where a student is first exposed to examining a person's gait or for research interests. This can of course also be a useful visual aid to the patient by helping them to understand their situation. For example, the use of Smartphones speeds up that process where appropriate consents have been obtained and provides a swift and handy option which can be instantly made available to the patient and practitioner for ease of reference.

An individual's musculoskeletal system can take time to adjust to treatment and which can vary from person to person, with some patients benefitting from treatment more quickly than others. For example, when wearing foot orthoses (also known as 'orthotics'), it may well be some weeks or months following the issuing of foot orthoses before the individual experiences the beneficial effects of improvement in their symptoms and gait. Hence, the logic for gradually introducing the use of foot orthoses incrementally over a period of a few weeks when initially wearing them, in order to help minimise any adjustment aching/discomfort as the person's body adapts to a new position. Ankle braces may also be utilised with the treatment of injuries and instability. Flexibility exercises and strengthening exercises are often part of an overall treatment programme that can include foot orthoses. Such exercises are often commenced before the introduction of the foot orthoses and continued thereafter. In brief, foot orthoses are shoe insert devices designed to alter the function of an individual's foot and lower limb or other aspects of the musculoskeletal system and in relation to the individual's gait. Orthoses can range from relatively inexpensive 'off the shelf' devices to chair side, semi-bespoke or fully customised. Podiatrists also use plaster casting techniques, take plaster impression moulds of feet and may use 'CAD/CAM' (computer-aided design/computer-aided manufacture) scanning equipment, capturing the contours of the foot which can then be used in the manufacturing process of orthoses. The results of orthotic treatment are dependent upon a variety of factors, including the assessment and diagnosis of the patient's condition; the general and particular analysis of the individual's biomechanics and gait; clinical biomechanical measurements and their interpretation; understanding the orthotic prescription form for laboratory interpretation; appreciating the range of materials for the manufacture of suitable orthoses and how these meet with the patient's activities, footwear, expectations and needs. There is, of course, the requirement of appropriate information being provided to the patient; accurate record keeping; and crucially, patient compliance.

Other technical tools that can aid the podiatrist in gait analysis include 'in shoe' pressure monitoring devices. These are insoles that are linked to computer software to generate dynamic pressure maps of the foot during standing, walking, running and jumping. There are also pressure mats, again linked to computer software and applied to generate an image of the foot as it loads and propels during gait which can be used to assess walking pressures, with and without the use of footwear.

27

A thorough physical examination and medical history is required to support the clinical findings of gait analysis. These would also encompass assessing muscle flexibility, strength and assessing or measuring ranges of motion, which can involve a combination of analysing the individual walking, standing, sitting and laying down on their back (supine) or on their front (prone). A full body biomechanical assessment gives consideration to the many factors extrinsic to the foot which have a bearing on gait, including the lower limbs, knees, hips, pelvis and spinal positions; fixation and limitation of movements; upper limbs; shoulder and head position. All of these areas can display symptoms and where compensation for malalignment is exhibited.

When the podiatrist has formed a diagnosis they can develop a tailored treatment plan for the situation. This may also involve a multidisciplinary team approach and referral. As indicated, the treatment plan can include a number of elements, including prescribing specific stretching/flexibility exercises and muscle strengthening routines and rehabilitation; footwear advice; padding, strapping and taping techniques; soft tissue manipulation; electrotherapy; prescription only medicines; injection therapy; the provision of foot orthoses or surgery. Screening may also occur, particularly with those who have a family history of foot pathology or gait abnormalities. Many podiatrists have also developed other therapeutic skills, including joint mobilisation and manipulation techniques. Guides relating to the benefits of podiatry to patient care are available.

With their role in the diagnosis and treatment of musculoskeletal conditions related to foot function, podiatrists play a major role in relieving pressure on primary and secondary care settings and supporting people to manage their condition so that they can recover faster, stay in work and/or return to work earlier.[114]

As can be seen the development of gait analysis has been a slow and steady affair with significant breakthroughs in many areas over time contributing to the theories and tools utilised. In a fitting quote, Isaac Newton mirrored observations in his work by stating, 'If I have been able to see further it was because I stood on the shoulders of giants'.[115]

REFERENCES

1. Plato. *Timaeus* (360 BCE), web version translated by Benjamin Jowett. https://bit.ly/1xlhJS5 [Accessed 23 February 2020].
2. Porter, R. 1999. *The Greatest Benefit to Mankind: A Medical History of Humanity from Antiquity to the Present.* London: Fontana Press, pp. 64.

3. Plato. *Timaeus.*
4. Kenny, AJP; Amadio, AH. *Aristotle.* https://bit.ly/2rsaGKx [Accessed 23 February 2020].
5. Aristotle. 1978. *On the Motion of Animals, (350 B.C.E.), Part 3*, web version, translated by Farquharson, ASL. https://bit.ly/30flBYZ [Accessed 04 July 2019]. And: Nussbaum, MC. *Aristotle's De Moto Animalium.* Princeton, NJ: Princeton University Press.
6. Aristotle. *On the Motion of Animals (350 B.C.E.), Part 8*, web version translated by Farquharson, ASL. https://bit.ly/30flBYZ [Accessed 04 July 2019]. And: Braun, GL. 1941. Kinesiology: from Aristotle to the twentieth century. *Research Quarterly*, 12(2), pp. 163–173.
7. Sarton, G. 1953. *A History of Science: Ancient Science Through the Golden Age of Greece (1–2).* New York, NY: W.W. Norton & Co. Inc.
8. Kinematics. Oxford dictionaries online. Lexico. https://bit.ly/2XInvU3 [Accessed 23 February 2020].
9. Aruin, AS. *Biomechanics,* as defined in Encyclopedia Britannica, online version. https://bit.ly/2Ppwnrq [Accessed 23 February 2020].
10. Porter, R. ed. 1988. *Cambridge Illustrated History of Medicine.* Cambridge: CUP, pp. 62.
11. Galen. *De Motu Musculorum.*
12. Bastholm, E. 1950. The history of muscle physiology from the natural philosophers to Albrecht von Haller, Thesis. Copenhagen, pp. 77.
13. Anatomia homem leonardo. https://commons.wikimedia.org/w/index.php?curid=1440957 (US-PD -1923). [Accessed 23 February 2020].
14. Da Vinci, L. *Codex Atlanticus,* (Folio 815).
15. Da Vinci, L. *Codex Atlanticus.*
16. Vesalius, A. 1543. *De humani corporis fabrica libri septum.*
17. Porter, R. 1999. *The Greatest Benefit to Mankind: A Medical History of Humanity from Antiquity to the Present.* London: Fontana Press, pp. 179.
18. Vesalius, A. Image of skeleton with a skull from, *'De Humani Corporis Fabrica', by Vesalius,* (author), Jan van Stephan Calcar (illustrator, attributed) – Houghton Library at Harvard University, Public Domain. https://commons.wikimedia.org/w/index.php?curid=35797579 (US-PD-1923). [Accessed 23 February 2020].
19. Needham, D. 1971. *Machina Carnes.* Cambridge: CUP, pp. 118.
20. Santori, S. 1614. *De Statica Medicina.*
21. Ethier, CR; Simmons, CA. 2007. *Introductory Biomechanics: From Cells to Organisms.* Cambridge: CUP, pp. 4.
22. Martin, RB. *A Genealogy of Biomechanics,* Presidential Lecture. Pittsburgh, PA: American Society of Biomechanics. Delivered October 23, 1999. https://bit.ly/2RVjoyL [Accessed 23 February 2020].
23. Van Helden, A. *Galileo.* https://bit.ly/2nOW4D7 [Accessed 23 February 2020].
24. Hylton, J. *The Complete Works of William Shakespeare.* http://shakespeare.mit.edu/ https://bit.ly/P1WOSY [Accessed 23 February 2020].
25. Also in, Aldous Huxley's, *'Brave New World'* (Chapter 9), published 1932.

29

26. Hatfield, G. 2014. *René Descartes. Stanford Encyclopedia of Philosophy.* https://stanford.io/2np35Lg [Accessed 23 February 2020].
27. Borelli, GA. 1680. *De Motu Animalium.* Rome: A. Bernabo.
28. Riva, A; Toffoletto, E. *Marcello Malpighi, Italian Scientist. Encyclopedia Britannica.* https://bit.ly/2xrdv2P [Accessed 23 February 2020].
29. Borelli, GA. (De Motu Animalium book) [Public domain], *via Wikimedia Commons (US - PD-1923).* https://commons.wikimedia.org/wiki/File%3AGiovanni_Borelli_-_lim_joints_(De_Motu_Animalium).jpg [Accessed 23 February 2020].
30. Borelli Award. The American Society of Biomechanics. https://bit.ly/2xsoau2 [Accessed 23 February 2020].
31. Newton, I. 1664. *Quaestinoes Quaedam Philosophicae.*
32. Newton, I. 1687. *Philosophaie Naturalis Principia Mathematica.* London.
33. Swanson A. 2011. *Basic Biomechanics: Newton's Laws of Motion.* https://bit.ly/30aJkti [Accessed 23 February 2020].
34. The Editors of Encyclopedia Britannica. 2020. - Newton's laws of motion. *Physics.* https://bit.ly/2Lhy9rR [Accessed 23 February 2020].
35. Leupold, J. 1739. *Theatri Machinarum Supplementum.* Leipzig, pp. 16.
36. Encyclopedia.com. *Dufay (Du Fay), Charles-François Decisternai.* Complete Dictionary of Scientific Biography. https://bit.ly/2XITgN2 [Accessed 23 February 2020].
37. Andry, N. 1741. *L'Orthopedie.* Paris.
38. Andry, N. 1741. (engraver unknown) - Original source is Nicolas Andry, Orthopedie, immediate source is [1], Public Domain. https://commons.wikimedia.org/w/index.php?curid=8965114 (US-PD-1923) [Accessed 23 February 2020].
39. D'Alembert, J. 1743. *Traité de Dynamique.* Paris: Chez David L'Aine.
40. The Editors of Encyclopedia Britannica. *D'Alembert's Principle.* https://bit.ly/2Xp7qDG [Accessed 23 February 2020].
41. Lagrange, JL. 1788. *Mecanique Analytique.* Paris.
42. Terry, S; Science Photo Library. *Jean Jallabert.* https://bit.ly/2Jnxllj [Accessed 23 February 2020].
43. Wade, N; Piccolino, M; Simmons, A. 2011. *Robert Whytt.* Portraits of European Neuroscientists. https://bit.ly/309TrOP [Accessed 23 February 2020].
44. Whytt, R. 1751. *The Vital and Other Involuntary Motions of Animals.*
45. Rasch, PJ. 1958. Notes toward a history of kinesiology, (parts 1-3), p. 574. *Journal of American Osteopathic Association,* 572–574; 641–644 and 713–715.
46. Weber, W; Weber, E. 1836. *Die Mechanik der menschlichen Gehwerkzeuge.*
47. Cavanagh, PR. ed. 1990. *The Mechanics of Distance Running: A Historical Perspective, Biomechanics of Distance Running.* Champaign, IL: Human Kinetics Publishers, 1, pp. 1–34.
48. Davis, BL. Rana, MV. Levine, A. 2001. Human gait and joint mechanics: is the pendulum swinging back to passive dynamics? In: *Classics in Movement Science.* Edited by Mark L. Latash; Vladimir M. Zatsiotsky (Champaign, IL: Human Kinetics Publishers), pp. 88.

49. Davis, BL; Rana, MV; Levine, A. Human gait and joint mechanics: is the pendulum swinging back to passive dynamics? In: *Classics in Movement Science*. Edited by Mark L. Latash; Vladimir M. Zatsiotsky (Champaign, IL: Human Kinetics Publishers). pp. 89.
50. Rasch, PJ. Notes towards a history of kinesiology, parts 1-3. *Journal of American Osteopathic Association*, pp. 572–574; 641–644, 713–715.
51. Gilles de la Tourette, G. 1886. *Etudes Cliniques et Physiologiques sur la Marche*. Paris.
52. Acharya, HJ; Richard Camicioli, MD. 2005. The forgotten thesis of Gilles de la Tourette. *University of Alberta Health Sciences Journal*, 2(2), pp 32–33.
53. Marey, EJ. 1890–91. *Man Walking*. https://commons.wikimedia.org/w/index.php?curid=8471985 (US-PD-1923). [Accessed 23 February 2020.].
54. Ducroquet, R; Ducroquet, J; Ducroquet, P. 1968. *Walking and Limping: A Study of Normal and Pathological Walking*. Philadelphia, PA: J.B. Lippincott Company, pp. 6.
55. Gait during ambulation - See Marey, EJ., 1873. *La Machine Animale*. Paris: Librarie Germer Baillière. Marey, EJ. 1878. *La Méthode Graphique*. Paris: G. Masson Editeur. Marey, EJ. 1972. *Movement*. New York: Arno. (Original 1895). Marey, EJ. 1977. *La Photographie Mouvement*. France: Conservation des Musée de Beaune.
56. Cologne, ML. ed. 2007. *20th Century Photography*. Taschen.
57. By Photos taken by Muybridge, E. 1904. *Muybridge Race Horse Gallop*. Edit by User: Waugsberg. *[Public domain], via Wikimedia Commons, (US-PD- 1923)*. https://commons.wikimedia.org/wiki/File%3AMuybridge_race_horse_gallop.jpg [Accessed 23 February 2020.].
58. Muybridge, E. 1907. *The Human Figure in Motion: An Electro-Photographic Investigation of Consecutive Phases of Muscular Actions*. Third Impression. London: Chapman & Hall, pp. 9.
59. Muybridge, E. The Editors of Encyclopaedia Britannica. https://bit.ly/37Ni1sp [Accessed 23 February 2020.].
60. Nigg, BM; Herzog, W. ed. 2007. *Biomechanics of the Musculo-Skeletal System*. 3rd ed. Wiley-Blackwell.
61. Bernstein, NA. 1967. *The Co-ordination and Regulation of Movements*. 1st English ed. Pergamon Press.
62. Saunders, JB; Inman, VT; Eberhart, HD. 1953. The major determinants in normal and pathological gait. *Journal of Bone and Joint Surgery*, 35A, pp. 543–558.
63. Inman, VT; Ralston, HJ; Todd, F. 1981. *Human Walking*. Baltimore, MA: Williams & Wilkins.
64. Fondation Giacometti. Fragments and visions. https://bit.ly/2XoAA0D [Accessed 23 February 2020].
65. Scholl, W. 1915. *The Human Foot: Anatomy, Deformities and Treatment*. Chicago, IL: Foot Specialist Publishing Ltd.
66. Joseph, A; Burnett, EK; Gross, R. 1918. *Practical Podiatry*. New York, NY: First Institute of Podiatry, Chapter 23, pp. 343–356.

67. Joseph, A; Burnett, EK; Gross, R. 1918. *Practical Podiatry*. New York, NY: First Institute of Podiatry, Chapter 23, pp. 356. Note: also stated this chapter had been prepared by Luttinger, P. Professor of Bacteriology at the First Institute of Podiatry.

68. Root, ML; Orien, WP; Weed, JH. 1971. *Biomechanical Examination of the Foot. Vol. 1*. Los Angeles, CA: Clinical Biomechanics Corp.

69. Root, ML; Orien, WP; Weed, JH. 1977. *Normal and Abnormal Function of the Foot - Clinical Biomechanics Vol. 2*. Los Angeles, CA: Clinical Biomechanics Corp.

70. Valmassy, RL. ed. 1996. *Clinical Biomechanics of the Lower Extremities*. Foreword by Merton L. Root, Professor Emeritus. pp. vii. St Louis, MI: Mosby Inc.

71. Lee, WE. 2001. Podiatric biomechanics, an historical appraisal and discussion of the root model as a clinical system of approach in the present context of theoretical uncertainty. *Clinics in Podiatric Medicine and Surgery*, 18(4), pp. 555–684.

72. Dananberg, HJ. 1986. Functional hallux limitus and its relationship to gait efficiency. *Journal of the American Podiatric Medical Association*, 76(11), pp. 648–652.

73. Payne, CB; Dananberg, HJ. 1997. Sagittal plane facilitation of the foot. *Australasian Journal of Podiatric Medicine*, 31, pp. 7–11.

74. Dananberg, HJ. 2007. Gait style as an etiology to lower back pain. In: *Movement, Stability and Lumbopelvic Pain-Integration of Research and Therapy*. Edited by Vleeming, A; Mooney, V; Stoeckart, R. (Churchill Livingstone Elsevier).

75. Kirby, KA. 2001. Subtalar joint axis location and rotational equilibrium theory of foot function. *JAPMA*, 91(9), pp. 465–487.

76. Currie, S; Bursch, D; Glaser, E. 2010. Active stance: Orthoses – functional relevance of the arch. *Lower Extremity Review*. Online. March 2010. https://bit.ly/2VghZq8 [Accessed 23 February 2020]

77. Burrow, JG; Kelly, HD; Francis, BE. Forensic Podiatry - An Overview. *J Forensic Sci & Criminal Inves*. 2017; 5(3): 555666. DOI: 10.19080/JFSCI.2017.05.555666. https://bit.ly/3c3Bnwv [Accessed 23 February 2020].

78. Kelly, HD. 2014. Walk this way - forensic podiatrist identifies suspects by their gait. *RCMP Gazette*, 76(3), pp. 27.

79. Kelly, HD. 2019. *Forensic podiatry. Podiatry Now, College of Podiatry*, 22(1), pp. 16–18.

80. Guinness Book of World Records. 2009. *First Use of Forensic Gait Analysis Evidence in Court*. pp. 135.

81. Miles, C. 2001. Caught bow-legged: expert makes legal history. *Expert Witness Institute Newsletter*, Spring 2001, pp. 6–7.

82. Buncombe, A. 2000. Gang leader is unmasked by his bandy-legged gait. *The Independent*, 13 July, London, pp. 1.

83. BBC1 Television. August 2003. *Crimewatch Solved*. Interview and discussion with Haydn Kelly and his expert evidence on forensic gait analysis.

84. BBC1 Television. 11 June 2015. *Crimewatch Roadshow*. Live interview and discussion with Haydn Kelly, *Dean of Podiatric Surgery*, 2014–17 (UK), on forensic gait analysis and its uses and development illustrated with case examples.
85. EWN - EyeWitness News. Eliseev, A. 20 February 2015. *Busting Bad Guys: Movement Matters*. South Africa. https://bit.ly/2Xlk5mf [Accessed 23 February 2020.].
86. South Korea Television. 24 May 2013. *Interview with Haydn Kelly, Keynote Speaker, Daegu Forensic Conference, Daegu, South Korea*. https://bit.ly/2NKvjRN [Accessed 23 February 2020.].
87. Cowley, E. 2015. Opportunities in the world of podiatry. *Forensic Podiatry and Crime Fiction!* Podiatry with Plymouth University. Walk this way: an evening showcasing forensic podiatry with crime novelist Peter James & forensic podiatrist and Dean of Podiatric Surgery, Haydn Kelly and Plymouth University. https://bit.ly/2RVCAwd [Accessed 23 February 2020.].
88. Theakstons Crime Writing Festival. 22 July 2016. Harrogate. *Set a Scientist to Catch a Killer*. Panel discussion with audience Q&A.
89. *Theakstons Crime Writing Festival 2016*. Harrogate, UK. July 2016. https://bit.ly/2XoWi9H [Accessed 23 February 2020.].
90. Shreeve, J. 2010. The birth of bipedalism. *National Geographic*. July 2010. pp. 63–67.
91. Harmon, K. 2009. Long-awaited research on a 4.4-million-year-old hominid sheds new light on last ommon ancestor. 01 October 2009. *Scientific American*. https://bit.ly/32bRALs [Accessed 23 February 2020.].
92. Harmon, K. How human like was "Ardi"? 19 November 2009. *Scientific American*. https://bit.ly/2Xn8ms9 [Accessed 23 February 2020.].
93. Ward, CV. 2002. Interpreting the posture and locomotion of *Australopithecus afarensis*: where do we stand? *American Journal of Physical Anthropology*, Suppl 35, pp. 185–215.
94. *AL 288–1. "Lucy"*. Updated: November 15, 2018. Smithsonian National Museum of Natural History. https://s.si.edu/1xYuBAN [Accessed 23 February 2020.].
95. *Laetoli Footprint Trails*. Updated: October 23, 2018. Smithsonian National Museum of Natural History. https://s.si.edu/2zJZ51z [Accessed 23 February 2020.].
96. Crompton, RH; Pataky, TC; Savage, R; D'Août, K; Bennett, MR; Day, MH; Bates, K; Morse, S; Sellers, WI. 2012. Human-like external function of the foot, and fully upright gait, confirmed in the 3.66 million year old Laetoli hominin footprints by topographic statistics, experimental footprint-formation and computer simulation. *Journal Royal Society Interface*, 9(69), pp. 707–719.
97. Masao, FT; Ichumbaki, EB; Cherin, M; Barili, A; Boschian, G; Iurino, DA; Menconero, S; Moggi-Cecchi, J; Manzi, G. 2016. New footprints from Laetoli (Tanzania) provide evidence for marked body size variation in early hominins. *eLife*. https://bit.ly/2YtzxOm [Accessed 23 February 2020.].

98. Hatala, KG; Demes, B; Richmond, BG. 2016. Laetoli footprints reveal bipedal gait biomechanics different from those of modern humans and chimpanzees. *Proceedings on the Royal Society B*, 283(1836). https://bit.ly/2KXwLxV [Accessed 23 February 2020.].

99. *Footprints from Koobi Fora, Kenya*. Updated: February 9, 2016. Smithsonian National Museum of Natural History. https://s.si.edu/2Yz5x3y [Accessed 23 February 2020.]

100. Ashton, N; Lewis, SG; De Groote, I; Duffy, SM; Bates, M; Bates, R; Hoare, P; Lewis, M; Parfitt, SA; Peglar, S; Williams, C; Stringer, C. 2014. Hominin footprints from early pleistocene deposits at Happisburgh, UK. *PLOS ONE*. https://bit.ly/2YtCHlm [Accessed 23 February 2020.].

101. Shreeve, J. 2015. This face changes the human story. But how? *National Geographic*. Published, 10 September 2015.

102. Hatala, KG; Wunderlich, RE; Dingwall, HL; Richmond, BG. 2016. Interpreting locomotor biomechanics from the morphology of human footprints. *Journal of Human Evolution*, 90, pp. 38–48.

103. Pontzer, H. 2019/2020. Evolved to Exercise. *Scientific American*, Special Edition. Vol. 28, Number 5, Winter 2019/2020. pp. 60–67. Scientific American, New York.

104. Daley, J. 2019. Hundreds of ancient footprints reveal a snapshot of neanderthal family life. *Smithsonian Magazine*. https://bit.ly/32hmiTA. [Accessed 23 February 2020.]

105. Bustos, D. et al. 2018. Footprints preserve terminal Pleistocene hunt? Human-sloth interactions in North America. *Science Advances*, 4(4).

106. Kruesi, L. 2019. First human steps, chapter two: human footprints. *The Moon*. Celebrating the 50th Anniversary of Apollo 11. Washington, DC: National Geographic.

107. James, P. Books listed here published by Macmillan. *"Not Dead Yet"* (2012); *"Dead Man's Time"* (2013); *"Want You Dead"* (2014); *"You Are Dead"* (2015); *"Love You Dead"* (2016); *"Need You Dead"* (2017); *"Dead If You Don't"* (2018); *"Dead at First Sight"* (2019); *"Find Them Dead"* (2020).

108. Davenport, J. 2015. Burka robbers exposed by their walk. *Evening Standard (London)*, 28 August 2015, pp. 1 & 4.

109. Strathy, GM; Chao, EY; Laughman RK. 1983. Changes in knee function associated with treadmill ambulation. *Journal of Biomechanics*, 16(7), pp. 517–522.

110. Andriacchi, TP; Alexander, EJ. 2000. Studies of human locomotion: past, present and future. *Journal of Biomechanics*, 33(10): 1217–1224.

111. Riley, PO; Paolini, G; Della Croce, U; Paylo, KW; Kerrigan,DC. 2007. A kinematic and kinetic comparison of overground and treadmill walking in healthy subjects. *Gait & Posture*, 26(1): 17–24.

112. Fischer, A, Debbi, E, Wolf, A. 2015. Effects of body weight unloading on electromyographic activity during overground walking. *Journal of Electromyography and Kinesiology*, 25(4), pp. 709–714.

113. Schache, AG; Blanch, PD; Rath, DA; Wrigley, TV; Starr, R; Bennell, KL. 2001. A comparison of overground and treadmill running for measuring the three-dimensional kinematics of the lumbo-pelvic-hip complex. *Clinical Biomechanics*, 16, pp. 667–680.
114. Kim, Y; Lim, JM; Yoon, B. 2013. Changes in ankle range of motion and muscle strength in habitual wearers of high heeled shoes. *Foot & Ankle International*, 34(3), pp. 414–419. doi: 10.1177/1071100712468562.
115. Letter from Isaac Newton to Robert Hooke, February 1676.

2

Observational Gait Analysis – Progression and Application

Contents

INTRODUCTION

In this chapter we will consider the clinical use of observational gait analysis (OGA) in contemporary practice. As identified in other chapters herein, interest in locomotion is not a modern phenomenon. Hippocrates (c.460–370 BCE) emphasised the application of observation, experience and rational science as he made numerous observations following 'dislocations of the articulations' described in the gaits a clinician might observe.[1] It was however with the emergence of new technologies that photographic imaging was first used in gait analysis, and the depth of analysis increased considerably.

In the mid-twentieth century, the clinical value of video in gait analysis became apparent to paediatric orthopaedic surgeon David Sutherland (1923–2006), who began measuring kinematic (joint movement) angles from cinematic film to aid surgical decision-making.[2] Since Sutherland's early work, video aided observational gait analysis has remained a commonly used tool in laboratory settings, but also increasingly in primary care clinical settings. Additionally, two-dimensional digitisation software, which was costly at the outset in the 1980s and 1990s (as new technologies often are until their wider deployment), can now be much more easily obtained on smartphones or other handheld devices, thereby adding the instant ability to digitise video. This enables quantification of joint angles in paused frames of the recorded footage – a facility that somewhat blurs the boundaries between quantitative, objective laboratory analysis and subjective clinical OGA.

In the twentieth and twenty-first centuries, video further developed and has become a commonly applied technology in gait analysis, and by its existence, allowed for the advent of forensic gait analysis in 2000.

Less than 150 years since the zoopraxiscope movie showing horse gait, technology has now progressed to a point where, by 2021, it is estimated 40% of the world's population is projected to own a smartphone,[3] each having the ability to record instantaneous video with just a few button presses straight from their pocket. Whilst Muybridge was projecting monochrome movies in low frame rates from a heavy table-top zoopraxiscope, smartphone users can record and play back up to 4K resolution or high definition 240 frames per second (fps) colour movies with small, image stabilised handheld devices. Undoubtedly, such technology will not end there.

DEVELOPMENT OF GAIT ANALYSIS IN PODIATRY

Within the fields embraced by podiatry, applied biomechanics, referred to as 'podiatric biomechanics', became core to daily podiatric practice in addressing musculoskeletal pain and pathology of the foot and lower limb, in both diagnosis and treatment.[4]

The USA first began teaching the principles of podiatric biomechanics during the 1950s and 1960s, culminating in the publication in 1971 by Sgarlato of *A Compendium of Podiatric Biomechanics*[5] and the text by Root, Orien, Weed and Hughes entitled, *Biomechanical Examination of the Foot: volume 1.*[6] In 1977, Root and his colleagues added a second volume entitled, *Normal and Abnormal Function of the Foot.*[7] These seminal early texts offered students and practitioners of podiatry clear models for assessment and treatment with the use of mechanical therapies – namely functional foot orthoses – to address mechanical foot related pain and pathology.

The era of evidence-based medicine emerged in the 1970s, but the technology with which it would be possible for scientists to challenge podiatric biomechanical models had yet to fully develop. The models proposed by Root et al.[7] were widely adopted by the profession with the outcomes they observed, but patients who did not respond to the therapies as well as expected and which could not easily be explained from the standpoint or the 'Root' approach, led to other researchers challenging the model.[8,9] Podiatrists continued to problem solve the biomechanics of the lower limb and foot, and new conceptual papers were published in the American literature.[10-16] These offered clinicians alternative assessment and treatment models based on modelling the foot as a lever system to balance rotational equilibrium or by facilitating sagittal plane movement through the joints of the foot. The new models were well received and offered an alternative to the 'Root' approach in assessment and treatment of mechanical foot and lower limb conditions traditionally managed with foot orthoses. This period drew podiatrists towards embracing the functional anatomy of the foot and drawing on articles from the 1950s and 1970s[17,18] to add greater understanding about the basis of human movement.

The tissue stress theory proposed by McPoil and Hunt in 1995[19] arguably helped move podiatry on to another level of critical thinking. By considering all of the podiatric biomechanical models, the functional anatomy, the theories learned from the seminal texts, the new science then emerging from two-dimensional (2D) motion analysis, use of pedobarographs and electromyography, as well as the knowledge through education, training and clinical experience, podiatrists were able to critically reason mechanisms of injury and therapy – that is identify the problem and the solution.

Podiatric biomechanics conferences were hives of pioneering thinkers pinning together old and new knowledge and skills to form hypotheses for musculoskeletal conditions, causation, progression and, importantly, the solution via novel approaches in biomechanical therapy.

Now in the era of evidence-based medicine and with the technology more fully developed, podiatrists and other clinicians are further able to refine and explain the models and approaches of the last century moving towards a more person-centred, stratified medicine paradigm when considering musculoskeletal conditions of the foot and lower limb. The foundation training at podiatry undergraduate level combines many areas, including anatomy, physiology, medicine, pathology, musculoskeletal growth and development, neurology, gait analysis, imaging, human movement and biomechanics, dermatology, pharmacology, rheumatology, footwear design and technology and more,[20,21] all of which inform and are underpinned by skills in critical thinking. This contributes to the accuracy of clinical diagnosis, treatment and rehabilitation, adding detail and thereby bringing more good quality evidence to the environment.

With the hindsight of early podiatric biomechanics and its clinical successes and failures, as well as the insight of current emerging clinical and scientific evidence, podiatrists are expertly equipped to hypothesise and critically reason around the observations they make in OGA to determine likely causes for the patterns of movement displayed by individuals.

Gait analysis performed by podiatrists involves information gathering, assessment and analysis of that information and evaluation of the data about an individual's locomotion. This includes consideration and comparison of the material obtained at the initial and subsequent consultations with a patient, which is helpful in assessing the patients' progress when comparing their situation pre-treatment, during treatment and post-treatment. This has applications across all areas of podiatric practice, including general clinical practice, podiatric surgery, forensic podiatry, sports injuries and research and development. During the career of the podiatrist, there develops a particular blend of knowledge, understanding, skill sets and experience to approach assessment, analysis and treatment of the musculoskeletal system, including clinical tests and gait analysis in a unique way, which prepares them ideally for observing gait in a forensic capacity.

DEFINITION AND CONTEXTS

Gait is defined as 'a manner of walking, stepping or running'.[22]

The gait of an individual is a coordinated series of complex movements involving the musculoskeletal system from the head to the foot. Human gait analysis has been variably defined and Kirtley[23] notes that people refer to it in their own frame of reference: observational, computerised and instrumented often without qualification. It is therefore important to communicate how gait analysis has been conducted when reporting the results beyond the frame of reference. For example, a clinical gait analysis report submitted by a podiatrist or other healthcare professional in clinical practice; that by a biomechanics laboratory; a gait analysis report for medico-legal purposes such as personal injury or clinical negligence claims in the civil courts; or that for identification purposes in the criminal justice system, will all be geared differently according to the requirements. One should be mindful that an individual's knowledge, training and experience will also affect the content of a gait report and how that is then displayed and considered.

Although an understanding by the reader here of gait analysis is already presumed, it may be helpful to briefly discuss some of the fundamentals to assist readers who may not have clinical expertise in performing gait analysis but who may find it useful to have an appreciation of some terms used in this area.

Step – The movement of the body during the period from when one foot contacts the ground to when the foot of the opposite side contacts the ground.

Stride – The movement of the body that occurs during two successive steps.

Cadence – A term which defines the number of steps per minute.

Gait Cycle – Refers to the movement of the body during one single stride[24,25]

The gait cycle identifies, describes, analyses and evaluates all aspects of gait and lists sequential events that occur in one limb during one complete stride (i.e. from the initial heel contact (heel strike) of one foot to the initial heel contact of the same foot at the start of the next stride).[26]

41

The gait cycle is divided into two phases:

1. **Stance phase**: When any part of the foot is in contact with the supporting surface. The stance phase approximates 60% of a gait cycle.
2. **Swing phase**: When the foot is swinging from one episode of ground contact to the next. The swing phase approximates 40% of a gait cycle.

For general ease of understanding and for the reader who may not be so familiar with gait analysis: in the traditional podiatric model of gait analysis, the stance phase can be subdivided into three periods: contact, mid-stance and propulsion. Each of these may be subdivided further into early, middle and late.

There is also what is known as the 'Rancho Los Amigos' terminology,[27] broadly adopted across multiple clinical disciplines, which describes the stance phase with five events: initial contact, loading response, mid-stance, terminal stance and pre-swing; whilst the swing phase is divided to initial swing, mid-swing and terminal swing and this we will revisit later in the chapter.

Anatomical Planes/Planes of Motion

Human movement is a complex process involving coordinated actions of the musculoskeletal system and occurs about the body's anatomical planes, which are three in number. These are the *sagittal plane, transverse plane* and the *coronal plane* (see Figure 2.1). The coronal plane may also be referred to as the 'frontal' plane, but this should not to be confused with the descriptor of a 'front view' of an individual.

Joints glide and roll to produce clinically detectable movement, as follows:

Sagittal plane – Contains the movements of dorsiflexion (upwards) and plantar flexion (downwards).
Transverse plane – Contains the movements of abduction and adduction. Abduction is movement away from the mid-line of the body (known as 'out-toed' when referring to the feet). Adduction is movement towards the mid-line of the body (or 'in-toed' when referring to the feet).
Coronal (frontal) plane – Contains the movements of eversion (dorsiflexion + abduction) and inversion (plantar flexion + adduction).

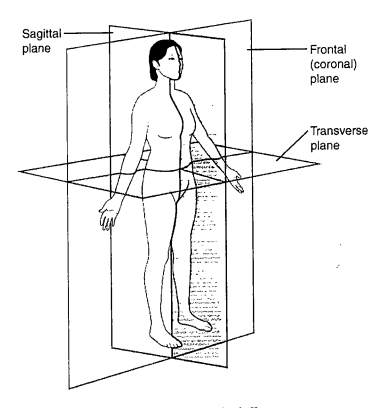

Sagittal plane

Frontal (coronal) plane

Transverse plane

Figure 2.1 Anatomical planes of the human body.[29]

Whilst there is no internationally agreed definition of the terms *prona-tion* and *supination* in the research literature, in clinical contexts these are frequently understood to mean tri-planar and tri-axial movements of the foot on the leg.[6]

In weight-bearing, pronation is comprised of relative dorsiflexion and abduction of the forefoot on the rearfoot, and eversion of the heel. Supination is comprised of the opposite: plantar flexion and adduction of the forefoot on the rearfoot, and inversion of the heel. The movements cou-ple with leg rotation – pronation and internal leg rotation occur together – supination with external leg rotation.[6] There are also a series of other movements that normally occur throughout the musculoskeletal system that help facilitate a person's gait, but we do not need to go into the details here. A more general and relatively recent definition might be to describe pronation as 'motion of the foot articulations that allow the foot to become more prone to the support surface thereby increasing the ground contact surface area of the foot'.[28]

At What Age Does Adult Human Gait Occur?

Adult human gait, that is a mature walking action with an upright bipedal gait and reciprocal heel-toe pattern, has been reported to occur from around the age of 2–4 years.[30–32] However, normal gait during childhood varies with age,[33,34] and some children do not demonstrate a fully symmetrical mature gait by 13 years of age.[35,36] Similarly, childhood growth and development issues as well as pathology can affect gait, and variability is demonstrated to be at its greatest under the age of 7 years.[37,38] Generally, walking with assistance occurs at around 12 months, walking independently by 12–15 months, and running by 18 months.[39] All children do of course differ and such ages are determined by broad criteria.

The bones of the various body segments ossify and reach skeletal maturity at different stages,[40] during which appearances may alter. For example, as seen with 'growth spurts' where musculoskeletal conditions or malalignments may appear, such as genu valgum (knock-knee) or genu varum (bowing of knee), which may then remain, reduce, accentuate or disappear as growth and development continue.[4,39] Such changes in alignment need to be considered in context and have relevance both when analysing and comparing video footage of individuals' gait or features of their gait in the diagnosis and treatment of clinical conditions and for forensic purposes.

Function of Gait

The primary purpose of walking or running is to transport the human body safely and efficiently across the ground, on the level, uphill and downhill, negotiating obstacles as necessary. In order to transport the body safely, the neuromuscular control system must also provide appropriate shock absorption, prevent collapse and maintain balance of the upper extremity and achieve a safe foot trajectory.[41,42] Human gait, whether walking or running, has the characteristic of bilateral symmetry; that is, when an individual walks or runs, the leading leg and arm have an opposite reciprocal placement. For example, when the left leg swings forward (anterior), the right arm swings behind (posterior). Conversely, when the right leg swings forward (anterior), the left arm swings behind (posterior). Figure 2.2 gives an illustration of reciprocal arm and leg movements during gait.

Figure 2.2 Illustration of adult human gait.

It should be remembered that walking and running have important bio-mechanical differences,[43,44] One obvious difference, even to the untrained eye, is that in running there is a period in which both feet are simultaneously off the ground, but not so with walking. Of course, running gait activities differ themselves. By way of example, consider that of 100 m sprinters, hurdlers, marathon runners, multi-directional activities such as football, rugby, tennis, basketball or other activities involving jumping or throwing, all have different styles.

There is much written in the literature on human gait and its components,[4,25,42,45–50] including but not limited to the areas of kinematics, kinetics, biomechanics, balance, movement and motor control. The relationship with a person's step length and step frequency[51] and the correlation between step length and step frequency and how one affects the other is understandably of interest in human walking.[52,53] Acoustically observable properties of adult gait have been developed by an approach extracting human gait parameters from micro Doppler sonar grams. Key parameters included average speed of walking, torso velocity, walk cycle time and peak leg velocity and illustrate similarities and dissimilarities between female and male gait; males tend to walk with larger walk cycle times and peak leg velocities than females.[54]

Kirtley[23] notes that in podiatry the influences of Root et al. remain strong although these are being replaced by what he refers to as 'new biomechanics' enlightened with nuances following bone pin studies, advanced clinical motion analysis and finite element modelling. Healthcare professionals appreciate the importance of gait analysis for patients and the worth that multidisciplinary approaches can bring to the patients' benefit.

It is therefore important that whoever is reading and interpreting a gait analysis report is clear about the emphasis the practitioner is likely to have taken, based upon their clinical background. Should they not have the knowledge, education and experience of using gait analysis in diagnosis and treatment, and where the understanding of normal and pathological gait is significant, one needs to comprehend where the

45

gaps and disadvantages may be, apart from the theoretical and different skill sets. The common ground, however, among many definitions of gait analysis is the observation or measurement of gait and performance parameters that informs a report. Reports are written according to the context and might include emphasis in skeletal biomechanics and posture, muscular tone and coordination, athletic performance and form, orthotic and prosthetic function, all according to the matter and task in hand.

OBJECTIVE AND SUBJECTIVE GAIT ANALYSIS

The fundamental difference between instrumented gait analysis and observational gait analysis (OGA) is objectivity versus subjectivity. Highly accurate instruments in the gait laboratory offer numerical data with a known system error, whereas in OGA, the instrument outputting data is the practitioner. While quantitative data is undeniably helpful, such as in surgical decision-making or reducing the risk, for example, of foot ulceration in diabetics, it is the clinical experience and knowledge of the practitioner that decides the usefulness of the data and the interpretation for clinical decision-making. It is the human synthesis of objective plus subjective clinical judgement that ultimately leads to the most ideal choice for all involved – human interaction modulates a set of graph data in the clinical decision-making process. As technology improves, it is likely that the barrier of time in a busy clinic could disappear with automated reporting and faster software workflows.

Where no instrumentation (or video alone) is used, the methods to analyse gait can become entirely subjective. Where there is no quantification of data, human interpretation and judgement are the only contributors to the gait report. If humans were as consistent as machines, this would not be a problem, but the differences in expertise, experience and ability to quantify events and angles by eye can vary between practitioners reporting of gait.[55,56] Whilst it may not be expected to be challenging in seeking agreement on identifying a particular feature of gait from practitioners with appropriate knowledge, education and training, it could be more so when seeking agreement for a more exact measurement of a specific feature or form of gait. In such circumstances, and depending on the matter in hand, it could be helpful to seek agreement on whether a measurement is within a defined range. However, opinions could perhaps be expected to vary more so when two or more people from different spheres or professions (and therefore training) are asked to provide an opinion on the same item.

The past twenty years or so in the scientific literature has, therefore, been somewhat focused on demonstrating methods to improve upon non-standardised OGA with instrumentation and tools for use with OGA such as proformas.[55,57–59]

Whilst instrumentation improves clinical gait analysis, particularly with measurements, time constraints in primary and secondary care settings can often lead to such instruments being used sparingly. Whilst OGA provides a much more rapid means of gait analysis, it may be the only tool the clinician immediately has available in gait analysis to add to the information needed as part of the clinical decision-making process in diagnosis and treatment. Of course, as already mentioned, nowadays smartphones can also have a role.

Patla[60] reported that OGA was the most commonly used method of clinical gait analysis, and this likely remains true today given the assertion by Perry and Burnfield[61] in 2010 that:

> all professionals involved in the management of the lower extremities use some form of gait analysis. The simplest approach is a generalised screening to note gross abnormalities in a person's walking pattern.

Acknowledging the pragmatism that leads to the employment of OGA in many clinical environments, they add a caveat saying:

> The observer is more likely to make the appropriate determinations, however, if the analysis proceeds in a systematic fashion.

A significant foundation of undergraduate training in gait analysis within podiatry in fact relates to OGA techniques for this reason, with instrumentation being added throughout the degree courses to delineate the value and drawbacks of each method.

INTRA-RATER AND INTER-RATER RELIABILITY FOR OBSERVATIONAL GAIT ANALYSIS

Studies have repeatedly drawn attention to the impact of experience in orthopaedic and neurological OGA, since it could be hypothesised that a practice effect may improve intra-rater and inter-rater reliability[56,59,62–64]

Brunnekreef and colleagues confirmed this in a study of four inexperienced, four experienced and two expert observational gait analysts.[59] Each were shown 30 gait movies (15 male and 15 female, aged between 15 and 62 years) with patients demonstrating mild to severe gait deviations due to orthopaedic impairment. The patients were all wearing shorts and walked several, 15m laps in a straight line and in a semi-circle. Results are displayed in Table 2.1.

Intra Class Correlations (ICCs) are deemed to be very good above 0.7.[65] The only time this was achieved overall was in the 'Expert' intra-rater (test-retest) reliability. The next nearest being the 'Experienced' intra-rater reliability at 0.63. However, the ranges include one experienced practitioner performing equally to the experts and one performing worse than the inexperienced ones.

Table 2.1 Table to Summarise Intra- and Inter-Rater Reliability of Variably Experienced Gait Analysts in the Estimation of Moderate to Severe Gait Deviations, from Pelvis to Ankle, among Orthopaedic Patients (Brunnekreef et al [59])

Expertise Level	Intra-Rater Reliability ICC (95% CI)	Inter-Rater Reliability ICC (95% CI)
Expert	0.70 and 0.74	0.54 (0.48–0.60)
Experienced	0.63 (0.57–0.70)	0.42 (0.38–0.46)
Inexperienced	0.57 (0.52–0.62)	0.40 (0.36–0.44)

Table 2.2 displays an orthopaedic gait proforma for intra-rater and inter-rater reliability testing in observational gait analysis similar to that used by Brunnekreef et al.[59]

Brunnekreef et al. also reported that whilst overall reliability varies between practitioners, this can be refined to show how variability exists in the ability to assess specific gait parameters and characteristics. Table 2.3 shows some examples of such parameters and characteristics. The test-retest reliability for specific gait parameters in   practitioners of varying experience in orthopaedic OGA is also displayed.

Table 2.3 also illustrates intra-rater reliability of observational gait analysis over various parameters with increasing levels of experience.[56,59,66]

Table 2.2 Table to Show an Orthopaedic Gait Pro-Forma for Intra-Rater and Inter-Rater Reliability Testing in Observational Gait Analysis (Similar to That Used by Brunnekreef et al[59]).

	Factor	Question	Limb	Stance Phase			Swing Phase	
				Early	Midstance	Late	Early	Late
General	1	Shortened stance phase?	Left	Yes No	Yes No	Yes No		
			Right	Yes No	Yes No	Yes No		
Trunk	2	Trunk anterior to the hips?	Left			Yes No		
			Right			Yes No		
	3	Trunk posterior to the hips?	Left			Yes No		
			Right			Yes No		
	4	Lateral flexion present?	Left	Yes No	Yes No	Yes No		
			Right	Yes No	Yes No	Yes No		
	5	Arm swing reduced?	Left			Yes No		
			Right			Yes No		
Pelvis	6	Posterior rotation excessive?	Left			Yes No		
			Right			Yes No		
Hip	7	Extension reduced?	Left			Yes No		
			Right			Yes No		
Knee	8	Extension reduced?	Left					Yes No
			Right					
	9	Flexion absent?	Left			Yes No		
			Right					
	10	Flexion reduced?	Left		Yes No			
			Right					
Ankle	11	Extension absent?	Left		Yes No	Yes No		Yes No
			Right					
	12	Plantar flexion reduced?	Left			Yes No	Yes No	Yes No
			Right					

Table 2.3 Table to Show Intra-Rater Reliability of Observational Gait Analysis over Various Parameters with Increasing Levels of Experience[56,59,66]

Gait Parameter	Intra-rater Reliability Expert	Intra-rater Reliability Experienced	Intra-rater Reliability Moderately experienced	Intra-rater Reliability Inexperienced	Study
Shortened stance phase	ICC=0.86	ICC=0.54	—	ICC=0.50	Brunnekreef et al.[59]
Trunk anterior to hips	ICC=0.87	ICC=0.81	—	ICC=0.53	Brunnekreef et al.[59]
Lateral flexion	ICC=0.82	ICC=0.68	—	ICC=0.74	Brunnekreef et al.[59]
Reduced arm swing	ICC=0.75	ICC=0.75	—	ICC=0.81	Brunnekreef et al.[59]
Posterior rotation of pelvis excessive	ICC=0.65	ICC=0.13	—	ICC=0.45	Brunnekreef et al.[59]
Hip extension reduced	ICC=0.63	ICC=0.59	—	ICC=0.47	Brunnekreef et al.[59]
Knee extension reduced	ICC=0.66	ICC=0.65	—	ICC=0.63	Brunnekreef et al.[59]
Knee flexion absent	ICC=0.82	ICC=0.58	—	ICC=0.36	Brunnekreef et al.[59]
Knee flexion reduced	ICC=0.82	ICC=0.42	—	ICC=0.54	Brunnekreef et al.[59]
Knee extension absent	ICC=0.52	ICC=0.58	—	ICC=0.22	Brunnekreef et al.[59]
Ankle plantar flexion reduced	ICC=0.66	ICC=0.30	—	ICC=0.37	Brunnekreef et al.[59]
Abnormal rearfoot movement	—	—	Kappa=-0.12 to 0.59	—	Keenan and Bach[56]
Out toe foot position	—	—	64-73%	—	Geradts et al.[66]

Interpretations:

ICC = 1–0.7 is excellent to very good

ICC = 0.6–0.4 is fair

ICC = 0.3–0 is poor to very poor

Kappa = negative number to 0 is no tester agreement

Kappa = 0.01–0.2 is poor to fair

Kappa = 0.21–0.4 is fair

Kappa = 0.41–0.6 is moderate

Expert = senior clinicians with exceptional knowledge of gait impairments associated with orthopaedic conditions and extensively used a gait proforma in a clinical environment.

Experienced = senior clinicians with prior gait training and minimum 10 years clinical experience, including 5 years using a gait proforma.

Moderately experienced = junior or senior clinician with limited or no experience of using a gait analysis proforma.

Inexperienced = no experience of gait analysis or use of a gait analysis proforma.

Some gait parameters, however, have been shown to be more universally well agreed in moderately experienced gait analysts.[60]

- Genu valgum (90%)
- Genu varum (81%)
- Shortened stride length (93%)

WORKFLOW IN OBSERVATIONAL GAIT ANALYSIS

Lord et al.[58] developed a gait proforma to ensure a systematic approach in clinical gait analysis and found that reliability was improved with its use.

Perry and Burnfield[61] also advocate the use of a proforma along with a systematic workflow with three discrete components:

1. Information organisation
2. Established sequence of observation (data acquisition)
3. A format for data interpretation

They advocate a logical approach with anatomy and the phases of the gait cycle forming the focus, starting with the first point of contact with the ground. Since this happens in the foot, they begin data acquisition from this segment but enter it onto a form laid out like the anatomy; hips before knees in the list. The form is completed from the bottom of the form upwards. Such a method includes a two-step approach.

A two-step approach is that which is commonly carried out by podiatrists.

1. Firstly, by considering the global (or general) movement patterns of the individual.
2. Secondly, by then focusing on the anatomical segments.

This process of OGA is classically that performed by podiatrists and other clinicians, involving observation from the front, rear and sides of the person walking at their preferred speed.[67] During the process of observation, the clinician attempts to identify gait abnormalities by comparing what they observe to an optimal pattern and sequence of events based on data of what they would expect to observe in a normal gait.[24] Gait analysis needs a holistic procedure and each body segment of the individual needs to be viewed and considered, and examination involves both static and dynamic evaluation. Whether one starts at the foot or the head for the analysis of the anatomical segments may vary, depending on the practitioner. What matters is the method adopted by the practitioner is consistent across the subjects they are assessing.

One needs to be mindful that where a person is aware of being observed, such as in a clinic or laboratory setting, the person being observed may modify or improve an aspect of their behaviour in response to their heightened awareness of being observed. This is a phenomenon known as the *Hawthorne effect*.[68] Clinicians are aware of such behaviour and will often re-assure patients and encourage them in a mild and relaxed manner. As patients walk for longer, they usually tend to relax and their normal gait pattern can be observed.

A particularly useful aspect for forensic gait analysis when viewing CCTV footage, surveillance footage, custody suite footage or other environments is the generally reduced awareness of the individual being recorded when compared to that of video recording a patient in a clinical setting.

We have already seen that proformas are helpful to ensure a systematic approach in the gait analysis performed and which improves reliability. But proformas can vary in the body segments they consider. What is important is that the practitioner selects a proforma that assesses all body segments involved in gait from the head to the foot. Whether the practitioner begins at the head or the foot in the analysis of the body segments is an individual choice. Again, what matters is consistency in the process adopted.

It must be remembered that in order to correctly assess the normality of gait, a sound knowledge of normal movements in the observed population is required.

Since children and adults vary within gait parameters, as do adults with and without neurological conditions that affect an individual's gait, for example Parkinson's disease, the examiner should become *au fait* with the normal objective parameters for healthy gait where available in the literature, prior to commencing gait analysis and be well versed at performing such analyses of patients. Deviations of any gait parameter can then be identified and estimated using Observational Gait Analysis.

In an attempt to describe the events of the gait cycle in more detail, one example, as mentioned earlier, is that offered by the Rancho Los Amigos (RLA) Gait Analysis Committee, who constructed a new system with less specific terminology.[69] Instead of heel strike, they refer to 'initial contact' followed by a description, 'initial contact achieved by forefoot heel strike'. Figure 2.3 displays an illustration aligning the traditional or 'classic' podiatric terminology[70] and that of RLA. The aim of the RLA terminology acted as a 'catch all' for existing terminology so that heel strike could still be referred to if present at initial contact. The RLA option divides the gait cycle into two periods in the same way as is classically understood: *stance phase* and *swing phase*. The tasks within these phases are weight acceptance, single limb support and limb advancement and the

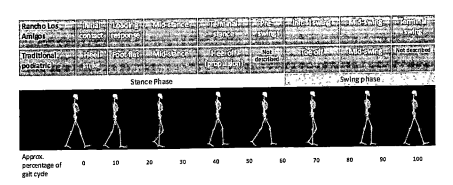

Figure 2.3 Illustration to display aligning of traditional podiatric gait analysis and RLA.[69,70]

phases are initial contact, loading response, mid-stance, terminal stance, pre-swing, initial swing, mid-swing and terminal swing.

Both timing and joint angles are important to the acquisition and recording of data in gait analysis, since they are intrinsically linked to the tasks of gait. For example, failure to have knee extension at heel strike (initial contact) could result in a fall. Such actions or events can be seen when performing OGA. Having the capability to reliably quantify the amount of knee flexion that occurred as per this example could then allow for a more precise statement to be made.

However, the proforma that accompanies the RLA system only notes body segments from the toes up to the trunk. The head, neck, shoulders and arms are not included. Such a gait proforma is *not* ideally suited for podiatry practice as the podiatrist needs to give consideration to all body segments when conducting gait analysis, due to the impact that overall posture and movement has on the centre of mass and foot function.

In 1996 a core undergraduate textbook in Podiatry by Valmassy was published, *Clinical Biomechanics of the Lower Extremities*,[4] and conveys that gait analysis is apportioned into two important parts: "static and dynamic". It also includes a shorthand system for displaying dynamic gait analysis and provided a skeleton type illustration for recording observable details of gait analysis. Referred to as 'GHORT' (Gait Homunculus Observed Relational Tabular),[71] the human kinetic chain is depicted in segmented form, head to feet. Such an approach is useful as many generations of ergonomic studies have demonstrated that shorthand systems such as Fischer projections of organic molecules[72] tend to become a preferred method for representing and compressing data.[73] (Fischer Projections allow for 3D molecular structures to be represented in a 2D environment without changing their properties and/or structural integrity.) Using simple strikes of a pen, the clinician would draw lines against the GHORT diagram to indicate deviations in postures during stance or gait. Most of the individuals using the system were able to understand information recorded by other clinicians and draw the same conclusion on what another recorder has observed. Familiarisation studies revealed that, after about the fifth evaluation, most clinicians seemed to have easily mastered the (GHORT) form.[71] The system continues to have utility.

Video Playback

When recording details of a person's gait, the option of video playback can be of considerable benefit. It is an improvement over having only the option of normal time (also known as *real time*) clinical gait analysis, as it provides recorded footage for repeated analysis, which can be analysed in normal time, slow motion and still frame pictures. This also has the benefit of being able to be shown to a patient and in a similar way that a surgeon may do, for example, of a patient's hip or knee replacement.

The option of video playback in a clinical setting may be regarded as of more use when initially studying and learning about the subject of clinical gait analysis – and perhaps less so to an experienced practitioner in clinical practice where the added time element of using video playback does not always allow, or in situations where it does not add significantly to the clinical decision-making process. The advent of having video easily available on smartphones allows for brief clips of gait to be obtained and a playback facility allows such footage to be displayed and discussed efficiently with the patient as needs be, there and then at the time of the consultation or treatment. That can be a helpful tool whether for illustrative purposes or as an aid in diagnosis and treatment, where local clinical governance policy/patient consent allows.

PARAMETERS IN ANALYSIS OF GAIT FROM VIDEO FOOTAGE

In addition to the kinematic parameters, other clinical gait analysis techniques transfer well when gathering data from video. People not only have a gait pattern determined by age or joint pathology but other variables from their genetic inheritance, musculoskeletal development, joint morphology and geometry, soft tissue restrictions or hypermobility, acquired injuries, systemic medical conditions affecting the limbs and idiosyncrasies to make up a unique overall style of walking.[74]

Clinical research has identified clear links between human gait characteristics and different medical conditions.[75] Some characteristics of gait and posture are more frequently described than measured in a clinical setting. Examples include classifications of postures where qualifiers of + or – are helpful in emphasising the extent of the characteristic. The presence of genu varum, for example, may be described either qualitatively or in some cases quantitatively. Where clothing is not obscuring the view, or parallax error an issue, genu varum could be described as mild, moderate or severe, or the internal tibiofemoral angle could be measured using digitisation software. Measurements have the advantage over descriptors of being more easily comparable to existing data where available, to describe the measurement in standard deviations and the mean for a population.

The qualitative or quantitative parameters using CCTV footage include:

- Global patterns or styles of movement
- Joint kinematics 2D/3D
- Static and/or dynamic postures
- Anthropometrics
- Temporal spatial characteristics

PERCEPTION AND OBSERVATIONAL GAIT ANALYSIS

The performing of OGA brings the 'pros and cons' of not only the practitioner's wealth of knowledge, experience and expertise, but also that of the human visual system. The human primary visual cortex is one of the most primitive parts of the human brain and is particularly sensitive to movement and pattern recognition.

Recent fMRI studies have revealed a dedicated centre in the human brain – the superior temporal sulcus (STS), which specifically detects and discerns human locomotion movement. The STS is, however, also sensitive to social context and is stimulated further where social context is added as opposed to sterile gait videos with no background detail or when human-like robots are seen walking.[76]

The practitioner should always be mindful of their innate brain function when commenting on video gait footage, since it is reasonable to expect that some of their perception may have been affected by selective attention. This phenomenon refers to the instance when focus is set on a particular area of a screen or scenario and other events in the same visual frame are missed. A famous exercise demonstrating the optical illusion of selective attention was constructed by Chabris and Simons[77] and the 'Invisible Gorilla' experiment. This builds on Posner and Presti's original work on orientation of attention.[78] The Invisible Gorilla experiment shows how 50% of observers, when trying to count basketball passes between actors as they watch a film, fail to notice a gorilla walking across the centre of the screen. Even those wise to the ruse and who know to watch for the gorilla will see the gorilla but frequently miss other unexpected changes such as the colour of the backdrop. Given the selective attention used in gait analysis when the practitioner focuses intently on a particular segment of anatomy, it is possible for them to miss a significant event in a part of the screen that they are not focused on. For this reason, taking a step-wise, systematic approach to segmental analysis of a subject can help in minimising missing any 'gorillas' or important movements in the footage.

The Invisible Gorilla experiment illustrates how the physiological limitations and mechanisms of the human visual system can impact interpretation of video footage. It is therefore important to be aware of the same when carrying out such tasks, especially when fatigued.

OTHER FACTORS TO CONSIDER IN OBSERVATIONAL GAIT ANALYSIS

Observational gait analysis can be affected by numerous, often transient, internal and external factors and the podiatrist needs to be aware of the possible effects these can have when compiling a gait report. Camera equipment, frame rate, lighting and environment, all can affect image quality. Alcohol, drugs, injury, medical conditions, body weight, clothing, environment, footwear and mood can also affect gait. These are considered further in other chapters.

SUMMARY

Gait analysis in the forensic context draws heavily on the preparation given to podiatrists, which commences during their undergraduate training and extends into their clinical working environments. With a knowledge base, a systematic scientific approach in workflow, experience, an understanding of the forensic subject and the requirements of the legal system, including report writing, courtroom skills along with the duties and responsibilities of an expert to the court, the practitioner has a firm foundation and structure upon which to prepare unbiased, reliable forensic gait analysis reports for use in the legal systems. Remember, all experts in any area have a duty and responsibility to remain within their area of expertise. Or, put another way, although an expert may have expertise in one area, it does not follow that they may do so in another.

REFERENCES

1. Adams, F. *On the Articulations, Parts 52 and 53.* (2009). Available at: http://cla ssics.mit.edu/Hippocrates/artic.52.52.html (part 52) and http://classics.mit. edu/Hippocrates/artic.53.53.html (part 53).

2. Kaufman, K; Chambers, HG. David H. Sutherland, MD (1923–2006). *Gait Posture* **24** (1), 1–3 (2006).

3. Holst, A. 2018. Smartphones industry: Statistics and Facts. Available at: http://www.statista.com/topics/840/smartphones/.

4. Valmassy, RL. *Clinical Biomechanics of the Lower Extremities.* (St. Louis, MO: Mosby-Year Book Inc., 1996).

5. Sgarlato, T. *A Compendium of Podiatric Biomechanics.* (California College of Podiatric Medicine, 1971).

6. Root, ML; Orien, WP; Weed, JH. *Biomechanical Examination of the Foot: Volume 1.* (Clinical Biomechanics Corporation, 1971).

7. Root, ML; Orien, WP; Weed, JH. *Normal and Abnormal Function of the Foot. Clinical Biomechanics: Volume 2.* (Clinical Biomechanics Corporation, 1977).

8. Findlow, AH; Nester, CJ; Bowker, P. Foot kinematics in patients with two patterns of pathological plantar hyperkeratosis. *J. Foot Ankle Res.* **4**, 7 (2011).

9. Jarvis, HL; Nester, CJ; Bowden, PD; Jones, RK. Challenging the foundations of the clinical model of foot function: further evidence that the root model assessments fail to appropriately classify foot function. *J. Foot Ankle Res.* **10**, 7 (2017).

10. Kirby, KA. Subtalar joint axis location and rotational equilibrium theory of foot function. *J. Am. Pod. Med. Assoc.* **91**, 465–487 (2001).

11. Kirby, KA. The medial heel skive technique. *J. Am. Pod. Med. Assoc.* **82**, 177–188 (1992).

12. Kirby, KA. Rotational equilibrium across the subtalar joint axis. *J. Am. Pod. Med. Assoc.* **79**, 1–14 (1989).

13. Dananberg, HJ. Gait style as an etiology to chronic postural pain. Part I. Functional hallux limitus. *J. Am. Pod. Med. Assoc.* **83**, 615–623 (1993).

14. Dananberg, HJ. Sagittal plane biomechanics. *J. Am. Pod. Med. Assoc.* **90**, 47–50 (2000).

15. Dananberg, HJ; Guiliano, M. Chronic low-back pain and its response to custom-made foot orthoses. *J. Am. Pod. Med. Assoc.* **89**, 109–117 (1999).

16. Dananberg, HJ. Gait style as an etiology to chronic postural pain - part II postural compensatory process. *J. Am. Pod. Med. Assoc.* **83**, 615–624 (1993).

17. Hicks, B. The mechanics of the foot. *J. Anat.* **88**, 25–31 (1954).

18. Bojsen-Møller, F. Calcaneocuboid joint and stability of the longitudinal arch of the foot at high and low gear push off. *J. Anat.* **129**, 165–176 (1979).

19. McPoil, TG; Hunt, GC. Evaluation and management of foot and ankle disorders: present problems and future directions. *J. Orthop. Sport. Phys. Ther.* **21**, 381–388 (1995).

20. Benchmark statement: health care programmes, Podiatry (Chiropody).

21. Blakeman, P. et al. *Benchmark Statement: Podiatry (Chiropody).* (2001).

22. Dictionary.com. Gait. Available at: https://bit.ly/2Jsb5qb [Accessed 23 February 2020].

23. Kirtley, C. *Gait Analysis: Theory and Practice.* (Churchill Livingstone, 2006).

24. Watkins, J. Basic biomechanics of gait. In: *Neale's, Disorders of the Foot*, 8th edition (eds. Frowen, P; O'Donnell, M; Lorimer, D; Burrow, G) (Churchill Livingstone Elsevier, 2010).

25. Levine, D; Richards, J; Whittle, M. *Whittle's Gait Analysis*. (Elsevier, 2012).

26. Mooney, J; Campbell, R. Adult foot disorders. In: *Neale's Disorders of the Foot*, 8th edition (eds. Frowen, P; O'Donnell, M; Lorimer, D; Burrow, G) (Churchill Livingstone Elsevier, 2010).

27. Pathokinesiology Service and Physical Therapy Department, Rancho Los Amigos National Rehabilitation Center. *Observational Gait Analysis*. (Downey, CA, Rancho Los Amigos Research and Education Institute, 2001.)

28. Horwood, AM; Chockalingam, N. Defining excessive, over, or hyper-pronation: a quandary. *Foot* **31**, 49–55 (2017).

29. Planes of body. *Connexions*. Available at: https://commons.wikimedia.org/wiki/File:Planes_of_Body.jpg. (Accessed 23 February 2020.).

30. Sutherland, DH; Olshen R; Cooper L; Woo SL. The development of mature gait. *J. Bone Jt. Surg. [Am.]* **62**, 336–353 (1980).

31. Adolph, KE; Vereijken, B; Shrout, PE. What changes in infant walking and why. *Child Dev.* **74**, 475–497 (2003).

32. Malina, RM; Bouchard, C; Bar-Or, O. *Growth, Maturation, and Physical Activity*. (Human Kinetics, 2004).

33. Inman, VT; Ralston, HJ; Todd, F. *Human Walking*. (Williams & Wilkins, 1981).

34. Smith, L. Limp and the pediatric patient. In: *Clinical Biomechanics of the Lower Extremities* (ed. Valmassy, RL) (St. Louis, MO: Mosby-Year Book Inc, 1996).

35. Lythgo, N; Wilson, C; Galea, M. Basic gait and symmetry measures for primary school-aged children and young adults whilst walking barefoot and with shoes. *Gait Posture* **30**, 502–506 (2009).

36. Lythgo, N; Wilson, C; Galea, M. Basic gait and symmetry measures for primary school-aged children and young adults. II: walking at slow, free and fast speed. *Gait Posture* **33**, 29–35 (2011).

37. Dusing, SC; Thorpe, DE. A normative sample of temporal and spatial gait parameters in children using the GAITRite 1 electronic walkway. *Gait Posture* **25**, 135–139 (2007).

38. Sala, DA; Cohen, E. Gait component changes observed during independent ambulation in young children. *Indian J. Pediatr.* **80**, 397–403 (2013).

39. Goel, K; Watt, GF. Paediatric podiatry and genetics. In: *Neale's Disorders of the Foot* (eds. Frowen, P; O'Donnell, M; Lorimer, D; Burrow, G) (Churchill Livingstone Elsevier, 2010).

40. Gómez-Martín, B. et al. Age estimation based on a radiographic study of the growing foot. *J. Am. Podiatr. Med. Assoc.* **107**, 106–111 (2017).

41. Winter, D. *The Biomechanics and Motor Control of Human Gait*. (University of Waterloo Press, Canada, 1987).

42. Winter, D. *Biomechanics and Motor Control of Human Movement*. (John Wiley and Sons Inc, 2009).

43. Thordarson, DB. Running biomechanics. *Clin. Sports Med.* **16**, 239–247 (1997).

44. Ounpuu, S. The biomechanics of walking and running. *Clin. Sports Med.* **13**, 843–63 (1994).
45. Gore,TA; Higginson, GR; Stevens, J. The kinematics of hip Joints. *Clin. Phys. Physiol. Meas.* **5**, 233–252 (1984).
46. Berg, K; Norman, KE. Functional assessment of balance and gait. *Clin. Geriatr. Med.* **12**(4), 705–723 (1996).
47. Anglin, C; Wyss, P. Review of arm motion analyses. *Proc. Inst. Mech. Eng. H.* **214**, 541–555 (2000).
48. Sutherland, D. The evolution of clinical gait analysis - part II - kinematics. *Gait Posture* **16**, 159–179 (2002).
49. Watkins, J. *An Introduction to Biomechanics of Sport and Exercise.* (Churchill Livingstone, 2007).
50. Nigg, BM; Herzog, W. *Biomechanics of the Musculo-Skeletal System.* (Wiley-Blackwell, 2007).
51. Zatsiorky, VM; Werner, SL; Kaimin, MA. Basic kinematics of walking step length and step frequency: a review. *J. Sports Med. Phys. Fitness* **39**, 109–134 (1994).
52. Chau, T; Parker, K. On the robustness of stride frequency estimation. In: *IEEE Transactions on Biomedical Engineering*, pp. 294–303. (2004).
53. Li, L; van den Bogert, ECH; Caldwell, GE; van Emmerik, REA; Hamill, J. Coordination patterns of walking and running at similar speed and stride frequency. *Human Movement Science*, 18:67–85. (1999).
54. Bradley, M; Sabatier, JM. Acoustically-observable properties of adult gait. *J. Acoust. Soc. Am.* **131**, EL210–EL215 (2012).
55. Krebs, DE; Edelstein, JE; Fishman, S. Reliability of observational kinematic gait analysis. *Phys. Ther.* **65**, 1027–1033 (1985).
56. Keenan, A-M; Bach, T. Video assessment of rearfoot movements during walking: a reliability study. *Arch. Phys. Med. Rehabil.* **77**, 651–655 (1996).
57. Coutts, F. Gait analysis in the theraputic environment. *Man. Ther.* **4**, 2–10 (1999).
58. Lord, SE. et al. Visual gait analysis: the development of a clinical assessment and scale. *Clin. Rehabil.* **12**, 107–119 (1998).
59. Brunnekreef, JJ; van Uden, CJT; van Moorsel, S; Kooloos, JGM. Reliability of videotaped observational gait analysis in patients with orthopedic impairments. *BMC Musculoskelet. Disord.* **6**, 17 (2005).
60. Patla, AE; Proctor, J; Morson, B. Observation on aspects of visual gait assessment: a questionnaire study. *Physiother. Canada* **39**, 311–316 (1987).
61. Perry, J; Burnfield, JM. *Gait Analysis: Normal and Pathologcial Function.* (Slack Incorporated, 2010).
62. McGinley, JL; Goldie, PA; Greenwood, KM; Olney, SJ. Accuracy and reliability of observational gait analysis data: judgments of push-off in gait after stroke. *Phys. Ther.* **83**, 146–160 (2003).
63. Eastlack, ME; Arvidson, J; Danoff, JV; Charles, L. Interrater reliability of videotaped observational gait-analysis assessments. *Phys. Ther.* **71**, 465–472 (1991).

64. Viehweger, E. et al. Influence of clinical and gait analysis experience on reliability of observational gait analysis (Edinburgh Gait Score Reliability). *Ann. Phys. Rehabil. Med.* **53**, 535–546 (2010).

65. Cicchetti, DV. Guidelines, criteria, and rules of thumb for evaluating normed and standardized assessment instruments in psychology. *Psychol. Assess.* **6**, 284–290 (1994).

66. Geradts, ZJ; Merlijn, M; De Groot, G; Bijhold, J. Use of gait parameters of persons in video surveillance systems. In: *SPIE 4709, Investigative Image Processing II* (2002). doi:10.1117/12.474735

67. Perry, J. Pathologic gait. In: *Instructional Course Lectures* (ed. Greene, WD), pp. 325–331 (American Academy of Orthopaedic Surgeons, Rosemont, IL, 1990).

68. McCarney, R; Warner, J; Iliffe, S; van Haselen, R; Griffin, M; Fisher, P. The Hawthorne Effect: a randomised, controlled trial. *BMC Med. Res. Methodol.* **7**(30)(2007). https://doi.org/10.1186/1471-2288-7-30

69. Rancho Los Amigos Medical Center. *Observational Gait Analysis.* (2001).

70. Hughes, J; Jacobs, N. Normal Human Locomotion. *Prosthetics and Orthotics International,* **3**, 4–12. (1979).

71. Southerland, CC. Gait evaluation in clinical biomechanics. In: *Clinical Biomechanics of the Lower Extremities* (ed. Valmassy, RL) (St. Louis, MO: Mosby-Year Book Inc, 1996).

72. Morrison, RT; Boyd, RN. *Organic Chemistry.* (Allyn & Bacon, 1976).

73. Chem.libretexts.org. *Fischer Projections.*

74. Larsen, PK; Simonsen, EB; Lynnerup, N. Gait analysis in forensic medicine. *J. Forensic. Sci.* **53**, 1149–1153 (2008).

75. Hodgins, D. The importance of measuring human gait. *Med. Dev. Technol.* **19**(5):42, 44–7 (2008).

76. Pelphrey, KA; et al. Brain activity evoked by the perception of human walking: controlling for meaningful coherent motion. *J. Neurosci.* **23**, 6819–6825 (2003).

77. Chabris, C; Simons, D. *The Invisible Gorilla: And Other Ways Our Intuition Deceives Us.* (Harper Collins, 2010).

78. Posner, M; Presti, D. Selective attention and cognitive control. *Trends Neurosci.* **10**, 13–17 (1987).

3

Neurological Disorders Affecting Gait

Contents

Many neurological diseases impair the execution of coordinated muscle activity required in stepping and moving without loss of balance when walking. This chapter gives a general overview on the area. Understanding the effects of neurological disease requires knowledge of the nervous systems' anatomical structure, function and the likely effects of pathology at different sites. The information obtained from a careful history of a patient's walking difficulties, detailed observation of their gait starting when they first enter the examination room and a more general examination can then be interpreted to reach a likely diagnosis. The more general neurological or medical examination will provide further clues to the possible underlying causes of the patients' problem.[1]

It should be appreciated that gait problems become increasingly prevalent with age. At least one fifth of elderly people who are not institutionalised have walking difficulties, require assistance or walking aids[2] and often have multiple co-morbidities.[3] For elderly hospital inpatients falls are associated with significant morbidity. In England and Wales around 5000 inpatients suffer a fracture as a result of a fall each year.[4,5] Gait instability is recognised as a significant risk factor for falls, particularly if combined with confusion, advanced age, urinary infection or the adverse effects of medication.[6]

ANATOMICAL CONSIDERATIONS

When walking or carrying out other motor tasks visual information from the environment, vestibular information and sensory information about the body's position in space arising from muscle, tendons and joints (proprioception) are integrated to maintain balance and to adapt to environmental changes.

Muscles involved in standing, walking, running and other movements are innervated through a final common pathway. This final common pathway extends from motor neurones in the spinal cord through a peripheral motor nerve to the neuromuscular junction. Injury to this final common pathway, or lower motor neurone, produces flaccid weakness with a loss of muscle tone and reduced or absent reflexes. Activation and coordination of this final lower motor neurone pathway and muscle activity depends on upper motor neurone systems. These include structures in the spinal cord and brainstem, the cerebellum, subcortical structures including the basal ganglia, and the cerebral cortex.[7]

It should be appreciated that coordinated stepping movements may be generated within the spinal cord by neuronal networks, referred to as 'central pattern generators', in the absence of input from the brain or other higher levels.[8] These stereotyped movements can be seen in spinally transacted animals placed on a treadmill[9] and in patients recovering from spinal cord injury.[10,11] Higher control of these central pattern generators and regulation of the postural reflexes required to maintain balance are normally mediated through the brainstem. The cerebellum coordinates the smooth, precise execution of muscle activity required for walking. Cerebellar Purkinje cells fire rhythmically to coordinate muscle activation in different parts of the step cycle and cerebellar injury results in an unsteady, uncoordinated, broad based ataxic gait.[12]

Output from the basal ganglia includes important pathways to both the midbrain and the frontal cortex influencing posture, balance and movement.[13] Disease of the basal ganglia results in impaired or reduced (hypokinetic) movement as in Parkinson's disease or abnormal (hyperkinetic) involuntary movements. Either may disrupt normal walking. Hyperkinetic movement disorders include chorea, characterised by brief, irregular, involuntary movements, and dystonia in which sustained involuntary muscle contraction produces abnormal postures or movement.

The sensorimotor area of the brain cortex is required to produce fine movement and precise placement of the feet in stepping. Impulses travelling through the corticospinal tract mediate voluntary individual limb movement and initiate and modify activity in spinal pattern generators and other lower structures.[14] These lower spinal cord structures in turn are responsible for the rhythmic muscle activation required to maintain balance and to walk. Limb movement is controlled by information arising from the contralateral (opposite) side of the brain, travelling from the cortex through the corticospinal tract which crosses to the ipsilateral (same) side as the limbs at the level of the medulla in the lower brainstem, before descending in the spinal cord. A stroke or other injury to the brain affects limbs on the opposite side of the body; while trauma or compression of one side of the spinal cord produces weakness and motor signs on the same side of the body.

HISTORY AND EXAMINATION

It is usually possible to form an impression of an individual's walking and balance at the initial meeting or assessment. It is important to be alert for subtle neurological abnormalities. An example is the unilaterally reduced arm swing or mild unsteadiness on turning which may be evident in individuals with early Parkinson's disease. Observing an individual entering the examination room may suggest a spastic or hemiplegic gait, ataxia or a neuropathic disorder. These observations are explored through the more detailed examination and history of an individual's problems to identify clues to the underlying cause.

An account or a clinical history of the time course and the onset of walking difficulties from the person or a family member can provide important information about likely causes and helps direct the examination. Unsteadiness, walking 'like a drunk', slowing, falling or tripping are common. The onset, progression and time course of walking difficulties is particularly important. Symptoms may arise suddenly in a stroke or be gradually progressive in degenerative disease. Other symptoms or signs such as the speech disturbance, characteristic of cerebellar disease, or urinary difficulties in spinal cord disease may also give clues to the underlying diagnosis. It is important to be aware of the patient's medical and family history. For example, a peripheral neuropathy might commonly be caused by diabetes or alcohol, or might be inherited and present with walking problems.

Observation of the affected individual while talking and sitting is also important, noting problems with balance or clues to underlying neurological or other disorders that might affect gait.

Difficulty rising from a chair without pushing with the arms may suggest proximal muscle weakness, typically seen with muscle disease or myopathy. These individuals have difficulty rising from a crouched position without assistance, climbing stairs or getting out of the bath. Cognitive difficulties or central coordination problems in dementia, stroke or Parkinsonism may also impair the ability to rise and initiate walking.

Delay or hesitation on starting to walk, described as 'gait ignition failure',[15] initial short hesitant steps and a tendency to become stuck or 'freeze' are seen in disorders of the basal ganglia such as Parkinson's disease. Occasionally, similar gait problems are also evident in frontal lobe and subcortical disease after multiple strokes.

A high stepping gait or foot drop suggests weakness of ankle and toe dorsiflexion. The affected person has difficulty lifting the foot which may slap on the ground or catch on steps. This may result from a lower motor neurone lesion at a number of possible anatomical sites. Most commonly this is the fifth lumbar (L5) nerve root or common peroneal nerve. Conversely, weakness of calf muscles (gastrocnemius and soleus) impairs ankle plantar flexion and leads to walking on the heel, described as a calcaneal gait.[16] Weakness of ankle dorsiflexion and plantar flexion may be evident if the patient is asked to walk on heels or toes, respectively.

Regular symmetrical stepping may become uncoordinated and irregular if interrupted by involuntary movements such as chorea, in hemiparesis and spasticity after a stroke, or in Parkinson's disease.

Ataxia is a clinical description referring to imbalance and uncoordinated movement seen in a variety of diseases.[17] Poor balance from either impaired sensory input (sensory ataxia) or cerebellar disease (cerebellar ataxia) produces an unsteady, broad based, ataxic gait as individuals attempt to improve stability by walking with their feet widely separated. Balance difficulties may be more evident on turning, or when asked to walk heel to toe (tandem gait). Improved balance with visual input may help distinguish sensory from cerebellar ataxia. This is demonstrated if an individual maintains balance when standing with the feet together and eyes open, but then sways or falls when the eyes are closed (Romberg's test), suggesting a sensory or proprioceptive deficit. These individuals are using visual information to compensate for proprioceptive loss from a peripheral sensory neuropathy (for example in diabetes) or spinal dorsal column disease (for example in vitamin B12 deficiency).

When considering a possible neurological cause for gait disorders, it is important to observe other associated movements while the person walks, particularly of the arms and head. An arm may adopt a typical hemiplegic posture after unilateral upper motor neurone injury to the corticospinal tract in the brain or spinal cord. In this the shoulder is adducted (pulled towards the midline), the elbow, wrist and fingers flexed. Increased tone, extension of the affected knee with plantar flexion at the ankle, causes the hemiplegic leg to move in a semicircle (circumduction) during walking.[18,19] This is most frequently seen after a stroke[20] but also with tumours, injury or inflammatory diseases such as multiple sclerosis (MS). Bilateral injury or disease affecting the spinal cord or higher nervous system may similarly produce a paraplegia and spastic increase in tone in both legs.[21,22] Increased tone and shortening of hip adductors causes paraplegic patients to walk with a narrow base or crossing of the legs (a scissor gait) and a tendency to drag or scrape the toes.

Involuntary movements of the arms such as the rapid, irregular movements of chorea or a tremor may be evident. Individuals with vestibular or inner ear balance problems who complain of vertigo may prefer to avoid sudden head movements when walking and appear stiff or rigid.

Other aspects of the clinical examination are important in identifying underlying problems responsible for poor gait. Multi infarcts (repeated small strokes) affect gait and cause dementia. Poor visual acuity and double vision may explain unsteadiness and falls. Slurred speech (dysarthria) is seen in cerebellar and other disorders of higher function. Examination of the limbs will identify weakness, but other sensory and motor abnormalities are relevant. The incoordination of cerebellar disease may affect the ability to accurately perform rapid alternating hand movements, finger-nose or heel-shin tasks. Movements associated with Parkinson's disease are slow and of small amplitude. Apraxia (difficulty performing a motor task in the absence of motor weakness, sensory deficit or incoordination)[23] of gait is suspected if a person has difficulty taking steps and walking but performs cycling and other leg movements normally when lying on the couch. Reflex testing helps to distinguish lower motor neurone from higher level injuries. As described earlier, individuals with lower motor neurone lesions will typically have weak, wasted muscles with reduced or absent reflexes. Upper motor lesions involving the corticospinal tract produce increased muscle tone with brisk reflexes. Sensory examination is important when balance is impaired.

In assessing an individual with walking difficulties caused by neurological disease, it is also necessary to be aware of other possible complicating medical conditions. As discussed earlier, multiple medical problems are common in the elderly population and these often worsen gait problems and increase the risk of falls.

COMMON NEUROLOGICAL DISORDERS AFFECTING GAIT AND BALANCE

An understanding of common diseases which are likely to affect walking is helpful when interpreting an abnormal gait pattern. Different diseases produce additional difficulties which can affect balance or coordination. Accurate diagnosis of a patient's underlying condition has implications for progression or changes in gait patterns and is important in planning treatment and rehabilitation strategies.

Stroke

Stroke describes the symptoms and disability suffered by a patient when the blood supply to the brain or spinal cord is suddenly impaired.[24] Defined as a rapidly developing focal neurological deficit caused by vascular disease, most often infarction or death of brain tissue occurs when a blood clot either forms in an artery affected by atheroma (thrombosis) or travels from another site in the circulation such as the heart (embolism).[24] The term transient ischaemic attack (TIA) is used to describe symptoms which resolve within 24 hours.[25] Less often ischaemia occurs during a catastrophic failure to maintain brain blood circulation, for example in a cardiac arrest. About 15% of strokes are caused by an intracerebral haemorrhage.[26]

About 150,000 people each year in England and Wales suffer from a stroke, the third most common cause of death after heart attack and cancer. In 2016, a report from the American Heart Association stated, in the United States 800,000 people each year have a stroke with an estimated annual cost in medical care and lost productivity of 33 billion US dollars.[27] One in 10 men and 1 in 20 women aged 45 can expect to suffer a stroke by the age of 65. Stroke is a major cause of disability in an ageing population with about half of stroke survivors requiring care or assistance from others.[28] This highlights the importance of managing factors which increase the risk of stroke. The most important of these are hypertension, smoking,[29] diabetes and atrial fibrillation.[30] Stroke risk is directly related to blood pressure[31] and diabetes doubles the risk of stroke.[32] Raised blood lipids,[33] alcohol excess and obesity are other important and treatable risk factors.[27]

The effect of a stroke depends on the underlying pathology (infarction or haemorrhage), its location and size.[34] Internal carotid arteries supply blood to the eye and anterior part of the brain through their anterior and middle cerebral branches. Vertebral arteries ascend in the posterior part of the neck close to the spine before forming the basilar and posterior cerebral arteries, supplying blood to the brainstem, cerebellum and posterior cerebral hemispheres.

Ischaemic stroke associated with narrowing of the internal carotid artery in the neck may be preceded by repeated TIAs including transient visual loss (amaurosis fugax). These patients require urgent assessment as about 10% will have a stroke within the next 90 days.[35] The middle cerebral artery (MCA) is a common site for occlusive stroke.[36] Complete MCA occlusion may produce a large area of brain infarction causing weakness or paralysis of the opposite arm and leg. The arm and hand are usually most severely affected since the leg area of the cerebral cortex receives a blood supply from the anterior cerebral artery. Those affected who are able to walk have a typical hemiplegic gait but may also suffer loss of gaze or vision and neglect (loss of awareness) to the affected side of the body.

69

These additional disabilities may severely limit mobility and rehabilitation. Stroke affecting the dominant (usually left) hemisphere of the brain often causes problems with speech and understanding language (aphasia) while persistent neglect is more frequent in non-dominant hemisphere strokes.[37]

Vascular occlusion in the posterior circulation involves vertebral and basilar arteries. Several different clinical pictures arise depending on the precise arterial involvement.[38] For example, unilateral ataxia affecting gait and hand function associated with loss of pain and temperature sensation on the same side of the face but opposite side of the body, a small pupil and eyelid drooping (Horner's syndrome), jerky eye movements (nystagmus), or paralysis of the palate and vocal cords, all suggest a lateral medullary or Wallenberg's syndrome following occlusion of the posterior inferior cerebellar branch of the vertebral artery.[39] Basilar artery stroke may cause an asymmetrical quadriplegia with complex eye movement disorders and in severe cases those affected may be in coma or conscious but paralysed ('locked in').

Lacunar strokes often present differently to the single large vessel occlusions described above. A lacunar stroke is a small stroke or infarct up to 15 mm in diameter. These most commonly occur if deep penetrating branches of the middle cerebral or basilar arteries occlude, typically in individuals with hypertension or diabetes. A lacunar stroke may present with an isolated focal deficit such as a pure motor weakness or sensory loss[40,41] but often these are asymptomatic with cumulative damage to deep brain structures and widespread small vessel disease.[36] Those affected in this way have difficulty initiating gait, short shuffling steps and poor balance, often tending to fall backwards. This gait disorder may be mistaken for Parkinsonism, although patients with small vessel disease often have poor attention and evidence of dementia.

Strokes affecting the spinal cord are much less common and the anterior spinal artery is most often involved. Infarction of the anterior part of the spinal cord produces a sudden flaccid paraparesis with loss of pain and temperature sensation but preserved vibration and joint position sense.[36]

Attention to gait, balance and assessment of fall risk are important aspects of post-stroke rehabilitation with up to 70% of stroke patients having a fall in the first six months after hospital discharge.[40,41] Motor functions such as walking have some neurological control from both sides of the brain. Motor functions with this bilateral representation often show significant improvement after a stroke.[42]

70

Parkinson's Disease

Parkinson's disease is a progressive neurological disorder characterised by slowness, rigidity, tremor and impaired balance. Specific areas of the brain are affected by loss of neurones and the presence of characteristic intracellular protein deposits termed Lewy bodies. Cells producing the neurotransmitter dopamine in the substantia nigra area of the brainstem are particularly affected. The substantia nigra innervates a part of the basal ganglia, the dorsal striatum (caudate nucleus and putamen), involved in motor function.[43,44] The cause of Parkinson's disease is unknown but likely to result from an interaction of environmental and genetic factors.[45,46]

Individuals with Parkinson's disease often present with tremor, slowing, loss of facial expression and an abnormal gait with shuffling or a tendency to drag one leg. In established disease, a number of signs may be evident when the person walks or is at rest. The principal feature of Parkinson's disease is akinesia in which movement is reduced, of small amplitude (hypokinesia) and slowed (bradykinesia). Repetitive alternating movements demonstrate fatigue and are reduced in amplitude. The majority of those affected demonstrate stiffness or rigidity of their muscles and tremor. Although there are many neurological causes of tremor,[47] in Parkinson's disease this typically occurs at rest and is reduced by movement. Tremor of the fingers with flexion of the thumb produces a characteristic 'pill rolling' appearance when the individual is relaxed.[48] This tremor may be seen when the person walks, or it emerges when the arms are held outstretched. The other major feature of Parkinson's disease which has particular significance for gait and balance is postural instability, particularly in more advanced disease. Individuals may stumble, cannot regain their centre of balance and are at risk of falling.

Problems with gait may be subtle at presentation. Clinical signs are usually asymmetrical and the person may initially complain of generalised slowing, drag one leg or a tendency to shuffle. Individuals may become 'stuck' or frozen when on their feet and struggle to start walking, a phenomenon termed 'gait ignition failure'.[15] With progression of symptoms, a typical short stepped or festinating gait, flexed truncal posture and poor balance cause the patient to accelerate or fall[49] It is important to observe other features during walking such as reduced arm swing on the affected side with tremor or a flexed posture. Other clues are difficulties with fine motor tasks such as fastening buttons or writing and family members may have noticed the individual has reduced facial expression and a general slowing up. As mobility and gait problems become more

71

advanced in Parkinson's disease, abnormal postures may be adopted. These include camptocormia, a severe forward flexion of the thoracolumbar spine when the patient stands and walks but which may disappear when laying on the couch.[50.]

Non-motor features of Parkinson's disease are increasingly recognised as important causes of disability. These include drooling, urinary symptoms, depression and autonomic symptoms. In 'rapid eye movement (REM) sleep behaviour disorder' (RBD), the usual loss of muscle tone during sleep and dreaming is absent, so the patient may act out violent or frightening dreams and nightmares. RBD may precede other symptoms of Parkinson's disease by many years. Pain is a common complaint and might be mistakenly attributed to back or other limb problems. Impaired judgement as a result of cognitive decline and dementia are significant factors affecting independence.[51]

The gait of people with Parkinson's disease is affected by treatment which may improve symptoms but produce side effects, including abnormal movements and gait patterns. Levodopa, converted to dopamine in the brain, is the most effective treatment. This is usually combined with a peripheral enzyme (decarboxylase) inhibitor which blocks the conversion to dopamine outside the brain and reduces peripheral side effects. Dopamine agonist drugs (such as ropinirole and pramipexole) mimic the effect of dopamine by stimulating dopamine receptors in the striatum directly. Other enzyme blocking drugs increase the availability of levodopa or dopamine (entacapone, rasagiline) while anticholinergics or amantadine act on alternative neural pathways. With long-term medication and disease progression, the treatment response fluctuates. As described earlier, episodes of 'freezing' occur when the patient becomes immobile or 'stuck'.[52] This may alternate with excessive abnormal involuntary movements, or dyskinesia, when gait is disturbed by sudden irregular choreiform jerks, sustained dystonic postures or disabling violent ballistic movements.[53]

Neurodegenerative Disease and Other Movement Disorders

A number of abnormal movement disorders are likely to affect walking and balance. Some less common neurodegenerative diseases have akinetic features and rigidity resembling Parkinson's disease, termed Parkinsonism, but with other prominent neurological problems. Marked dementia, confusion and hallucinations early in the disease course are characteristic of Lewy body dementia[54]; frequent early falls and abnormal eye movements suggest progressive supranuclear palsy (PSP)[55]; patients with corticobasal degeneration have apraxia of limb movement[56]; while autonomic features or ataxia are seen in multisystem atrophy (MSA)[57]. Abnormal postures affecting gait occur in several forms of Parkinsonism or as adverse effects of drugs, particularly antipsychotic medication. These include lateral deviation of the spine and a tendency to lean to one side when walking, the Pisa syndrome.[58]

Alzheimer's disease and neurodegenerative disorders which progressively impair cognitive function most often present with dementia, although unsteadiness and ataxia may be additional early features of some prion diseases.[59] Prion diseases are rare neurodegenerative conditions caused by an infectious prion protein and occur spontaneously, through infection, or are inherited.[60] They include Creutzfeldt-Jakob disease (CJD) and bovine spongiform encephalopathy (BSE),[61] conditions which are invariably progressive and fatal.[62]

Difficulty walking, dementia and urinary incontinence form a clinical triad which may suggest normal pressure hydrocephalus (NPH). NPH is a poorly understood condition, usually affecting the elderly, in which enlarged cerebrospinal fluid (CSF) spaces are seen on brain scans.[63] The gait disorder is usually a form of gait apraxia and individuals complain of being unable to move their feet which seem stuck to the floor. Recognition of the condition is important as a minority of affected individuals benefit from removal of CSF through lumbar puncture or a shunt.[64,65]

Chorea describes sudden, irregular randomly distributed involuntary movements.[66] Sydenham's chorea (also known as Saint Vitus' dance) mostly affects children[67] and occurs after common streptococcal infections which can also cause rheumatic fever.[68] Abnormal movements start suddenly and affect the facial muscles, limbs and trunk. The child's gait is unsteady and they may fall. The condition is usually self-limiting with resolution of symptoms by six weeks, although some children have a more prolonged illness, cardiac or psychiatric complications[69] which may develop later.[70]

Huntington's disease (HD) is a neurodegenerative disorder in which abnormal choreiform movements, cognitive deterioration with psychiatric symptoms and progressive motor impairment are prominent features.[71,72] This is an inherited, progressive and ultimately fatal neurodegenerative disease characterised by significant gait variability[73] and falls.

Dystonia may produce striking and bizarre abnormalities of gait and posture.[74,75] Involuntary muscle spasms result from the co-contraction of agonist and antagonist muscles, sometimes producing slow writhing

73

movements termed athetosis. Dystonia has many inherited or acquired causes but it is important to recognise the condition as some of these causes such as dopa responsive dystonia (an inherited disease responsive to levodopa)[76] or Wilson's disease (a disorder of copper metabolism) are treatable.[77]

Other abnormal movements such as myoclonus (sudden involuntary muscle jerks) or tics (rapid, brief involuntary movements or vocalisations seen in conditions such as Gilles de la Tourette syndrome[72]) are less likely to present with obvious gait problems.

Multiple Sclerosis

MS is an inflammatory disease of the brain and spinal cord character-ised by a relapsing illness with an unpredictable but usually progressive course.[78] The cause is unknown but an increased incidence in close rela-tives suggests an inherited predisposition and many studies have explored possible environmental triggers.[79] These have included exposure to infec-tions in childhood, particular viruses, vitamin D and sunlight exposure.[80]

Balance and walking impairments are frequent,[81] affecting the major-ity of MS sufferers depending on the extent and distribution of lesions within the central nervous system (CNS).[82] Since MS lesions may involve any part of the central nervous system, an individual's gait may be unsteady or ataxic if the brainstem or cerebellum are involved.[83] More commonly, involvement of the spinal cord produces a progressive paraparesis with a spastic increase in muscle tone, weakness, stiffness and muscle spasm. Those affected often have bladder and bowel symptoms with brisk reflexes and positive Babinski response (the reflex extension of the first toe to stim-ulation of the sole of the foot) on examination. Simple clinical measures of walking speed and strength correlate with brain corticospinal tract pathol-ogy demonstrated by sophisticated imaging techniques.[82]

Although those individuals who remain mobile benefit from exercise training[84] and gait rehabilitation,[85] the functional problems due to balance and gait difficulties are often compounded by other effects of MS. In par-ticular, memory, attentional, information processing and other cognitive difficulties[86] increase the likelihood of falls and injury.[87,88]

Non-organic and Psychogenic Gait Disorders

Psychogenic movement disorders often present with gait abnormalities which are dramatic and striking. Investigations to exclude alternative causes may be important but diagnosis rests on careful observation and clinical assessment of gait. A combination of positive findings help with diagnosis, including inconsistencies over time or between reported disability and observed physical signs. Disability may be distractible or fluctuating during examination with the presence of other non-organic signs. Inexplicable excessive slowness, hesitation and sudden 'buckling' of the knees are suggested as other signs.[89] Anxiety and depression are often present.[90] A history of psychiatric illness or medico-legal involvement in compensation claims is common[91] but do not exclude an organic cause.[92,93]

Peripheral Neuropathies

Gait is affected by many diseases affecting the peripheral nervous system from lumbosacral nerve roots through the lumbosacral plexus to peripheral nerves. Disease or injury produces weakness and sensory loss with pain, muscle wasting or other signs.

Peripheral nerve injuries, including those related to sporting activity,[94] and muscle disease are often identified by typical physical signs and abnormal gait patterns. The patient with an abnormal gait caused by peripheral nerve injury may also complain of sensory symptoms such as a feeling of 'walking on stones', shooting or burning pains. Although there are many causes of bladder dysfunction, diarrhoea and impotence, these may also be a clue to involvement of the autonomic nervous system as part of a peripheral neuropathy.

If an abnormal, high stepping gait is due to one of the common inherited neuropathies, or Charcot-Marie-Tooth disease (CMT), those affected most usually have a long history of gradually progressive problems with motor weakness and sensory loss. There may not always be a family history of similar problems, although the most common forms of CMT are dominantly inherited (so that one parent is likely to be affected to some degree). In patients with CMT, gait problems typically arise in childhood or adolescence[95] and examination reveals reduced or absent reflexes. There may be symmetrical wasting of lower leg muscles or longstanding deformity such as pes cavus (very high arching of the foot which does not flatten when standing with weight taken on the heel and ball of the foot). Sensory loss is usually in a symmetrical, distal 'stocking' distribution.

Most generalised neuropathies are acquired rather than inherited. Diabetes mellitus, a metabolic condition characterised by abnormally raised blood glucose levels, is the commonest cause of peripheral neuropathy in the developed world.[96] The neuropathy usually presents with slowly progressive sensory loss[97]. Poor metabolic control is associated with progression to neuropathy[98]. Loss of sensation, poor metabolic control and impaired blood supply in diabetic peripheral neuropathy all predispose to foot ulceration and injury[99,100] which further affect gait patterns.[101] This is evident on gait analysis and important to consider in preventing and managing falls, loss of mobility and conservative or surgical treatments for diabetic foot offloading.

Toxic and drug related neuropathies are also common, although in many cases no cause is found. Inflammatory neuropathies may develop more rapidly. The commonest inflammatory neuropathy is Guillain-Barré syndrome (GBS) in which weakness or paralysis ascends from the legs over three or four weeks. Patients may also experience pain or sensory symptoms and respiratory paralysis may lead to artificial ventilation. Many patients do not fully recover with residual weakness restricting mobility and gait.[102]

Focal Nerve Damage and Foot Drop

Focal nerve damage occurs as a result of trauma or local compression at a vulnerable anatomical site. Diabetes or other factors may predispose to injury.[103] Localisation is helped by knowledge of basic anatomy and common sites of peripheral nerve injury.

This can be illustrated by the individual who presents with an isolated foot drop. Very often this is caused by injury to the common peroneal nerve, which is vulnerable to compression or injury as it passes superficially around the head of the fibula below the outer knee. Prolonged crouching, leg crossing, local fractures or wearing plaster casts may all cause a common peroneal palsy at this site. The nerve innervates muscles responsible for dorsiflexion of the foot at the ankle, eversion of the foot and extension of the toes (tibialis anterior, extensor halluces longus, extensor digitorum longus and peronei muscles). Sensory loss at this site may involve the outer lower leg and dorsum of the foot. The common peroneal nerve does not innervate muscles responsible for inversion or plantar flexion of the foot, and weakness of these movements therefore suggests injury at other sites, commonly the sciatic nerve or L4, L5 and S1 nerve roots.[104]

Swelling in one of the closed muscle compartments of the lower leg, usually due to bleeding or oedema after trauma, can produce severe pain with muscle and nerve damage. Those affected have weakness or a foot drop and management of this compartment syndrome can require urgent surgical decompression to restore blood flow.[105]

Clinical examination will give clues to other conditions affecting the peripheral nervous system.

Disorders of the Neuromuscular Junction

Myasthenia gravis is a condition in which circulating antibodies target the acetylcholine receptor at the neuromuscular junction. Symptoms are fatigue and worsen with sustained effort. Blurred or double vision, eyelid drooping (ptosis), respiratory or swallowing problems becoming worse later in the day are the most usual presentations, although limbs and gait may be involved.[106]

Motor Neurone Disease

Motor neurone disease is a progressive degenerative disease of anterior horn cells and the central nervous system.[107] The diagnosis may not be immediately obvious in those who present with mild foot drop until progressive muscle wasting, fasciculation and more widespread involvement become apparent.[108] Most often affected individuals have a combination of upper and lower motor neurone signs with a spastic or paraplegic gait and distal flaccid weakness and wasting.[109] It is often this combination of signs and a rapidly progressive clinical course which suggest the diagnosis.[110]

Muscle Disease

Individuals with primary muscle disease often present with complaints of difficulty when walking and weakness. There are many genetic, degenerative or inflammatory conditions which cause myopathy and very often diagnosis is delayed as other conditions are considered and subtle clinical signs missed.[111-113] Muscle pain, cramps, stiffness or fatigue may provide clues in a patient who is weak. Examination may demonstrate muscle wasting and testing of strength identifies weakness in individual muscles or muscle groups. Any pattern of muscle involvement may be seen, particularly in inherited muscle disease, but typically proximal limb muscles are involved. People with a myopathy have difficulty rising from a crouching position, they complain of problems rising from a low chair when starting to walk or get stuck in the bath. This weakness can be demonstrated by asking the person to rise from a crouching position or even a low chair without using their arms or other support to push themselves up.[114] Those with significant weakness of proximal muscles supporting the pelvic girdle have a myopathic or 'waddling' gait. Weakness of hip abductor muscles produces a lurching or Trendelenburg gait as the opposite hip drops during the standing phase of the gait cycle.[115] It is important to recognise that myopathy may be caused by medication, including widely prescribed drugs such as statins or steroids, and the medical history should include an account of treatment for other disorders seemingly unrelated to walking and balance problems.[116]

The diagnosis of these disorders may require specialist investigations, including blood tests and neuro-imaging with magnetic resonance (MRI) or computerised tomography (CT). Neurophysiology tests, nerve conduction studies (NCS) and electromyography (EMG) are most useful in evaluating peripheral nerves and muscles. Occasionally it may be necessary to biopsy a peripheral nerve or muscle to establish a precise diagnosis, to inform the likely prognosis and guide optimal treatment.

Ataxia

The clinical characteristics and examination findings in individuals with a sensory or cerebellar ataxia have been described earlier. It is important to recognise that many of the inherited and acquired disorders which predominantly cause ataxia present with poor balance and gait problems.

Numerous genetic mutations have been identified in the group of degenerative and inherited spinocerebellar ataxias (SCA).[117] The most common affects the frataxin gene, inherited in an autosomal recessive pattern in patients with Friedreich's ataxia. Friedreich's ataxia may present in adult life but is usually clinically evident by the late teenage years with an ataxic gait and sensory peripheral neuropathy.[118] Another genetic disorder, ataxia telangiectasia, usually presents in childhood with unsteadiness and poor balance. This is a complex disorder with associated immune deficiencies and a predisposition to develop cancer.[119]

Acquired ataxia is common and the cerebellum is sensitive to damage or the direct effects of a variety of auto-immune disorders,[120] drugs and toxins.[121] These include drugs used to treat epilepsy,[122] solvents and most commonly alcohol. As well as the effects of acute alcohol intoxication, chronic alcohol abuse may produce an irreversible progressive gait and limb ataxia, slurred speech (dysarthria) and a peripheral neuropathy. Tabes dorsalis, one of a number of late neurological complications of syphilis, is a much less common cause of sensory ataxia. Involvement of the spinal dorsal columns causes lightning pains and paraesthesia, those affected may also have pupillary abnormalities and progress to dementia.[123,124]

REFERENCES

1. Brodal A. *Neurological Anatomy in Relation to Clinical Medicine*, 3rd ed. New York: Oxford University Press, 1981.
2. Ostchega Y, Harris TB, Hirsch R, Parsons VL, Kington R. The prevalence of functional limitations and disability in older persons in the US: data from the National Health and Nutrition Examination Survey III. *J Am Geriatr Soc* 2000;48:1132–1135.
3. Alexander NB, Goldberg A. Gait disorders: search for multiple causes. *Cleve Clin J Med* 2005;72:586, 589–590, 592–584 passim.
4. Morris R, O'Riordan S. Prevention of falls in hospital. *Clin Med (Lond)* 2017;17:360–362.
5. Oliver D, Healey F, Haines TP. Preventing falls and fall-related injuries in hospitals. *Clin Geriatr Med* 2010;26:645–692.
6. Oliver D, Daly F, Martin FC, McMurdo ME. Risk factors and risk assessment tools for falls in hospital in-patients: a systematic review. *Age Ageing* 2004;33:122–130.
7. Thompson PD. Gait disorders. In: Daroff RB, Jankovic J, Mazziotta J, Pomeroy S, eds. *Bradley's Neurology in Clinical Practice*, 7th ed. Philadelphia: Elsevier, 2015.
8. Dimitrijevic MR, Gerasimenko Y, Pinter MM. Evidence for a spinal central pattern generator in humans. *Ann N Y Acad Sci* 1998;860:360–376.
9. Jiang W, Drew T. Effects of bilateral lesions of the dorsolateral funiculi and dorsal columns at the level of the low thoracic spinal cord on the control of locomotion in the adult cat. I. Treadmill walking. *J Neurophysiol* 1996;76:849–866.
10. Pepin A, Ladouceur M, Barbeau H. Treadmill walking in incomplete spinal-cord-injured subjects: 2. Factors limiting the maximal speed. *Spinal Cord* 2003;41:271–279.
11. Pepin A, Norman KE, Barbeau H. Treadmill walking in incomplete spinal-cord-injured subjects: 1. Adaptation to changes in speed. *Spinal Cord* 2003;41:257–270.
12. Stolze H, Klebe S, Petersen G, et al. Typical features of cerebellar ataxic gait. *J Neurol Neurosurg Psychiatr* 2002;73:310–312.
13. Groenewegen HJ. The basal ganglia and motor control. *Neural Plast* 2003;10:107–120.
14. Barthelemy D, Grey MJ, Nielsen JB, Bouyer L. Involvement of the corticospinal tract in the control of human gait. *Prog Brain Res* 2011;192:181–197.
15. Atchison PR, Thompson PD, Frackowiak RS, Marsden CD. The syndrome of gait ignition failure: a report of six cases. *Mov Disord* 1993;8:285–292.

16. O'Brien SE, Karol LA, Johnston CE, 2nd. Calcaneus gait following treatment for clubfoot: preliminary results of surgical correction. *J Pediatr Orthop B* 2004;13:43–47.

17. Subramony SH. Ataxic disorders. In: Bradley WG, Daroff RB, Fenichel GM, Jankovic J, eds. *Neurology in Clinical Practice*, 4th ed. Philadelphia: Butterworth Heinemann, 2004.

18. Sheffler LR, Chae J. Hemiparetic gait. *Phys Med Rehabil Clin N Am* 2015;26:611–623.

19. Marque P, Gasq D, Castel-Lacanal E, De Boissezon X, Loubinoux I. Post-stroke hemiplegia rehabilitation: evolution of the concepts. *Ann Phys Rehabil Med* 2014;57:520–529.

20. Balaban B, Tok F. Gait disturbances in patients with stroke. *PM R* 2014;6:635–642.

21. Vyshka G, Muzha D, Papajani M, Basho M. Recent advances in acute paraplegia. *J Acute Dis* 2016;5:445–449.

22. Scivoletto G, Tamburella F, Laurenza L, Torre M, Molinari M. Who is going to walk? A review of the factors influencing walking recovery after spinal cord injury. *Front Hum Neurosci* 2014;8:141.

23. Meyer JS, Barron D. Apraxia of gait: a clinico-physiological study. *Brain* 1960;83:261–284.

24. Sacco RL, Kasner SE, Broderick JP, et al. An updated definition of stroke for the 21st century: a statement for healthcare professionals from the American Heart Association/American Stroke Association. *Stroke* 2013;44:2064–2089.

25. Easton JD, Saver JL, Albers GW, et al. Definition and evaluation of transient ischemic attack: a scientific statement for healthcare professionals from the American Heart Association/American Stroke Association Stroke Council; Council on Cardiovascular Surgery and Anesthesia; Council on Cardiovascular Radiology and Intervention; Council on Cardiovascular Nursing; and the Interdisciplinary Council on Peripheral Vascular Disease. The American Academy of Neurology affirms the value of this statement as an educational tool for neurologists. *Stroke* 2009;40:2276–2293.

26. Bamford J, Sandercock P, Dennis M, Burn J, Warlow C. A prospective study of acute cerebrovascular disease in the community: the Oxfordshire Community Stroke Project--1981–86. 2. Incidence, case fatality rates and overall outcome at one year of cerebral infarction, primary intracerebral and subarachnoid haemorrhage. *J Neurol Neurosurg Psychiatr* 1990;53:16–22.

27. Writing Group Members, Mozaffarian D, Benjamin EJ, et al. Executive summary: heart disease and stroke statistics--2016 update: a report from the American Heart Association. *Circulation* 2016;133:447–454.

28. Adamson J, Beswick A, Ebrahim S. Is stroke the most common cause of disability? *J Stroke Cerebrovasc Dis* 2004;13:171–177.

29. Kernan WN, Ovbiagele B, Black HR, et al. Guidelines for the prevention of stroke in patients with stroke and transient ischemic attack: a guideline for healthcare professionals from the American Heart Association/American Stroke Association. *Stroke* 2014;45:2160–2236.

30. Sandercock P, Bamford J, Dennis M, et al. Atrial fibrillation and stroke: prevalence in different types of stroke and influence on early and long term prognosis (Oxfordshire community stroke project). *BMJ* 1992;305:1460–1465.
31. Rothwell PM, Howard SC, Dolan E, et al. Prognostic significance of visit-to-visit variability, maximum systolic blood pressure, and episodic hypertension. *Lancet* 2010;375:895–905.
32. Kaplan RC, Tirschwell DL, Longstreth WT, Jr., et al. Vascular events, mortality, and preventive therapy following ischemic stroke in the elderly. *Neurology* 2005;65:835–842.
33. Stone NJ, Robinson JG, Lichtenstein AH, et al. 2013 ACC/AHA guideline on the treatment of blood cholesterol to reduce atherosclerotic cardiovascular risk in adults: a report of the American College of Cardiology/American Heart Association Task Force on Practice Guidelines. *Circulation* 2014;129 Supplement 2:S1–S45.
34. Luengo-Fernandez R, Gray AM, Bull L, et al. Quality of life after TIA and stroke: ten-year results of the Oxford Vascular Study. *Neurology* 2013;81:1588–1595.
35. Giles MF, Rothwell PM. Risk of stroke early after transient ischaemic attack: a systematic review and meta-analysis. *Lancet Neurol* 2007;6:1063–1072.
36. Southerland AM. Clinical evaluation of the patient with acute stroke. *Continuum (Minneap Minn)* 2017;23:40–61.
37. Stone SP, Halligan PW, Greenwood RJ. The incidence of neglect phenomena and related disorders in patients with an acute right or left hemisphere stroke. *Age Ageing* 1993;22:46–52.
38. Tarnutzer AA, Berkowitz AL, Robinson KA, Hsieh YH, Newman-Toker DE. Does my dizzy patient have a stroke? A systematic review of bedside diagnosis in acute vestibular syndrome. *CMAJ* 2011;183:E571–E592.
39. Hosoya T, Watanabe N, Yamaguchi K, Kubota H, Onodera Y. Intracranial vertebral artery dissection in Wallenberg syndrome. *AJNR Am J Neuroradiol* 1994;15:1161–1165.
40. Batchelor F, Hill K, Mackintosh S, Said C. What works in falls prevention after stroke? A systematic review and meta-analysis. *Stroke* 2010;41:1715–1722.
41. Winstein CJ, Stein J, Arena R, et al. Guidelines for adult stroke rehabilitation and recovery: a guideline for healthcare professionals from the American Heart Association/American Stroke Association. *Stroke* 2016;47:e98–e169.
42. Cramer SC, Crafton KR. Somatotopy and movement representation sites following cortical stroke. *Exp Brain Res* 2006;168:25–32.
43. Braak H, Ghebremedhin E, Rub U, Bratzke H, Del Tredici K. Stages in the development of Parkinson's disease-related pathology. *Cell Tissue Res* 2004;318:121–134.
44. Ruitenberg MFL, Abrahamse EL, Santens P, Notebaert W. The effect of dopaminergic medication on conflict adaptation in Parkinson's disease. *J Neuropsychol* 2017.
45. Nalls MA, Saad M, Noyce AJ, et al. Genetic comorbidities in Parkinson's disease. *Hum Mol Genet* 2014;23:831–841.

81

46. Noyce AJ, Bestwick JP, Silveira-Moriyama L, et al. Meta-analysis of early nonmotor features and risk factors for Parkinson disease. *Ann Neurol* 2012;72:893–901.

47. Edwards MJ, Deuschl G. Tremor syndromes. *Continuum (Minneap Minn)* 2013;19:1213–1224.

48. Elias WJ, Shah BB. Tremor. *JAMA* 2014;311:948–954.

49. Forsyth AL, Paul SS, Allen NE, Sherrington C, Fung VS, Canning CG. Flexed truncal posture in Parkinson disease: measurement reliability and relationship with physical and cognitive impairments, mobility, and balance. *J Neurol Phys Ther* 2017;41:107–113.

50. Doherty KM, van de Warrenburg BP, Peralta MC, et al. Postural deformities in Parkinson's disease. *Lancet Neurol* 2011;10:538–549.

51. Schrag A, Jahanshahi M, Quinn N. How does Parkinson's disease affect quality of life? A comparison with quality of life in the general population. *Mov Disord* 2000;15:1112–1118.

52. Bloem BR, Hausdorff JM, Visser JE, Giladi N. Falls and freezing of gait in Parkinson's disease: a review of two interconnected, episodic phenomena. *Mov Disord* 2004;19:871–884.

53. Fahn S. The spectrum of levodopa-induced dyskinesias. *Ann Neurol* 2000;47 Supplement 1:S2–S9; discussion S9–S11.

54. McKeith IG, Boeve BF, Dickson DW, et al. Diagnosis and management of dementia with Lewy bodies: fourth consensus report of the DLB Consortium. *Neurology* 2017;89:88–100.

55. Boxer AL, Yu JT, Golbe LI, Litvan I, Lang AE, Hoglinger GU. Advances in progressive supranuclear palsy: new diagnostic criteria, biomarkers, and therapeutic approaches. *Lancet Neurol* 2017;16:552–563.

56. Erkkinen MG, Kim MO, Geschwind MD. Clinical neurology and epidemiology of the major neurodegenerative diseases. *Cold Spring Harb Perspect Biol*, 2018 Apr 2;10(4). pii: a033118.

57. Laurens B, Vergnet S, Lopez MC, et al. Multiple system atrophy - state of the art. *Curr Neurol Neurosci Rep* 2017;17:41.

58. Barone P, Santangelo G, Amboni M, Pellecchia MT, Vitale C. Pisa syndrome in Parkinson's disease and parkinsonism: clinical features, pathophysiology, and treatment. *Lancet Neurol* 2016;15:1063–1074.

59. Lloyd SE, Mead S, Collinge J. Genetics of prion diseases. *Curr Opin Genet Dev* 2013;23:345–351.

60. Collinge J. Mammalian prions and their wider relevance in neurodegenerative diseases. *Nature* 2016;539:217–226.

61. Wroe SJ, Pal S, Siddique D, et al. Clinical presentation and pre-mortem diagnosis of variant Creutzfeldt-Jakob disease associated with blood transfusion: a case report. *Lancet* 2006;368:2061–2067.

62. Collinge J. Prion diseases of humans and animals: their causes and molecular basis. *Annu Rev Neurosci* 2001;24:519–550.

63. Relkin N, Marmarou A, Klinge P, Bergsneider M, Black PM. Diagnosing idiopathic normal-pressure hydrocephalus. *Neurosurgery* 2005;57 Supplement:S4–S16; discussion ii–v.
64. Klinge P, Marmarou A, Bergsneider M, Relkin N, Black PM. Outcome of shunting in idiopathic normal-pressure hydrocephalus and the value of outcome assessment in shunted patients. *Neurosurgery* 2005;57 Supplement:S40–S52; discussion ii–v.
65. Krauss JK, Faist M, Schubert M, Borremans JJ, Lucking CH, Berger W. Evaluation of gait in normal pressure hydrocephalus before and after shunting. *Adv Neurol* 2001;87:301–310.
66. Degnan AJ, Capek E, Bowman A. Chorea in the older adult: a full blooded answer. *J R Coll Physicians Edinb* 2016;46:244–246.
67. Sanger TD, Chen D, Fehlings DL, et al. Definition and classification of hyperkinetic movements in childhood. *Mov Disord* 2010;25:1538–1549.
68. Cucca A, Migdadi HA, Di Rocco A. Infection-mediated autoimmune movement disorders. *Parkinsonism Relat Disord* 2018;46 Suppl 1:S83-S86.
69. Ridel KR, Lipps TD, Gilbert DL. The prevalence of neuropsychiatric disorders in Sydenham's chorea. *Pediatr Neurol* 2010;42:243–248.
70. Ekici F, Cetin H, Cevik BS, et al. What is the outcome of rheumatic carditis in children with Sydenham's chorea. *Turk J Paediatr* 2012;54:159–167.
71. Liu D, Long JD, Zhang Y, et al. Motor onset and diagnosis in Huntington disease using the diagnostic confidence level. *J Neurol* 2015;262:2691–2698.
72. Hirschtritt ME, Lee PC, Pauls DL, et al. Lifetime prevalence, age of risk, and genetic relationships of comorbid psychiatric disorders in Tourette syndrome. *JAMA Psychiatr* 2015;72:325–333.
73. Moon Y, Sung J, An R, Hernandez ME, Sosnoff JJ. Gait variability in people with neurological disorders: a systematic review and meta-analysis. *Hum Mov Sci* 2016;47:197–208.
74. Jinnah HA, Berardelli A, Comella C, et al. The focal dystonias: current views and challenges for future research. *Mov Disord* 2013;28:926–943.
75. Defazio G, Gigante AF. The environmental epidemiology of primary dystonia. *Tremor Other Hyperkinet Mov (N Y)* 2013;3: tre-03-131-3076-1.
76. Maas R, Wassenberg T, Lin JP, van de Warrenburg BPC, Willemsen M. l-Dopa in dystonia: a modern perspective. *Neurology* 2017;88:1865–1871.
77. Bandmann O, Weiss KH, Kaler SG. Wilson's disease and other neurological copper disorders. *Lancet Neurol* 2015;14:103–113.
78. Huang WJ, Chen WW, Zhang X. Multiple sclerosis: pathology, diagnosis and treatments. *Exp Ther Med* 2017;13:3163–3166.
79. Goldenberg MM. Multiple sclerosis review. *P T* 2012;37:175–184.
80. Alharbi FM. Update in vitamin D and multiple sclerosis. *Neurosciences (Riyadh)* 2015;20:329–335.
81. Forsberg A, von Koch L, Nilsagard Y. Effects on balance and walking with the CoDuSe balance exercise program in people with multiple

sclerosis: a multicenter randomized controlled trial. *Mult Scler Int* 2016;2016: 7076265.

82. Fritz NE, Keller J, Calabresi PA, Zackowski KM. Quantitative measures of walking and strength provide insight into brain corticospinal tract pathology in multiple sclerosis. *Neuroimage Clin* 2017;14:490–498.

83. Wilkins A. Cerebellar dysfunction in multiple sclerosis. *Front Neurol* 2017;8:312.

84. Edwards T, Pilutti LA. The effect of exercise training in adults with multiple sclerosis with severe mobility disability: a systematic review and future research directions. *Mult Scler Relat Disord* 2017;16:31–39.

85. Held Bradford E, Finlayson M, White Gorman A, Wagner J. Maximizing gait and balance: behaviors and decision-making processes of persons with multiple sclerosis and physical therapists. *Disabil Rehabil* 2018;40(9):1014–1025.

86. Rouleau I, Dagenais E, Tremblay A, et al. Prospective memory impairment in multiple sclerosis: a review. *Clin Neuropsychol* 2018;32(5):922–936.

87. Kalron A, Allali G. Gait and cognitive impairments in multiple sclerosis: the specific contribution of falls and fear of falling. *J Neural Transm (Vienna)* 2017;124(11):1407–1416.

88. Kalron A. Association between gait variability, falls and mobility in people with multiple sclerosis: a specific observation on the EDSS 4.0–4.5 level. *NeuroRehabilitation* 2017;40:579–585.

89. Lempert T, Brandt T, Dieterich M, Huppert D. How to identify psychogenic disorders of stance and gait. A video study in 37 patients. *J Neurol* 1991;238:140–146.

90. Sudarsky L. Psychogenic gait disorders. *Semin Neurol* 2006;26:351–356.

91. Hallett M. Functional (psychogenic) movement disorders - clinical presentations. *Parkinsonism Relat Disord* 2016;22 Suppl 1:S149–S152.

92. Parees I, Kojovic M, Pires C, et al. Physical precipitating factors in functional movement disorders. *J Neurol Sci* 2014;338:174–177.

93. Peckham EL, Hallett M. Psychogenic movement disorders. *Neurol Clin* 2009;27:801–819, vii.

94. Olivo R, Tsao B. Peripheral nerve injuries in sport. *Neurol Clin* 2017;35:559–572.

95. Kennedy RA, Carroll K, McGinley JL. Gait in children and adolescents with Charcot-Marie-Tooth disease: a systematic review. *J Peripher Nerv Syst* 2016;21:317–328.

96. Hughes RA. Peripheral neuropathy. *BMJ* 2002;324:466–469.

97. Menz HB, Lord SR, St George R, Fitzpatrick RC. Walking stability and sensorimotor function in older people with diabetic peripheral neuropathy. *Arch Phys Med Rehabil* 2004;85:245–252.

98. Paisey RB, Darby T, George AM, et al. Prediction of protective sensory loss, neuropathy and foot ulceration in type 2 diabetes. *BMJ Open Diabetes Res Care* 2016;4:e000163.

99. Chadwick P, Edmonds M, McCardle J, Armstrong DG. Best practice guidelines: Wound management in diabetic foot ulcers [online]. *Wounds Int* 2013. Available at: https://www.woundsinternational.com/resources/details/b

est-practice-guidelines-wound-management-diabetic-foot-ulcers. https://bit.ly/2Pb2ewM. [Accessed 21 February 2020.]

100. Boulton AJ, Vileikyte L, Ragnarson-Tennvall G, Apelqvist J. The global burden of diabetic foot disease. *Lancet* 2005;366:1719–1724.
101. Raspovic A. Gait characteristics of people with diabetes-related peripheral neuropathy, with and without a history of ulceration. *Gait Posture* 2013;38:723–728.
102. Seidel J, Mathew B, Marks J. Bilateral ankle and subtalar joint fusion secondary to Guillain Barre-induced foot drop. *J Foot Ankle Surg* 2016;55:260–262.
103. Vinik A, Mehrabyan A, Colen L, Boulton A. Focal entrapment neuropathies in diabetes. *Diabet Care* 2004;27:1783–1788.
104. Reife MD, Coulis CM. Peroneal neuropathy misdiagnosed as L5 radiculopathy: a case report. *Chiropr Man Therap* 2013;21:12.
105. Frink M, Hildebrand F, Krettek C, Brand J, Hankemeier S. Compartment syndrome of the lower leg and foot. *Clin Orthop Relat Res* 2010;468:940–950.
106. Gilhus NE. Myasthenia gravis. *N Engl J Med* 2016;375:2570–2581.
107. Brown RH, Al-Chalabi A. Amyotrophic lateral sclerosis. *N Engl J Med* 2017;377:162–172.
108. Lenglet T, Camdessanche JP. Amyotrophic lateral sclerosis or not: keys for the diagnosis. *Rev Neurol (Paris)* 2017;173:280–287.
109. Al-Chalabi A, Hardiman O, Kiernan MC, Chio A, Rix-Brooks B, van den Berg LH. Amyotrophic lateral sclerosis: moving towards a new classification system. *Lancet Neurol* 2016;15:1182–1194.
110. Statland JM, Barohn RJ, McVey AL, Katz JS, Dimachkie MM. Patterns of weakness, classification of motor neuron disease, and clinical diagnosis of sporadic amyotrophic lateral sclerosis. *Neurol Clin* 2015;33:735–748.
111. Iyadurai SJ, Kissel JT. The limb-girdle muscular dystrophies and the dystrophinopathies. *Continuum (Minneap Minn)* 2016;22:1954–1977.
112. Katzberg HD, Kassardjian CD. Toxic and endocrine myopathies. *Continuum (Minneap Minn)* 2016;22:1815–1828.
113. Tarnopolsky MA. Metabolic myopathies. *Continuum (Minneap Minn)* 2016;22:1829–1851.
114. Venance SL. Approach to the patient with hyperCKemia. *Continuum (Minneap Minn)* 2016;22:1803–1814.
115. Gottschalk F, Kourosh S, Leveau B. The functional anatomy of tensor fasciae latae and gluteus medius and minimus. *J Anat* 1989;166:179–189.
116. Ramachandran R, Wierzbicki AS. Statins, muscle disease and mitochondria. *J Clin Med* 2017;6(8):75.
117. Subramony SH. Degenerative ataxias: challenges in clinical research. *Ann Clin Transl Neurol* 2017;4:53–60.
118. Burk K. Friedreich ataxia: current status and future prospects. *Cerebellum Ataxias* 2017;4:4.
119. Rothblum-Oviatt C, Wright J, Lefton-Greif MA, McGrath-Morrow SA, Crawford TO, Lederman HM. Ataxia telangiectasia: a review. *Orphanet J Rare Dis* 2016;11:159.

120. Baizabal-Carvallo JF, Alonso-Juarez M. Cerebellar disease associated with anti-glutamic acid decarboxylase antibodies: review. *J Neural Transm (Vienna)* 2017;124(1): 1171–1182.

121. van Gaalen J, Kerstens FG, Maas RP, Harmark L, van de Warrenburg BP. Drug-induced cerebellar ataxia: a systematic review. *CNS Drugs* 2014;28:1139–1153.

122. Fife TD, Blum D, Fisher RS. Measuring the effects of antiepileptic medications on balance in older people. *Epilepsy Res* 2006;70:103–109.

123. Singh AE, Romanowski B. Syphilis: review with emphasis on clinical, epidemiologic, and some biologic features. *Clin Microbiol Rev* 1999;12:187–209.

124. Ghanem KG. Review: Neurosyphilis: a historical perspective and review. *CNS Neurosci Ther* 2010;16:e157–168.

4

Emotions and Gait

Contents

INTRODUCTION

The human brain responds to both internal and external stimuli, known as 'psychophysics' and the field of experimental psychology has studied such matters for a long time, going back to ancient philosophers alluding that human behaviours were influenced by our five senses. However, the complexities of our human body and the way we behave go far beyond the biological and biomechanical understanding in terms of establishing links between emotions and gait. The aim of this chapter is to give an essence of the connection in the areas of emotions and gait.

As our mind can take control of the way we think and the way we process emotions, these impact our behavioural responses. Our body systems have many other sophisticated sensory and motor mechanisms in addition to our senses of smell, vision, touch, hearing and taste, which also influence human behaviour and gait. For instance, the sense of motion or kinaesthetic sense (controlled by receptors in the muscles, tendons and joints), the sense of balance (commanded by receptors in the vestibular organs in the inner ear) and many other sensory receptors found in the circulatory and digestive systems. Additionally, the brain stem has regulatory centres to monitor basic body functions such heart rate, blood pressure and breathing. The brain stem plays an important part in regulating respiratory and cardiac functions and is highly sensitive to changes in blood chemistry and body temperature.[1]

On the one hand, when we perceive any internal biological and/or biomechanical stimuli, it is down to the individual's state of mind at the time to process the way the information is received by the brain. Subsequently, the way it is interpreted determines the choices that one can make at both cognitive and emotional levels prior to expressing a motor response. On the other hand, science could congruently argue that there is a strong correlation between the structural and physiological brain changes and the physical body affecting gait. For example, the pattern of gait observed in an elderly person who may be afraid of having a fall as a result of the natural ageing process, or the gait pattern observed by someone suffering from a neurological disorder.

Mental processes including emotions and thoughts can independently take control of the way individuals respond emotionally and physically to stimuli. The ability to attribute to humans a mental state, emotions and behaviours pertinent to each individual is what has been referred to as the theory of the mind.[2] This theory also relates to the understanding that each individual has a set of original systems of beliefs, emotions, desires, intentions and knowledge. This view enables an understanding of everyday human behaviours, social interactions and the limitations involved in placing an objective judgement and/or making predictions about emotional responses and behaviours, which are not directly communicated from mind to mind. Our inability to communicate directly from mind to mind can introduce bias in the way we make assumptions and interpretations about others.

BASIC CONCEPTS OF THE RELATIONSHIP BETWEEN EMOTIONS AND GAIT (PERCEPTION–PROCESSING–EXPRESSION)

'Emotion' is a term commonly used and therefore it could become rather confusing when it comes to the distinction between conscious and unconscious processes.

Emotion is defined as 'A strong feeling deriving from one's circumstances, mood, or relationships with others'.[3]

Gait is defined as, 'manner of walking or running; bearing'.[4]

Emotional states are interrelated with the human gait, for example, at the time the brain registers highly challenging situations, such as danger, a set of physiological responses are put in motion involving both brain and body processes. Both unconscious and conscious responses activate a series of automatic physiological actions involving endocrine, autonomic and musculoskeletal functions. Whilst we are unaware of some mental processes, we are aware of others, and both of these impact the way we perceive, process, interpret and elicit an emotional and physical response. Feelings such as anger, elation, sadness, happiness and fear also involve our conscious perception of somatic (bodily) sensations. For example, an unpleasant bodily sensation such as 'pain' could trigger negative thinking; this could then trigger a range of emotions such as fear and anger, which in turn influences behaviours and body movement.[1]

Human motion reflects human behaviour and informs human activity recognition, human motion tracking and detection, along with movement analysis of the human body.[5] The current understanding of human motion linking emotions and gait would benefit from further work in contributing to a more in-depth understanding. Humans can consciously or unconsciously influence the way body language and gestures are expressed. For example, someone could be observed smiling and appear very relaxed having just committed a heinous crime. In this sense, there is no congruence between this individual's emotional or mental state and the gait observed. This lack of correlation demonstrates the potential bias involved when it comes to understanding and analysing the complex relationship between emotions and gait.

The human body has a highly sophisticated and adaptive system to perform automatic body movements directly controlled by the nervous system. This refers to body movements outside our conscious control. Body movements and postural adjustments are the outcome of how our brain processes information and establishes the intricate connections between cognition (thought processing), personality, emotions and motor behaviours.[6] Like a computer, our brain is constantly processing and automatically making appropriate adjustments to our behaviours and motor responses. Simultaneously, our brain is constantly processing our ability to think and reason[2] and act or respond, or not.

BASIC NEUROANATOMY AND NEUROPHYSIOLOGY

The activity of human locomotion involves highly interconnected motor cortical areas of the brain with the basal ganglia, the cerebellum and the spinal inter-neuronal networks. This interconnected neuronal network processes sensory and motor signals travelling up and down the spinal cord, which enables us to automatically regulate muscle tone and rhythmic limb movements in the absence of conscious awareness. It also allows us to generate limb trajectory to achieve accurate foot placement and to make gait modifications by adjusting our body posture or motor alignment.[1]

Emotional responses according to how our brain processes information have a meaningful, subjective significance to each individual. Deep in our brain there is a highly sophisticated, complex and somewhat primitive area known as 'The Limbic System' (Figure 4.1). This is a group of structures which presides over emotions and behaviour.[7] The limbic system is involved in emotions, memories and instinctive responses, thereby facilitating different mental or psychological reactions expressed by people and these play a central role in the way we behave, both individually and socially. The limbic system is formed by several parts of the brain which are found above the brain stem and the cerebrum (the section of the brain responsible for thinking and movement). Each part of the limbic system has a highly specialised function involved in the role of movement and behaviour, like an

The Limbic System

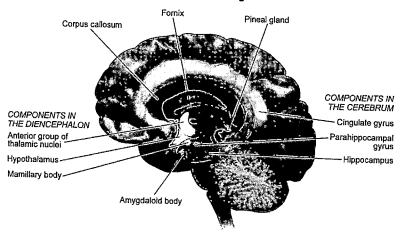

Figure 4.1 The limbic system.

'emotional motor system'. In brief, this system is responsible for the experience and expression of emotion involving an interconnected system of neurons. For example, our reactions to immediate danger such as running – part of the so-called 'fight or flight' response – whereby certain hormones such as adrenaline, noradrenaline and cortisol are released by the sympathetic nervous system. The release of these stress hormones escalates key activities controlled by the autonomic nervous system such as the increase of heart and breathing rate, the slowdown of the digestive functions and the re-direction of blood flow to major muscles groups to give to the body a burst of energy and strength.[1] The way our brain responds to emotions such as danger is like a computer programme triggering a defence system that assists us to face such hazards and threats. Neuroscientist, Joseph LeDoux, described how emotions are hardwired biological functions of the central nervous system (CNS), which are effective for survival.[1] The stimulation of this emotional motor system affects every organ of the body. This reflects the complexities involved in our understanding of the intricate relationship between body, mind and environment. The limbic system is part of a larger neuronal circuit, including major interconnected parts of the brain, namely, the amygdala, hippocampus, thalamus and hypothalamus as well as many other key brain structures such as cortical areas.

The amygdala is a small area of the brain located in the temporal lobe which constantly receives sensory links from various external stimuli such as visual, auditory, olfactory (relating to sense of smell) and touch, but it is also intricately interconnected with all our emotional activity and the physiological functioning of our body. This assists an understanding of how sensory information coming into our brain gets expanded to other key internal brain connections. The amygdala is an integrated centre that is involved in processing emotions, emotional behaviour and motivation and is like the 'brain centre' which triggers our response to fight, flight or freeze. The amygdala is involved in forming sophisticated associations between external stimuli with internal mental processes, which enable humans to adapt highly sophisticated behavioural responses or adapt responses to basic stimuli such as sound, food and thirst (pavlonian associations). Therefore, the amygdala instrumentally influences behaviours.[1]

The hippocampus is involved in the formation of short- and long-term memory and spatial navigation. The thalamus and hypothalamus play important roles in linking the limbic system with other areas of the CNS and endocrine systems. A very basic example of how all these areas of the limbic system integrate is when we face imminent danger, such as being chased by a dangerous animal. This triggers fear – the emotional

example: 'I am having a serious illness', 'I am worthless', 'I did something wrong', 'I cannot be trusted', 'I am inadequate'. These are strongly linked to the way an individual expresses and copes with emotional distress and are in turn associated with behavioural patterns.[9]

Several studies have suggested a link between children exposed to chronic stress and anxiety with the development of adulthood psychological and mental disorders such as generalised anxiety disorder, mood disorders and depression. Functional magnetic resonance imaging (fMRI) of the brain has shown an increase in the amygdala size and connectivity in children and adults exposed to high anxiety. Animal studies have shown the same findings when animals have been exposed to chronic stress.[10] Recent studies have also suggested strong evidence of the limbic system involvement in body movement or motor response in patients suffering from Parkinson's disease. These revealed associations between visual stimuli with the cognitive processing (thinking process), which influence gait initiation.[11]

PSYCHOLOGICAL AND PSYCHIATRY CONDITIONS AFFECTING GAIT

The examination of human gait is known to have a long history of investigation, but what is perhaps less well understood, in some areas, is the individual traits exhibited during movement. Recent studies have suggested that our body movements may give clues about the individual's personality and/or mental health – advocating that each person has an 'individual motor signature' (IMS) and that movement gives an indication of one's behavioural characteristics.[12] One recent work combining motion capture of gait, personality testing and questionnaire assessing the level of aggression, suggests that disposition may be observed in a person's gait.[13] However, another way to consider this is to appreciate the way some individuals walk could simply be a function of their socio-cultural environment.

In addition to other forms of person identification, such as face recognition, the use of gait to identify an individual's emotional state of mind has become an area of interest. It has been argued that useful information regarding an individual's emotional state could be specifically correlated to an individual's body pattern movement. However, as we have mentioned earlier, locomotor activity involves complex biological and biomechanical variables that go beyond the body's physical state (this

93

includes normal and abnormal anatomy, physiology, injury), as it is also influenced by the individual's state of mind[2] and the sociocultural environment. Therefore, it is not surprising that an attempt to identify strong emotions by gait analysis requires a bio-psycho-social approach, which is a systematic approach to consider complex interactions between biological, psychological and social factors involved in health and illness. There are several variables involved in the analysis of the relationship between emotions and body movements. In addition to the bio-psycho-social variables, the use and abuse of alcohol, recreational substances, prescribed medication, electroconvulsive therapy and psychotherapy to treat mental disorders could also impact the correlation between body pattern movements and emotions.

A study carried out by Birch et al.,[14] based on the previous work of Montepare et al.,[15] presents some thought provoking outcomes. Participants in this study were provided with scripts designed to elicit five emotions: pride, happiness, neutral, fear and anger. A group of observers were asked to identify the emotion expressed by the walker on video footage. Overall, the observers in the study correctly identified all five emotions more often than would be expected by chance. The emotions of neutral, fear and anger were more frequently and correctly identified than pride and happiness. There were also variations in the observer's confidence rating of emotions. For example, anger showed tendencies towards a strong confidence rating when compared with the other emotions. Neutral showed that the lowest number of strong confidence selection and happiness was often misidentified for neutral or pride.[14] Although it is possible for an observer to identify some emotions from gait more regularly than other feelings, the outcomes of this small study provide food for thought and help to inform future, more substantive studies regarding the complex links between emotions and gait.

Other studies have suggested that the gait pattern in depressed patients improves with antidepressant medication, therefore establishing a correlation between mood and body pattern movement.[16] It has also been suggested that there is a direct correlation between the pattern of gait and low mood when normal individuals have been induced to experience sadness.[16] Furthermore, other studies using sophisticated three-dimensional technology and transcranial magnetic stimulation have suggested that individuals exposed to highly unpleasant images have induced changes in the pattern of body movement. Individuals exposed to anxiety provoking images have triggered behavioural responses such as avoidance and these have been correlated to changes in the pattern of body movement, such as a reduction in the length and speed of steps. These studies have also argued that even during the anticipation state of someone suffering from extreme anxiety, individuals have exhibited a pattern of psycho-motor agitation. The outcome of studies utilising transcranial magnetic stimulation have suggested that the effect of emotions on the motor system reflects responses on behaviours and neurophysiological processes. In other words, this could suggest that our motor system anticipates and is prepared for action.[17]

Emotions and cognitions are intertwined and previous research has looked at the physiology of emotions, particularly facial expressions.[18] Ekman's work has suggested that there are six basic universal emotions identified cross-culturally. These are sadness, fear, disgust, anger, surprise and happiness. Negative thoughts or cognitions are powerful and they just happen automatically and without much effort. Negative cognitions lead to powerful emotions and they in turn have a direct influence on how mood states are expressed.[9]

In fact, Charles Darwin had already suggested that emotions were part of an evolutionary adaptive process in man and animals and that 'primal emotions', such as fear, are associated with pre-mammals' ancient parts of our brain.[19] This could have improved our chances of survival by adapting behaviours in preparation for a rapid response in combination with psychological and physiological processes. Other studies consider pleasant and unpleasant emotional states with body movement and demonstrate the links between 'highly arousing unpleasant' and 'low arousing pleasant' stimuli with the speed and quality of emotional response to initiate body movement, including reaction time, motor displacement, velocity of the centre of pressure (COP) trajectory, length and velocity of the first and second steps. How emotional conflict could affect gait initiation, such as the amplitude of early postural response, has also been looked at. These studies serve to further inform the intricate links between emotions and motor behaviour impacting gait.[20,21] Others suggest links of gait and basic emotions.[22] Video footage and detailed gait measurements have been carried out on patients suffering from affective disorders and compared to the normal population, which consistently found differences in body pattern movements. These also found evidence of non-verbal cues that can be assessed by psychomotor analysis (psychomotor retardation vs. psychomotor agitation) on individuals with low and agitated moods.[23,24]

There are several publications which have looked at how emotions would impact on the different stages and variables involved in human motion. This includes a study carried out by Fawver et al., which looked at the impact of motor behaviour on normal individuals exposed to self-generated or self-induced affective states. It was found that self-induced affective states such as happiness, sadness, anger and fear affected forward gait initiation when compared to individuals expressing neutral affect.[20] It identified that individuals exposed to happiness and anger showed greater posterior-lateral displacement and velocity of their centre of pressure during the first, second and final phases of gait when compared to those experiencing sadness and fear.

Pain exerts a strong influence on the neuro-motor expressions of gait linked to the individual's emotional states. This mood related aspect could influence body posture and muscle activity, rather than being directly influenced by the pain alone. Strong emotions such as fear and anger associated to high states of anxiety and mood change may be expressed in maladaptive behaviours such as avoidance and catastrophising, and this impacts muscle activity during gait.[24]

The cerebral cortex (visible external area of the brain) and subcortical structures (below the cerebral cortex) are closely intertwined in both structure and function. The cerebral cortex controls the movement of the muscles and subcortical structures such as the basal ganglia, limbic system, thalamus, hypothalamus, tectum, tegmentum, cerebellum, reticular formation, and both gross and fine motor skills. The nervous system during the process of its development generates gender-specific-related behaviours. It is suggested that this process is still not totally understood as there are genetic and social determinants that are yet to be identified and that recent advances in imaging and genetics have provided better understanding about specific links of neural pathways and social behavioural differences between males and females.[1] Furthermore, recent neuroimaging studies have shown gender differences in the process of structural brain development.[25]

Gross motor development starts at birth and they are more prominent during the first years of life (crawling, walking, jumping, maintaining balance). Gross motor skills become almost automatic as the child grows. Fine motor skills require refined and precise control such as holding an object between the thumb and the finger, writing and moving the tongue.[1]

In psychiatry conditions, dysfunctions taking place at the cerebral cortex and subcortical areas of the brain can influence changes in gait or body movements. Most psychiatry conditions are associated with behavioural and emotional changes, which are not in keeping with the individual's base-line behaviours or socio-cultural background. Individuals suffering from mental health disorders process the functions of the mind differently when compared to the general population regardless of socio-cultural environment. Strictly speaking, emotions and behaviours are the outcome of sophisticated mental processes or appraisals, which are highly interconnected and like two sides of the same coin. Understanding the difference between the two could assist one to change unhealthy behaviours. Altered emotional states and behaviours are common in psychiatry patients, as they may not be able to regulate the way emotions such as happiness, sadness, irritability, anger and fear are expressed. The individual may exhibit behaviours that are extreme (intense) or prolonged. Whilst they may also 'know' what they do, they do not/may not 'realise' what they do.

A book edited by Kirkcaldy compiled comprehensive studies linking altered human movement with mental illness, schizophrenia and affective disorders.[6] (pp25–26) However, it is also suggested that movement characteristics associated to mental disorders are more indicative of the degree of psychopathology and less of the type of disorder.[6] (pp133) Furthermore, Kirkcaldy's book describes studies suggesting that children who suffered psychiatry illness later in life were observed to have motor symptoms in childhood. The motor symptoms mentioned in these studies included marked hyperactivity, rigidity, abnormal gait, poor coordination and impaired attention.[6] (pp112).

There are also several scientific publications suggesting a relationship between motor performance and mental disorder, rather than looking at the links between normal personality traits and motor skills and/or responses.[27] In addition, the pattern of body movements from someone suffering from a mental disorder could be influenced by the side-effect of psychotropic medication (antipsychotic medication) affecting the musculoskeletal system. This could include muscle jerks, stiffness and shakiness, uncomfortable feeling of internal restlessness (akathisia), movements of the jaw, lips and tongue (tardive dyskinesia), alongside sleepiness and slowness (see Table 4.1). The links between mental disorder and psychological disorders with body movement are complex.

The CNS monitors the body's normal functions and will automatically send an alert to the brain when attention is needed, for example chest pain. Bodily sensations become a symptom when a patient or medical practitioner believes it could be the manifestation of physical illness. There are times when an individual could become focused or fixated on bodily sensations, in such a way that causes high anxiety and worry to the individual. Medically 'unexplained symptoms' could imply an undiagnosed condition which may or may not resolve, or may imply

Table 4.1 Mental Health Disorders and Altered Body Movements

Mental Health Disorder	Pathology and Abnormal Behaviour/Emotion	Abnormal Gait/Body Movements
Affective or mood disorders (depressive illness)	Pervasive and persistent low mood, sleep disturbance, lack of appetite, lack of motivation and enjoyment. It is different to a state of unhappiness. It is associated with neurochemistry changes of the brain. Socially withdrawn.	Depressed patients walked with a lifting motion of the leg, while normal individuals were observed to be propelling themselves forward. Reduced walking speed, reduced arm swing and vertical head movement. Decreased facial expressions, poor eye contact and psychomotor retardation. Overall body posture could be affected and both body language and gait return to standard body movements once the illness is treated.
Affective or mood disorders (bipolar or manic-depressive Disorder)	Incongruent affect, mood could be elated (psychomotor agitation), irritable, fearful or low.	Abnormal liveliness of movement, socially disinhibited, distractible and overfamiliar.
Schizophrenia	The aetiology is multifactorial. It is a psychotic mental illness where an individual perceives themselves and the world around them outside of the norm. It is associated with structural brain changes and neurochemistry dysfunction. Incongruent affect, mood could be elated (psychomotor agitation), fearful or low. Bizarre behaviours, including responding to unheard or unseen external stimuli (auditory and visual hallucinations).	It could be associated with mild Parkinsonism like body movements and ataxia, slow gait, reduction of the stride length. Tandem gait could also be mildly impaired regardless of antipsychotic medication. Inappropriate eye contact. Unusual body postures, which can be maintained for hours or days, e.g. waxy flexibility observed in catatonic states. Abnormal body movements associated to the side effects of psychotropic medication. *Echopraxia* copying of a movement performed by someone else. *Extrapyramidal effects* *Acute Dystonia*: torticollis, grimacing, tongue protrusion, muscle jerks. *Akathisia*: the individual experiences an unpleasant bodily feeling of internal restlessness and therefore needs to move leading to an inability to keep still. *Parkinsonian like movements* *Tardive dyskinesia*: chewing and sucking facial movements, grimacing, choreoathetoid movements (involuntary sudden and random twist, contraction and contortions of muscle groups).

(Continued)

Table 4.1 (Continued) Mental Health Disorders and Altered Body Movements

Mental Health Disorder	Pathology and Abnormal Behaviour/Emotion	Abnormal Gait/Body Movements
Alcoholism	The nervous system is highly sensitive to alcohol. The prolonged abuse of this toxic substance affects the nervous system and consequently affects gait at every level. Alcoholism causes damage to the structure and function of the brain, causing cognitive and motor dysfunctions as well as behavioural difficulties. It can also induce several dysfunctions or deficits, including impairment of the individual's mental processes.	*Ataxia* Loss of full control of motor leg movement (cerebellar ataxia) due to alcoholic cerebellar degeneration causing wide-based gait, poor tandem gait. Usually legs are more affected than arms. Loss of the sense of body position (sensory ataxia). *Asterixis* Abnormal tremor of the hand when the wrist is extended (like a bird flapping its wings). *Wernicke-Korsakoff syndrome* Caused by thiamine (Vit. B1) deficiency. Impairment of cognition and motor functions. The latter including abnormal function of the muscles that control eye movement. *Alcoholic Neuropathy* Damage of peripheral nerves of the body causing sensorial and motor impairment. It induces an abnormal and unpleasant sensation when touched (dysaesthesia), which discourages walking. *Abnormal muscle function* Alcohol causes myopathy (muscle weakness and consequently abnormal muscle function).
Other psychiatry and psychological disorders	*Anxiety*: subjective sense of internal tension. *Mannerism*: repetitive non-goal-directed body motion. *Stereotypic movements*: repetitive purposeless movements, which interfere with normal activity and may cause bodily harm. *Tic*: sudden, involuntary and rapid muscle movement, which are difficult to control.	It is associated with autonomic nervous system arousal such as tachycardia, sweating, dry mouth, pale skin, coarse tremor of hands and fidgeting. Unusual hand movements when shaking hands or any other unusual greeting, e.g. hand waving, rocking, head-banging. Blinking, shoulder-shrugging, neck-jerking, tends to be more frequent in the upper part of the body. Tics could also be vocal such as throat clearing, sniffing and hissing, barking. Tics are key features on Tourette's syndrome.

99

a psychological cause where no medical cause is found to be associated to the symptoms, despite exhaustive medical investigations with nothing abnormal being established. There are three related clinical presentations of medically unexplained symptoms which could impact one's gait. These are: somatisation disorder, factitious disorder and malingering. Somatisation disorder involves unconscious processes where the individual expresses emotional or psychological distress in physical body symptoms, for example when an individual clinically presents a dysfunctional limb resembling the paralysis of a limb (this involves an unconscious process). Factitious disorder is a mental health disorder in which the individual acts as if he or she is suffering from a physical or mental illness. This involves a conscious process and the individual has deliberately created the clinical picture. This mainly serves for the purpose of attracting or seeking attention, and there is no malingering motive or secondary gain involved. It is mainly attaining a patient role. Munchausen's syndrome is a rare factitious disorder. Individuals affected by this disorder fake physical or psychological symptoms in order to seek sympathy, attention or reassurance for themselves. In Munchausen syndrome by proxy, it is the caregiver who fabricates, exaggerates or causes illness or physical injury to someone in their care, to gain sympathy, attention or reassurance for themselves. Malingering is the fabrication of a mental disorder or physical illness, which has the purpose of obtaining a secondary gain, for example financial compensation.

MEDICAL ASSESSMENT AND INVESTIGATIONS OF GAIT

Observational gait analysis (OGA) is a helpful and important tool for clinicians in the diagnosis and treatment of conditions, and there are numerous medical conditions that can exhibit subtle or marked gait alterations and disturbances.

The gait abnormality rating scale (GARS) is a tool that can be used to identify patients with abnormal gait at risk of falling. Other investigations include blood tests, dynamic electromyography, X-ray, magnetic resonance imaging (MRI) and computerised tomography (CT). Kinematic and kinetic studies can also be deployed, although for the vast majority of conditions seen with patients, this is considerably more time consuming in a busy clinical setting. Video analysis and playback can be performed and reviewed easily on smartphones, which is a useful way to show to a patient and for later comparison, provided appropriate consents have

100

been obtained. A more detailed coverage of OGA is encompassed in other chapters.

DISCUSSION

The initiation of human locomotion is triggered by signals arising from either volitional processing in the cerebral cortex or emotional processing in the limbic system. Regardless of whether human gait is initiated by volitional or emotional processes, it involves automatic controlled movement processes such as the adjustment of postural muscle tone and rhythmic limb movements. Human gait is a purposeful, goal-directed behaviour and is the result of complex interactions of anatomical structures, physiology and in particular neurology and neurophysiology. In addition to this, pathology and injury can and do alter the pattern of body movements. Therefore, human gait represents a basic pattern of movement that is expressed by the peculiarities of the individual. Another idiosyncrasy that has raised scientific debate during experimental behavioural studies is that of participants altering their performance, which could influence the outcome of the behaviours analysed. The Hawthorne Effect is a form of reaction that occurs when an individual alters facets of their behaviour when conscious of being observed. Recent systematic review has called for new scientific concepts to be introduced on future behavioural studies to avoid the influence of confounding factors.[28]

In addition to the Hawthorne Effect, a study using sophisticated brain imaging, known as fMRI, looked at how the superior temporal sulcus (STS) area of the human brain (with multisensory processing capabilities) and a more specific part of the visual brain (area V5 where the visual brain is organised anatomically, functionally and perceptually) operate or are stimulated when the observer watches biological motion (human locomotion) and compared to that of non-biological motion (robotic/mechanical motion). It was shown that biological motions evoked larger responses in the STS area than did non-biological motion. However, strong activation was also noticed in a region corresponding to the motion area V5, but this area did not show any preference for the biological motion stimuli. The study concluded that the STS area of the human brain is sensitive to the distinction between biological and non-biological motion and speculates that the STS region could play a role in the way our brain processes social information.[29] Furthermore, a recent study has also shown the potential for new highly computerised technology such as the use of a wearable 'smart' bracelet device to recognise human emotions, including anger, happiness and neutral. The study used human gait data collected from this device to build classification models to differentiate various emotions, which could benefit future research in the computerised automatic recognition of human emotions.[30]

In terms of human pathology affecting gait, there is an interesting recent genetic study suggesting a strong genetic correlation of comorbidity affecting the brain structure and function between Parkinson's disease and Schizophrenia.[31] The pathology of these two conditions is clearly evidenced in body pattern movements. Furthermore, this study also found genetic correlations between Parkinson's disease and Crohn's disease. This suggests that both Crohn's disease and Schizophrenia could be genetic risks associated with Parkinson's disease comorbidity.

Body language represents an essential element of non-verbal communication, and the ability to recognise and adequately interpret emotional states in others plays a fundamental role in regulating social interaction. The relationships between emotions and gait are also highly complex and sophisticated. The objective analytical assessment linking the emotional state with motor behaviours can be a demanding task. It requires consideration of all the components of motor and mental processes, which are influenced by internal mental activities and the impact of the environment around us. The neural networks that underlie the processing and expression of emotions reflected in human locomotion would benefit from further understanding. Objective assessment in connecting emotions and gait is a challenging area that will require further levels of research and thereby for a more extensive understanding.

REFERENCES

1. Kandel ER; Schwartz JH; Jessell TM; Siegelbaum SA; Hudspeth AJ. (Eds). 2013. *Principles of Neural Science*. 5th edition. The McGraw-Hill Companies, Inc.
2. Premack D; Woodruff G. 1978. Does the chimpanzee have a theory of mind? *Behavioral and Brain Sciences*, 1(4), 515–526. doi:10.1017/S0140525X00076512.
3. Emotion. Lexico.com, UK Dictionary online. https://bit.ly/2TUulCg [Accessed 11 March 2020].
4. Gait. 2016. *Aa Collins ENGLISH DICTIONARY*. 12th edition reprinted. HarperCollins Publishers, Glasgow.
5. Wang L; Hu W; Tan T. 2003. Recent developments in human motion analysis. *Pattern Recognition*, 36(3), 585–601.

102

6. Kirkcaldy B. 1989. Normalities and abnormalities in human movement. *Medicine and Sport Science*, 29, 3–25–26–112–133.
7. MedlinePlus. Limbic system. https://bit.ly/2PJfXd7 [Accessed 21 February 2020.].
8. Cannon WB. 1927. The James-Lange theory of emotions: a critical examination and an alternative theory. *The American Journal of Psychology*, 39(1/4), 106–124. doi:10.2307/1415404
9. Westbrook D; Kennerley H; Kirk J. 2011. *An Introduction to Cognitive Behavioural Therapy: Skills and Applications*. pp 8–9. SAGE Publications.
10. Bergland C. 2013. The size and connectivity of the amygdala predicts anxiety. *Psychology Today*. https://www.psychologytoday.com/us/blog/the-athletes-way/201311/the-size-and-connectivity-the-amygdala-predicts-anxiety (posted: 20 Nov 2013). [Accessed 21 February 2020.].
11. Lagravinese G; Pelosin E; Bonassi G; Carbone F; Abbruzzese G; Avanzino L. 2018. Gait initiation is influenced by emotion processing in Parkinson's disease patients with freezing. *Movement Disorders*, 33(4):609–617
12. Słowiński P; Zhai C; Alderisio F; Salesse R; Gueugnon M; Marin L; Bardy GB.; di Bernardo M; Tsaneva-Atanasova K. 2016. Dynamic similarity promotes interpersonal coordination in joint action. *Journal of the Royal Society Interface*, 13(116). https://royalsocietypublishing.org/doi/full/10.1098/rsif.2015.1093.
13. Satchell L; Morris P; Mills C; O'Reilly L; Marshman P; Akehurst L. 2016. Evidence of big five and aggressive personalities in gait biomechanics. *Journal of Nonverbal Behavior*, 41, 35–44. doi:10.1007/s10919-016-0240-1
14. Birch I; Birch T; Bray D. 2016. The identifications of emotions from gait. *Science & Justice*, 56(5), 351–356. doi:10.1016/j.scijus.2016.05.006
15. Montepare JM; Goldstein SB; Clausen A. 1987. The identification of emotions from gait information. *Journal of Nonverbal Behavior*, 11, 33–42.
16. Michalak J; Troje NF; Fischer J; Vollmar P; Heidenreich T; Schulte D. 2009. Embodiment of sadness and depression-gait patterns associated with dysphoric mood. *Psychosomatic Medicine*, 71(5), 580–587. doi:10.1097/PSY.0b013e3181a2515c
17. Coombes SA; Tandonnet C; Fujiyama H; Janelle CM; Cauraugh JH; Summers JJ. 2009. Emotion and motor preparation: a transcranial magnetic stimulation study of corticospinal motor tract excitability. *Cognitive, Affective, & Behavioral Neuroscience*, 9(4), 380–388. doi:10.3758/CABN.9.4.380
18. Ekman P. 1977. 'Biological and cultural contributions to body and facial movement', in *The Anthropology of the Body*. Vol. 1, ed. Blaikie A. (London: Academic Press), 34–84.
19. Darwin C (author); Ekman P (Ed). 1999. *The Expression of the Emotions in Man and Animals*. 200th Anniversary edition. Harper Collins, United Kingdom.
20. Fawver B; Hass CJ; Park KD; Janelle CM. 2014. Autobiographically recalled emotional states impact forward gait initiation as a function of motivational direction. *Emotion*, 14(6), 1125–1136. doi:10.1037/a0037597

21. Gélat T; Coudrat L; Le Pellec A. 2011. Gait initiation is affected during emotional conflict. *Neurosci Letters*, 497(1), 64–67. doi:10.1016/j.neulet.2011.04.030
22. Greenberg LS. 2002. Evolutionary perspectives on emotion: making sense of what we feel. *Journal of Cognitive Psychotherapy*, 16, 331–347.
23. Sloman L; Pierrynowski M; Berridge M; Tupling S; Flowers J. 1987. Mood, depressive illness and gait patterns. *Canadian Journal of Psychiatry*, 32(3), 190–193.
24. Pakzad M; Fung J; Preuss R. 2016. Pain catastrophizing and trunk muscle activation during walking in patients with chronic low back pain. *Gait & Posture*, 49, 73–77. doi:10.1016/j.gaitpost.2016.06.025
25. Blakemore SJ. 2012. Imaging brain development: the adolescent brain. *Neuroimage*, 61(2), 397–406. doi:10.1016/j.neuroimage.2011.11.080
26. Mednick SA; Mura M; Schulsinger F; Mednick B. 1971. Perinatal conditions and infant development in children with schizophrenic parents. *Social Biology*, 18, S103–S113.
27. Lipskaya-Velikovsky L; Elgerisi D; Easterbrook A; Ratzon NZ. 2018. Motor skills, cognition, and work performance of people with severe mental illness. *Disability and Rehabilitation*, 2018, 1–7. doi:10.1080/09638288.2018.1425744
28. McCambridge J; Witton J; Elbourne DR. 2014. Systematic review of the Hawthorne effect: new concepts are needed to study research participation effects. *Journal of Clinical Epidemiology*, 67(3), 267–277. doi:10.1016/j.jclinepi.2013.08.015
29. Pelphrey KA; Mitchell TV; McKeown MJ; Goldstein J; Allison T; McCarthy G. 2003. Brain activity evoked by the perception of human walking: controlling for meaningful coherent motion. *The Journal of Neuroscience*, 23(17), 6819–6825. doi:10.1523/JNEUROSCI.23-17-06819.2003
30. Zhang Z; Song Y; Cui L; Liu X; Zhu T. 2016. Emotion recognition based on customized smart bracelet with built-in accelerometer. *PeerJ*, 4, e2258. doi:10.7717/peerj.2258
31. Nalls MA; Saad M; Noyce AJ; Keller MF; Schrag A; Bestwick JP; Traynor BJ; Gibbs JR; Hernandez DG; Cookson MR; Morris HR; Williams N; Gasser T; Heutink P; Wood N; Hardy J; Martinez M; Singleton AB; International Parkinson's Disease Genomics Consortium (IPDGC); Wellcome Trust Case Control Consortium 2 (WTCCC2); North American Brain Expression Consortium (NABEC); United Kingdom Brain Expression Consortium (UKBEC). 2014. Genetic comorbidities in Parkinson's disease. *Human Molecular Genetics*, 23(3), 831–841. doi:10.1093/hmg/ddt465

5

Video Image Analysis

Contents

INTRODUCTION

The aim of this chapter is to provide a general overview of what is involved in video image analysis. The use of moving pictures has long been of benefit to the analysis of motion and events. The human eye is often incapable of recording an accurate log of fast-moving episodes as they happen in real time, but the ability to review an occurrence in slow motion allows the eye to determine the exact movements and the order in which they occurred. A good example of this is illustrated by the fatal air crash at the Farnborough, UK air show in 1952 that resulted in the death of test pilot, John Derry, his observer Anthony Richards and 29 spectators, with many more injured. The accident was witnessed by thousands of people and many eye witness accounts described how during a high-speed pass, the tail and engines broke away from the aircraft and fell into the crowd. Subsequent review of cine film of the incident showed that it was caused by a failure in the wing, not the tail. What the witnesses had in fact seen was the most ferocious element of the separation – the last stage of events. None had noticed the initial cause of 'the break-up' which happened in less than a second and too fast to recall with any accuracy.[1]

Challenging observer's perception of reality is not new. It was also a thoughtful area of artist René Magritte (1898–1967) illustrated by his work, *The Treachery of Images*. The picture displays a pipe below which Magritte painted, '*Ceci n'est pas une pipe*' (French for, 'This is not a pipe'). At first this may appear as a contradiction, but actually it is true. The work is not a pipe – it is an image of a pipe. As Magritte said, 'I'm not an artist. I'm a man that thinks'.[2]

WHAT IS VIDEO?

To understand how we have ended up with the video technology of today, we need to look at the history behind television. Video is the recording, reproducing or broadcasting of moving visual images, or the recording of moving visual images made digitally or on videotape.[3] Television is a system for converting visual images (with sound) into electrical signals, transmitting them by radio or other means and displaying them electronically on a screen.[4] Both video and television have their roots firmly set in the motion picture (film) industry.

The creation of the illusion of a moving image is generated by presenting a number of still pictures in quick succession. This illusion occurs because of two optical phenomena known as 'persistence of vision' and 'phi phenomenon'. *Persistence of vision* causes the brain to retain images projected upon the retina of the eye for a split second beyond their disappearance from the field of sight.[5] *Phi phenomenon* creates apparent movement between images when they succeed one another rapidly.[6]

Figure 5.1 Eadweard Muybridge's phenakistoscope, 1893.

Moving images were initially seen as more of an entertainment piece than a major communications medium, and were first produced in the 1830s using revolving drums and disks containing a number of images. These included inventions such as the stroboscope, phenakistoscope, zoetrope, zoopraxiscope and other instruments (see Figure 5.1).

Right from the early years, moving pictures were used to analyse motion and perhaps the most renowned early applications of this was the series of images showing a galloping horse produced by Eadweard Muybridge (alias Edward Muggeridge), who was retained by the US railroad magnate, Leland Stanford. The images displayed that during a particular moment in a galloping horse's gait, all four feet are simultaneously off the ground. Muybridge used a battery of cameras and a special shutter he developed that gave an exposure of 2/1000 of a second.[7] This arrangement gave satisfactory results and proved Stanford's contention.

107

Cameras were soon designed to take multiple pictures per second and record each picture on a continuous strip of transparent film. *Film* is a thin flexible strip of plastic or other material coated with light-sensitive emulsion for exposure in a camera and used to produce photographs or motion pictures.[8] Video is similar to film only in that it is also the creation of the illusion of a moving image, by presenting a number of still pictures in quick succession.

In 1897, Thomas Edison obtained a patent for *kinetoscope*.[9] This instrument was designed for films to be viewed by one individual at a time by looking through a peephole at the top of the device. The kinetoscope (Figure 5.2) introduced the basic approach that would become the standard for all cinematic projection in creating the illusion of movement by conveying a strip of perforated film bearing sequential

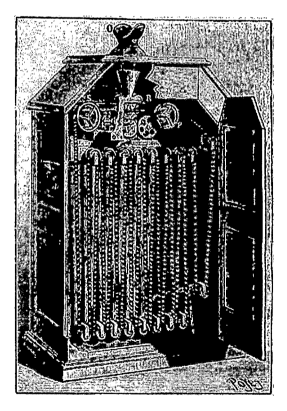

Figure 5.2 Illustration showing the rear of a kinetoscope.

108

pictures over a light source incorporating a shutter and projecting it onto a viewing screen. The effect on the human eye is to perceive this as a continuous motion.

Also, in the 1890s and following the invention of kinetoscope, brothers Auguste and Louis Lumière began work in Paris on what is known as a *cinématographe*, initially a camera and projector in one.[10] In the early 1920s, a great many scientists in several countries were working on an electronic equivalent of film, capable of transmitting moving pictures over wire. In 1922 in France, Edwin Belin – an Englishman, demonstrated a mechanical scanning device that was an early precursor to modern television. Up until Belin's demonstration the concept behind television was established, but it was not until the invention of the electronic scanning of imagery (the breaking up of images into individual elements for transmission over radio waves) that modern television received its birth. Many have laid claim to the origination of television and much debate over who invented television has continued since. The credit as to who was the inventor of modern television probably does not sit with only one person, as there were many pioneers and people involved either working alone or together over time that led to its evolution. Notable input on this in the 1920s and 1930s came from two different people in two different places, both working on the same problem at around the same time: Vladimir Kosma Zworykin, a Russian-born American inventor working for Westinghouse in the USA, and Philo Taylor Farnsworth, a privately backed individual from the state of Utah, USA.[11] Another well-known inventor associated with early television was John Logie Baird, a Scottish engineer and entrepreneur who also in the 1920s achieved and demonstrated his first transmissions of simple face shapes using mechanical television; he also demonstrated colour television and a process for recording sound and vision which he called 'Phonovision'[12] and made the first transatlantic television transmission. In 1936, the British Broadcasting Corporation (BBC) started the world's first regular service from Alexandra Palace in London using the Baird system, though it was abandoned one year later in favour of a system developed by Marconi-EMI which was a fully electronic system comprising 405 lines[13] of information.

CLOSED-CIRCUIT TELEVISION (CCTV) SYSTEMS

In the more modern era of 1960s onwards, let's step forward past the various incarnations to more recent years and the standard definition 625 line technology adopted in the design of most CCTV systems. These systems are able to provide a closed loop system where cameras feed a recording device typically over a hard wire or via a transmitted link. An example of a CCTV system is displayed in Figure 5.3.

Components of a typical CCTV System

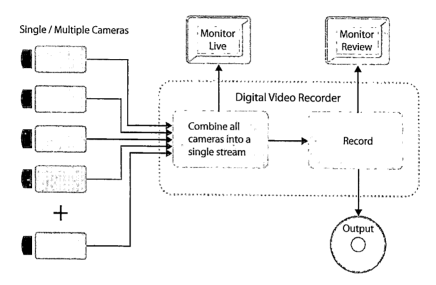

Figure 5.3 Illustration showing the components of a CCTV System.

Whilst the increasing use of digital recordings is becoming more commonplace, CCTV work continues to be carried out on standard definition systems, which can still be fed by analogue cameras, so we will concentrate here on the worse case scenario of legacy systems and not on the latest High Definition technology, mentioned later. The inherent limits of CCTV systems fall into two main categories:

1. Limits in detail recorded or 'resolution'
2. Limits in the ability to resolve motion – that is, the number of images/pictures recorded, the 'frame rate'.

The image is scanned in a number of lines running left to right and top to bottom of the image. In the PAL (Phase Alternating Line) CCTV system used in the UK, there are 625 scanning lines in the system but only 576 actually contain picture information. In the USA, the National Television

Standards Committee (NTSC) system has 525 scanning lines of which 480 contain picture information. The lines that are not used for picture information are used to synchronise the start and end of lines, fields and frames. Video is captured at 25 frames per second (fps) in the UK (PAL system) and 30 fps (NTSC system) in the USA.[14]

Human vision is sensitive to abrupt local changes in brightness.[15] If we return to film again for a moment, when individual still pictures used to create the illusion of a moving image are not presented quickly enough, then the eye detects the gaps (light) between successive images and sees this as *flicker* on the moving image. This flickering effect is often apparent on early films. In films traditionally, the rate of 24 fps became customary but the refresh rate is upped with the use of a shutter interrupting the light for each frame, thereby effectively doubling or trebling the effective frame rate.

FRAME RATE AND INTERLACING

The term *frame rate* refers to the number of individual frames that are displayed in 1 second (fps). This is the frame rate frequency which is also expressed as Hertz (Hz). The term *frame rate*, or *frame frequency*, equally applies to computer graphics, video cameras, film cameras and motion capture systems. Frame rate is not a measure of quality of the image (which is measured by resolution) but a measure of how any given scene is captured in terms of motion.[16] While the human visual system can process 10–12 images per second and perceive them individually, higher rates are perceived as motion.[17] The human eye may be excellent at detecting brightness changes, but it is not as good at detecting detail. Hence, for television it was found that if the video frame was split into two 'parts' called *fields* – comprising odd lines and even lines – and only half of the scan lines were displayed at a time, then the eye did not detect the lack of individual picture detail. Instead, with the two fields being displayed alternately, the eye sees a much smoother and flicker free image. This is known as *interlacing*. Two successive fields are called a *frame*. The frame rate for NTSC systems is 29.97 fps (rounded up to 30 fps); or 25 fps for PAL systems. Where video is not interlaced, it is termed *progressive video*, in which each picture is one complete frame.

For NTSC systems, each frame contains two fields or images producing an actual rate of 60 images/pictures per second (60 fields, 30 frames). In PAL systems, it is 50 images/pictures per second (50 fields, 25 frames). The fact that only half of the image lines are being displayed is not noticeable

111

on the moving image, but this becomes an important factor when carrying out any detailed image analysis or if the signal is subjected to *time lapse* recording or *multiplexers*, as often found in CCTV systems. Newer technology that allows for high definition 1080 lines and progressively scanned (so no interlacing) is now standard in the domestic market and is finding its way into newer CCTV systems. On the domestic and professional market, 4 K systems (4000 lines) are becoming established and with 8 K output being available, the development of such technology would be expected to continue to advance.

Time lapse is a security industry term for reduced frame rate recording.

We have already seen that NTSC video runs at 30 fps or 60 pictures/fields per second; and PAL video runs at 25 fps or 50 pictures/fields per second. In the security industry, these frame rates are commonly referred to as *real-time* recording. Typically, a requirement in the days of VHS videotape was to have the videotape last for 24 hours. This was achieved by running the video recorder at approximately 1/8th speed giving a frame rate of approximately 6.25 pictures per second, based on a 3-hour VHS tape. In standard video there is a 0.02 second gap between successive pictures, but in 24 hour time lapse video there is approximately a 0.16 second gap between successive pictures. This rate is fine for recording general movements, but for analysis of high-speed dynamic events, where even 50 or 60 pictures per second can limit accurate analysis, there may be information missing to allow for an accurate assessment of the individual actions or the sequence of events. The greater the number of frames per second used, the greater the amount of information available regarding motion. Consider this for example, in a forensic context. An incident is seen on CCTV footage but because of the large gap between successive pictures (in this example, approximately 1.5 seconds), the actual point of contact between one person's boot and another's body was not recorded. At court it was argued that there was in fact no evidence of an assault. This was accepted and the case thrown out. The investigators in the matter did not commission an analysis that would have been able to explain the technical limitations of the system, in addition to examining the images either side of when the alleged injury occurred. Of course, not all recordings have a significant loss of information.

Larsen et al. indicated that 15 Hz (fps) is an ideal recording frequency for examining some dynamic features of gait and that lower frequencies of 5 Hz and 2 Hz could also be sufficient to yield useful information for identification.[18] A study by Birch et al. looked at frame rates in the range of 0.25 fps to 25 fps and concluded that frame rate affects the ability of experienced practitioners to identify characteristics of gait captured on CCTV footage. It was acknowledged that although all the participants had been trained in observational gait analysis as part of their pre-registration education, were experienced in the clinical application of the technique and had an understanding of its purpose and use for forensic gait analysis, their level of forensic gait analysis experience was inevitably variable and this may have impacted on their proficiency in identifying the features of gait from the CCTV footage.[19] The frame rates* considered in the participants' scores were expressed as: 0.25 fps; 0.5 fps; 1 fps; 2 fps; 4 fps; 6 fps; 8fps; 12.5 fps and 25 fps. Generally, the results trend there showed from the nine frame rates considered and eight participants, increasing the frame rate had an affirmative outcome on identifying features of gait displayed on CCTV footage. Interestingly, the results also revealed that whilst the two highest frame rates of 25 fps and 12.5 fps yielded the two highest total number of correct identifications (differing by one), there was variation across the results and correct identifications were still possible at all of the lower frame rates tested by seven of the eight participants, including the lowest frame rate of one frame every 4 seconds (expressed in the participant scores as 0.25 fps). The results may also generally reflect that *frame rate* is not a measure of the quality of the image (which is measured by resolution) but a measure of how any given scene is captured in terms of motion.

The American Public Transportation Association, CCTV Standards Working Group, published guidelines which relate to both analogue and digital video system and include recommendations for camera frame rates. A minimum of 5 fps (4 fps for PAL-based systems) is recommended in low-traffic areas or areas where only walking pace motion is likely, for access control, and for on-vehicle passenger areas. Fifteen frames per second (12 fps for PAL) are recommended for trackside operations and platform areas, ticket office desks, pay machines and vehicle passenger areas where emergency call operated or in the area of doorways. For vehicle traffic areas, parking garages or forward-facing cameras on trains, trams and buses, a minimum of 30 fps (25 fps for PAL) is recommended.[20]

---

* 0.25 fps and 0.5 fps are representations of 1 frame every 4 seconds; and 1 frame every 2 seconds, respectively. For the avoidance of misunderstanding, some areas may express frame rates when less than 1fps as a decimal fraction, for example, 0.25 or 0.5. It is helpful to bear in mind the minimum number of frames required for an image to be displayed is one frame

ACTUAL FRAME RATE AND COPIED CCTV MATERIAL

One common area of misunderstanding is the actual frame rate of copied CCTV material. For ease of viewing and to present an easy to understand picture of an event captured on multiple systems and cameras, CCTV material is often ingested into an editing system so that the relevant parts from each camera can be isolated and made into a compilation video. The edited video can then be output onto a memory stick, or DVD (Digital Video Disc) or other common storage formats such as Audio Video Interleaved (AVI) file, or MOV (a multimedia data storage file). Many of these compilations contain material at a variety of frame rates which may often be quite low. However, the compilation is invariably output at 25/30 fps, so frames from the original, low rate, clips are replicated to fit in with the standard frame rate. It is important to assess the actual frame rate – that is how many individual frames are seen per second – rather than looking at the compilation metadata and seeing 25/30 fps and assuming that is the correct rate. Ideally, the image analyst should gain access to the original CCTV download material and view that at its native frame rate.

CCTV AND MULTIPLEXERS

In CCTV things are further complicated by the addition of multiplexers – devices that are designed to take analogue or digital input signals from multiple cameras and send them into a single picture stream. The transmission process that allows this to occur is known as multiplexing.[21] This approach allows multiple cameras to be connected to the same recording device. The effect, in most cases, is to further reduce frame rates. The net result is that there can be a significantly increased time between successive pictures, and the motion that occurs between successive pictures is not recorded. To put this into context, a camera designed for use in high-speed motion analysis can record in the region of 7000 pictures per second. Some CCTV systems may only record one frame per second – a frame rate that would limit the amount of information and the extent of any meaningful analysis that can be performed.

IMAGE COMPRESSION

In the early days, CCTV systems used VHS (Video Home System) tapes to store data but these had a rather limited duration resulting in the need to compress more information onto the tape, as very few facilities could have an operator on standby to change the tape for each recorder every 3 or 4 hours.

114

In addition, it was often not practical to have a separate recorder for each camera. This led to the use of long play (1/2 speed) and time lapse recording – recordings running at a greatly reduced frame rates and video multiplexers. These requirements still hold true with modern digital recording systems.

With increased emphasis and value being placed on security world-wide, new approaches and systems are always evolving according to the needs of the time. Newer CCTV systems often incorporate a digital sys-tem. An added problem to image quality can occur with digitisation and in most cases, compression of the imagery for these digital recordings. Digitisation, compression of images and conversion to more flexible for-mats such as AVI can cause image loss which on time lapse footage can be significant, depending on the task in hand. These do not only limit *resolu-tion* (the term used to represent the smallest detail that can be resolved by a system), but can also create unwanted artefacts within the image. Digitisation splits each picture line into a number of pixels, where a pixel is a digital point of a single value. This can be done as interlaced or pro-gressive scan. The term *pixel* is actually short for 'picture element'.[22]

The fewer the number of pixels in the image, the less fine detail appears on that image. Therefore, the ability to detect fine detail that may confirm or eliminate persons, movements or objects may be limited accordingly. Conversely, the greater the number of pixels in the image, the more fine detail appears on that image. A common cause of a 'pixelated' image is resizing an image to make it larger. That alters the size of image but not the resolution. An image that has been scanned may look pixelated too. Can you recognise the face in Figure 5.4?

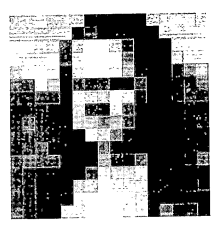

Figure 5.4   Pixelated face (Image modified from a shutterstock.com sourced image.)

115

To increase the storage capacity of the system, compression is applied to the images in order to reduce the amount of data required to store each image. Depending on the method of compression used, there are further issues that can arise in the resolution of fine or moving detail. Particular attention must also be given to distinguishing the image content from any possible artefacts caused by the compression. These often manifest themselves as a 'block' pattern on uniform areas of the image, illustrated in Figure 5.5. Image analysts can advise upon such matters.

Figure 5.5   Compression can result in artefacts appearing on the image with a 'block pattern' effect.

IMAGE DIMENSION

Guidelines aimed at installers of CCTV are to help ensure the CCTV system is fit for purpose. These have been based on standard definition CCTV and that to recognise, not identify, a person known to you, that person should occupy at least 50% of the screen height. In other words, if the person's feet are at the bottom of the image, proportionally their head would be half way up the screen. This should not preclude a human being able to identify a person from images where that person occupies less than 50%. Equally, there is no guarantee that individuals will be identifiable just because they occupy up to 100% of the screen. The purpose of

116

these categories was to suggest appropriate image sizes to aim towards when specifying a system to meet a particular requirement, rather than to define a minimum standard.[23]

HIGH DEFINITION, 3D, 4K AND 8K

High Definition (HD) systems are fast taking over the domestic scene and in CCTV. HD vastly increases the number of lines in the image and hence the ability to resolve fine detail. A Full HD system can provide 1080 scanning lines per image and by using progressive scanning, it displays each complete frame of information and avoids the use of interlacing. Further developments include systems such as 4K and the even more impressive Super Hi-Vision or Ultra High Definition (UHD) 8K with a staggering 7680×4320 pixels – twice the resolution of 4K UHD and some 16 times as many pixels as Full HD.[24] High definition systems address both limitations of standard definition (in that they can provide more lines = more detail) and a faster picture update. Such technology allows a greater degree of analysis capability. 3D is another technology that is well established in some sectors, but, unlike HD, has not as yet found wide acceptance in the security (CCTV) industry. The developments with camera technology are fascinating and it has been suggested that future generations of super smart cameras might be able to see behind walls.[25,26]

IMAGE ENHANCEMENT

Image enhancement using digital signal processing techniques has been used in forensic video since the early 1980s and for longer in military, medical and industrial applications with many of the techniques that were developed still having utility. Enhancement can bring benefits to image analysis by allowing the image analyst and others to see the full extent of the image data available and to thereby have a better appreciation of the content. When enhancement techniques were first mentioned in courts, objections were raised that enhancement is 'changing' the image and should not be allowed, and imaging experts had a tough time explaining the use of these techniques on the effect on the imagery. Fortunately, the benefit of correctly applied image enhancement is now more widely appreciated as a means of extracting the best data available.

The emphasis here is on 'correctly applied', as the incorrect application of image enhancement could lead to the outcome of court cases being overturned on appeal. Enhancement must be applied by appropriately trained personnel and any technique must be checked to ensure the image is not changing, removing or obscuring any relevant detail. It is vital that if the image processing system does not have an audit trail, then meticulous contemporaneous notes must be made of any settings and all work done as these may be required for examination in cases presented at court.

Calibration of equipment throughout its lifetime is also important to confirm the equipment will reliably and repeatability produce the results expected. The aim of calibration is to minimise uncertainty from measurements to an acceptable level.

The British Security Industry Association has published a code of practice and associated guidance on planning, design, installation and operation of CCTV surveillance systems.[27] In England and Wales, published guidelines are also available in *Forensic Image Comparison and Interpretation Evidence: Guidance for Prosecutors and Investigators*.[28] European Network of Forensic Science Institutes (ENFSI) has a best practise manual for facial image comparison[29] which considers enhancement of imagery. The Scientific Working Group on Digital Evidence (SWGDE) in the USA has also published guideline information in relation to video.[30]

PICTURE NOISE AND PERCEPTION OF DETAIL

The main aspects of image enhancement involve removing unwanted artefacts such as the 'grainy' picture noise seen on many CCTV images, and then increasing the perception of detail within the image by edge and contrast enhancement. Because the digital image has the lines split into a number of discreet picture points (pixels), this is done by applying algorithms to pixels or groups of pixels and modifying their value in accordance with predetermined mathematical rules and the values of the surrounding pixels.

Much of the perception of detail in an image is by the recognition of 'edges'. Edges are represented by changes in grey level or colour, and the more rapid the change, the sharper the edge appears. If the edges can be more easily found, then the image analyst can make a more accurate assessment of the features and structures. These filters can be designed to increase the rate of change of an 'edge' to make it appear sharper to the eye, by speeding up the rate of change, to sharpen edges in a particular direction or to smooth random or structured picture noise. Multiple filters are often used in conjunction to address different aspects of the image. A *noise reduction filter* is one that will effectively 'smooth' fine detail and reduce the grainy effect, and then an *edge sharpening filter* can be applied to boost the relatively coarse edge detail.

Many images are subject to 'picture noise' of some sort and usually manifest as a grainy effect superimposed onto the image. The most common in CCTV is 'random picture noise', which is a high frequency interference superimposed onto the image and typical of a camera operating in low light conditions. This obscures detail in the image and can hinder the perception of image features. It can appear poor on a moving image when the human eye's persistence of vision will tend to average the noise out, but can appear worse on a 'freezed'/paused image or still picture. There are several noise reduction techniques available for both still images and moving images using filters, real-time filters or recursive processing. These are designed to remove both structured and random noise. If picture noise is not removed it will be subjected to whatever enhancement is applied and its damaging effect is then increased. The danger is differentiating between what is noise and what is relevant edge detail. Too much noise reduction can soften or remove edge detail, for example, removing a fine feature on a face, or can also cause 'motion blur' on moving imagery making detailed analysis of dynamic events more difficult.

Should an expert in forensic gait analysis receive video footage that appears 'grainy' or where there may be other image quality issues that make initial assessment of the material for that purpose seem difficult, then it is appropriate for the footage to be passed to an image analyst to consider whether the quality of the imagery can be improved. Thereafter the video footage can be reviewed again as to consider whether the material is suitable for forensic gait analysis and if so, whether any meaningful analysis can be performed.

CONTRAST ENHANCEMENT

In broadcast television, the video signals are adjusted to fit within strictly defined parameters. Cameras and broadcast equipment are constantly adjusted to maintain the signal within these limits irrespective of the material and lighting conditions. This is illustrated by a person rarely needing to adjust the settings on their television screen after they have initially set them to their personal preference, because every channel has a signal that conforms to the quality level. However, many CCTV systems may not be set up in such a way and the picture may look good for part of the day, but varying light conditions can cause degradation in the image quality. Poor lighting is the most common factor that degrades the quality of video images.[31]

A dismal camera set up means there is often more detail in the image than can be displayed without adjusting the contrast, brightness and gamma, often collectively referred to as *contrast enhancement,* to show the full extent on the image content. *Gamma* is a particularly useful correction, as it is a non-linear adjustment used to encode and decode luminance,[32] unlike contrast and brightness which are linear. Gamma adjusts the image in a way more like the human eye response. Log and exponential curves can boost or reduce mid tones without affecting the peak light and dark tones.

As displayed by the example in Figure 5.6 before contrast enhancement has occurred and in Figure 5.7 after contrast enhancement has taken place. Note on Figure 5.7 the additional vertical lines that are present and can be seen within the image (on the left of the greyscale).

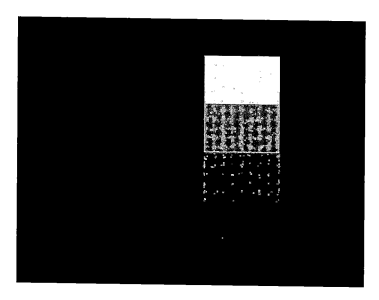

Figure 5.6   Before contrast enhancement.

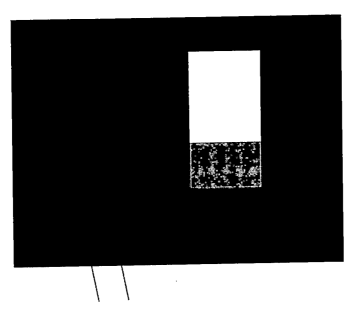

Figure 5.7   After contrast enhancement.

Again, there is a potential to change or distort image detail if these techniques are applied without care. Special attention must be given to avoid over application on areas of interest resulting in detail becoming 'whited' out or merged into a dark background. This sounds obvious but when images are incorrectly processed in this way, it undesirably leads to finished products with incorrectly set contrast levels that can mask vital image data. Enhancement can be a big benefit, but in its application the opportunity to make significant unwanted changes must be constantly monitored.

To summarise the use of image enhancement, this is a vital tool in the analysis and interpretation of video imagery. This process can allow detail to be more easily viewed and interpreted by experts and others, but it can also be a double-edged sword if techniques are incorrectly or inappropriately applied. Such misuse of the processes can remove, modify or alter vital detail and lead the image analyst to make inaccurate conclusions, which can then result in others receiving inaccurate information and evidence. Being mindful of such aspects can be helpful in avoiding unsuitable application of such techniques.

Figures 5.8 and 5.9 illustrate Before and After correct image enhancement. The After enhancement addresses picture noise (grain), contrast levels and edge detail.

Figure 5.8 Before correct image enhancement.

Figure 5.9   After correct image enhancement.

LENSES AND DISTORTION

The images displayed can also be affected by the lens on the imaging device. For example, a zoom lens commonly used to record objects at a distance will tend to foreshorten 'the third dimension' – the distance of the object from the camera. In terms of analysing events, for example a dangerous tackle in sport, participants can often appear to be much closer together on the imagery than they actually were in real life. *Radial or curvilinear distortion*[33] such as *barrel distortion* is seen with fish-eye lenses where straight lines at the edge of an image bow outwards; *pin-cushion distortion* is where straight lines bend inwards, often when long telephoto lenses are used; *moustache distortion* is a mixture of both barrel and pin-cushion distortions, where wide-angle zoom lenses can cause straight lines on the image to appear wavy. Another potential distortion that can be more marked with the use of wide-angle lenses is *chromatic distortion*, also known as *chromatic aberration*. This phenomenon distorts image details by introducing magnification error, defocus blur and colour fringes.[34] The effect is due to the lens not being able to focus all wavelengths of light (colours) to the same point of convergence and appears as a coloured halo at the edges of subjects. This can also affect black and white images, which then appear blurred. *Vignetting* is another form of distortion where the outer edge of the image has reduced brightness and appears darker compared to that at the centre of the image. *Vignetting* refers to the fall-off pixel intensity from the centre towards the edges of the image[35] and there are several types.[36] Camera angles, position of the object/subject and the effect of *parallax* can also affect the information displayed on images. *Parallax* is the apparent displacement of an observed object due to a change in the position of the observer.[37]

FORENSIC IMAGERY ANALYSIS

The information provided by CCTV systems on identification, order of events or motion was invariably not set up at the outset specifically for examination of the material in a court of law. Traditionally, the setup of CCTV systems was geared more towards monitoring activity, safety and other objectives such as a deterrent or for insurance purposes – a sort of 'one size fits all' design and not particularly geared to provide high-quality images of individuals and actions. As mentioned earlier, images can be limited in terms of resolution (detail) and frame rate (number of pictures) and as we have seen, the image analyst has to take into consideration various factors that can affect the images displayed.

It was reported that a survey commissioned by the British Security Industry Association (BSIA) in 2013 estimated that the UK had up to 5.9 million CCTV cameras.[38] By 2020, it is estimated that 6.1 billion people will have phones with picture-taking capabilities. Meanwhile, in a single year, an estimated 106 million new surveillance cameras are sold.[39] That is a considerable development from 1949 when an American company released the first commercially available CCTV system, followed by in 1951 when Kodak introduced its Brownie portable movie camera.[40] The high concentration of cameras is such that CCTV imagery will often play a significant investigative and evidential role in today's legal cases.

The camera never lies – perhaps a familiar phrase but one that probably deserves its place alongside the equally well-known phrase: *payment has been sent*. The reality is that a camera is quite capable of being perceived in this way for a variety of reasons. Whilst modern life bombards our eyes with different sources of imagery whether it be television, advertising or social media, there is an inherent danger in taking these images at face value. It is also useful to keep in mind that two-dimensional imagery is nothing like the human eyes binocular vision and its depth of perception. The advent of digital photography and home computing has resulted in people being far more familiar with handling and viewing imagery, and the 'airbrushing' techniques used by some industries are now well known. With airbrushing, spots and blemishes can be removed by borrowing neighbouring skin tone pixels and placing them over the area in question or, in the hands of a skilled operator, waistlines, legs and arms can be sculpted for the desired effect. It is the role of the trained and experienced image analyst to identify whether the imagery presented for examination is reliable and, if not, then to what extent they may be deceiving the observer and whether that can be rectified. To take a typical scenario, Person X is recorded on a betting shop CCTV system in the act of robbing the cashier. Subsequently, an individual is arrested as a Suspect for the robbery. Whether instructed by the prosecution or the defence, the forensic imagery analyst will be requested to test the contention that Person X and the Suspect are/are not the same individual. Firstly, it is essential for the image analyst to be provided with a copy of the CCTV footage in the original format. This must be a direct copy in the native format that the material was originally recorded in. Confirming the authenticity of the video recording is an important step and to ensure there has been no editing[41] or abnormality of the recording apparatus.[42] With CCTV systems, there are literally hundreds of formats used by the system manufacturers. Some of these are standard formats and others are proprietary to the manufacturer. Most will need a software viewer to allow the material to be replayed and these are often used to convert the material to a 'standard' type format, so that it can be reviewed, analysed and ultimately displayed in court.

The forensic imagery analyst should always be conscious about the effects of using any 'converted' material when performing the analysis, as there can be unknown effects of the conversion, such as changes to the aspect ratio (the ratio between the width and the height of the picture), frame rate, different degrees of compression (previously discussed) and image degradation.

Where there are gross changes between adjoining frames, this can often be identified visually by the image analyst. Where such changes are more subdued, for example, where there are smaller changes in compression, minor sensor artefacts, inter-frame differences between adjoining images or other modifications, then any slight variation in pixilation may not be optically determined.[43] There are a variety of techniques to detect such differences.[44] The forensic imagery analyst must base an opinion on the images in the original format and if this is not available, then the potential for any inaccuracies in the conversion process must be considered in the analyst's conclusion. Where there is a digital recording of the footage that can be directly downloaded from a hard drive on which the incident is originally recorded, this can be less of an issue providing there is no significant compression of the material in question, for the task in hand. However, whilst digital recordings are replacing analogue ones, the formats are not always compression free and the image analyst needs to be conscious of this also. A more detailed exegesis of compression systems is not needed for the purposes of this chapter and is available elsewhere.[45] Video footage can also be viewed directly from a web link to the original footage, although such facility varies in its availability. Such a route is quicker, less costly and could be expected to be adopted more widely as platforms advance in a modern technological world.

It has been demonstrated that in the specific task of CCTV monitoring, trained CCTV operators show greater consistency in fixation location and greater consistency in suspiciousness judgements than untrained observers. Howard et al. reported that training appears to increase between-operators consistency by learning 'knowing what to look for' in these scenes.[46]

When considering the minimum duration of image observation that is required to detect meaning, the human visual system has the extraordinary capacity to swiftly do so. With image recognition, Potter et al. showed that participants recognised a specific image in a rapid serial visual presentation (RSVP) of different images at 13 milliseconds[47]; Maguire and Howe found reliable recognition to occur when each image in the sequence was presented for 53 ms but not when each image was presented for 27 ms.[48] Nevertheless, these time frames reflect a near instantaneous understanding of the images displayed and which has uses in persons being able to perform immediate responses when needed.

Images of perpetrators on CCTV video footage are used as evidence in courts and the work of an image analyst in the forensic arena encompasses a number of different tasks including clothing comparison, vehicle and object analysis, event analysis, tattoos, piercings, general physical

126

characteristics such as height assessment and facial image comparison (sometimes referred to as facial mapping). Essentially, the role of the forensic imagery expert is the same as any other expert insofar as to assist the court in understanding what can be learned from the evidence *in their area of expertise* and to provide an informed and impartial assessment which helps the court with that particular aspect of the case. As with all types of forensic work, forensic image analysis needs to be carried out carefully[49] and is intended to avoid any sentimental responses to an image and for the material to be examined in a scientific manner, that being knowledge based, systematic and reproducible. It is generally understood that experience in any area makes for better practice: White et al. reported forensic examiners with many years of experience in comparing face images have been shown to outperform untrained individuals and computer algorithms, and when scores were averaged across all facial forensic examiners, the experts achieved a 'near-perfect' mark of 0.997.[50,51] Norel et al, looked at comparing correct identifications for forensic experts and non-trained individuals in facial image comparisons and the impact of image quality, which found forensic experts arrived at their conclusions with notably less mistakes than the non-trained individuals; the forensic experts were also better compared to beginners at deciding when two high-quality images portrayed the same individual; and lower image quality led to more cautious conclusions by the forensic experts, but not for the non-trained individuals.[52] In relation to gait analysis, a study by Birch et al. had seven participants from multiple disciplines ('podiatry, physiotherapy and biomechanics'), each with a minimum of five years' experience in performing observational gait analysis as part of their main area of work. It was reported that none of the participants engaged in forensic gait analysis as their central area of practice. The results overall showed that the participants correctly identified individuals by their gait pattern displayed on video recordings from closed-circuit television cameras in 71% of cases (124 of 175 cases). The participants had a success rate of 79% (22 of 28 cases) when performing comparisons of the 'suspect walker' and 'target walker' recorded from the same angle; and 69% (102 of 147 cases) correct decisions when the 'target walker' and 'suspect walker' were not recorded from the same angle. Interestingly, there was a 94% (33 of 35 cases) precision in distinguishing between a 'suspect walker' and a 'target walker' when the suspect walker was of a different gender.[53]

With any image analysis task, the first step is to assess the imagery for the purpose of the analysis to be performed. That includes determining whether the *quality* of the footage is *suitable* for the type of analysis that is to be undertaken. For the image analyst, as we have seen, that also requires

127

consideration as to whether any appropriate techniques can improve the quality of the images, when required. It is helpful to bear in mind that whilst the quality of the imagery is generally an important consideration, it is not absolute in determining whether material is suitable for analysis. For example, a piece of CCTV footage contains high-quality images, but the subject or object of interest is significantly occluded, which renders the material unsuitable for that examination. On the other hand, for example, it may be the imagery quality is poor, but an aspect or feature of the subject or object is so *distinctive*, which renders the material suitable for that examination. Providing the imagery is suitable for the analysis that is to be performed, the analysis can then proceed. For the forensic imagery analyst, this begins with observing the CCTV footage (the 'unknown' or 'questioned' material) and the selection and capture of suitable still images (stills). When carrying out the same task on the footage displaying the 'Suspect' (that is the 'known' or 'reference' footage), comparator photographs should include angles that, as far as possible, replicate those seen of the perpetrator in the CCTV imagery relating to the incident. In any comparison that follows (and by the very meaning of the word comparison, that includes similarities and dissimilarities), a clear significant difference would allow for an individual or object to be excluded.

The riots seen in the UK during the summer of 2001 in Bradford[54,55] and in 2011 in a number of locations in the UK[56,57] generated a rise in the requirements for image comparison work. However, a significant proportion of the imagery evidence was not suitable for facial comparison purposes. As a result, many reports were produced detailing the limitations of the imagery evidence which the defence successfully used to cast doubt on the identification of their clients. Nixon et al. reported that a unique advantage of 'gait' is that it is not restricted where other biometrics can be in being able to provide recognition at a distance or low resolution.[58] Gait also has uses in cases where other biometrics may not be suitable, or where there is attempt to disguise.[59] An advantage of gait analysis in forensic investigations is that gait, unlike the face,[60] is hard to conceal.[61] Stevenage et al. showed that humans can recognise people by their gait using video and that even under adverse conditions and where illumination or length of exposure were affected, gait could still be perceived.[62]

 The extent of any image analysis and the degree of confidence expressed in any conclusions is primarily dependent on the image quality. Good quality imagery that presents a high level of fine-feature detail will enable comprehensive and solid comparisons to be made, whereas lesser quality imagery may perhaps only result in a statement of broad similarity or dissimilarity between the subjects, or no analysis or comparison being possible at all. Determining image quality is a subjective assessment by the image analyst and which should be made clear in reports for use in the legal systems. As such, it is somewhat dependent on the knowledge, training and experience of the practitioner. However, as is mentioned later, a framework for determining 'Levels of Support' when performing image comparisons is available and such guidance has a direct relationship to image quality.

Forensic casework involves a jigsaw of evidence which vary in the amount and different types of forensic material available to help resolve any matter, and as determined on a case by case basis. Hence, it is important to appreciate the skills of the image analyst are complementary alongside other areas of expertise and which assist one another. For example, whilst an image analyst may generally observe a person's gait on CCTV footage as part of the variety of tasks an image analyst may carry out, reporting on the specific details of a person's gait or features of gait and significance thereof is the province of those with appropriate knowledge, training and skill in that area. However, particularly distinctive gaits or features of gait may be so obvious and simply require referral. Similarly, it would be unusual for a 'gait expert' to perform the detailed tasks of the image analyst, as these are largely two separate areas of expertise, albeit with some overlap. Another illustration could perhaps be an 'expert' in one specific area of science or social sciences who ventures into clothing or object analysis, facial imagery analysis, gait analysis or other areas of expertise such as in medicine, surgery or other sectors. Clearly, these are all different areas of expertise and it is unhelpful to the courts and in the interests of justice for people to stray outside of their area of expertise and irrespective of their enthusiasm to do so. The courts have been very clear and continue to be so, that just because an expert has, or is perceived to have, expertise in one area, it does not follow that they do so in another. However, that does not seem on occasion to prevent legal counsel when cross-examining an expert in trying to lure the expert into commenting upon matters outside their area of expertise – a devilish trick that may catch out the unwary or inexperienced expert in any area!

R V Stockwell [1993][63] is the first known reported case of facial image comparison evidence in the UK. This area of expertise is also acknowledged by the Court of Appeal,[64,65,66] and the Attorney General.[67,68]

R V Atkins and Atkins [2009] EWCA Crim 1876[69] is a case concerning facial mapping evidence. Hughes LJ, at para 31:

> We conclude that where a photographic comparison expert gives evidence, properly based upon study and experience, of similarities and/or dissimilarities between a questioned photograph and a known person (including a defendant) the expert is not disabled either by authority or principle from expressing his conclusion as to the significance of his findings, and that he may do so by use of conventional expressions, arranged in a hierarchy, such as those used by the witness in this case and set out in paragraph 8 above. We think it preferable that the expressions should not be allocated numbers, as they were in the boxes used in the written report in this case, lest that run any small risk of leading the jury to think that they represent an established numerical, that is to say measurable, scale. The expressions ought to remain simply what they are, namely forms of words used. They need to be in an ascending order if they are to mean anything at all, and if a relatively firm opinion is to be contrasted with one which is not so firm. They are, however, expressions of subjective opinion, and this must be made clear to the jury charged with evaluating them.

The Forensic Imagery Analysis Group FIAG was established in the UK in 2003 (later renamed FIAD – Forensic Imagery Analysis Division), in order to develop common practice and provide direction and guidance to practitioners. This endorsed guidance for evaluating levels of support designed to compare facial images[70] and a six-point scale was created (No Support; Limited Support; Moderate Support; Support; Strong Support; Powerful Support) in order to provide the image analyst with a framework on which to base their conclusions. This would then result in some form of statement in the image analyst's report to help the courts with understanding the strength of (subjective) opinion evidence on the imagery and the degree of support for dissimilarities and similarities between two individuals or objects. (Also see chapter on Interpreting and Communicating Forensic Statistics.) The conclusion scale applied in casework for forensic imagery comparison is understood, at the time of writing, in the process of being updated in order to provide analysts with an improved framework on which to base conclusions and to reflect the relationship between image quality and the strength of evidence which can be easily understood by the legal system. The aim is to help reduce variation between different practitioners when applying the levels of support to casework.

According to the European Network of Forensic Science Institutes (ENFSI) Best Practise Manual (BPM) issued in 2018 for Facial Image Comparison.[71] morphological analysis is recommended for the task of facial image comparison. Empirical evidence indicates this method improved accuracy in facial comparison tasks.[72] Morphological analysis has been defined by the Facial Identification Scientific Working Group (FISWG) as:

> Morphological analysis as a comparison method is based on the assessment of correspondence of the shape, appearance, presence and/or location of facial features. These features include global (corresponding to the overall face), local (including anatomical structures such as the nose or mouth and their components, e.g. nose bridge, nostrils, ear lobes) and discriminating characteristic facial marks such as scars or moles.[73]

When performing the tasks involved with facial imagery examinations, the ACE (V) workflow is recommended and can help to avoid confirmation bias.

ACE (V) represents: Analysis, Comparison, Evaluation and Verification. These are subjective tasks and should be stated in any subsequent Report provided by the image analyst. The workflow can be also represented by the acronym, ACE (V) R which incorporates the report (R) element.

The facial image comparison tasks carried out by the image analyst consider all of the facial components and features that are available to view both generally and more specifically with subclass characteristics (e.g. the nose). As already mentioned and worthy of repeat here, any comparison by its very nature is for similarities and dissimilarities – that is resemblances *and* differences. The 'singularity' of any similarity/dissimilarity, or combination of similarities/dissimilarities will depend on the population being examined and the nature or permanence of a given feature. Some similarities or dissimilarities will add more weight than others to the contention that two individuals or objects are/are not the same. It should of course be remembered that all forms of identification are based on probability.

There are indications that facial mark patterns have a geometric distribution capable of differentiating individuals.[74] Facial imaging computer software products are also entering the market and this area is known as *facial recognition*, which uses computer database references or matching. This is to be distinguished from the skill and tool of *facial image comparison*.

Another feature regarded as having potential for singularity is the ear.[75-77] Note the variations, for example, in Figure 5.10. However, at the time of writing, retrieved CCTV footage is often not of sufficient quality to exploit the full potential of this appendage.

Figure 5.10 Illustration to display some examples of ear morphology.

As imaging technology develops and the practical issues of recording high resolution imagery are overcome, the potential of CCTV footage for investigative and evidential purposes would be expected to increase.

In recent years, there has been much publicity regarding the subject of facial recognition software which inevitably raises the question of whether the human eye could be taken out of the identification process in favour of an automated replacement. Whilst these systems can perform well with controlled imagery acquired specifically for the purpose of facial recognition, a reliable and widely available automatic facial recognition system for uncontrolled CCTV footage could well be achieved in the future. The almost limitless number of potential variables involved in recording a face on CCTV imagery is such that, for use as comparison evidence, the human element currently remains crucial as the information will continue to need to be explained to investigators, legal counsel and the courts. Who knows, perhaps those tasks will eventually be replaced by an automaton, or if the machines rise high, then perhaps it may be the human who will continue to be deployed? Finally, that face, did you recognise the Mona Lisa?

Within the field of military reconnaissance, the concept of Automatic Target Recognition (ATR) software was considered by some as the way forward for processing the vast amounts of aerial imagery data available to the modern military. It was interesting to see that when the true complexity of imagery analysis had been realised by the software developers, the phrase, 'Assisted Target Recognition', began to be used as a more appropriate term to describe the software's capability. Software that is able to narrow down a search and provide a limited number of potential candidate faces is undeniably valuable but, for now, the complexities of facial and other image comparison will still require the skills of the trained and experienced imagery analyst to convey the information, in much the same way as other areas require experts in the fields. The ongoing general trend is for the continued expansion of surveillance tools. As is to be expected with many entities involving the development of technology, some understandably would be expected to get there swifter and slicker with much less flicker.

REFERENCES

1. Brookes AJ. 1991. *Crash! Military Aircraft Disasters, Accidents and Incidents*. Ian Allan Publishing, Horsham, UK.
2. Surreal Artists. 2017. *René Magritte the Surrealist Master*. May 24, 2017. https://bit.ly/2XlDqUd [Accessed 21 February 2020].
3. Video. Oxford dictionary online. Lexico. https://bit.ly/2xso2Ln [Accessed 21 February 2020].
4. Television. Oxford dictionary online. Lexico. https://bit.ly/2Yy3e0L [Accessed 21 February 2020].
5. Trundle E. 1988. *Newnes guide to Television & Video Technology*. Newnes. Oxford, UK.
6. Wertheimer M. 1989. Experimentelle Studien uber das Sehen von Bewegung (Experimental studies on the seeing of motion), 1912, as cited in Viktor Sarris, Max Wertheimer on seen motion: Theory and evidence. *Psychological Research*, 51(2): 59.
7. Muybridge E. 1955. *The Human Figure in Motion*. ppviii. Dover Publications, Inc., Mineola, NY.
8. Film. Oxford dictionary online. Lexico. https://bit.ly/2JbmbB9 [Accessed 21 February 2020].
9. America's Story from America's Library. Thomas Edison patented the kinetoscope. https://bit.ly/1junGV6 [Accessed 21 February 2020].
10. Bergan R. 2011. *The Film Book: A Complete Guide to the World of Cinema*. DK, London, UK.
11. PhysLink.com. Physics and astronomy online. Who is the inventor of television. https://bit.ly/2JtOvgW [Accessed 21 February 2020].
12. McLean DF. 2013. The Dawn of TV. *The Mechanical Era of British Television*. https://bit.ly/2KY8sjb [Accessed 21 February 2020].
13. History of the BBC. The story of BBC television - the contest. https://bbc.in/2uV5BkU [Accessed 21 February 2020].
14. Trundle E. 1988. *Frame rate. Newnes Guide to Television & Video Technology*. Newnes. Oxford, UK.
15. Russ JC. 2007. *The Image Processing Handbook*. 5th ed. CRC Press/Taylor & Francis Group, Boca Raton, FL.

16. APTA Standards Development Program. Recommended Practice. 2011. *Selection of Cameras, Digital Recording Systems, Digital High-Speed Networks and Trainlines for Use in Transit-Related CCTV Systems.* pp9–10. CCTV Standards Working Group, American Public Transportation Association, Washington, DC. https://bit.ly/2LAhQsJ [Accessed 21 February 2020].
17. Read P; Meyer M-P; Gamma Group. 2000. *Restoration of Motion Picture Film.* pp24–26. Butterworth-Heinemann.
18. Larsen PK; Simonsen EB; Lynnerup N. 2008. Gait analysis in forensic medicine. *Journal of Forensic Sciences,* 53(5): 1149–1153.
19. Birch I; Vernon W; Burrow G; Walker J. 2014. The effect of frame rate on the ability of experienced gait analysts to identify characteristics of gait from closed circuit television footage. *Science and Justice,* 54(2014): 159–163.
20. APTA Standards Development Program. Recommended Practice. 2011. *Selection of Cameras, Digital Recording Systems, Digital High-Speed Networks and Trainlines for Use in Transit-Related CCTV Systems.* pp10. CCTV Standards Working Group, American Public Transportation Association, Washington, DC. https://bit.ly/2LAhQsJ [Accessed 21 February 2020].
21. Dean T. 2013. *Network+ Guide to Networks.* 6th ed. *Chapter 3, Transmission Basics and Networking Media, Multiplexing.* Cengage Learning, Boston, MA.
22. Pixel definition. Techterms. https://bit.ly/2v70k9H 21 February 2020. [Accessed 21 February 2020].
23. Cohen N; Gattuso J; MacLennan-Brown K. *CCTV Operational Requirements Manual 2009.* Home Office Scientific Development Branch. Publication No. 28/09. 5.0. ISBN: 978-1-84726-902-7.
24. 8K resolution. Wikipedia. https://bit.ly/305Luds [Accessed 21 February 2020].
25. Faccio D; McLaughlin S. 2018. The next generation of cameras might see behind walls. *The Conversation.* January 22, 2018. https://bit.ly/2xrXKJ2 [Accessed 21 February 2020].
26. Faccio D; McLaughlin S. 2018. The next generation of super smart cameras might be able to see behind walls. *iNewspaper (UK),* 25 January 2018.
27. British Security Industry Association (BSIA). 2014. Issue 4. Planning, design, installation and operation of CCTV surveillance systems code of practice and associated guidance. https://bit.ly/2Vd6I9Z [Accessed 21 February 2020].
28. Forensic Science Regulator. 2016. Issue 2. Forensic image comparison and interpretation evidence: guidance for prosecutors and investigators. https://bit.ly/2XTuCtf [Accessed 21 February 2020].
29. ENFSI. 2018. *Best Practice Manual for Facial Image Comparison. 5.2.3, Enhancement of Imagery.* pp10–11. ENFSI-BPM-DI-01. Version 01 June 2018.
30. Scientific Working Group on Digital Evidence (SWGDE). https://bit.ly/2LCGBo7 [Accessed 21 February 2020].
31. APTA Standards Development Program. Recommended Practice. 2011. *Selection of Cameras, Digital Recording Systems, Digital High-Speed Networks and Trainlines for Use in Transit-Related CCTV Systems.* pp15. CCTV Standards Working Group. American Public Transportation Association, Washington, DC. https://bit.ly/2LAhQsJ [Accessed 21 February 2020].

32. Poynton AC. 2003. *Digital Video and HDTV: Algorithms and Interfaces*. Morgan Kaufmann Publishers/Elsevier.
33. van Walree P. 2001–2015. Distortion. https://bit.ly/2xu14Dk [Accessed 21 February 2020].
34. Korneliussen JT; Hirakawa K. 2014. Camera processing with chromatic aberration. 23(10): 4539–4552. *IEEE Trans Image Process.* doi: 10.1109/TIP.2014.2350911.
35. Kordecki A; Palus H; Bal A. 2016. Practical vignetting correction method for digital camera with measurement of surface luminance distribution. *Signal, Image and Video Processing*, 10(8): 1417–1424. Springer. doi: 10.1007/s11760-016-0941-2.
36. Goldman DB. 2010. Vignette and exposure calibration and compensation. *IEEE Transactions on Pattern Analysis and Machine Intelligence*, 32(12): 2276–2288. doi: 10.1109/TPAMI.2010.55.
37. Parallax. Dictionary.com. https://bit.ly/30dsmds [Accessed 21 February 2020].
38. BBC Newsround, UK. 11 July 2013. 5.9 million CCTV cameras in UK. https://bbc.in/39SNZoo. [Accessed 22 February 2020].
39. Draper R. 2018. They are watching you. *National Geographic*, February 2018, *Journal of the National Geographic Society*, 233(2): 41.
40. Draper R. 2018. They are watching you. *National Geographic*, February 2018, *Journal of the National Geographic Society*, 233(2): 38.
41. Weise M; Weynand D. 2007. *How Video Works*. 2nd ed. Focal Press, Amsterdam, pp164–176, 253–254.
42. Lacey DS; Koenig BE. 2012. Identification of identical and nearly identical frames from a Lawmate PV-500 digital video-audio recorder. *Journal of Forensic Identification*, 62(1): 36–46.
43. Koenig BE; Lacey DS; Richards GB. 2012. Video frame comparisons in digital video authenticity analyses. *Journal of Forensic Identification*, 62(2): 165–182.
44. Brunetti J. 2007. Analyzing pre and post-event surveillance video frames. *Journal of Forensic Identification*, 57(3): 338–347.
45. Shi Y; Sun H. 2008. *Image and Video Compression for Multimedia Engineering: Fundamentals, Algorithms and Standards*. 2nd ed. CRC Press, Boca Raton, FL.
46. Howard CJ; Troscianko T; Gilchrist ID; Behera A; Hogg DC. 2013. Suspiciousness perception in dynamic scenes: a comparison of CCTV operators and novices. *Frontiers in Human Neuroscience*, 22 August 2013. doi: https://doi.org/10.3389/fnhum.2013.00441.
47. Potter MC; Wyble B; Hagmann CE; McCourt ES. 2014. Detecting meaning in RSVP at 13 ms per picture. *Attention, Perception, & Psychophysics*, 76(2): 270–279. Springer. doi: 10.3758/s13414-013-0605-z.
48. Maguire JF; Howe PDL. 2016. Failure to detect meaning in RSVP at 27ms *Attention, Perception, & Psychophysics*, 78, 1405–1413 (2016). https://doi.org/10.3758/s13414-016-1096-.
49. Oxlee GJ. 2006. Chapter 14: facial recognition and imagery analysis. In *Forensic Human Identification: An Introduction*, Eds, Black S; Thompson T. CRC Press, Boca Raton, FL.

135

50. White D; Phillips PJ; Hahn CA; Hill M; O'Toole AJ. 2015. Perceptual expertise in forensic facial image comparison. *Proceedings of the Royal Society B Biological Sciences*, 282(1814): 20151292. doi: 10.1098/rspb.2015.1292.

51. National Institute of Standards and Technology, U.S. Department of Commerce. 2015. Study reveals forensic facial examiners can be near perfect. Released September 28, 2015. Updated January 08, 2018. https://bit.ly/2JcJtqp [Accessed 22 February 2020].

52. Norell K; Läthén KB; Bergström P; Rice A; Natu V; O'Toole A. 2015. The effect of image quality and forensic expertise in facial image comparisons. *Journal of Forensic Sciences*, 60(2): 331–340. doi: 10.1111/1556-4029.12660.

53. Birch I; Raymond L; Christou A; Fernando MA; Harrison N; Paul F. 2013. The identification of individuals by observational gait analysis using closed circuit television footage. *Science and Justice*, 53(2013): 339–342.

54. Demetriou D. 2001. Two stabbed as race riots flares in Bradford. *The Telegraph*. 08 July 2001. https://bit.ly/2XqdmqU [Accessed 22 February 2020].

55. 2001. Race riots ignite Bradford. *The Guardian*. 08 July 2001. https://bit.ly/304FDVU [Accessed 22 February 2020].

56. BBC News UK. 2011. England riots: Maps and timeline. 15 August 2011. https://bbc.in/30cL8C4 [Accessed 22 February 2020].

57. Geddes L. 2011. UK riots: why respectable people turned to looting. *New Scientist*. 12 August 2011. https://bit.ly/2XGmFaA [Accessed 22 February 2020].

58. Nixon MS; Tan TN; Chellappa R. 2006. *Human Identification Based on Gait*. Springer.

59. Buncombe A. 2000. Gang leader is unmasked by his bandy-legged gait. *The Independent*. 13 July 2000, pp1.

60. Ricanek K; Savvides M; Woodard DL; Dozier G. 2010. Unconstrained biometric identification: emerging technologies. *Computer*, 43(2): 56–62. IEEE Explore.

61. Yang SX; Larsen PK; Alkjoer T; Simonsen EB; Lynnerup N. 2014. Variability and similarity of gait as evaluated by joint angles: implications for forensic gait analysis. *Journal of Forensic Sciences*, 59(2). doi:10.1111/1556-4029.12322.

62. Stevenage SV; Nixon MS; Vince K. 1999. Visual analysis of gait as a cue to identity. *Applied Cognitive Psychology*, 13(6): 513–526.

63. *R V Stockwell* [1993].

64. *R V Stockwell* [1993] 97 Cr App R 260.

65. *R V Clarke* [1995] 2 Cr App R 425.

66. *R V Hookway* [1999] Crim LR 750.

67. *Attorney General, No.2 of 2002* [2002] EWCA 2373.

68. Forensic Science Regulator. 2016. *Issue 2. Forensic Image Comparison and Interpretation Evidence: Guidance for Prosecutors and Investigators*. pp8. https://bit.ly/2XTuCtf [Accessed 21 February 2020].

69. *R v Atkins and Atkins* [2009] EWCA Crim 1876, para 31.

70. Bromby MC; Plews S. 2006. Guidance for evaluating levels of support (March 22, 2006). Last revised: 2 Mar 2010. Available at SSRN: https://ssrn.com/abstract=1550752.
71. ENFSI. 2018. *Best Practice Manual for Facial Image Comparison. ENFSI-BPM-DI-01.* Version 01 - January 2018.
72. Towler A; White D; Kemp RI. 2017. Evaluating the feature comparison strategy for forensic face identification. *Journal of Experimental Psychology: Applied,* 23(1): 47–58.
73. Facial Identification Scientific Working Group, (FISWG). 2012. *Guidelines for Facial Comparison Methods.*
74. Srinivas N; Flynn PJ; Vorder Bruegge RW. 2016. Human identification using automatic and semi-automatically detected facial marks. *Journal of Forensic Sciences,* 61 Suppl 1: S117–S130. doi: 10.1111/1556-4029.12923.
75. Hoogstrate AJ; Van den Heuvel H; Huyben E. 2001. Ear identification based on surveillance camera images. *Science & Justice,* 41(3): 167–172.
76. Junod S; Pasquier J; Champod C. 2012. The development of an automatic recognition system for earmark and earprint comparisons. *Forensic Science International,* 222(1–3): 170–178. doi: 10.1016/j.forsciint.2012.05.021.
77. Asmaa Sabet A; Ghany KKA; Elmahdy H. 2015. Human ear recognition using geometrical features extraction. *Procedia Computer Science,* 65: 529–537. Elsevier. doi: 10.1016/j.procs.2015.09.126.

137

6

Gait Analysis in Identification

Contents

INTRODUCTION

This chapter is designed to provide an insight into gait analysis and its role in human identification; this is not designed to be a full topic review detailing all of the various and specific medical and musculoskeletal conditions which can affect an individual's gait or features of gait, and which is suitably covered elsewhere. The practitioner in forensic gait analysis would be expected to have such knowledge, understanding and experience of prior to embarking upon forensic gait analysis casework. Without such comprehension the practitioner is disadvantaged.

The skills and expertise required in gait analysis as part of the clinical process with the diagnosis, treatment and management of conditions is a more demanding task when compared to that of forensic gait analysis where the examiner is observing for gait styles and features of gait displayed on CCTV or other video footage. It is worthy of remembering that when carrying out any type of gait analysis, an examiner is noting effects, and not causes, although in the clinical situation they will also be utilising their knowledge, skills, training and experience to arrive at a diagnosis – that being the cause of the effect and then deciding how this is to be treated and managed. Clinician's will also be comparing the effects of such treatment on the individual's gait over time and making any adjustments, as deemed appropriate. The gait pattern observed is what remains when body's compensatory mechanisms are finished.[1] Nevertheless, whilst the tasks differ, they share commonalities. It is a reasonable expectation for a practitioner in forensic gait analysis to have understanding of functional anatomy, physiology, medicine and surgery, which all make up the components of how a person walks and therefore gait. It is also helpful in emphasising that some gaits and features of gait may be the result of injury or where surgery was required. For example, when considering the gait style or features of gait displayed on video footage of a known suspect it may be possible for examination of medical records to assist in determining the possible cause of such features of gait with any underlying medical conditions, injury or surgery.

It is also worthy of mention that the legal systems can be excellent tools for teasing out an expert's true credentials and capabilities in any area of expertise, illustrating the need for the 'expert' to be properly prepared. Such experience also serves to expand the education of practitioners and 'experts' and would be expected to widen their horizons and make a better practitioner. *Reflective practice* is a long established part of clinical practice. Those who are experienced with many years in diagnosing and treating musculoskeletal conditions with clinical gait analysis and other clinical or surgical skills are accustomed to recognising and understanding normal gait, features of gait, gait abnormalities and how these are affected by and respond to treatment. To those who are perhaps not directly engaged in clinical areas with the diagnosis, treatment and management of conditions, or not having clinical autonomy on such aspects, then understandably, there could well be significant gaps to be addressed.

A basic principle of forensic science is that of *Locard's Exchange Principle*[2,3] – that the perpetrator of a crime brings something into the scene and leaves with something from it and that both can be used as forensic evidence. Science cannot tell us what is or what is not, only what is more or less likely based on the information we have.[4]

The area referred to as 'automatic gait recognition' (AGR) – that is the identification of an individual without the use of pre-placed markers, whilst a subject area which the author is well acquainted, is not a topic that will be largely explored here. However, we will see more of such automation in the future with identifying individuals by their gait compared to the current human manual process, and that trajectory is appreciated. Nevertheless, humans (at least for a while) are likely to continue to be needed to carry out tasks and explain findings.

WHAT IS GAIT?

Gait is the defined as the manner of walking or running; bearing[5]; manner of walking or stepping; a going; a walk, a march; a way[6]; manner or style of walking, including rhythm, pattern, cadence and speed.[7]

The understanding of abnormal gait has the pre-requisite of being able to comprehend normal gait.[8] Murray reported that 'normal gait is characterised by both smooth forward translation and wide ranges of comfortable walking speeds'.[9] Purposes for observing and analysing human motion have altered with time as advancements have given rise to new requirements on our essential learning and understanding. Andriacchi and Alexander reported, 'The ability to observe and interpret measurements of human movement have been the primary factors limiting growth of the field'. 'The advancement of the study of locomotion remains dependent on the development of new tools for observation'.[10]

Gait analysis is separated into two significant parts: "static and dynamic"[11] and includes the appearance of the body and the dynamics of human walking motion. Gait analysis is performed by qualitative and quantitative methods.[12-14] Techniques for the observation of gait produce large datasets.[15] Observational gait analysis begins with an initial general assessment and then becoming more specific.[16] Conducting observational gait analysis brings upsides and drawbacks; not only the practitioner's skills and abundance of a body of facts accumulated over time, but as a reminder of the significance of the visual cortex area of the human brain, which is shown to be acutely responsive to context, motion and pattern recognition.[17]

WHAT IS FORENSIC GAIT ANALYSIS?

Definition

Forensic Gait Analysis was first defined by Kelly in 2000 as 'The identification* of a person or persons by their gait or features of their gait, usually from closed circuit television (CCTV) footage and comparison to footage of a known individual'.[18-21] In the more general sense, Kelly refers to forensic gait analysis as, 'the application of gait analysis knowledge to legal matters/problems'.[22] Grant, in 2006 provided a definition of forensic gait recognition

---

* Identification in this context is that of 'sharing characteristics with another person'. Vernon et al. 2009. Forensic podiatry: Role and scope of practice (in the context of forensic human identification), International Association for Identification, USA.

as, 'The process of identifying people by the unique characteristics of their manner of walking' in which 'features are extracted from a person's gait in order to recognize them'.[23] Other definitions are also available.

"Forensic Gait Analysis" was created and deemed relevant and admissible evidence in criminal law in 2000, [*R V Saunders*] at the Old Bailey Central Criminal Court, London. Subsequently, forensic gait analysis opinions have been sought and provided more widely and in other jurisdictions. Figure 6.1 illustrates some key components of forensic gait analysis.

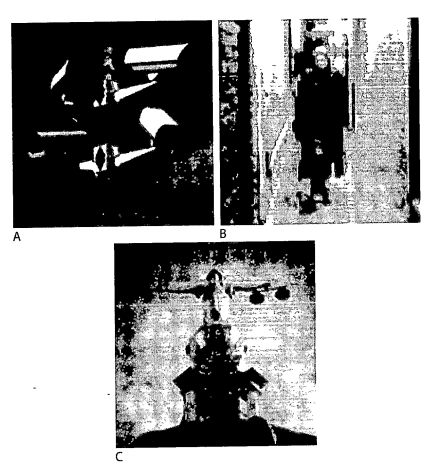

A   B

C

Figure 6.1 A, B and C. Displays three images depicting key components of forensic gait analysis: CCTV imagery, individual/s, and the justice systems.

An adversarial legal system is by nature one that is combative and which can therefore have both positive and negative effects. Experts, whether instructed by the prosecution or defence in the criminal justice system, or for the claimant or respondent in the civil justice system, need to be provided with and consider the *same* material insofar as it relates to their area of expertise, and prior to preparing their reports and giving evidence at court. When that does not occur, it leads to an imbalance and a greater risk of the expert's reports being further apart than perhaps they otherwise would be. Whilst that may suit some more than others, it is unwelcome for the experts and can place individuals in unnecessarily difficult situations which they should not be.

Forensic gait analysis was created and evolved out of the knowledge, skills and experience of the author long deployed in podiatry practice with gait analysis. Gait analysis is utilised by podiatrists and other healthcare professionals in the diagnosis and treatment/management of conditions. A main difference is that the quality of the video images utilised with clinical applications is usually greater than those available from lower resolution CCTV images for forensic purposes to assist in the identification of individuals. What is significant is the clinician's ability to observe and recognise the many attributes or aspects of normal gait and how these can be affected by pathology, illness, injury and treatment. Also, in recognising those presenting clinically or surgically, who have no observable gait abnormality amongst their symptoms. When observing gait or features of gait, one is observing effects, not causes. That said, features of gait may lead to symptoms in an individual. By way of illustration (but not the only one), consider the patient who presents with patella-femoral knee pain or ankle pain and who requires foot orthoses to help control the underlying excessive foot pronation responsible for their symptoms, in that instance.

The extent of gait analysis carried out by clinicians varies and is according to the particular focus and range of services. This is where it can be useful for those seeking to instruct an 'expert' to enquire at an early stage regarding the scope of their practice or area of expertise, as the courts generally prefer to hear from 'experts' who are in current practise. By way of illustration, it could be that a hospital services manager may not have treated patients for many years, but seeks to provide reports on clinical or other matters for use in the legal systems but is de-skilled in the area, no longer current, and may lack the necessary experience. Not vastly different perhaps to the academic lawyer who for decades has not represented a client, if ever at all, but constantly churns out practise articles. These are of course merely illustrations to help emphasise the important point of expert's having appropriate credentials and experience for the task performed. This is where a suitable examination of the expert's curriculum vitae is better placed early on, rather than perhaps when arriving at court to be met in cross-examination with a most unedifying experience in the witness box. The requirements of experts is further considered in other chapters.

ANATOMICAL GUIDE

It is important to have knowledge and understanding of the following:

- Body planes: sagittal, coronal, transverse and the various medical conditions and features of gait which may be displayed in the body planes
- Clinical biomechanics and anatomy of the human body
- Normal gait
- Gait abnormalities and pathomechanics
- Orthopaedics and Neurology
- Effects on gait arising from medical conditions and surgery
- Other factors affecting gait

There are three body planes about which motion occurs. (Figure 6.2)[24] These are the *Sagittal, Coronal* and *Transverse* planes.[25] The coronal plane may (perhaps somewhat confusingly) also be referred to as the 'frontal' plane. This is *not* to be misinterpreted with a 'front view', which is in the sagittal plane. The transverse plane view is also known as an 'axial' view. Figure 6.3 shows front, rear and side views of the human body. Figure 6.4 illustrates the three body types also known as 'somatotypes', these being, ectomorph, mesomorph and endomorph.

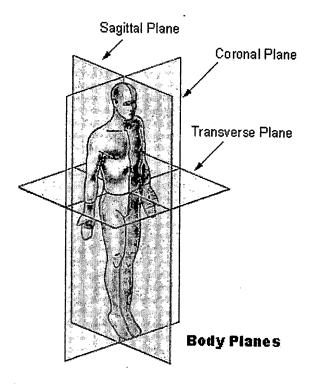

Figure 6.2   Anatomical planes of the human body.[24]

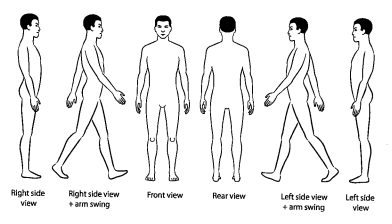

Right side view | Right side view + arm swing | Front view | Rear view | Left side view + arm swing | Left side view

Figure 6.3   Illustration to show front, rear and side views of the human body.

Body types

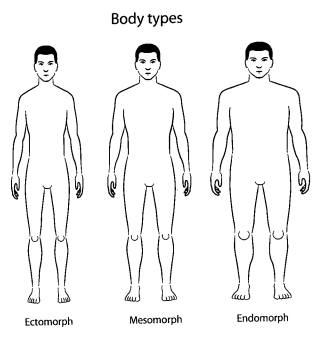

Ectomorph   Mesomorph   Endomorph

Figure 6.4 Body types (somatotypes). Ectomorph, Mesomorph and Endomorph.

Features of Gait

When performing forensic gait analysis, a feature of gait or gait style is either observable or it is not. The word *feature* is defined as a distinctive attribute or aspect of something.[26] By way of example, an individual limping is a feature of their gait; tibial varum (bow-legged position) and abducted foot position are also examples of a feature of gait.

The aim of this section is to provide general information for a broad readership and who may have engagement with gait analysis in legal matters. Working along a general anatomical guide with each segment aims to assist the reader's general knowledge of the anatomical areas considered with forensic gait analysis. Alignment of the body segments is followed from the head to the feet. Equally, some may prefer start at the feet in the process and work upwards to the head (also see section on *proforma*). What matters is that each segment is considered in a systematic, knowledge-based way that is organised, reliable and repeatable/reproducible. Ensuring that is straight forward and easy to follow should aid

147

when describing and explaining forensic gait analysis in a given matter, as an expert in court or elsewhere.

Alongside considering the positional aspects of an individual's gait and features of gait are the magnitudes thereof. A more detailed understanding of the aforementioned areas should already be a given for the practitioner carrying out forensic gait analysis. Note: Of those who have or are carrying out such casework, most had circa ten years of clinical experience before embarking upon medico-legal casework in the civil justice systems. Whilst not an absolute prerequisite, such a timeframe nevertheless gives a steer to the extent of clinical experience one may wish to consider having on board prior to undertaking duties and responsibilities of expert witness work – and includes being sufficiently resilient for encountering the inevitable tests presented in giving oral expert evidence.

What is relevant and significant in any given matter regarding an individual's gait or feature of gait is determined on a case by case basis from the material available. The forensic gait analysis expert should follow the same format when performing such examinations of material, allowing for modifications as further knowledge becomes available.

- Head and Neck
- Shoulders
- Torso and Spine
- Arms
- Hands
- Pelvis
- Lower Limbs
- Feet
    - Angle and Base of Gait

Head and Neck

Individuals are normally envisaged to have an erect head on their body when standing upright. Instead, they may present with a head tilt to the left or right side. Or, they may have a *forward head posture* (also known as 'head poke', 'turtle neck' or 'chicken head posture'), that is extension of upper cervical spine and flexion of the lower cervical spine. This results in the centre of gravity of the head being shifted forwards.[27,28] Forward head posture can be related to the use of computers,[29] and by smartphone use which can be improved by exercises.[30] The feature of forward head posture can be most easily observed on a side view (lateral view). (See Figures 6.5 and 6.6).

Figure 6.5 Forward head posture.

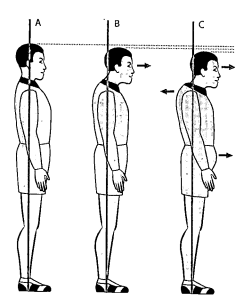

Figure 6.6 (A) Head erect. (B) Forward head posture. (C) Forward head posture with other musculoskeletal effects.

Shoulders

The shoulders move about a vertical axis and rotate in the opposite direction to that of the pelvis during normal gait. Otherwise, the shoulders and hips can move in the same direction.

A shoulder drop/tilt can occur forwards, backwards or laterally. The feature may also appear to present with an apparent longer arm on the 'dropped' side, thereby giving the appearance of a shorter arm on the opposite side (Figure 6.7A and Figure 6.7B).

150

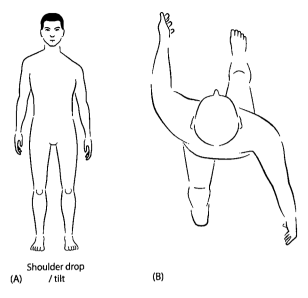

Shoulder drop
(A)   / tilt   (B)

Figure 6.7 (A) Shoulder drop/tilt.   (B) Axial view from above to show alternating position of shoulders with arms and legs.

Torso and Spine

Having considered the body type (somatotype[31-33]) displayed on the images (ectomorph, mesomorph and endomorph, Figure 6.4), conditions affecting the curvature of the spine such as scoliosis, kyphosis and lordosis should also be considered and whether such features are observable, and if so, to what extent. Examples of features also include *forward lean* (also known as anterior lean or forward bending of the torso) and *posterior lean*, these being most easily observed on a side view. *Lateral leaning* or bending of the torso (trunk) can be unilateral or bilateral, the latter exhibiting a *waddling gait*, where the torso bends from side to side towards the supporting limb during locomotion. These are most easily observed when viewed from the front or rear. Figure 6.8 displays (two dimensional) illustrations of some spinal alignments.

When examining video images in forensic practice, the observation of spinal conditions may be challenging when concealed by clothing. Generally, the greater the malalignment, the more difficult it is for clothing to obscure. One should be aware that video footage presented for human/manual forensic gait analysis is often two dimensional, and therefore some aspects may not always be observable in the way that they would be when observed in three dimensions.

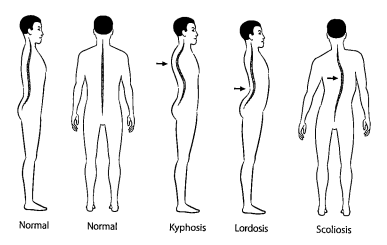

Normal   Normal   Kyphosis   Lordosis   Scoliosis

Figure 6.8 Illustration (two-dimensional) to show normal spinal alignment, kyphosis, lordosis and scoliosis.

Arms and Hands

During normal gait, the arms and lower limbs move in opposite directions. For example, as the right arm swings forwards, so does the left leg. In turn, as the left arm swings forwards, so does the right leg. Although arm swing is not essential for normal human gait, the alternating movements act to help counterbalance the body throughout locomotion.[34]

Moving the arms faster helps the feet move faster. In order to move the arms faster, an individual bends the elbows to shorten the swing, thereby reducing the duration of arm swing back and forth from the shoulder.[35] As walking speed increases, the frequency of arm movements gradually alters from mainly synchronising on the step frequency to the stride frequency, and this is an illustration of the various patterns of coordination which exist within human walking.[36] Loss of arm swing or asymmetrical arm swing can be a sign, for example, of Parkinson's disease, vascular dementia, prosthesis or concealment. Side views or angled side views often provide better perspectives from which to observe arm swing. Front or rear views may display other aspects. Also consider hand positions and whether or not particularly distinctive features are observable.

Figure 6.9 illustrates a right and left side view; right and left side view with arm swing; front and rear view. Figure 6.7B also illustrates the reciprocal movements of the arms and legs.

152

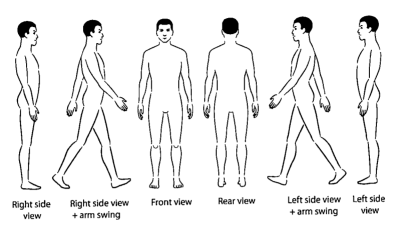

Right side view | Right side view + arm swing | Front view | Rear view | Left side view + arm swing | Left side view

Figure 6.9   Illustration depicting front, rear, right and left side views of the body.

Figure 6.10 and 6.11   Figure 6.10 displays a front view of an individual. Figure 6.11 displays a front left side angled view of the same individual as they move forwards, altering the angle of the individual in relation to the camera. Note the distinctive arm positions. Figure 6.11 also displays the individual's very abducted left foot.

Figure 6.10 displays a front view of an individual. Figure 6.11 displays a front left side angled view of the same individual as they move forwards, altering the angle of the individual in relation to the camera. Note the distinctive arm positions. Figure 6.11 also displays the individual's very abducted left foot.

153

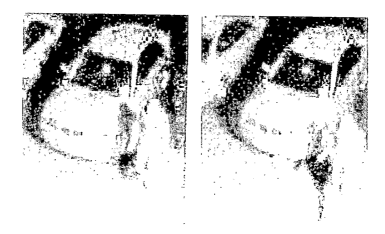

Figure 6.12 and 6.13 These are the images displayed in Figure 6.10 and Figure 6.11, but with 40% increase in brightness and contrast.

Figures 6.12 and 6.13 are the images displayed in Figures 6.10 and 6.11 but with 40% increase in brightness and contrast. Figures 6.14 and 6.15 are the images displayed in Figures 6.10 and 6.11 but with 40% decrease in brightness and contrast.

Figure 6.14 and 6.15 Figure 6.14 and Figure 6.15 are the images displayed in Figure 6.10 and Figure 6.11, but with 40% decrease in brightness and contrast.

154

Pelvis

The illustration in Figure 6.16 displays a left sided pelvic tilt/drop in the individual. Note also how in this example, the knee on that shortened limb exhibits increased internal (medial) rotation. Foot positions in this case are unaltered, but can be affected.

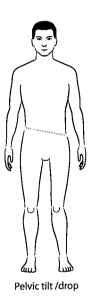

Pelvic tilt /drop

Figure 6.16   A left sided pelvic tilt/drop in the individual.

Figure 6.17 displays three images A, B and C representing bony remains. Note the unusually large circular area of erosion displayed in the acetabulum on the left and right side of the pelvis. Can you predict the gait style? What are the white areas?

155

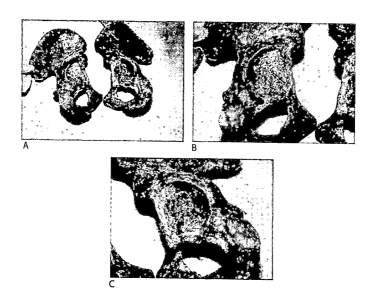

Figure 6.17 The three images A, B and C represent bony remains. Note the unusually large circular area of erosion displayed in the acetabulum on the left and right side of the pelvis. Can you predict the gait style? What are the white areas?

Lower Limbs

Consider the following:

- **Femur** – e.g. normal position; varus or valgus position; bowing in sagittal plane.
- **Knees** – e.g. normal position; genu varum; genu valgum; genu recurvatum.
- **Patella** – (kneecap) may be obscured by clothing.
- **Tibia** – e.g. normal position; tibial varum (bowing); tibial valgum.

Figure 6.18 Rear view of an individual. Note the distinct appearance of the right lower limb – a full limb prosthesis (e.g. following above knee amputation). Also, the equally abducted left and right foot positions. The lateral incline of the pavement, in this example, has no effect on the musculoskeletal observations.

157

Figure 6.19 illustrates a selection of lower limb features.

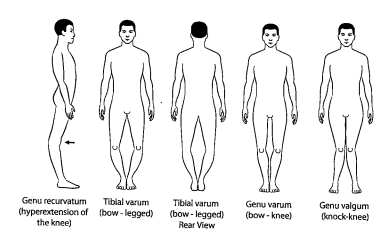

| Genu recurvatum (hyperextension of the knee) | Tibial varum (bow - legged) | Tibial varum (bow - legged) Rear View | Genu varum (bow - knee) | Genu valgum (knock-knee) |

Figure 6.19 Illustrates a selection of lower limb features. Genu recurvatum (hyperextension of the knee – most easily observed from a lateral/side view); Tibial varum (bow-legged) – front and rear views; Genu varum (bowing at the knee) and Genu valgum (knock-knee).

Figures 6.20 (A) and (B). Rear view of the individual. Image B is an enlarged version of image A. The individual's head is more clearly seen turned to right in image B. Left leg: tibial varum. Right leg: tibial varum. Note the trouser creasing (circled) at the lateral aspect of the right knee. Also, note the foot positions. Left foot forward and straight. Right foot behind and very abducted.

159

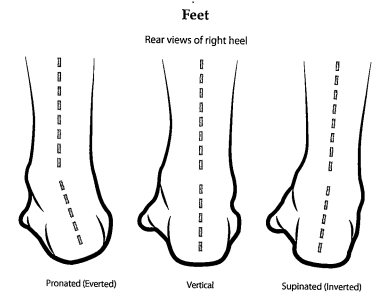

Feet

Rear views of right heel

Pronated (Everted)   Vertical   Supinated (Inverted)

Figure 6.21   Rear view illustration of some right rear foot positions with lower leg alignments.

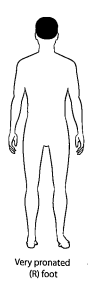

Very pronated
(R) foot

Figure 6.22   Rear view illustration of the body and very pronated right foot.

Angle and Base of Gait

Angle of Gait

The *angle of gait* (or *foot placement angle*) is formed by the longitudinal bisection through the heel and midline of the foot, and the line of progression in the sagittal plane (Figure 6.23). The method in determining the angle of gait can vary according to the study.[37] The approach of Dougan is one that is long established with shoeprints.[38] Normal angle of gait is reported in the ranges of 7 and 10 degrees of abduction of each foot.[39–43] Curran et al. reported no significant differences ($p < 0.0001$) when comparing the angle of gait from static and dynamic footprints.[44]

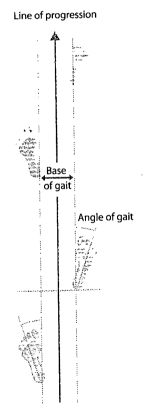

Figure 6.23   Axial view illustrating angle of gait and base of gait.

Base of Gait

This is determined by measuring the horizontal distance between the bisection of the left and right heel on two successive steps, as per Wilkinson et al.[45] There are variations on the lines of reference utilised according to the studies performed. Curran et al. reported that when comparing the *base of gait* in adults there were significant differences between the static and dynamic states of walking, the larger values seen in the static state of base of gait being attributed to the supportive wider base of gait adopted by individuals during static stance.[46] Levine et al. report the *walking base* (base of gait) usually between 5 centimetres and 13 centimetres (0.05 m and 0.13 m), which may be increased or decreased by pathology.[47] Angle and base gait have also been shown to be affected in individual's carrying load[48] (also see section on 'Body weight'). Figures 6.23 and 6.24 illustrate the angle of gait and base of gait.

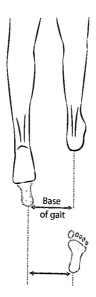

Figure 6.24 Rear view illustrating base of gait.

162

Base of Gait and Centre of Mass (CoM)

During walking, the body's centre of mass moves.[49] As walking speed increases, the base of gait narrows, the vertical transfer (upwards and downwards) of the centre of mass increases and the horizontal displacement (side to side) transfer of the centre of mass decreases with increased walking speed[50] (Figures 6.25 and 6.26).

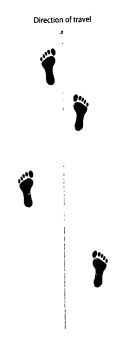

Figure 6.25 Transverse (axial) view illustrating variation in the horizontal transfer of the centre of mass (CoM) with an increase and decrease in base of gait.

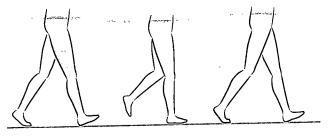

Figure 6.26 Lateral view illustration to show the vertical transfer of the centre of mass (CoM) during normal gait.

163

Transverse Plane Foot Positions

The following terminology is to assist the reader who may not be familiar with the descriptors in context:

Abducted = out-toed. Foot positioned away from the midline of the body.
Adducted = in-toed. Foot positioned towards the midline of the body.
Straight = foot is neither abducted nor adducted.
Windswept = one foot abducted (out-toed) and one foot adducted (in-toed).

Transverse plane foot positions are usually most easily observed on a front view of the individual (Figure 6.27). When transverse plane foot positions are large in magnitude, they can also be observed on rear or side views (Figures 6.28 and 6.29).

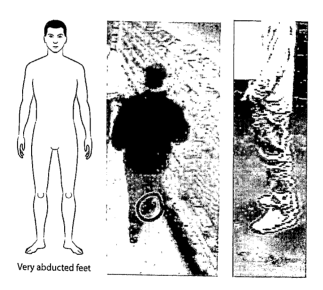

Very abducted feet

Figure 6.27, 6.28 and 6.29 Front view – both feet very abducted. Rear view – left foot straight; right foot very abducted. Left side view – both feet very abducted.

Diagrams to illustrate transverse plane foot positions are displayed in Figures 6.30 to 6.35.

164

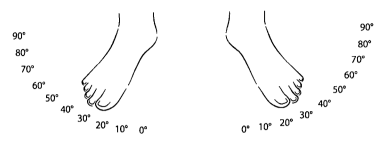

Figure 6.30 Both feet very abducted.

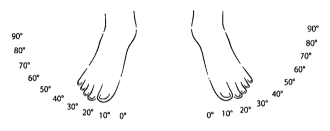

Figure 6.31 Both feet moderately abducted.

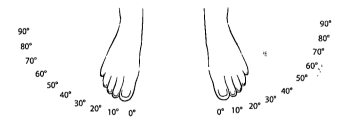

Figure 6.32 Both feet mildly abducted.

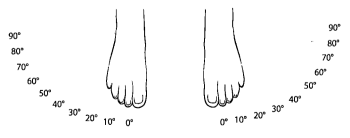

Figure 6.33 Both feet straight.

165

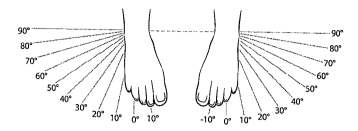

Figure 6.34 Both feet mildly adducted.

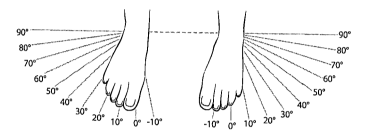

Figure 6.35 Windswept – one foot abducted, one foot adducted.

Figure 6.36 displays a selection of abducted foot positions with rear, front, side and angled views.

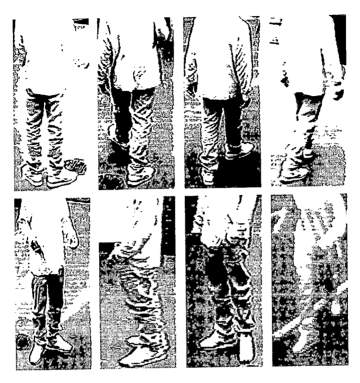

Figure 6.36 Displays a selection of abducted foot positions with rear, front, side and angled views.

And Figure 6.17, did you predict the gait? *Circumducted gait*, where there is an arc movement outwards of the lower limb away from the mid-line of the body, rather than a straight line when stepping forwards. Could also present as a *waddling gait* where the torso shifts from side to side. The white areas represent mould.

FACTORS AFFECTING FORENSIC GAIT ANALYSIS

- Quality and Suitability of video images
  e.g. frame rate: real time and time lapse, resolution, lighting.
- Parallax – camera angle/distortions
- Anatomical planes
- Medical conditions/injury – temporary and permanent
- Alcohol/Drugs
- Emotions

167

- Body weight
- Terrain
- Footwear
- Clothing
- Equipment: hardware (e.g. viewing screen/monitor) and software
- Disguised gaits?

[Further information on the quality and suitability of video material is available later in this chapter, with aspects also detailed in Chapter 5. Chapters 2, 3 and 4 also contain information with relation to areas of the above list.]

Body Weight

The effects of altered load on gait is reported on individuals across a range of parameters such as healthy controls,[51] military,[52,53] treadmill walking, which is also known to affect gait,[54,55] and the postural effects of load carriage on young people.[56,57] A small study by LaFiandra et al.,[58] limited to transverse plane kinematics, concluded there to be some counterbalancing of the upper and lower aspects of the body when carrying load. They also reported compatibility with the findings of Wagenaar and Beek,[59] in that 'increasing walking speed during unloaded walking was associated with a linear increase in stride length, stride frequency, and transverse trunk rotation'. Gillette et al. looked at the effects of a range of body weight loadings, the effects of which were found to be most noticeable with a loading of 20% body weight. They also reported that age could have affected the alterations observed in lower limb kinematics.[60]

Severely obese people often walk abnormally to accommodate their weight and widen their stance, making walking less steady and stressing the joints.[61] Meng et al.[62] looked at alterations in overground walking patterns in obese and overweight adults, which revealed gait variables to be more dependent with body mass index (BMI) and body mass rather than percentage body fat. Fischer and Wolf examined the unique effects of body weight unloading (BWU) on biomechanical parameters of healthy subjects walking overground at comfortable speed. The study showed that up to 30% of BWU reduces joint loads without notably modifying gait curvature patterns or the plantar flexion angle.[63] Fischer, Debbi and Wolf conducted experiments that replicated daily walking while controlling for speed variability, with a mechanical device designed to pull the BWU system at a constant speed. The controlled study assessed the unique effects of BWU on gait electromyography of healthy subjects and concluded that overground gait with up to 30% BWU reduces joint loads without modifying the muscle activation patterns.[64] Fischer and Wolf also assessed the distinctive effects of BWU modifications on the frontal plane in healthy subjects walking overground. The findings revealed a notable inverse relationship between increased BWU levels (0–30%) and decreased hip and knee adduction moments and impulses and increased lateral shift of the foot centre of pressure.[65]

Anness and Curran performed a pilot study of 15 participants (3 males and 12 females) into the effect on the angle and base of gait when a person carries a weight. The participants carried various weights up to 15 kg. It was concluded that when carrying a 15 kg weight to the front of the body, the base of gait increased and the non-dominant (left) foot abducted more than the opposite (right) side. When a 15 kg weight was carried to the left side of the body, a reduction occurred in the base of gait and the non-dominant (left) foot abducted, and the opposite (right) foot adducted.[66] Whilst acknowledged as a small study, the results are of interest and provides a steer to further work in that area.

Terrain

Consider by way of example, an individual walking or running on a soft, dry sandy beach, recently ploughed field, wet or dry grass meadow, concrete sidewalk, and snow covered or icy street. Also consider whether or not the walking surface has a significant incline or decline; uphill, downhill or sideways camber to the direction of travel (Figures 6.37–6.39), which significantly affects the gait or features of gait observed. Also keep in mind the imagery may not always display such angulation of the walking surface. It may be useful on occasion to visit the scene at which the video footage was recorded, particularly where the footage displays an alteration in gait which may be explained by an incline in the walking surface. Studies have shown that gait adaptation on inclined surfaces is attained by altering the pattern of movement in the lower limbs.[67–69] Adjustments to posture are specific to the assignment, which varies with standing and walking on an inclined surface.[70]

Many factors can be involved in slipping,[71] and the interaction of the walking surface and footwear is important.[72,73] A key aspect is the coarse texture shared by the two contact surfaces.[74] The coefficient of friction shared by the walking surface and the footwear being worn by an individual, along with other forces, affect slipping. Slipperiness or slipping has been shown to be related to occupational fall injuries.[75] The evaluation of the slip resistance of footwear under varying conditions is a useful tool in the prevention of slips and falls.[76] Heel strike and toe off phases during gait can be risky periods for an individual slipping.

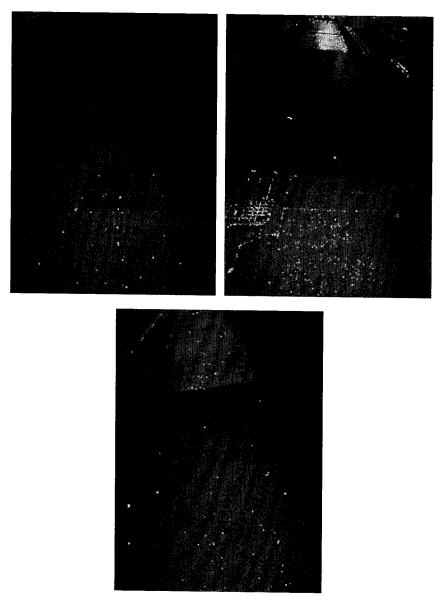

Figure 6.37, 6.38 and 6.39   These images display sideways angulation of the walking surface. Note these remain observable with reduced/night time lighting conditions in these examples. Figure 6.37 also shows the incline/decline at the sidewalk edge.

Footwear

This is an overview of footwear in the context of gait analysis, and which aims to give some understanding of the relationship of gait analysis and footwear. This is not designed to be a full topic review of forensic footwear examination, which is a separate area on which further reading is recommended.

- History and Functions

During the last 200,000 years humans have continually endeavoured at improving their existence by attempting to make all things more straightforward and easier. However, with some items there can be a long-lasting anticipation betwixt the empirical and that which is symbolic – and on footwear it is perhaps the symbolic that has become more significant.[77] The use of footwear by humans goes back a long time as illustrated by the discovery in Spain of paintings dated 12,000–15,000 years BCE, displaying a woman wearing boots made of fur and a man wearing boots from skin.[78] Footwear is worn by humans for various reasons and primarily to protect themselves from the environment, but also as an item of fashion, status, as a sexual signal[79] and costume.[80] One type of footwear with a lengthy social history is that of wooden shoes and clogs, thought to be one of oldest forms of footwear known[81] Whilst footwear is primarily a creation of necessity to shield us from the elements, for centuries and in differing cultures, it has taken a vast array of forms indicating that the role of footwear is more than simply protection. It is acknowledged that footwear in the world is influenced by fashion and that in turn can enable or hamper comfort, health and ease of movement.[82] In the late 1800s, Northampton shoemaker, *Church's*, introduced the concept of left and right shoes in the *Adaptable* model being available in assorted widths, materials and half sizes.[83]

In approaching the period around the most recent 200 years or so of footwear design, from the 1830s creation of the *Plimsoll* by the then Liverpool Rubber Company (later Dunlop) to 2008 and the *Melissa Shoe*, a collaboration of architect Zaha Hadid and Brazilian footwear manufacturer Melissa, the shoe clearly exerts a fascination on the popular imagination.[84] For designers such as Alexander McQueen, the allure of shoe styles from other cultures and periods in history lay in their transformative capacity. No longer shoes in the conventional sense, they had become an organic part of the wearer. McQueen's footwear creation in 2010, the '*Armadillo*' boot, pushed the boundaries of the traditional shoe shape.[85] These examples provide only but a glimpse of the vast array of shoe designs and how footwear can address such aspects as comfort and creativity, fashion and one's identity, contentment and technology, and not necessarily in that order.

The choice of one's footwear facilitates activities and occupational functions.[86] Footwear improves foot health and can aid a person to prevail over a lower limb abnormality, for example, limb length discrepancy where modifications to footwear facilitate a more natural and efficient gait.[87] The need for therapeutic footwear is often the only course of action or the most successful way of treating a condition.[88] Abnormal gait and impaired mobility may be helped by the prescription of therapeutic footwear.[89]

- Footwear and Gait

Footwear can also be the cause of symptoms and pathology when it is ill-fitting or unsuitable for the task being performed.[90-92] The 1915 text of Dr William Scholl, *The Human Foot: Anatomy, Deformities and Treatment,* addressed 'Mechanical Consideration of the Human Foot', in which is described not only the action of walking and how that could lead to various foot abnormalities and impairment, but also considered the impact of footwear on walking.[93] Footwear can influence gait[94] and has been shown to affect numerous walking gait parameters including balance[95] and speed of walking.[96] To what extent those effects occur and, when they do, to what level they are observable need to be considered on an individual basis. Kinematic and temporal spatial effects of footwear include increased step/stride length, decreased cadence, less flatfoot placement and decreased knee flexion.[97] Whether these are frequently seen as significant effects or alterations when performing observational gait analysis of an individual should be considered on a case by case basis. The practitioner should be mindful as to the 'seasonality' of footwear being worn that may obscure, restrict or enhance movement and the level to which that effect varies, if any. Of course, such factors may not affect observational gait analysis of an individual and again should be considered on a case by case basis. Careful examination of the shoe can serve to confirm a diagnosis of structural abnormalities of the foot. Where relevant, footwear should therefore be assessed during a person's initial visit when seeking treatment and bearing in mind the footwear worn by a person on a day when visiting a podiatrist may or may not be reflective of the footwear worn by the person for the majority of the time. It is applicable to enquire whether any symptoms experienced are aggravated or enhanced by particular footwear and activities. Hence, the need to examine the person's gait and observe for any alterations in their stance and gait.

Examination of footwear necessitates considering how the normal and abnormal foot functions in footwear – and how normal and abnormal gait is reflected on footwear. When managing the foot and its related

172

structures, it is important to address how any abnormalities being examined can translate to the footwear during stance and gait. Inspection of the location and extent of wear occurring on footwear can provide information about the gait of the wearer, and comparison of the wear marks on a person's footwear to those regarded as normal can also be of assistance.[98]

- Relevance of Wear Patterns

Anomalous wear on the heels and soles of footwear gives a steer as to the gait and weight-bearing patterns during locomotion.[99] It has been submitted that some wear patterns suggest particular gait patterns.[100] By way of example, a circular wear pattern on the sole of the shoe generally indicates an increased transverse plane movement such as circumduction or rotation.

Also, consider for example, a person who has a high arched foot type in comparison to that of an excessively pronated foot type (in some instances referred to as a 'flatfoot' or 'flatfeet', albeit a common term that is used as a broad descriptor). Here, a high arched foot type (also known as a 'supinated' or 'inverted' foot type) could generally be expected to display excessive wear on the *lateral* (outside) plantar aspect of the heel of the shoe; and the excessively pronated foot type perhaps being expected to display increased wear on the *medial* (inside) plantar aspect of the shoe? Well, let's pause for a moment as one has to be careful about misinterpretation. An excessively pronated foot type may actually display excessive wear on the lateral (outside) plantar aspect of the heel of the footwear, when that area is first to make contact with the ground at heel strike during gait. When an excessively pronated foot contacts the ground with heel strike on the medial (inside) plantar aspect, then it would be the corresponding medial aspect of the shoe which would display increased wear at that location. Consider this with Newton's third law of motion: 'When one body exerts a force on a second body, the second body simultaneously exerts a force equal in magnitude and opposite in direction on the first body'.[101] The statement means that in every interaction, there is a pair of forces acting on the two interacting objects – in this case the interacting objects being the respective heel area of the shoe and the ground. Or, put another way, the size of the force applied by the foot to the ground is equal to and opposite the force exerted by the ground on the foot.

The initial use of footwear impression evidence in criminal proceedings was in Scotland in the eighteenth century[102] and further material is available in more recent times on footwear impression evidence.[103-108] The deterioration of footwear increases with use, and whilst the general wear displayed on footwear may seem alike on the shoes of the same individual, it may also

173

seem alike between shoes owned by different individuals. Therefore, such general wear in isolation should not be used to identify a shoe as the particular source of a footwear impression and be mindful that attrition of the outsole on shoes is influenced by numerous components, including (but not limited to) the way a person stands and walks.[109] It has also been proposed that wear patterns on footwear[110–119] suggest that specific foot pathologies produce characteristic wear patterns on the outsoles of footwear. However, it has been recognised that such deductions can be accompanied by complications and uncertainty, as it became evident that outsole wear patterns could not be exactly correlated to specific foot pathologies as had formerly been thought. By contrast, a range of factors can affect outsole wear patterns on footwear.[120,121] Although wear marks should not be considered as standard, some abnormalities and gait patterns can have a tendency in presenting with representative patterns of wear.[122]

Whilst acknowledging that there can be links between outsole wear patterns and specific foot pathologies, one cannot reliably state in every case a solitary outsole wear pattern has an individual relationship to a specific foot pathology. Rather, an array of options can exist. Linking or disassociating outsole wear patterns on footwear to a wearer, or multiple wearers, can have value in the process of human identification. Appreciating such aspects, for example, as the amount of wear appearing on 'new' shoes will appear different to footwear that has been worn repeatedly over many months or years, is but one item to consider when examining footwear. It is also useful to bear in mind the same footwear may be worn by more than one individual.

Another confounding variable can be the deliberate alteration of gait.[123] Whether any intentional alteration in one's gait is able to be continually sustained is another matter. There are situations where other elements are helpful to consider alongside the gait identification evidence. For example, if an individual is seen to have a limp, then examination of the medical records may assist as to the relevance of any pre-existing injury, surgery, other treatment, including prostheses, orthoses and footwear.

Footwear impressions, such as those created in sand or other mediums, move into 3D analysis of footwear impressions, whereas photos of such impressions would be 2D. Video recordings of the footwear impressions created could be in 2D or 3D, depending upon the equipment deployed. Such footwear impressions, or barefoot impressions, that display a gait pattern/positions of the feet may be useful when also considering those observed on CCTV or other video footage, for example footwear patterns left at different crime scenes, and gait patterns/positions of the feet seen on CCTV, surveillance or other video footage. When available, these can be useful in serving to exclude or include an individual's from matters. CCTV footage can provide images of footwear that have the potential to be useful for investigations.[124]

It is important to be aware of prudence being needed when carrying out examinations and not to be conducted in a perfunctory way. Given that wherever there are a range of factors to contemplate, there is also the risk of forming incorrect conclusions, and more so if one is unaware of significant factors. As with all forensic material, footwear also has *chain of custody* requirements that need to be followed. Chain of custody is the documentation that tracks evidence on each occasion it changes hands or is moved between locations.[125]

Forensic gait analysis, footwear and bare footprints are separate tools in the forensic toolbox. That said, there may be occasion where these forensic instruments combine to be useful in the same case, depending on the material available and the matter in hand, and in a similar way that a whole raft of other forensic tools can be used as part of the wider jigsaw of evidence, and as determined on a case by case basis. This is not dissimilar in approach in some ways to how a multidisciplinary care team functions where different skills sets can be combined to the benefit of the patient (for example in diabetes). As indicated earlier, the purpose of this section is to provide the reader with a brief overview of how footwear and gait can be related and not to go into all the details of what is performed in a forensic footwear examination, which is a separate area of expertise.

Clothing

Whilst it may not normally be expected for an expert in forensic gait analysis to have specialised knowledge or training on all aspects of clothing, one would reasonably anticipate a basic awareness of how different types of clothing can affect observations of an individual's gait. In a clinical setting, for example, the increased bulk of an individual's rolled-up trousers or other tightly fitting clothing may be uncomfortable and/or restricting to a joint or segment movement, which may result in gait adaptation where the test becomes less useful, or on occasion useless.

Focused questioning of the patient will discern if this is a factor when analysing gait and if so, the gait examination repeated after alleviation of any such impeding factors. It can therefore be preferable to conduct such gait analysis in an environment that allows the patient to change into shorts or similar attire to avoid the potential problem of tight fabric

175

apposition. Of course, for some people tight fitting clothing is comfortable and preferable and for others not so. When considering forensic gait analysis from CCTV video recordings, the option of the practitioner selecting suitable clothing does not exist, which may enhance or disable the expert from being able to provide a meaningful opinion, depending on whether or not the clothing is significantly affecting the individual's gait or features of gait. Where there are video recordings of a 'suspect', it may be possible to simulate/request apparel nearer to that initially observed on the CCTV footage.

Equipment

In carrying out Forensic Gait Analysis, it is necessary for the practitioner to utilise a screen(s) or other monitor on which video images can be viewed and inspected. Technology around such equipment nowadays advances swiftly with numerous manufacturers with a broad range of products available. Visual equipment features, including normal play, pause, slow motion, rewind and fast forward allow for material to be examined in detail beyond a general overview.

Alterations in brightness and contrast can also be beneficial in assisting with observing the clarity of the images and the detail contained therein. As we have seen earlier, CCTV and other video material is provided in a variety of formats. In the early days of forensic gait analysis, analogue videotapes were the main format for recording material. These were superseded by CDs, DVDs and memory sticks, and subsequently video footage being available via weblinks, and the associated ease and savings that also brings with time and expense.

Nowadays there is a considerable range of computers, monitors/ screens and other equipment available, which can affect the clarity of the images displayed and observed. Hence, when compiling a forensic gait analysis report (or in the contemporaneous notes), refer to the equipment on which the footage was viewed and examined. It could be that more than one screen/monitor is used in the process of a different manufacturer. If the visual aids in the courtroom equipment are not of the same specification to that on which the analysis was conducted by the examiner, it may present challenges when explaining the visual evidence, particularly where sufficient clarity is not available to observe relevant detail of the images. In situations where the images are not of a high quality, it may be helpful to inspect the footage on a different screen to determine whether that has any observable effect on the clarity displayed.

Whilst the resolution may well be the same for two or more pieces of equipment, it could well be that the screens display a different clarity of the images simply due to a difference in the screen material, e.g. glass or other material.

Calibration of equipment also matters, so there is confidence in the results being measured throughout the lifetime of the equipment being used. There are also health and safety[126,127] factors when observing material on computer screens and appropriate rest breaks.

Whether or not the video material provided has been subjected to 'compression' – a technique performed to increase the amount of material stored on devices – but which can also result in the loss of information (images), which may not always be immediately apparent. In cases where images may need *enhancement* before being determined whether or not they are suitable for the purpose of forensic gait analysis, this enters into another area of expertise which is that of the 'Image Analyst', who should be consulted in such situations accordingly. Further information is available and recommended for reading in Chapter 5.

APPLICATIONS OF FORENSIC GAIT ANALYSIS (IN THE CONTEXT OF HUMAN IDENTIFICATION)

- Excluding or including individuals from an investigation/inquiry
- Identifying perpetrators at the scene
- Identifying perpetrators pre- and post-event
- Identifying masked/disguised individuals
- Verifying alibis – presence or absence at locations
- Comparing the effects of drugs/alcohol on gait
- Tracking persons of interest
- Reduce time in analysing CCTV in locating persons of interest
- Providing information where other tools are not suitable or available
- Suspicion to arrest

USES OF FORENSIC GAIT ANALYSIS

- **Evidential**
  Comparing the gait or features of gait of an individual displayed on closed circuit television (CCTV) footage ('unknown' person) to that of an individual displayed on other footage such

as custody suite footage or surveillance footage (referred to as 'control' footage or 'known' footage).

- **Investigative**

  Providing assistance in locating an individual. Here the individual's gait or features of gait can be cross-matched to various pieces of video footage to include or exclude them from being at a particular location. Or put another way, the presence or absence of an individual's gait, or features of gait, can allow for the important aspect of excluding individuals from an investigation. This can also assist where there may be a series of offences or where there is a question as to whether or not there is one or more perpetrator.

- **Pre-event or Prevent**

  Gait is a behaviour. This is a useful consideration when an individual's gait or features of gait are displayed, which may represent suspicious or unwelcome activity, subsequent to which an appropriate alert can occur elsewhere. In order to *prevent*, it is necessary to be able to *predict*.

CONSIDERATIONS IN PERFORMING FORENSIC GAIT ANALYSIS

- Receiving video footage and maintain *chain of custody* requirements relating to the material. For example, signing and dating receipt of items and ensuring they are locked for safe keeping if the material is to be retained.

- View and assess the video footage and determine whether it is of a *Quality* that is *Suitable* for the purpose of the analysis to be performed, that is forensic gait analysis.

- Determine whether any meaningful *Investigative* or *Evidential* product (report) can be produced from the material provided. When material is clearly of such poor quality and not suitable for analysis, that should be a relatively straight forward task for the expert to address. There may be instances where the footage provided does not take the matter any further forwards, in any direction. In such circumstances that should be stated at an early stage (in writing) with reason by the expert to those instructing them. This approach can save time and expense later on. Bear in mind that on occasion when some of the video footage appears to be of a quality unsuitable for analysis, it does not follow that all of the video footage is not suitable. Hence the importance of initially examining all of the material provided in its entirety prior to arriving at a conclusion on the suitability of the material. Also, if not already carried out prior to one's receipt of the material, consider whether or not the material could benefit from being examined by an image analyst for enhancement of the footage. This is an example of where separate areas of expertise can assist jointly.

- Think carefully about what information can be derived from the footage and whether it is relevant to your area of expertise.

- When providing evidence for use in the legal systems, ensure the duty and responsibility as an expert witness is understood, including court rules and good practise guidelines as they apply to the relevant jurisdictions.*[128–139]

Quality and Suitability of the Material

In the context of forensic gait analysis, this relates to the *quality* and *suitability* of the video footage which is usually in the form of CCTV, custody suite, surveillance or other video footage. Also see Chapter 5.

Information contained within the motion of the video footage may sometimes appear to be of a better quality than still images or still frame picture prints taken from the footage. Therefore, the (moving) video footage should primarily be used when the examination is being conducted. Nevertheless, still images or still frame picture prints can be useful to assist in explaining some visual aspects, but beware of blurring to the image which can occur when the image is paused or 'freezed'. A bundle of still frame picture prints in sequence can be helpful for the court to have sight of alongside the video footage, or before viewing the video footage as an aid to what they are to be observing on the motion video footage.

The following qualitative guide is to assist the forensic gait analysis expert with the initial process of determining whether video footage is of a *quality* that is *suitable* for the analysis that is to be undertaken. *Note:* It is important that when a forensic gait analysis expert is unsure of whether the quality of the imagery is suitable for the purpose, then opinion is to

---

* A primer on forensic gait analysis was first published in 2017 as part of a collaborative project on judicial primers for the courts in the UK on a range of forensic areas. The first two primers were for DNA and forensic gait analysis. As a 'living document' an updated version is to be welcomed with experts experienced in forensic gait analysis casework.

be sought from an 'image analyst' with the relevant imagery expertise.[140] Remember, take time and do not rush when carrying out examinations of the material and when preparing a report (see Chapter 10).

- *Good quality and suitable for analysis*
  Where the individual's gait and/or features of gait are clearly displayed. In such instances the material is suitable for forensic gait analysis. (For example, see Figure 6.40).

- *Reasonable quality and suitable for analysis*
  Where the individual's gait and/or features of gait are displayed with some reduced quality of the images, but not to the extent to impede the expert's ability to observe the gait or features of gait displayed. In such instances the material is suitable for forensic gait analysis (for example, see Figure 6.41).

- *Poor quality but suitable for analysis*
  Where the individual's gait and/or features of gait are displayed with reduced quality of the images, to the extent that only a particularly distinctive gait or features of gait can be observed. On such occasion this can override the significance of the general quality of the footage. In such instances the material is suitable for forensic gait analysis (for example, see Figure 6.42).

- *Poor quality and not suitable for analysis*
  Where the individual's gait and/or features of gait are not displayed with significantly reduced quality of the images, to the extent that no discernible gait or features of gait can be observed. In such instances the material is not suitable for forensic gait analysis (for example, see Figures 6.43 and 6.44).

Note: Factors relating to image quality such as frame rate (real time/time lapsed), resolution and lighting are important considerations when determining whether the quality of the video footage is suitable for analysis (see Chapter 5). For example, a high resolution image with a low frame rate recording may not be suitable for forensic gait analysis. Gait is a repetitive action and repeatability of movement is a factor to consider when assessing the quality and suitability of material.

Figure 6.40 The image is of good quality and suitable for analysis. Rear view. Note the distinct feature of the right lower limb, a full limb prosthesis. Left foot abducted. Right foot abducted. The lateral incline of the pavement in this illustration has no effect on the musculoskeletal observations.

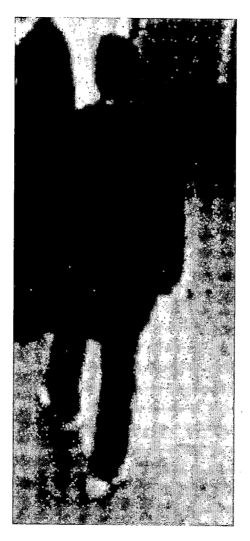

Figure 6.41 The image is of reasonable quality and suitable for analysis. Rear view. Head turned to the right. Left leg: tibial varum. Right leg: tibial varum. Note the trouser creasing at the lateral aspect of the right knee. Left foot forward and straight. Right foot behind and very abducted.

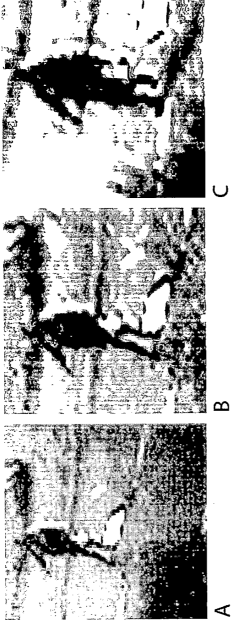

Figure 6.42 Displays three images A, B, C. Front left side view. Image B is an enlarged version of A. In this example, the effect of enlarging image A results in a lower quality image B. Note the individual's distinctive right arm position. The individual is carrying an object in their left hand. The distinctive right arm position remained when carrying and not carrying the object. The images are of poor quality but suitable for the purpose of forensic gait analysis. It is significant to bear in mind that 'still frame' images or printed still images, may display as lower quality images than the actual motion video footage.

Figure 6.43 Displays a left side view of an individual. The image is of poor quality and not suitable for the purpose of forensic gait analysis. No meaningful analysis can be performed.

Figure 6.44 Displays a right side view of an individual. The image is of poor quality and not suitable for the purpose of forensic gait analysis. No meaningful analysis can be performed.

184

The process performed for forensic gait analysis (in the context of human identification) utilises *class level characteristics* and recognising that some gait styles or features of gait are more distinctive than others. The preparation of a report should be a straightforward systematic, knowledge-based task that is reliable and repeatable in assessing and analysing the material and performing comparisons of the relevant imagery, arriving at conclusions and an opinion formed. Such a process can also be represented by the process of Analyse, Compare, Evaluate (ACE). This is an acronym introduced by Huber in the 1950s for describing hypothesis testing as it is related to the comparative sciences. The ACE terminology was subsequently used across various areas and Ashbaugh of the Royal Canadian Mounted Police (RCMP), a modern pioneer, introduced the process to the forensic discipline of fingerprints.[141]

In order to help ensure depiction of incorporating the essential initial assessment on whether or not the *quality* (Qu) of the video footage is suitable for the purposes of forensic gait analysis, the author suggests the acronym *Qu-ACE-VR*.

Qu: Is the *quality* of the material *suitable* for the analysis that is to be undertaken

A: Analysis of the unknown (CCTV) footage. Analysis then performed on the known (control/suspect) footage

C: Comparisons of the unknown (CCTV footage) to known (control/suspect footage)

E: Evaluation of the findings (Conclusions)

V: Verification

R: Report

Having determined the video footage is suitable for the purpose of forensic gait analysis, the analysis of the material can then proceed. This commences with analysis of the 'unknown' (CCTV) footage followed by analysis of the 'known' (control/suspect) footage. It is *crucial* that the unknown (CCTV) footage is *always* viewed prior to any known (control/suspect footage) in order to avoid *confirmation bias*. Not following such a process may render a report inadmissible as evidence at court.

Analysis of Unknown (CCTV) Footage

To reiterate, the 'unknown' material must first be examined prior to that of the 'known' (control/suspect) material. Unknown material is usually regarded as the CCTV footage from the crime scene. It may also include other material.

Initially, a *general* assessment is performed of the video footage observing for any distinctive gait or features of gait displayed on the video footage. This is followed by a more *particular* detailed examination of each of the body segments displayed on the relevant individual(s) seen on the footage.

All observations should be recorded in the expert's contemporaneous notes for preparing a report. The expert's notes are part of the evidence and are often requested by counsel as part of proceedings. Hence, the importance for the expert's contemporaneous notes to be recorded at each stage from initial contact and receipt of the material, whether in a physical or online format.

Analysis of Known (Control/Suspect) Footage

This may include custody suite, overt, covert or other footage where the identity of the individual(s) is known. When one is unsure as to whether the footage is deemed 'unknown' or 'known' footage, then confirmation should be sought from those providing the instruction. Again, an initial general assessment is performed of the footage, observing for any distinctive aspects displayed on the video footage. This is followed by a more particular and detailed analysis of the material and all observations should be recorded.

Comparisons

A comparison considers similarities and dissimilarities. That is resemblances *and* differences. The comparative process in forensic gait analysis is one of comparing the unknown to known and progressing for each corresponding area on the body systematically and sequentially until all areas have been compared. Starting at the head and working down through the skeleton is a logical system. But it could be from the feet upwards to the head, and is an individual choice for the examiner. What matters is that the same process is conducted and repeated throughout (see proforma).

When performing comparisons for forensic purposes, it is imperative for the *unknown* material to be compared *to* the *known* material (and not the reverse). That helps avoid the risk of introducing 'confirmation bias'. Carrying out such a process of comparing the unknown material to that of the known material also displays a considered, sensible approach with balance and understanding in the decision-making process.

It could be that in some cases a series of unknown clips of video footage are also requested to be compared to one another, perhaps to consider whether or not there is any link between events.

Evaluation (Conclusions)

As part of any conclusions and having performed the comparisons for similarities and dissimilarities of the gait and features of gait displayed on the video imagery, consideration should *equally* be given as to whether or not there is any gait information displayed on the CCTV (unknown) footage to suggest the known person (e.g. person on the custody suite footage or surveillance footage) is not the person described on the CCTV footage. The strength of similarity or dissimilarity is expressed by scale when considering the two propositions.

Expression of the expert's opinion may include reference to relevant material in the literature such as journals, texts, publications; clinical/empirical data; observational/field studies, and databases, as appropriate. Also, consider the 'class level of evidence' (e.g. I–IV, where level 1 represents the highest level of evidence and level IV the lowest level, when classifying the overall quality of an individual study,[142]) where that is relied upon in supporting the propositions. Observational/field studies can provide some information as a guide to the prevalence of gait styles or features of gait displayed in the footage examined. In many observational studies, the samples will be independent of one another.[143] When such information is not already available and an observational study is required and commissioned by the instructing party, this is likely to incur further resources. In such situations, the expert may need to address that later at court, including if one expert conducted such a study, then the other side should also be able to carry out such a study to avoid potential imbalance. Where one side chooses not to instruct an expert in the same discipline, or no opposing expert at all, that is perhaps a matter for the court to consider. Another option would be where experts are instructed by both sides, for both experts to jointly conduct an observational study where relevant, should the court request or order the same.

Datasets come in many formats. Care is required as data collections have imperfections or 'holes' in them and are not perfect which may affect results and lead to misinterpretation. It follows that experts may well attach differing probabilities to the same observations. When significant factors are not properly considered or communicated then misunderstanding can follow, particularly where individuals are unfamiliar and have no qualifications nor expertise in a specialism, but engage on it anyway. For example, with patient data – which is itself a database – it can be rightly argued that information is not necessarily representative of the whole population (adult or otherwise). One needs to also be aware that what is statistically significant in one area may not necessarily be so in another area. It is well understood by clinicians who use gait analysis in the diagnoses and management of conditions that individuals do not always display an altered gait. As indicated elsewhere and in Chapter 9, whilst acknowledging practitioners may have some familiarity with statistical methods, that is a specialist area and area of expertise.

A 'strength of support' scale is often deployed by those providing expert evidence when considering the two propositions. Likelihood ratios may be used, if or where appropriate, but caution again needs to be applied and the language used (see Chapter 9). Practitioners/experts need to stick to their area of expertise and not digress into other fields in which they are not appropriately qualified, nor into the realms of advocacy[144]; nor must they consider only one proposition.[145] Being aware of one's limitations is important. Rest assured, counsel in cross-examination can be masters at addressing such things.

Verification

Verification aims to demonstrate the practitioner has acceptable and satisfactory skills and knowledge in providing reasonable and justifiable information in performing the task.

The term *verification* may lead one to have a mistaken sense of understanding as there can be several potential problems with the term (confusion being one), as the expression can be interpreted as being *synonymous with confirmation*.[146]

It should be a given that any expert should in the first instance perform a 'double check' themselves on the content of their report before finalising and signing. A report is not to take the shape of some form of 'quick e-mail' but instead is a comprehensive legal document upon which others rely. This requires and deserves patience, time and a conscientious approach in the production thereof (see Chapter 10).

True verification is actually about looking at the first examiner's conclusions to see if those hold true. That is not about simply confirming or agreeing with what another practitioner has performed and concluded, who they may know or work alongside, which could in itself be deemed as *bias* and/or having *conflicts of interest*. Conflicts of interest can arise when enacting peer review, and there can be some confusion between the replicability of results and reliability of the evidence.[147]

Honesty and integrity are fundamental requirements of the legal system and includes experts. Ideally and where resources are no obstacle, a complete 'blind' review on each and every aspect of a report should be welcomed, but which is likely to bring further costs in time and expense to re-evaluate all elements of a report. Instead, a 'critical findings check' can reduce such costs. When a report is finalised and having been disclosed to the other side, joint discussions between experts in the same area of expertise can be directed by the court to assist in 'narrowing the issues'. This is formatted in a joint statement by the experts. Cross-examination in court is an effective mechanism of testing evidence where there are significant discrepancies between experts.[148] Sometimes one side or the other may not call an expert to give oral evidence at court which opposes the other side's report. Such decisions are for the advocates and the courts to consider, not the experts.

In the Civil Courts of England and Wales, verification of an expert's report by another expert is not currently (at the time of writing) a requirement of the Civil Procedure Rules. Nevertheless, duties and responsibilities remain upon experts including that their duty is to the court. A thorough dissection of an expert's report is to be expected in cross-examination in the courts and is a well-established test in the adversarial legal system.

Report

The preparation of a report is the product of the expert's findings. As mentioned earlier, contemporaneous notes need to be maintained which commences from the time of initial contact from those providing the instruction. This is so that the court can follow the expert's workings of what they did, when they did it with times and dates and where it was performed. In addition to the expert's report(s), contemporaneous notes form part of the expert evidence and which may well be examined as evidence at court (see Chapters 10 and 11).

On occasion it may be requested by counsel in cross-examination of an expert when giving oral evidence at court, for the expert to perform a detailed analysis of video footage, as a test. This is not acceptable and to be resisted by the expert. The courtroom is not an acceptable environment in which to carry out such work and in unscientific conditions. That is a very different task to an expert answering questions on their report and observing video footage in court which they have previously analysed, and which is a normal part of what is required of experts when giving oral evidence in court.

189

Validation

The methods employed for validation will vary depending on whether a quantitative or qualitative method is used. Jurisdictions may vary in their requirements. Experts should be familiar with the requirements/guidelines and court procedure rules of the legal system in the relevant jurisdiction, insofar as it relates to the expert's duty and their responsibilities.
Some points to consider:

- A first step in the validation process is whether the examiner considered the video footage to be of a quality that is suitable for the analysis to be undertaken. How is this accomplished? For example, are the resolution, frame rate and lighting adequate for the observation of gait and features of gait, rather than a sequence of still images.
- Having determined the footage is suitable for the analysis that is to be undertaken, then is that process repeatable by another examiner.
- Where the process is repeatable by another examiner, will the examiner, or is the examiner likely to, arrive at the same result.

  [*Note:* There may be some instances, for example, where the video footage is generally of a poor quality but suitable for the purpose of forensic gait analysis where a particularly distinctive gait or feature/s of gait is displayed. On such occasion, be mindful that in the adversarial legal system, this aspect may be argued the other way by another examiner/expert, and if so, they will also have to justify their position. So, be sure in such situations the distinctive gait or feature/s gait are observable before proceeding. Otherwise, the footage should be deemed unsuitable for the analysis being undertaken.]

- Providing the process is reliable and repeatable, then the first part of the process is validated. If there is only one examiner in the process (e.g. sole practitioner/trader), then their process can be regarded as validated on condition that they could repeat the process consistently, and if they were given the same video footage at a later stage they could arrive at the same decision.
- The process of validation is applied to each stage in the examination of the material.

Further information on validation is available.[149]

190

Proforma

A proforma is a document used to standardise the recording of data collected. This can be devised for an individual to repeatedly use for data collection or analysis and from which other information, or patterns, can be determined. A proforma for general use by practitioners or communities is aimed to ensure everyone is collecting on the same data points. When constructing a proforma for wider general use or where assessment guidelines do not exist, seeking expert opinion through consensus gathering is a useful initial step to developing recommendations.[150] Additional information can also arise and a proforma should not restrict this and instead allow for other relevant factors to be accommodated when the data is being collected or analysed. In the creation of a proforma, consultation needs to occur amongst the practitioners with appropriate expertise and to agree on what questions need to be addressed and therefore what data needs to be collected for a particular task or survey.

A musculoskeletal template is illustrated by the acronym 'GHORT' (Gait Homunculus Observed Relational Tabular) as referred to by USA Podiatrist, Southerland [Ed. Valmassy], in order to express features of pathomechanical gait that are *observable, interpretable and reproducible*. This was developed as a framework to display and record dynamic gait cycle observations from head to feet with static measurements also recorded.[151] Such a process makes for a systematic, knowledge-based way that is reproducible and one for clinicians to be able to view, analyse and interpret the recordings of other clinicians, and which continues to have utility.

There are many benefits to communities using a single data collection form being consensus based, systematic and standardised and which supports consistency in communications amongst professionals.[152] When considering, for example, the variability in footwear impression comparison conclusions, it has been found that when experienced examiners use the same conclusion scale and compare the same features, there is reportedly little variability within their stated findings.[153] In order to achieve consensus when creating a proforma, various processes can be deployed, including wide and mature co-operation amongst the community. For example, whilst recognising the Delphi survey technique is a valid method to determine consensus, the process of a Delphi survey has also been subject to concerns with the existence of consensus or agreement not necessarily ensuring correctness.[154] Avoiding collusion and ensuring anonymity are important considerations for participants in Delphi surveys. Criteria set for 'expert' within Delphi panels are there to ensure contributors have acknowledged expertise within their professions.[155] Whilst obtaining consensus amongst a range of expertise in any area may be challenging, individual experts should have their own pro-forma where no universally agreed proforma exists.

Bias

The courts in England have permitted experts to give opinion evidence from around the middle of the sixteenth century[156] and the important question of how legal systems can best effectively utilise expert knowledge also has a long history, having courted debate for centuries.[157] The issue of expert evidence and the quality thereof is also not a new phenomenon, as illustrated by the then Lord Chancellor regarding a case in the 1800s: 'this confirms the opinion I have entertained, that hardly any weight is to be given to the evidence of what are called scientific witnesses; they come with a bias on their minds to support the cause in which they are embarked'.[158] The courts continue to search for ways that will allow them to distinguish between good and bad science.[159] The actual quality and level of expertise in cases may only transpire as a result of extensive dissection by advocates or counsel, on the basis of specialised knowledge on the subject matter from the opponent's expert, where cross-examination is a natural part of the adversarial system. The assumption that science (particularly forensic science) is itself objective was successfully challenged in a large body of research in 2003 in the USA relating to crime laboratory practice, showing how bias was universally present in scientific analysis.[160] This along with other considerations have in recent years prompted a review in the standards in forensic practice.

In the USA, the Frye test and later the Daubert principle are a guard to ensure that only suitable testimony is put before the Courts in which a criteria of 'soundness' is incorporated into the concept of 'knowledge and skills'. This led to the US Supreme Court justifying the employment of the concept of reliability as a precondition of evidential accountability and is thus provided by Rule 702 of the Federal Rules of Evidence (see Chapter 11).

In the UK, the duty and responsibilities of experts are as per the relevant court procedural rules, that is the Civil Procedure Rules and Criminal Procedure Rules applicable in the jurisdiction of England and Wales (also see Chapters 10 and 11).

Bias can occur at different stages and comes in many different forms with over 100 types listed.[161,162] *Confirmation bias, cognitive bias, selection bias, performance bias, attrition bias, detection bias, reporting bias* are but a small handful of the many types of bias that may be encountered. Examples of cognitive bias are the *'Halo'* effect and the opposite *'Horn'* effect, both types relating to perception error. For example, the *'Halo'* effect is where an individual who likes one aspect of something then decides they like everything about it. Conversely with the *'Horn'* effect, if an individual dislikes one aspect of something they then choose to dislike everything about it.

People are faced with bias in some form each day and as human beings some will find it more challenging than others to escape from those. What is significant for 'experts' is to have the capacity to shift the paradigm in their way of thinking and to avoid being trapped by bias. Many experts can probably recite cases of those who can apparently present their proposition as being the 'right one' and that any other way cannot be correct or true. Whilst there is no place for such a course, it does not follow that it does not exist. Visualising 'the scales of justice' can be one simple and useful way to help consider balancing the merit of what we are told or presented with – that is weighing up what is on one side and giving equal and *balanced* consideration to the other proposition, and consider doing one's own analysis before arriving at a conclusion. We also need to enquire why others seek to manipulate support for their own ends from those around them and at times from some 'scientists' who are regarded as supposedly 'unbiased'. When one has or develops expertise in an area, one should enquire how narrow (and in some areas very narrow) or wide is that particular area of expertise. Sticking to one's areas of expertise is a must, whilst portraying to be an expert in other areas is for the birds, and phrases such as 'the mad scientist' or 'the mad professor' are not unknown.

Having an appreciation of bias and how it impacts an area of expertise is important. An understanding of bias and how it affects results is essential for the practice of evidence-based medicine,[163] and a useful classification of biases is also described in the Cochrane handbook.[164] There are some sources of bias that are relevant only in certain circumstances and there may be derivations of bias only found in a particular setting. For example, 'in-group' bias, where there is a propensity to give favourable behaviour towards those perceived to be members of 'their' own group; another example could be, what relations of the editor at a time and those submitting a publication. This becomes even more disturbing when those practicing act to disguise or justify conduct as acceptable and try to influence the peer review processes of publications, particularly when not carried out on a *'double-blind'* basis (that is, where the reviewer and those instructing the reviewer are both unaware of the identity of the submitting authors of an article in the peer review process prior to its publication). Amongst the many other forms of bias is the *'Dunning-Kruger'* effect, in which there is the tendency for unskilled individuals to overestimate their own ability and the tendency for experts to underestimate their own ability.[165] Is the reverse also true, we may also enquire. Many find it challenging to objectively assess their own abilities and the vast majority of accidents in the workplace being ascribed to *'overconfidence'*.[166,167]

- Confirmation bias

This is defined as 'the tendency to search for, interpret, focus on and remember information in a way that confirms one's preconceptions'.[168] In forensic gait analysis, an area where confirmation bias can occur as alluded to earlier is when an examiner is initially considering video material. At such times, it is crucial for the 'unknown' footage (e.g. CCTV footage) to be viewed prior to any 'known' footage (e.g. custody footage of a suspect). If the examiner views the known footage *prior to* the unknown footage, then in such situation confirmation bias is introduced. It means that no matter how 'objective' the examiner may believe they are, the fact they have not viewed nor analysed the unknown footage prior to the known footage could later present significant problems at court, including whether the evidence be deemed admissible.

It may be argued that the examiner/expert who has been instructed or tasked with a matter is motivated, or inherently biased, towards wishing to satisfy those by whom they have been instructed or who are responsible for their fees! The UK courts are clear that an expert's duty is to the court and not those who instruct them or responsible for their fees. As experts and scientists, the temptation 'to please' must be resisted and adhering to the facts in a non-partisan way is paramount. Whilst appreciating that no system is perfect, one would expect that when an expert presents evidence which is clearly contrary to reason, then the courts would be expected to see that for what it is. Those who are instructing experts need to know what the facts are as early as possible in a case. One can consider the question of whether or not is it possible that those contending *confirmation bias* and *contextual bias* are themselves only seeing what they want to see in their own work? Perhaps such situations are culpable of 'the Texas sharpshooter fallacy – firing shots at the barn door, drawing a circle around the best group, then declaring that to be the target'.[162] Keep in mind that a *logical fallacy* is an error in logical argument, but a *cognitive bias* is a genuine deficiency or limitation in one's thinking – a flaw in judgement arising from memory errors, social attribution and miscalculations.

INTERPRETATION AND CONTEXT

The application of *gait* knowledge to legal matters in the justice systems in the UK is not new with 'expert evidence' being widely deployed as part of civil proceedings involving, for example, musculoskeletal injuries which may occur in the workplace or in road traffic collisions (personal injury) and/or matters involving allegations of clinical negligence matters and where an expert is needed to opine upon prognosis and treatment. And more recently 'forensic gait analysis' in the context of expert evidence in criminal proceedings since *R v Saunders* [2000] at the Old Bailey in London.

There are long standing historical references to individuals being recognised by their 'gait' and referred to in many of Shakespeare's works,[169] and as described in Chapter 1. Studies of human locomotion also have a long history and human walking characteristics have been extensively investigated by experiments and simulations.[170-173] The science of gait analysis that began in the seventeenth century and continued beyond provided a solid scientific foundation for our current understanding of human walking.[170] As we have already seen, analysing the make-up of the human body, shape and movement goes back much further to the time of Plato and Aristotle, conveying the history and development of gait analysis and its uses have been a steady affair over a considerable period of time. Alphonse Bertillon (1853–1914) also appears to have utilised gait in some way in his system of body measurements based on anthropometry and photography in the 'Bertillon System',[174] an identification system based on physical measurements and supplanted as more cases became solved with fingerprint identification. The identification of functional characteristics is of exceptional interest to the clinician as this also relates to diagnosis and the management of conditions. Notwithstanding that advances in gait analysis over time have been considerable, in the words of Sutherland, 'we have barely scratched the surface of the development and potential contributions of clinical gait analysis'.[175]

The purposes of looking into human movement have altered over time and the study of such locomotion has contributed to the advancement of fundamental knowledge and applied fields ranging from military applications to healthcare; and there is substantial evidence some individuals adapt their gait to compensate for instability, pain or neuromuscular pathology.[176,177] As well as appreciating the important neurological and musculoskeletal considerations that relate to gait, why is it that an individual is able to walk or run? This can be addressed by considering the physics of a person's individual mass being less than that of planet earth. What does this mean? Well, let us contemplate by way of example, what occurs when an individual's foot contacts the ground (the earth) during walking or running. A force is applied when the individual's foot contacts the ground and an equal and opposite force is applied to the individual from the ground (see Newton's laws of motion). Given the earth has a vastly greater mass compared to that of the individual, it is the individual which then moves and not the earth. Movement is the result of the action – and force is the source of the action. Or, put another way, force is the cause and movement is the effect. Walking is a motor function involving the coordination of numerous muscles.[178] Man's bipedal mode of locomotion appears potentially rather testing, because only the rhythmic forward movement of the limbs keeps individual's from falling. Hence, the foot as the base of support of the skeletal framework has a significant role with a person's gait[179] and the human locomotor pattern has been shown to be highly adaptable to different environments.[180]

As we have already seen, a challenge when examining video footage for forensic purposes is whether an individual's gait or features of their gait can be observed, when considering the quality of the video material being examined in some situations can be less than ideal. In such instances where the video material is not of a quality that is suitable for the purpose, then forensic gait analysis may not be a useful instrument as determined on a case by case basis. Hence, the need for the video material to be of a quality that is suitable for the analysis that is to be undertaken. Circumstances where gait is partially displayed has the effect of evidential gait analysis being more challenging.[181]

It has been shown that both humans and computers are very good at recognising known gait patterns.[182] Forensic gait analysis utilises observational gait analysis with *class level characteristics*, recognising that some gait styles or features of gait are more distinctive than others. Browne et al. conducted a study considering thematic analysis and video of human gait and reported, 'a basic level experience or knowledge is required to provide a simple description of human gait. With more expertise came a richer description of observation of human gait by the "expert" group compared to basic observations by the "novice" group'.[183] Video imagery such as CCTV footage is frequently utilised as part of investigations by law enforcement[184] and has utility for corporate security. Knowledge on aspects that affect video imagery is also required, for example, compressed image formats[185] (also see Chapter 5). A person's gait cannot always be completely disguised,[186] and gait observations can be performed at distance and is a non-intrusive method with the capability to be performed without the knowledge of the individual.[187] It may not be easy for an observer to recognise a known individual at a distance when they are standing, but as soon as the person starts moving, the detection is much better due to the pattern of motion of the individual being observed.[188–190] There are numerous historical citations conveying the ability to recognise an individual by the way they walk, including in less than ideal lighting conditions of moonlight and in hazardous environments such as the events of World War II and the Normandy airborne landings in 1944 with the men of Easy Company of the US Army, as referred to by Stephen Ambrose in *Band of Brothers*.[191]

Stevenage et al. demonstrated that gait can be perceived in adverse lighting conditions and that individuals inexperienced in the task can recognise one another by their gait from video. The study showed an overall identification rate of 50% (greater than by chance alone when applying chi squared statistical testing). The study also revealed the participants had a higher detection rate for gender (33 from 48).[192] A study by Birch et al. showed that various practitioners with a minimum of five years of experience in performing observational gait analysis as part of their main area of practice had correct detection rate of 79% and a 94% precision in distinguishing between a 'suspect walker' and a 'target walker' when the suspect walker was of a different gender.[193] In a separate study by Birch et al., results showed increasing the frame rate (frequency) in the range of 0.25 frames per second (Hz) and 25 frames per second (Hz) had a positive effect on identifying features of gait viewed on CCTV footage, and that correct identifications were still possible at the lower frame rates.[194] Larsen et al. reported 15 Hz (fps) is the preferable recording frequency when looking at some dynamic features of gait, but that frequencies of 5Hz and 2Hz could also provide useful information for identification.[195] Larsen et al. also referred to the significance of the sagittal and frontal planes for obtaining useful information, as did Jokisch[196]; and Geradts[197] indicated the importance of an overhead view (transverse/axial) view) in order for step length to be examined.

Schöllhorn et al.[198] investigated general and specific human gait characteristics quantitatively in a small study of the lower limbs with three-dimensional kinematic and kinetic gait patterns of females wearing shoes of varying heel heights (14, 37, 54 and 87 mm). Both *time continuous* and *time discrete* artificial neural network data analysis procedures were deployed.

The results showed both of the procedures were able to identify individual gait characteristics and *recognition rates of 93.1–100%* for individuals in relation to each heel height state. The individual's gait characteristics were unaltered in changes to heel height up to 54 mm. They concluded, 'the results of this study demonstrated that gait pattern contain general and individual information', and that the time continuous procedure utilising artificial neural networks is useful in identifying particular and general human gait characteristics of the lower limb. The results support other outcomes on the individuality of distinct patterns of motion established in running, discus and javelin throwing.[199–201]

Nixon et al. reported that gait identification is a non-invasive mechanism and has the distinct benefit of being able to be used not only as an instrument for recognition at distance but also for dynamic identity. The recognition of gait can be based on the (static) human shape as well as on movement, suggesting a richer recognition cue.[202]

Horst et al.[203] reported in a study of 57 healthy adult individuals (29 female, 28 male) where the gait analysis data was by supervised 'machine learning' models, based on kinematic and kinetic variables. This was with a view to allow reliable automatic classifications of gait in clinical diagnosis. Subjects walked barefoot, for one stride per trial (in this instance one stride being from right foot heel strike to left foot toe off), and a total of 20 trials per subject were carried out in a single session on a 10 metre pathway at self-selected speed. Subjects wore reflective body markers (head to feet), and ten infra-red cameras recorded three-dimensional body marker trajectories. Two Kistler force plates were utilised to capture three-dimensional ground reaction forces. In brief, a most noticeable aspect of the results was that the tested 'machine learning' models were able to predict the correct class (subject) with a high mean prediction accuracy of 'above 95.4% for ground reaction forces, 99.9% for full body joint angles and 99.9% for lower body joint angles'. The results in the study 'verified the uniqueness of characteristics for individual gait patterns based on kinematic and kinetic variables'. The distinctive character of human gait signatures in this research was quantified using dissimilar linear and non-linear machine learning techniques. The findings substantiate earlier research on the individuality of human gait.[204–206]

Forensic gait analysis is part of a broad sphere of disciplines and techniques in forensic science which have utility in legal matters. Further understanding naturally brings expansion and refinement; these do not occur without that rarity of innovative ability at the outset and from which all else courses, and scientific discoveries have frequently met delay until somebody contemplates the new.[207] The creativity of new tools requires the vision, skills and know how. Imaginative innovation should not be discouraged nor restricted by unrealisitic controls and orders,[208] whilst correct guidance for good practice is sensible and should be followed. But development requires domain which facilitates its disposition. Satisfactory ways of discerning facts are pivotal without which even the facts become fictions.[209] It can also be helpful to bear in mind, as the mathematical area of calculus shows us, there is more than one solution to a problem. Perhaps consider those careful observations of Charles Darwin, including the 'mental powers and instincts of animals' where 'Even the headless oyster seems to profit by experience'.[210] We should appreciate the unchanging fact that, genuine scientific evidence is probabilistic.[211]

REFERENCES

1. Rose, GK. 1983. Clinical gait assessment: a personal view. *Journal of Medical Engineering & Technology*, 7: pp273–279.
2. Chisum, WJ; Turvey, BE. 2000. Evidence dynamics: Locard's exchange principle and crime reconstruction. *Journal of Behavioral Profiling*, 1 (1): pp1–15.
3. Burrow, JG. 2016. Is diurnal variation a factor in bare footprint formation? *Journal of Forensic Identification*, 66 (2): pp107–117.
4. Vosk, T; Emery, AF. 2015. *Forensic Metrology - Scientific Measurement and Inference for Lawyers, Judges and Criminalists*. CRC Press.
5. Collins Aa English Dictionary. 2016. *Twelfth Edition Reprinted with Changes*. Harper Collins Publishers, Glasgow.
6. Webster, N. *American Dictionary of the English Language*. Webster's Dictionary 1828 Online Edition.
7. Mosby's Medical Dictionary. 2017. 10th edition. pp736. Elsevier Inc.
8. Lehman, JF; et al. 1992. Biomechanics of normal gait. *Physical Medicine and Rehabilitation Clinics of North America*, 3: pp 125–138.
9. Murray, MP. 1967. Gait as a total pattern of movement. *American Journal of Physical Medicine*, 46 (1): pp290–333. Williams and Wilkins Co.
10. Andriacchi, TP; Alexander, EJ. 2000. Studies of human locomotion: past, present and future. *Journal of Biomechanics*, 33: pp1217–1224. Elsevier.
11. Southerland, CC. 1996. Gait evaluation in clinical biomechanics. In: Valmassy, RL (ed), *Clinical Biomechanics of the Lower Extremity*, pp152. Mosby.
12. Payton, C; Bartlett, R. Eds. 2008. *Biomechanical Evaluation of Movement in Sport and Exercise Sciences – The British Association of Sport and Exercise Sciences Guidelines*. 1st ed. Routledge, London, UK.
13. Bartlett, R. 2002. *Introduction to Sports Biomechanics*. Taylor and Francis Group.

199

14. Bartlett, R. 1997. *Introduction to Sports Biomechanics*. E & FN Spon, an imprint of Chapman and Hall.

15. Tingley, M; Wilson, C; Biden, E; Knight, WR. 2002. An index to quantify normality of gait in young children. *Gait & Posture*, 16: pp149–158.

16. Kirtley, C. 2006. *Clinical Gait Analysis Theory & Practice*. Churchill Livingstone Elsevier.

17. Pelphrey KA, et al. 2003. Brain activity evoked by the perception of human walking: controlling for meaningful coherent motion. *The Journal of Neuroscience*, 23: pp 6819–6825.

18. Guinness World Records. 2009. *First Use of "Forensic Gait Analysis" Evidence in Court*. pp135. Guinness World Records.

19. Miles, C. 2001. Caught bow-legged: expert witness makes legal history. *The Expert Witness Institute Newsletter*, Spring 2001, pp6–8.

20. Buncombe, A. 2000. Gang leader is unmasked by his bandy-legged gait. *The Independent*, July 2000, pp1.

21. Kelly, HD. 2000. *Old Bailey Central Court, London*. R v Saunders.

22. Kelly, HD. 2019. Forensic podiatry. *Podiatry Now, College of Podiatry*, January 2019, pp16–18.

23. Grant, MG. 2006. Gait. In: Thompson, T; Black, S (eds), *Forensic Human Identification, An Introduction*. pp343–362. CRC Press/Taylor and Francis Group, Boca Raton, FL.

24. Fig 6.2. https://commons.wikimedia.org/wiki/File:BodyPlanes.jpg [Accessed 1 March 2020].

25. Levine, D; Richards, J; Whittle, MW. 2012. *Whittle's Gait Analysis*. 5th ed. pp1–3. Elsevier.

26. Feature. https://www.lexico.com/en/definition/feature [Accessed 1 March 2020].

27. Gonzalez, HE; Manns, A. 1996. Forward head posture: its structural and functional influence on the stomatognathic system, a conceptual study. *Cranio*, 14 (1): pp71–80.

28. Griegel-Morris, P; Larson, K; Mueller-Klaus, K; Oatis, CA. 1992. Incidence of common postural abnormalities in the cervical, shoulder, and thoracic regions and their association with pain in two age groups of healthy subjects. *Physical Therapy*, 72 (6): pp 425–431.

29. Jung-Ho Kang; Rae-Young Park; Su-Jin Lee; Ja-Young Kim; Seo-Ra Yoon; Kwang-Ik Jung. 2012. The effect of the forward head posture on postural balance in long time computer based worker. *Annals of Rehabilitation Medicine*, 36 (1): pp98–104.

30. Yong-Soo Kong; Yu-Mi Kim; Je-Myung Shim. 2017. The effect of modified cervical exercise on smartphone users with forward head posture. *Journal of Physical Therapy Science*, 29 (2).

31. Encyclopedia Britannica. (eds). Somatotype. https://bit.ly/2H2i4po [1 March 2020].

32. Sánchez-Muñoz, C; Sanz, D; Zabala, M. 2007. Anthropometric characteristics, body composition and somatotype of elite junior tennis players. *British Journal of Sports Medicine*, 41 (11): pp793–799.

33. Sheldon, WH. 1954. *Atlas of Men: A Guide for Somatotyping the Adult Male at All Ages.* Harper, New York.

34. Murray, MP. 1967. Gait as a total pattern of movement. *American Journal of Physical Medicine,* 46 (1): pp291–333. Williams & Wilkins.

35. Mosby's Medical Dictionary. 2017. 10th edition. pp31. Elsevier Inc.

36. Wagenaar, RC; van Emmerik, REA. 2000. Resonant frequencies of arms and legs identify different walking patterns. *Journal of Biomechanics,* 33: pp853–861.

37. Levine, D; Richards, J; Whittle, MW. 2012. *Whittle's Gait Analysis.* 5th ed. Elsevier.

38. Dougan, S. 1924. The angle of gait. *American Journal of Physical Anthropology,* 7(2): pp275–279.

39. Root, ML; Orien, WP; Weed, JH. *Normal and Abnormal Function of the Foot. Clinical Biomechanics: Volume 2.* Clinical Biomechanics Corporation, 1977.

40. Morton, DJ. 1932. The angle of gait: a study based upon. *Journal of Bone and Joint Surgery Am,* 14: pp741–754.

41. Boenig, D. 1977. Evaluation of a clinical method of gait analysis. *Physical Therapy,* 57 (7): pp795–798.

42. Valmassy, RL. (Ed). 1996. *Clinical Biomechanics of the Lower Extremities.* pp35. Mosby.

43. Wilkinson, MJ; Menz, HB. 1997. Measurement of gait parameters from footprints: a reliability study. *The Foot,* 7 (1): pp19–23.

44. Curran, SA; Upton, D; Learmouth, ID. 2005. Dynamic and static footprints: comparative calculations for angle and base of gait. *The Foot,* 15: pp40.

45. Wilkinson, MJ; Menz, HB; Raspovic, A. 1995. The measurement of gait parameters from footprints. *The Foot,* 5 (2): pp84–90.

46. Curran, SA; Upton, D; Learmouth, ID. 2005. Dynamic and static footprints: comparative calculations for angle and base of gait. *The Foot,* 15: pp40–46.

47. Levine, D; Richards, J; Whittle, MW. 2012. *Whittle's Gait Analysis.* 5th ed. pp77. Elsevier.

48. Anness, R; Curran MJ. 2018. An investigation into the effect of weight on angle and base of gait. *Journal of Forensic Identification,* 68 (4), pp524–543.

49. Donelan, JM; Kram, R; Kuo, AD. 2002. Simultaneous positive and negative external mechanical work in human walking. *Journal of Biomechanics,* 35: pp117–124.

50. Orendurff, MS; Segal, AD; Klute, GK; Berge, JS; Rohr, ES; Kadel, NJ. 2004. The effect of walking speed on center of mass displacement. *Journal of Rehabilitation Research and Development,* 41 (6A): pp829–834.

51. Eckel, T; Abbey, AN; Butler, RJ; Nunley, JA; Queen, RM. 2012. Effect of increased weight on ankle mechanics and spatial temporal gait mechanics in healthy controls. *Foot and Ankle International,* 33 (11): pp979–983.

52. Attwells, RL; Birrell, SA; Hooper, RH; Mansfield, NJ. 2006. Influence of carrying heavy loads on soldiers' posture, movements and gait. *Journal of Ergonomics,* 49 (14): pp1527–1537.

53. Majumdar, D; Pal, MS; Majumdar, D. 2010. Effects of military load carriage on kinematics of gait. *Ergonomics,* 53 (6): pp 782–791.

54. Bhambhani, Y; Buckley, S; Maikala, R. 1997. Physiological and biomechanical responses during treadmill walking with graded loads. *European Journal of Applied Physiology and Occupational Physiology*, 76: pp544–551.
55. Riley, PO; Paolini, G; Della Croce, U; Paylo, KW; Kerrigan, DC. 2007. A kinematic and kinetic comparison of overground and treadmill walking in healthy subjects. *Gait & Posture*, 26 (1): pp17–24.
56. Steele, E; Bialocerkowski, A; Grimmer, K. 2003. The postural effects of load carriage on young people - a systematic review. *BMC Musculoskeletal Disorders*, 4: article 12.
57. Singh, T; Koh, M. 2009. Effects of backpack load position on spatiatemporal parameters and trunk forward lean. *Gait & Posture*, 29 (1): pp49–53. doi: 10.1016/j.gaitpost.2008.06.006.
58. LaFiandra, M; Wagenaar, RC; Holt, KG; Obusek, JP. 2003. How do load carriage and walking speed influence trunk coordination and stride parameters? *Journal of Bioemchanics*, 36: pp87–95.
59. Wagenaar, RC; Beek WJ. 1992. Hemiplegic gait: a kinematic analysis using walking speed as a basis. *Journal of Biomechanics* 25 (9): pp1007–1015.
60. Gillette, JC; Stevermer, CA; Miller, RH; Meardon, SA; Schwab CV. 2010. The effects of age and type of carrying task on lower extremity kinematics. *Journal of Ergonomics*, 53 (3): pp355–364.
61. 2004. *The Merck Manual of Medical Information*. 2nd ed. pp833. Pocket Books, Simon & Schuster Inc.
62. Meng, H; O'Connor, DP; Lee, B-C, Layne, CS; Gorniak, SL. 2017. Alterations in over-ground walking patterns in obese and overweight adults. *Gait & Posture*, 53: pp145–150.
63. Fischer, AG; Wolf, A. 2015. Assessment of the effects of body weight unloading on overground gait biomechanical parameters. *Clinical Biomechanics*, 30: pp454–461.
64. Fischer, AG; Debbi, EM; Wolf, A. 2015. Effects of body weight unloading on electromyographic activity during overground walking. *Electromyography & Kinesiology*, 25: 709–714.
65. Fischer, AG; Wolf, A. 2016. Body weight unloading modifications on frontal plane joint movements, impulses and center of pressure during overground gait. *Clinical Biomechanics*, 39: pp77–83.
66. Anness, R; Curran, MJ. 2018. An investigation into the effect of weight on angle and base of gait. *Journal of Forensic Identification*, 68 (4): pp524–543.
67. Wall, JC; Nottrodt, JW; Charteris, J. 1981. The effect of uphill and downhill walking on pelvic oscillations in the transverse plane. *Ergonomics*, 24: pp 807–816.
68. Lange, GW; Hintermeister, RA; Schlegel, T; Dillman, CJ; Steadman, JR. 1996. Electromyographic and kinematic analysis of graded treadmill walking and the implications for knee rehabilitation. *Journal of Orthopaedic & Sports Physical Therapy*, 23: pp294–301.
69. Leroux, A; Fung, J; Barbeau, B. 1999. Adaptation of the walking pattern to uphill walking in normal and spinal cord injured subjects. *Experimental Brain Research*, 126: pp359–368.

70. Leroux, A; Fung, J; Barbeau, H. 2002. Postural adaptation to walking on inclined surfaces: I. Normal strategies. *Gait & Posture*, 15: pp64–74.
71. Lockhart, TE; Smith, JL; Woldstad, JC. 2005. Effects of aging on the biomechanics of slips and falls. *Human Factors*, 47 (4): pp708–729. doi: 10.1518/0018720055775571014.
72. Li, KW. 2003. An ergonomics assessment of four female shoes: friction coefficients of the soles on the floors and electromyographic activities in the shank when walking. *Journal of the Chinese Institute of Industrial Engineers*, 20 (5): pp472–480.
73. Pollard, JP; Heberger, JR; Dempsey, PG. 2015. Slip potential for commonly used inclined grated metal walkways. *IIE Transactions on Occupational Ergonomics and Human Factors*, 3 (2): pp115–126. Published online 2015 Jul 16. doi: 10.1080/21577323.2014.1001501.
74. Chang, W-R; Leclercq, S; Lockhart, TE; Haslam, R. 2016. State of science: occupational slips, trips and falls on the same level. *Ergonomics*, 59 (7): pp1–23.
75. Courtney, TK; Sorock, GS; Manning, DP; Collis, JW; Holbein-Jenny, MA. 2001. Occupational slip, trip, and fall-related injuries - can the contribution of slipperiness be isolated? *Ergonomics*, 44 (13): pp 1118–1137.
76. Beschorner, KE; Iraqi, A; Redfern, MS; Cham, R; Li, Y. 2019. Predicting slips based on the STM 603 whole-footwear tribometer under different coefficient of friction testing conditions. *Ergonomics*, 62 (5): pp668–681. doi: 10.1080/00140139.2019.1567828.
77. Pearson, H. (Ed). 2015. *Pleasure and Pain. 'Objects of Desire: The Cult of Shoes'*. pp11. V&A Publishing, London.
78. McDowell, C. 1989. *Shoes Fashion and Fantasy*. 1st ed. Thames and Hudson, London.
79. Rossi, W. 1992. *The Sex Life of the Foot and Shoe*. 2nd ed. Krieger, Melbourne, FL.
80. Boucher, F. 1996. *A History of Costume in the West*. Thames and Hudson, New York.
81. Kippen, C. 2003. A brief social history of wooden shoes. *British Journal of Podiatry*, 6 (1): pp12–16.
82. Walford, J. 2007. *The Seductive Shoe*. pp9. Thames & Hudson Ltd, London.
83. Church's Footwear. 2018. The church's story. https://bit.ly/2XnTVnE [Accessed 1 March 2020].
84. Design Museum. 2012. *Fifty Shoes that Changed the World*. Conran Octopus Ltd.
85. McQueen, A. 2015. Edited by Claire Wilcox. *'Walking Out', by Helen Persson*. pp111–115. V&A, Publishing, London.
86. Kenwrick, P. 2003. Safety footwear. *Podiatry Now*, pp16–17. Translated summary of a study by Amblard, N; Cabanne, E; Huertas, C; Soulat, J-M. *Published in Le Podologue*. pp22–25.
87. Forrest, JD; Tyrell, W. 2010. *Neale's Disorders of the Foot*. 8th ed. Chapter 18, Footwear, pp455.
88. White, JM. 1994. Custom shoe therapy. *Clinics in Podiatric Medicine and Surgery*, 11 (2): pp259–270.

89. Forrest, JD; Tyrell, W. 2010. *Neale's Disorders of the Foot*. 8th ed. Chapter 18, Footwear, pp470.
90. Hendry, GH; Brenton-Rule, A; Barr, G; Rome, K. 2015. Footwear experiences of people with inflammatory arthritis. *Arthritis Care and Research, 67*: pp1164–1172.
91. Rome, K; Frecklington, M; McNair, PJ; Gow, P; Dalbeth, N. 2011. Footwear characteristics and factors influencing footwear choice in participants with gout. *Arthritis Care and Research, 63*: pp1599–1604.
92. Silvester, RN; Williams, AE; Dalbeth, N; Rome, K. 2010. Choosing shoes; a preliminary study into the challenges facing clinicians in assessing footwear for rheumatoid patients. *Journal of Foot and Ankle Research, 3*: pp24.
93. Scholl, W. 1915. *The Human Foot: Anatomy, Deformities and Treatment*. Foot Specialist Publishing Ltd, Chicago.
94. Linder, M; Saltzman, CL; 1998. A history of medical scientists on high heels. *International Journal of Health Sciences, 28* (2): pp201–225.
95. Arnadottir, SA; Mercer, VS; 2000. Effects of footwear on measurements of balance and gait in women between the ages of 65 and 93 years. *Physical Therapy, 80* (1): pp17–27.
96. Burnfield, JM; Few, CD; Mohamed, FS; Perry, J. 2004. The influence of walking speed and footwear on plantar pressures in older adults. *Clinical Biomechanics, 19* (1): pp78–84.
97. Franklin, S; Grey, MJ; Heneghan, N; Bowen, L; Li, F-X. 2015. Barefoot vs common footwear. A systematic review of the kinematic, kinetic and muscle activity differences during walking. *Gait & Posture, 42* (3): pp230–239.
98. Forrest, JD; Tyrrell, W. 2010. *Disorders of the Foot*. 8th ed. Chapter 18, pp 454. Churchill Livingstone Elsevier.
99. Burrow, G. 2010. *Neale's Disorders of the Foot*. 8th ed. Chapter 1, Examination and diagnosis in clinical management. pp7. Churchill Livingstone Elsevier.
100. Anderson, EG; Black, JA. 1997. Examination and assessment. In: Lorimer, D, et al. (eds), *Neale's Common Foot Disorders; Diagnosis and Management*. Churchill Livingstone.
101. Newton, I. 1687. Newton's laws of motion. In: *Philosophiæ Naturalis Principia Mathematica (Mathematical Principles of Natural Philosophy)*, first published in 1687.
102. Hamm, ED. 1989. Track identification: an historical overview. *Journal of Forensic Identification, 39* (6): pp333–338.
103. Cassidy, MJ. 1980. *Footwear Identification*. Royal Canadian Mounted Police, Canadian Government Publishing Centre, Hull, QC.
104. Bodziak, WJ. 2000. *Footwear Impression Evidence: Detection, Recovery and Examination*. 2nd ed. pp1–178; 197–374. CRC Press, Boca Raton, FL.
105. McCourt, FJ. 2000. A problem of attribution in forensic podiatry. *British Journal of Podiatry, 3* (4): pp107.
106. Vernon, W; Brodie, B; Dimaggio, J; Gunn, N; Kelly, H; Nirenberg, M; Reel, S; Walker, J. 2009. *Forensic Podiatry: Role and Scope of Practice (In the Context of Forensic Human Identification)*. International Association for Identification, USA.

107. DiMaggio, JA; Vernon, W. 2011. *Forensic Podiatry: Principles and Methods.* Humana Press.
108. Hilderbrand, DS. 2013. *Footwear the Missed Evidence.* 3rd ed. Staggs Publishing, Wildomar, CA.
109. Bodziak, WJ; Hammer, L; Johnson, GM; Schenck, R. 2012. Determining the significance of outsole wear characteristics during the forensic examination of footwear impression evidence. *Journal of Forensic Identification,* 62 (3): pp254–272.
110. Schuster, OF. 1915. Diagnostic points in cases of mechanical foot trouble. *Pedic Items,* 5(9): pp48–52.
111. Charlesworth, F. 1935. *Chiropody Theory and Practice.* 1st ed. Actinic Press Ltd, London.
112. Gottlieb, A. 1939. The foot in general practice. *The Chiropodist,* 26: pp316–323.
113. Lake, NC. 1943. *The Foot.* 3rd ed. Bailliere Tindall and Cox, London.
114. Hanby, JH; Walker, HE. 1949. *The Principles of Chiropody.* Bailliere, Tindall and Cox, London.
115. Gibbard, LC. 1958. The interpretation of wear marks on shoes as an aid to the diagnosis of foot troubles: part 1. *British Chiropody Journal,* 23(9): pp231–233a.
116. Gibbard, LC. 1958. The interpretation of wear marks on shoes as an aid to the diagnosis of foot troubles: part 2. *British Chiropody Journal,* 23(10): pp259–262.
117. Charlesworth, F. 1961. *Chiropody Theory and Practice.* Actinic Press Ltd, London.
118. Lucock, LJ. 1967. Identifying the wearer of worn footwear. *Journal of the Forensic Science Society,* 7(2): pp62–70.
119. Lucock, LJ. 1980. Identification from footwear. *The Chiropodist,* 35(9): pp343–350.
120. Vernon, W. 2000. The functional analysis of shoe wear patterns. PhD thesis. Sheffield Hallam University.
121. Vernon, W; Parry, A; Potter, M. 2004. A theory of shoe wear pattern influence incorporating a new paradigm for the podiatric medical profession. *Journal of the American Podiatric Medical Association,* 94 (3): pp261–268.
122. Forrest, JD; Tyrrell, W. 2010. *Neale's Disorders of the Foot,* Chapter 18, pp467. Churchill Livingstone Elsevier.
123. McCourt, FJ. 2000. A problem of attribution in forensic podiatry. *British Journal of Podiatry,* 3 (4): pp110.
124. Cheng, YK. 2016. CCTV footage used to link suspect to bloody footwear impression. *Journal of Forensic Identification,* 66 (6): pp517–525.
125. Bowen, TR. 2010. *Ethics and the Practice of Forensic Science.* CRC Press, Boca Raton, FL.
126. Health and Safety Executive (UK). 2008. *Work with Display Screen Equipment.* 2nd ed. reprinted. https://bit.ly/2sG9SV1 [Accessed 1 March 2020].
127. Health and Safety Executive (UK). 2013. Working with display screen equipment (DSE). A brief guide. https://bit.ly/1fyo1c5 [Accessed 1 March 2020].
128. *Criminal Procedure Rules.* October 2015 as amended April 2018 and April 2019. *Part 19. Expert Evidence.*

129. *Criminal Procedure Rules. Practice Directions.* April 2019.
130. *Civil Procedure Rules. Part 35 - Experts and Assessors.*
131. *Civil Procedure Rules. Practice Direction 35 - Experts and Assessors.* This practice direction supplements CPR part 35.
132. Forensic Science Regulator. 2016. Information. Legal obligations. *FSR-I-400.* Issue 4.
133. Forensic Science Regulator. 2017. Codes of practice and conduct. *For forensic science providers and practitioners in the Criminal Justice System.* Issue 4. February 2017.
134. Forensic Science Regulator. 2014. Guidance. Validation. *FSR-G-201.* Issue 1.
135. Forensic Science Regulator. 2017. Guidance on the content of reports issued by expert witnesses in the Criminal Justice System in England and Wales. *FSR-G-200.* Issue 1. Archived 14 February 2019.
136. Forensic Science Regulator. 2019. Guidance on the content of reports issued by expert witnesses in the Criminal Justice System in England and Wales. *FSR-G-200.* Issue 2. Archived 17 April 2019.
137. Forensic Science Regulator. 2019. Guidance on the content of reports issued by expert witnesses in the Criminal Justice System in England and Wales. *FSR-G-200.* Issue 3.
138. Academy of Medical Royal Colleges. 2019. *Acting as an Expert or Professional Witness. Guidance for Healthcare Professionals.* May 2019.
139. Abboud, R; Baker, R; Stebbins, J. 2017. *Forensic Gait Analysis a Primer for Courts.* 1st ed. The Royal Society of Edinburgh, London, UK.
140. Forensic Science Regulator (UK). 2019. *Image Enhancement and Image Comparison: Provision of Opinion.* Regulatory notice 01/2019. Effective date 17/07/2019.
141. Triplett, M; Cooney, L. 2006. The etiology of ACE-V and its proper use: an exploration of the relationship between ACE-V and the scientific method of hypothesis testing. *Journal of Forensic Identification,* 56 (3): pp345–355.
142. Dettori, J. 2012. Class or level of evidence: epidemiologic basis. *Evidence-Based Spine-Care Journal,* 3 (3): pp9–12. doi: 10.1055/s-0032-1327804.
143. Scally, AJ. 2014. A practical introduction to medical statistics. *The Obstetrician & Gynaecologist,* 16: pp121–128.
144. Cook, R; Evett, IW; Jackson, G; Jones, PJ; Lambert, JA. 1998. A hierarchy of propositions: deciding which level to address in casework. *Science & Justice,* 38 (4): pp231–239.
145. Wai-Ching Leung. 2002. The prosecutors fallacy: a pitfall in interpreting probabilities in forensic evidence. *Medicine, Science and the Law,* 42(1): pp41–50.
146. Triplett, M; Cooney, L. 2006. The etiology of ACE-V and its proper use: an exploration of the relationship between ACE-V and the scientific method of hypothesis testing. *Journal of Forensic Identification,* 56 (3): pp347.
147. Hirson, A. 2018. Forensic science. Death knell to UK forensic science. *Expert Witness Newsletter.* Summer 2018, pp8–9. Expert Witness Institute.

148. Hirson, A. 2018. Forensic science. Death knell to UK forensic science. *Expert Witness Newsletter*. Summer 2018, pp9. Expert Witness Institute.
149. Forensic Science Regulator. 2014. Guidance. Validation. *FSR-G-201*.
150. Hasson, F; Keeney, S; McKenna, H. 2000. Research guidelines for the Delphi survey technique. *Journal of Advanced Nursing*, 32 (4): pp1008–1015.
151. Southerland, CC. 1996. Gait evaluation in clinical biomechanics. In: Valmassy, R. (ed), *Clinical Biomechanics of the Lower Extremities*. Mosby-Year Book, Inc.
152. Cranage, S; Banwell, H; Williams, CM. 2016. Gait and lower limb observation of paediatrics (GALLOP): development of a consensus based paediatric podiatry and physiotherapy standardised recording proforma. *Journal of Foot and Ankle Research*, 9: pp8. doi: 10.1186/s13047-016-0139-4.
153. Hammer, L; Duffy, K; Fraser, J; Nic Daéid, N. 2013. A study of the variability in footwear impression comparison conclusions. *Journal of Forensic Identification*, 63 (2): pp205–218.
154. Jones, J; Hunter, D. 1995. Consensus methods for medical and health services research. *BMJ*, 311 (7001): pp 376–380.
155. Banwell, H; Macintosh, S; Thewlis, D; Landorf, K. 2014. Consensus based recommendations of Australian podiatrists for the prescription of foot orthoses for symptomatic flexible pes planus in adults. *Journal of Foot and Ankle Research*, 7 (1): pp49.
156. *Buckley v Rice Thomas*, 1554.
157. Hand, L. 1901. Historical and practical considerations regarding expert testimony. *Harvard Law Review*, 15: pp40–58.
158. Lord Campbell, Lord Chancellor, in the case of Tracey Peerage [1839,1843 X Clark & Finnelly 190–191].
159. Golan, T. 2007. *Laws of Men and Laws of Nature. The History of Scientific Expert Testimony in England and America*. Harvard University Press.
160. Saks, MJ; Risinger, DM; Rosenthal, R; Thompson, WC. 2003. Context effects in forensic science: a review and application of the science of science to crime laboratory practice in the United States. *Science and Justice*, 43 (2): pp77–90.
161. Bias. https://en.wikipedia.org/wiki/List_of_cognitive_biases [Accessed 1 March 2020].
162. Curtit, J. 2009. Confirmation bias. *Identification News*. 39(4), August/September, pp5.
163. Pannucci, CJ; Wilkins, EG. 2010. Identifying and avoiding bias in research. *Plastic and Reconstructive Surgery*, 126 (2): pp619–625.
164. Higgins, JPT Thomas J, Chandler J, Cumpston M, Li T, Page MJ, Welch VA (editors). 2011. *Cochrane Handbook for Systematic Reviews of Interventions*. Version 6.0 (updated July 2019). Available from www.training.cochrane.org/handbook. https://bit.ly/2VBQRC8 [Accessed 01 March 2020].
165. Kruger,J; Dunning, D. 1999. Unskilled and unaware of it: how difficulties in recognizing one's own incompetence lead to inflated self-assessments. *Journal of Personality and Social Psychology*, 77 (6): pp1121–34.
166. Taylor, SE; Brown, JD. 1998. Illusion and well-being: a social psychological perspective on mental health. *Psychological Bulletin*, 103(2): pp193–210.

167. Fitch, BF. 2010. Good decisions tips and strategies for avoiding psychological traps. *Auspol*, 3: pp18–21.
168. Oswald, ME; Grosjean, S. 2004. Confirmation bias. In: Pohl, RF (ed), *Cognitive Illusions: A Handbook on Fallacies and Biases in Thinking, Judgement and Memory.* pp79–96. Psychology Press, Hove, UK.
169. Hylton, J. *The Complete Works of William Shakespeare.* http://shakespeare.mit.edu/ https://bit.ly/P1WOSY [Accessed 01 March 2020].
170. Zajac, FE; Neptune, RR; Kautz, SA. 2002. Biomechanics and muscle coordination of human walking. Part I. Introduction to concepts, power transfer, dynamics and simulations. *Gait & Posture*, 16: pp215–232.
171. Cappozzo, A; Marchetti, M; Tosi, V. (eds). 1992. *Biolocomotion: A Century of Research Using Moving Pictures.* pp356. Promograph, Rome.
172. Cappozzo, A; Paul, JP. 1997. Instrumental observation of human movement: historical development. In: Allard, P; Cappozzo, A; Lundberg, A; Vaughan, C (eds), *Three-Dimensional Analysis of Human Locomotion.* pp1–25. Wiley & Sons, New York.
173. Tagawa, Y; Yamashita, T. 2001. Analysis of human abnormal walking using zero moment joint: required compensatory actions. *Journal of Biomechanics*, 34: pp783–790.
174. Bertillon, A. 1896. *Signaletic Instructions Including the Theory and Practice of Anthropometrical Identification.* Werner.
175. Sutherland, DH. 2001. The evolution of clinical gait analysis part1: kinesiological EMG. *Gait & Posture*, 14: pp61–70.
176. Andriacchi, TP; Alexander, EJ. 2000. Studies of human locomotion: past, present and future. *Journal of Biomechanics*, 33: pp 1217–1224.
177. Kagan, B. 2015. Forensic gerontology: a podiatrist's perspective of the dynamic "functioning" foot and the need for research to develop an interpretive approach. *Journal of Forensic Identification*, 65 (6): pp907–912.
178. Neptune, RR; Kautz, SA; Zajac, FE. 2001. Contributions of the individual ankle plantar flexors to support, forward progression and swing initiation during walking. *Journal of Biomechanics*, 34: pp1387–1398.
179. Rothbart, BA; Estabrook, L. 1988. Excessive pronation: a major biomechanical determinant in the development of Chondromalacia and pelvic lists. *Journal of Manipulative and Physiological Therapeutics*, 11 (5): pp373–379.
180. Andriacchi, TP; Andersson, GB; Fermier, RW; Stern, D; Galante, JO. 1980. A study of lower-limb mechanics during stair climbing. *Journal of Bone and Joint Surgery*, 62: pp749–757.
181. Yang, SX; Larsen, PK; Alkjaer, T; Simonsen, EB; Lynnerup, N. 2014. Variability and similarity of gait as evaluated by joint angles: implications for forensic gait analysis. *Journal of Forensic Sciences*, 59 (2): pp494–504.
182. Pataky, TC; Mu, T; Bosch, K; Rosenbaum, D; GoulermaS, JY. 2012. Gait recognition: highly unique dynamic plantar pressure patterns among 104 individuals. *Journal of the Royal Society Interface*, 9 (69): pp790–800.
183. Browne, T; Curran, MJ; Vernon, DW. 2015. How useful is thematic analysis as an elicitation technique for analyzing video of human gait in forensic podiatry? *Journal of Forensic Identification*, 65 (6): pp999–1012.

184. Yang, SX; Larsen, PK; Alkjaer, T; Simonsen, EB; Lynnerup. 2014. Variability and similarity of gait as evaluated by joint angles: implications for forensic gait analysis. *Journal of Forensic Sciences*, 59(2): pp494 doi: https://doi.org/10.1111/1556-4029.1232210.1111/1556-4029.12322.

185. Koenig, BE; Lacey, DS; Richards, GB. 2012. Video frame comparisons in digital video authenticity analyses. *Journal of Forensic Identification*, 62 (2): pp165–182.

186. Bouchrika, I; Goffredo, M; Carter, J; Nixon, M. 2011. On using gait in forensic biometrics. *Journal of Forensic Sciences*, 56 (4): pp 882–889.

187. Boulgouris, NV; Chi, ZX. 2007. Human gait recognition based on the matching of body components. *Pattern Recognition*, 40: pp1763–70.

188. Schollhorn, WI; Nigg, B; Stefanyshyn, DJ; Liu, W. 2002. Identification of individual walking patterns using time discrete and time continuous data sets. *Gait & Posture*, 15: pp180–186.

189. Cutting, JE; Kozlowski, LT. 1977. Recognising friends by their walk: gait perception without familiarity cues. *Bulletin of the Psychonomic Society*, 9: pp353–356.

190. Johansson, G. 1973. Visual perception of biological motion and a model for its analysis. *Perception & Psychophysics*, 14: pp201–211.

191. Ambrose, SE. 2016. *Band of Brothers*. pp74. Simon & Schuster, London.

192. Stevenage, SL; Nixon, M; Vince, K. 1999. Visual analysis of gait as a cue to identity. *Applied Cognitive Psychology*, 13: pp513–526.

193. Birch, I; Ray, L; Christou, A; Fernando, M; Harrison, N; Paul, F. 2013. The reliability of suspect recognition based on gait analysis from CCTV footage. *Science and Justice*, 53 (3): pp339–342.

194. Birch, I; Vernon, W; Burrow, G; Walker, J. 2014. The effect of frame rate on the ability of experienced gait analysts to identify characteristics of gait from closed circuit television footage. *Science and Justice*, 54 (2): pp159–163.

195. Larsen, PK; Simonsen, EB; Lynnerup, N. 2008. Gait analysis in forensic medicine. *Journal of Forensic Sciences*, 53 (5): pp1149–1153.

196. Jokisch, D; Daum, I; Troje, NF. 2006. Self recognition versus recognition of others by biological motion: viewpoint-dependent effects. *Perception*, 35 (7): pp911–920.

197. Geradts, ZJ; Merlijn, M; de Groot, G; Bijhold, J. 2002. Use of gait parameters of persons in video surveillance systems. In: *Proceedings of SPIE - The International Society of Optical Engineering*, 4709. pp16–24. doi:10.1117/12.474735.

198. Schöllhorn, WI; Nigg, BM; Stefanyshyn, DJ; Liu, W. 2002. Identification of individual walking patterns using time discrete and time continuous data sets. *Gait & Posture* 15: pp180–186.

199. Bauer, H-U; Schöllhorn, WI. 1997. Self-organising maps for the analysis of complex movement patterns. *Neural Processing Letters*, 5: pp 193–199.

200. Bauer, H-U; Schöllhorn, WI. 1998. Identifying individual movement styles in high performance sports by means of self-organizing Kohonen maps. In: Riehle, HJ; Vieten, M (eds), *Proceedings of the XVI ISBS 1998*. pp574–577. Konstanz University Press, Konstanz.

201. Schöllhorn, WI; Bauer, H-U. 1998. Erkennung von individuellen Lauf-mustern mit Hilfe von neuronalen Netzen (recognition of individual running patterns by means of artificial neural nets). In: Mester, J; Perl, J (eds), *Informatik im Sport. Cologne: Sport Buch Strauss.* pp169–176.
202. Nixon, MS; Carter, JN; Shuttler, JD; Grant, MG. 2002. New advances in automatic gait recognition. *Information Security Technical Report,* 7(4): pp23–25.
203. Horst, F; Lapuschkin, S; Samek, W; Müller, K-R; Schöllhorn, WI. 2019. Explaining the unique nature of individual gait patterns with deep learning. *Scientific Reports,* 9 (1): pp2391.
204. Horst, F; Mildner, M; Schöllhorn, WI. 2017. One-year persistence of individual gait patterns identified in a follow-up study – a call for individualised diagnose and therapy. *Gait & Posture,* 58: pp476–480.
205. Janssen, D; Schöllhorn, WI; Newell, KM; Jäger, JM; Rost, F; Vehof, K. 2011. Diagnosing fatigue in gait patterns by support vector machines and self-organizing maps. *Human Movement Science,* 30 (5): pp966–975.
206. Janssen, D; Lubienetzki, J; Folling, K; Kokenge, H; Davids, K. 2008. Recognition of emotions in gait patterns by means of artificial neural nets. *Journal of Nonverbal Behavior,* 32 (2): pp79–92.
207. Thouless, RH. 1974. *Straight and Crooked Thinking.* 3rd ed. pp83. Pan Books, London.
208. Evett, IW; Jackson, G; Lambert, JA; McCrossan, S. 2000. The impact of the principles of evidence interpretation on the structure and content of statements. *Science & Justice,* 40 (4): pp233–239.
209. Laing, RD. 1967. *The Politics of Experience and the Bird of Paradise.* Chapter 1. Persons and experience; experience as evidence. pp15. First published 1967, Reprinted in 1990. Penguin Books, London.
210. Darwin, C; Stauffer, RC. Edited from manuscript. 1987. *Charles Darwin's Natural Selection, Being the Second Part of His Big Species Book Written from 1856–1858. Mental Powers and Instincts of Animals.* pp472. Cambridge University Press.
211. O'Connor, C; Weatherall, JO. 2019/2020. Why we trust lies. *Scientific American.* Special Edition. 28 (5): pp110–115.

7

Height Estimation Using the Foot or Lower Limb as a Dimension

Contents

INTRODUCTION

Living stature is defined as the maximum height attained during one's lifetime.[1] Identification of dismembered human remains, in particular those of the foot or feet, in the case of forensic podiatry, can be of paramount importance in forensic/medico-legal investigations. Stature

211

estimation is one of the primary tasks before a forensic scientist/image analyst, but not necessarily for a forensic podiatrist. When an individual foot is subjected to forensic/medico-legal examination, areas such as somatometry (classification of people according to body form, physiological and psychological characteristics), osteology and radiology examinations can all assist in the determination of primary indicators of identification, such as gender, age and stature. This would usually be expected to fall into the area of forensic anthropology, and the forensic podiatrist can add further opinion in related aspects as deemed appropriate and on a case by case basis. For example, could aspects of the deceased's gait be commented upon from the presence of bony erosions in the hip or other joints; what could these erosions indicate with relation to the age of the deceased; are they likely to be caused by a metabolic, nutritional or other disorder, or by the ageing process. Where automated measurement systems are developed to perform tasks, then of course other skill sets and areas of expertise are needed in the production of algorithms utilised for such purposes.

As science and areas of expertise advance and research areas develop, this can help make the identification process more reliable.[2] Anthropometric techniques (anthropometry – the study of human body measurements, especially on a comparative basis) are commonly used by anthropologists and adopted by medical scientists to estimate body size for over a hundred years.[3] Interestingly, anthropology is described as having a relatively new role in the domain of identification of the living, although this area is still under represented in regard to research activity and seeks multi-disciplinary research and working relationships, suggesting a future goal for the anthropological community could be in the creation of working groups in order to coordinate research which applies traditional methods on different populations, so that results may be pooled and published in a homogeneous and coherent fashion.[3] This is an area in which forensic podiatry can input when it comes to height determination from feet, footprints and foot dimensions.

Podiatry is a profession in its own right and forensic podiatry is a specific area of podiatry. As with any area of practice, experts must remain within their area of expertise for whilst it is acknowledged that an expert can have expertise in one area, it does not follow that they do so in another. The courts are very clear on this. With that in mind, it is worthy of mention that all experts, whether healthcare professionals or otherwise, must be careful that they do not encroach on other areas of expertise in any way, as this may be used by counsel in court and risks the practitioner being in breach of regulatory codes of conduct or standards of practice (for example, the General Medical Council, General Dental Council, Health and Care Professions Council, Nursing and Midwifery Council and the like who have long regulated by law, practitioners standards of conduct, performance and ethics in the UK). It should of course be remembered that some areas of practitioners expertise may, on occasion, have an element of overlap.

A basic step in resolving a criminal case is the identification of the victim. This can be especially challenging when the remains are decomposed and poorly skeletonized.[4] When considering such cases, age, sex, population affinity and stature can provide essential information to start a criminal investigation.[5] *Locard's Exchange Principle*[6] (also known as *Locard's Principle*) is worthy of recall here as this confers that the perpetrator of a crime will bring something into the crime scene and leave with something from it – and that both can be used as forensic evidence, formulating the basic principle of forensic science that, 'every contact leaves a trace'.

Law enforcement officers may not be able to accept as accurate or do not have eyewitnesses who can provide height estimates of suspects in crime scene investigations. However, footprints, either of the barefoot or more commonly in the Western world, shoeprints (or the footprint on the insole of a shoe), could provide opportunities for estimating height as a characteristic in helping to identify, or, eliminate a suspect. Estimation of a living height can be made possible using various dimensions of the lower extremity. However, caution is needed as the forensic expert must consider differences between populations in order to apply functions as such to others. According to some estimations, characteristics display population-specific variation and therefore need further attention for major populations of the world[7].

In the area of closed-circuit television (CCTV) and forensic gait analysis, studies have been attempted in estimating height from images with some success – again careful reading of the research is needed before this can be used. For example, this can be illustrated by the phrase 'given unchanged camera settings', which is an important consideration in three-dimensional modelling of a crime scene. Forensic experts engaged in such work need to be familiar with such tools and which are possibly not available to most podiatry practitioners in this regard and should therefore be treated with caution.[8]

213

HEIGHT ESTIMATION USING THE
FOOT AND LOWER LIMB

Various lower limb areas have been utilised for comparison and estimations of height. For example, trochanteric height of the femur, thigh length, lower leg length, leg length, foot height, foot length and foot breadth,[9] the calcaneus,[10] foot length,[11,12] knee height[13] the femur,[14,15] tibia and ulnar,[16,17] metatarsals,[18,19] stride length,[20] footprints,[21] long bone lengths,[22] anterior superior iliac spines,[23] static and dynamic footprints,[24,25] foot and hand[26] or foot and shoe[27] measurements.

Different populations have also been studied such as Indo-Mauritian,[16] Sudanese Arabs,[28] South Africans of European descent,[10] South Africans,[18] Portuguese,[19] Egyptians,[29] Japanese,[30] Israeli,[31]Indian,[21,32] Turkish,[33] Thai,[34] Oriya population,[35] South Indians,[23] Bulgarians[36] and other population groups, e.g. Gujjars of North India,[37] Rajbanshi (North Bengal),[38] critically ill patients[13] and school aged children.[12] Height estimation of US people was conducted but was based on army cadets[39] and therefore could not be considered representative of the broader US population.

To date there is limited information regarding Caucasians and those of Europe, USA and UK as to which lower limb measurements would be useful to determine height estimation and therefore forensic podiatrists must be aware of the current limitations of the evidence base in this area. According to Reel et al., if a link is established between a crime and a footprint, and stature can be estimated from the dimensions of that footprint, then this can inform the case in conjunction with other evidence recovered at the scene.[24] Hens et al. state that despite a long history of investigation, stature estimation remains plagued by two methodology problems:

1. The choice of the statistical estimator
2. The choice of the reference population from which to derive the parameters[40]

The *anatomical* method, also referred to as the *fully* method, reconstructs stature by summing the measurements of the skeletal elements contributing to height (e.g. all the bones) and adding a correction factor for the soft tissues.

The *mathematical* method relates to the derivation of formulae applied directly to estimate stature from a given bone or part of the body. The mathematical method makes use of the high linear correlation between the body parts and stature, utilizing a regression equation that reflects the relationship between an individual's stature and the body part. This mathematical method uses both regression analysis and/or multiplication factor (MF) processes. Regression analysis is an approach used to examine the relationship between a dependent variable and one or more independent variables. In stature estimation, the approaches in the forensic anthropological literature typically consider stature as the dependent variable (y), which is predicted by independent variables such as a bone length (x). The correlation is not however perfect. When regression methods are employed, it is commonly reported with a 95% prediction interval, which indicates that 95% of individuals who have these same bone (or footprint) measurements will have a stature that falls within that interval. However, that indicates 5% of cases will fall out of that interval. It is important that regression approaches utilize formulae that are specific to the sex, ancestry and temporal cohort of the unknown individual. (Temporal cohort in this context is a group of people who were alive or existed during the same time period).

In anthropology, the main measurement used at the beginning of the last century was that of a percentage. For example, the foot or any body part could be comprised of a percentage of the full body height. According to Giles and Vallindigham, 'Martin' has been recognised as a standard reference for physical anthropologists who suggested foot length relative to height amounts to 15%, whilst Olivier suggested this should be 15.5% which could amount to a 6 cm variation.[39] Again, caution is needed as there is some evidence that the relationship between height and foot length is not constant throughout the life cycle and may alter with age – both at the beginning and the end of the life cycle. For example, there is a sex difference in reaching adult height: the median age for adult height in males is 21.2 years and for females is 17.3 years,[41] which may decrease as early as in the fifth decade when there is shrinkage in the vertebral column.[42] One may argue that as that research is from some years ago (1972 and 1977), that newer or more recent evidence is required to substantiate the findings, or otherwise.

One area to be considered is the 'error of estimate' in the various mathematical approaches employed. When the *multiplication factor process* in the mathematical model is used, the error of estimate is usually large and may be attributed to the fact that this method utilizes the mean values of stature and dimensions and does not take into consideration the range and variation in the data.[43] While ratios have been used to estimate stature, modern practice usually appears to use regression equations, both Model I and Model II:

Model I: Ordinary Least Squares (OLS)
Model II: Major Axis (MA) and Reduced Major Axis (RMA)

However, population-specific regression equations have been proposed. The literature is growing on stature estimation methods based on the total length of the foot or various foot measurements.[21,23,26,37,44,45,46] Given that the populations are small and specific, care is of course needed in the analysis, interpretation and usage of the data.

The results of any study must be carefully analysed. Some authors suggest that changes in physical stature may indicate changes in (net) nutritional status and that both the quality and quantity of food intake depend on economic conditions, particularly in economies in which food expenditure is an important component of the total budget.[47] In such economies, heights are influenced by economic activity. Perkins et al. suggest a positive association between socioeconomic position (SEP) and height, with lower SEP individuals being shorter and their results suggesting that inequalities in several health outcomes for low SEP adults may be reflected in inequalities in height, at least in India, albeit a cross-sectional study and a large sample size.[48]

The proportions of the different skeletal parts that comprise stature vary during growth. These proportions, it is suggested, can also be affected by external factors (e.g. nutrition and physical activity) and internal factors (e.g. genotype), and diachronic changes in stature at the population level can be related to short- to long-term stress and must be considered when making estimates of height/stature.[49]

Taking all these factors into account, podiatrists may receive enquiries from a variety of directions to consider estimating stature. On the whole, there will be two main areas that podiatrists may be able to help with on this determination:

1. Height estimation from images or CCTV footage.
2. Where footprints have been left or are found at a crime scene.

Footprints can be found as barefoot prints, socked footprints or as the foot outline located within footwear which could be found at a crime scene.

Although barefoot prints maybe less likely to regularly occur in some of the modern developed countries, with modern forensic techniques the proposition that they can be found is limited, mainly by the techniques used by the crime scene investigators and some lack of awareness of the possibility of such trace elements. One area in relation to this in which forensic podiatry still has to establish itself is that of the contribution it can make to crime scene investigations. Fingerprints are routinely sought at crime scenes and investigators are well aware of the need not to touch areas and to look for possible fingerprint evidence along with that of DNA

216

and other evidence, but little consideration seems to be given to the fact that *in almost all crimes the perpetrator needs to enter and exit and that is usually achieved by using their feet!*

HEIGHT ESTIMATION FROM IMAGES
OR VIDEO FOOTAGE

This is potentially the domain of the image analyst and, unless the forensic podiatrist is skilled and trained in such image analysis and image systems, could lead to challenges at court and in cross-examination, should one go beyond their area of expertise. Camera angles, positioning relative to the subject, as well as lens type can all affect an image and how it is viewed. For example, some lenses have *vignetting* at the edges, which is a reduction in brightness towards the periphery of the image compared to that at the centre. Other forms of distortion may also occur. All lenses have optical defects and create images that are not perfect copies of the subjects which they are pointed at. The amount of distortion a lens suffers is largely dependent on the type of lens and its construction. Cost plays a role, but factors such as the focal length are also important. The wider the angle of the lens, the more difficult it is for straight lines not to appear curved. For instance, zoom lenses are more prone to distortion than prime lenses, simply because it is highly demanding to correct for aberrations at every focal length. There are lots of distortions available in lenses, here are some common ones likely to be encountered which can affect height estimation.

Curvilinear Distortion

Curvilinear distortion or radial distortion comes in several different types, but the one seen most commonly is *barrel distortion.* This is relatively easy to spot when an ultra-wide lens has been used and causes straight lines at the edge of the frame to bow outwards (Figure 7.1). The effect is more obvious on a 'fisheye' lens, where these distortions are left uncorrected by design in order to have the widest possible field of view. Another form of distortion is that of *pin-cushion distortion*, often seen with the use of long telephoto lenses and causes straight lines to bend inwards. The effect is usually subtle and is not normally noticeable unless photographing rectangular subjects straight on. Some zooms can show signs of what is termed *moustache distortion* – where the image can show both

217

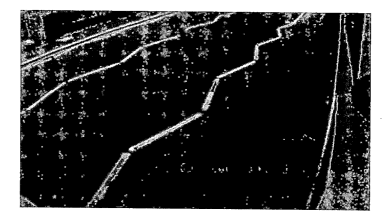

Figure 7.1 The image is a left side view (left lateral view) of an individual displaying the feature of 'forward lean'. Note the curvilinear distortion that appears on the right of the screen where the wall shows some *barrel distortion* which could affect how estimates of heights are undertaken.

barrel and pin-cushion distortion. Moustache distortion is most commonly seen where wide-angle zooms have been used and causes straight lines to appear wavy.

Chromatic Aberration

Lenses focus different wavelengths of light at slightly different distances. This creates colour fringing called *chromatic aberration* which can be seen as a coloured halo at the edges of subjects in an image. It is more marked with extremely wide-angled lenses.

Although there are some computer software programs available for video analysis that will assist the practitioner in measuring height, the original video/CCTV footage may still contain some of the aberrations mentioned which can make the estimation of height challenging. This will require the forensic practitioner to consider these factors when forming such estimations and is where validation of the equipment used is relevant.

VALIDATION

Validation, in this context, is demonstrating that a method is fit for the specific purpose intended and that the results can be relied upon. The requirement for this is that forensic reports submitted for use in the criminal justice system (in England and Wales, as stated by the forensic science regulator) should have some form of statement of the validation performed to provide those making decisions on the use of any results with a summary of the validation undertaken,[50,51,52] for example, where height estimation has been performed, has validation been conducted on the specific population group in this case or does it rely upon estimations using a different subgroup or population. The methods employed for validation will vary depending on whether a quantitative or qualitative method is used. Jurisdictions may vary in their requirements. Experts should be familiar with the requirements/guidelines and court procedure rules of the legal system in the relevant jurisdiction, insofar as it relates to the expert's duty and their responsibilities.

METHODS OF HEIGHT ESTIMATION FOR IMAGES OR VIDEO FOOTAGE

In the Netherlands, a method is suggested that might suit forensic image analysts, although it is doubtful that forensic podiatrists would utilize this method when asked to estimate height of a suspect.[53] Some authors state that while valid and reliable techniques have been established to determine vertical distances from video frames, there is a discrepancy between a person's true static height and their height as measured when assuming different postures or when in motion (e.g. walking).[54] For example, there may be a true discrepancy between the static height and the height measured of the unknown individual displayed in Figure 7.1 due to the unusual feature displayed of 'forward lean' posture.

Edleman et al.[8] suggest several methods for performing height estimations in images. These are currently beyond the scope of most forensic podiatrists and should otherwise be considered by image analysts. These being:

a) Reverse projection photogrammetry: Here a ruler is projected onto the questioned person to measure height.
b) Projective geometry: Vanishing points of parallel lines in the scene are used to obtain height measurements.
c) 3D modelling of the perpetrator: A 3D model of the questioned person is created out of synchronous images from different cameras.

d) 3D modelling of the crime scene: A 3D model of the scene is pro-jected onto the image to gain information about heights and dis-tances in the image.

Edelman and Alberink also suggested different modelling techniques, but again these are more likely to be limited to the skills of image analysts.[55]

Photogrammetry is the science of making measurements from photographs.[56]

In the field of forensics, photogrammetry has been deployed to help solve matters such as vehicle crush, map collision scenes, determine dimen-sions of a suspect from surveillance camera footage and measure the height of a suspect in a security video. Lynnerup and Vedel (2005)[57] suggest that by using photogrammetry, bodily measurements on comparison did not differ by more than 6 mm on average. Another study by Larsen et al. (2008)[58] used similar software and quantified the difference on height, as being within +/-1.5 cm for both intra- and inter-observer study. (Intra-observer studies are the agreement among repeated administrations of a test performed by a single observer, whilst inter-rater observer, inter-rater agreement or concor-dance is the degree of agreement among different observers.)

The following five points can be used as a quick check to determine if a photogrammetry analysis might be possible[59:]

1. There are several photos of the object to be measured from vary-ing camera angles. Most photogrammetry projects require two or more photos of the scene or object from different angles.
2. There are objects in the scene that have known reference dimen-sions or dimensions that can obtained after the photos were taken (e.g. there is a table in a photograph for which the length, width and height can be obtained, or a door frame).
3. The object to be measured is clearly visible in the photos and has distinguishable features (i.e. the object should not be blurred or out of focus).
4. The size of the object to be measured needs to be sizeable relative to the entire photograph (e.g. a skid mark that shows up as a tiny mark on a photograph way off in the distance cannot be mea-sured with accuracy).
5. Photos were taken with the same camera and same focal length (i.e. zoom) setting.

Another technique that can be used to estimate a person's height is by using a pedometer. A pedometer is an instrument that is often used by joggers and walkers to inform them of the distance they have travelled.[60] This is based on a ratio calculation (in this case approximately 0.4). To calculate the ratio, divide the individual's step length by their height (ensuring the same unit of measurement is used for both). Software can also provide a tool for practitioners to determine step length and thus indicate height estimation.

It has been suggested what people wear in terms of colour and thickness of clothing can affect measurements and accuracy in determining height estimation, thereby adding another dimension to the complexities of height estimation from CCTV images.[61] So, currently height estimation from either photographs or CCTV images may well be an estimation. However, it should be remembered that technology is always moving on and it would be no surprise to learn with time that height estimation can be more precisely discerned from such images.

FOOTPRINTS AND FOOTWEAR IN HEIGHT ESTIMATION

Other evidence found at crime scenes such as footprints or footwear may be useful in assisting in height estimation. Whether footprint or footwear evidence, similar techniques will be used for height estimation, for example, the foot outline or the footprint caused by either repeated foot impressions; or wear on the insole of the footwear; or an actual footprint left at the crime scene either barefoot or socked and 'lifted' by a scene of crime officer. It is likely that where a barefoot print or socked print is provided to a podiatrist for analysis, it is usually in the form of a photograph. In the case of footwear, it is likely to be items of footwear.

Where there is a photograph, the podiatrist will need to assure themselves the photograph is a true representation of the footprint, for example, is it a life size 1:1 print, has an appropriate scaled ruler been used and is that ruler shown in the photograph. Also, that the photographed print has been taken parallel to the subject and that a labelled scale which is of similar reflective value as the photograph should be used, such as greyscales, so that the exposure level does not have to be altered.[62] The ABFO No. 2 Standard Reference Scale is regarded as reliable and accurate reference scale for forensic work.[63]

Having received the actual item or the photograph of the footprint, the question then is which measurements should be used to estimate height? The first actual item to be considered here is that of a barefoot print, sometimes referred to as a dermatoglyphic footprint, as it clearly shows the individual ridges on the soles of the foot. Pawar and Pawar used the ink method, using printers' ink and a roller.[64] However, no information is given as to how the foot was printed and how the footprint was achieved. Measurements were taken using a vernier caliper between what is described as the 'Pternion' (mid-rear of the heel) and the tip of the hallux, or the second toe if that was longer. It is not clear how the Pternion was established and this method has some error which can affect the outcome. There is a lack of detail in the regression method used and the results raise debate, in that the correlation is stated as between 12.03% and 15.78%, but does not state the error rate or margin of error.

Barker and Scheur[65] agreed with the nineteenth-century findings of Topinard[66] over a hundred years earlier, who established foot length to height percentages of between 14.9% and 18.1% for various populations. However, Barker and Scheur do not appear to establish which height estimation ratio was determined and therefore which end of the Topinard spectrum their measurements were located.

Others also used foot length but did not encompass a footprint and appeared to use the standing foot and foot length, measured as a straight distance between the most posterior projecting point of the heel and the most anterior projecting point (whether the end of the great toe or second toe).[11] However, it is not stated how or with what tool this was measured. Linear and curvilinear regression equations were formulated and the data appeared to include males and females and both feet, compared to the previous study which included only the left foot of both genders. Foot breadth appears to also have been analysed, although no information as to how this was measured is included.

Kanchan et al. also used foot length and again did not use footprints, but instead measured the foot length from the 'Pternion' to the 'Acropodian' (from the most posterior and prominent aspect of the heel to the most anterior or longest toe) using an anthropometric rod compass as a straight-line distance between the two points[67]. The subject was standing upright with equal pressure distributed between both feet, although there is no information as to how this was measured. Foot breadth was also measured and information as to how this was measured is given. Various statistical tests were conducted and linear and multiple regression analysis conducted, which showed that multiple regression equations are preferred over linear regression when estimating stature. This is also supported in another paper.[43]

In reviewing various aspects of forensic investigation methods using the foot in a forensic context,[68] it is shown that most of the work and data produced rely on measurements taken whilst the foot has been weight bearing. Therefore, this is not applicable when a disarticulated foot is found and determining such things as gender or stature may be unreliable if using that data.

Zeybek et al. used the measurements of foot length, foot breadth, the navicular bone and malleoli height to correlate with stature.[69] That study does not state whether they were weight bearing or not and some figures used to illustrate methods would suggest that not all measurements were made weight bearing. The precise manner of the measurements is also lacking in detail. They concluded that as much as a 9–10 cm of deviation can be found when used according to gender, but as low as 4 cm when both genders are considered when using foot length with stature as an estimate. Using various body parts such as foot length, a single dimension can estimate the stature of an unknown person with a great accuracy and small standard error of less than 7 cm,[9] similar to Zeybek.

Various studies have different estimates with dissimilar confidence intervals and error rates. Table 7.1 displays some stature estimates using foot length.[25]

Table 7.1 Stature Estimation from Foot Length

	Stature Equation (in cm)	Confidence Interval of 70%
Males	$3.447 \times (\text{foot length}) + 82.206$	± 5.0
Females	$3.614 \times (\text{foot length}) + 75.065$	± 4.9

Ozden et al. used foot and shoe dimensions to determine stature and sex of the participants, but again little concrete information is given as to how the measurements were obtained. They suggested various formulae for shoe dimensions and foot dimensions depending on which foot (right or left) and which gender (male or female). Not surprisingly, they found significant differences between male and female relative to foot and shoe length and width along with size. They also suggest there is a better correlation between foot length measurements than foot width and stature estimation.[27]

Krishan, in assessing the foot dimensions of Gujjars, a North Indian endogamous group, showed that multiple regression analysis was the most accurate method of estimating stature using foot dimensions. Krishan also found the highest correlations between stature and foot dimensions in males was foot length, whilst it was foot breadth for females. Thus, it would appear from that study that gender identification needs to be addressed prior to determining stature.[37] All measurements were taken weight bearing and no footprints were taken, but the measurements were conducted using anthropometric devices.

Kanchan et al. conducted a study on footprints on an Indian population but it is unclear as to how the footprints were obtained. They used a glass plate uniformly 'smeared' with ink and subjects were asked to 'apply their feet' onto the plate and then transfer them to white paper. 'Regular pressure' was applied to the foot area to obtain the footprints. Therefore, it is not clear whether these footprints were taken weight bearing or non-weight bearing.[21] It is stated international standards were followed, although unclear who validated or approved those standards as they are taken from the now heavily criticised work of Robbins[70] and the landmarks are open to interpretation and error. However, instead of an overall foot length or breadth, they undertook a study using individual toe lengths from the heel to the tip of each toe. That is similar to the method created by Reel et al. and Gunn lines, used in casework in the UK when footprints are left at a crime scene.[24,71] Kanchan et al. also note that although a pooled samples method of multiple regression analyses showed a good result in estimating stature, regression models that are gender specific should be preferred and that any one of the measurements could be used.[26]

Jasuja and Manjula reported on a study whereby they measured stride length to estimate stature, however when reading the article, it becomes clear that they did not in fact estimate stature from stride length but step length.[72] Although the article starts by describing stride length correctly (a straight distance between the backward most points on the heels of two consecutive footprints), they appear to confuse the matter by then referring to the distance between right footprint and left footprint as right stride length, instead of right step length. In a similar study by Jasuja et al., step length is described as the straight distance between the rear most points in the heels of two consecutive footprints,[20] which in fact is the definition for stride length! The standard error recorded equates to 5.97 cm (2.5 inches approximately) and is similar to other studies using foot dimensions.

Krishan et al. suggest that in obtaining measurements and height estimations, the side from which the limb comes from is important, as there is an asymmetry between people generally and therefore it is important to introduce the correct regression analyses to the equations ensuring a more accurate result in estimation.[45] In a similar study, but using a different ethnic group, it is suggested by Moorthy et al. that regression equations must be made specific to the ethnic group.[73] This again could make life difficult if the ethnicity of the person is unknown. In another study by Krishan and

224

Sharma, it was found that the highest correlation and the lowest standard error of estimate (SEE) was foot length at 2–6 cm.[46]

Kanchan et al. looked at the problem of partial footprints being left at a crime scene and decided to determine the foot width at two points and seek a correlation between these and stature using the method described by Reel et al. to determine these measurements. This paper by Kanchan et al. in 2013 uses different techniques to those described previously as international standards. It is also interesting to note that Kanchan et al. now introduces the concept of static versus dynamic footprints, which has not been mentioned in previous papers[32]

In a study by Nor et al.[74] using Malaysian cadavers, foot length was again used as an indicator of stature estimation, but it is unclear how the foot length was taken, although it can be assumed that the foot length had to be non-weight bearing! In this study foot length did not show such good correlations as previous studies, which might be due to the methods used and the fact that non-living feet were used.

Hemy et al. suggest that foot length again is the most reliable measure of estimating stature from footprints. In this study, the left foot length was the most accurate. The footprints were collected using a podograph and the prints were static weight-bearing prints.[75] The Robbins method appears to have been used, although it is not specifically detailed.

In a UK study in 2012, Reel et al. found that the highest correlations with stature were the heel to the fourth toe print for static footprints and the heel to fifth toe print for the dynamic footprints.[24] They recommended that the calc-4th and calc-5th length measurements be utilized when estimating stature from footprint impressions. However, only one footprint was collected (the right foot) and it is therefore unclear if a different set of calculations is necessary for the left foot.

SUMMARY

The evidence to date shows that the foot has a role to play in estimating height/stature of unknowns and that care is needed when deriving stature from any measurement. In the case of the foot, gender appears to play a significant role as do the differences between right and left feet. So far, the methods employed all seem to vary making comparison between studies somewhat challenging. There appears to be differences in regression equations between different regression methods, different feet (left or right), whether static or dynamic footprints, whether foot outline or foot length, whether different individual foot length parameters are used, for example, calc4th or actual foot length using the Robbins method. On top of all the considerations around measurement, there are also aspects such as ethnicity, nutrition, socioeconomic factors and many others not analysed in detail.

The main message from this is that whilst the foot has a role to play in estimating stature, care is required and more research and studies of larger size are needed along with more consistency in methodology to allow greater accuracy and predictability for height estimation from foot measurements. The standard errors of estimate show varying amounts of accuracy/inaccuracy and considerable care is required not only in the methods employed, but also in the analysis and conclusions that can be drawn from any results obtained.

REFERENCES

1. Moore, MK. & Ross, AH. 2013. "Stature estimation". In: *Research methods in human skeletal biology*, ed. EA DiGangi & MK Moore, Elsevier Inc., pp. 151–179.
2. İşcan, MY. 2001. "Global forensic anthropology in the 21st century", *Forensic Science International*, Vol. 117, no. 1–2, pp. 1–6.
3. Cattaneo, C. 2007. "Forensic anthropology: Developments of a classical discipline in the new millennium", *Forensic Science International*, Vol. 165, no. 2–3, pp. 185–193.
4. Bilge, Y., Kedici, PS., Alakoç, YD., Ülküer, KÜ. & İlkyaz, YY. 2003. "The identification of a dismembered human body: A multidisciplinary approach", *Forensic Science International*, Vol. 137, no. 2–3, pp. 141–146.
5. Krogman, W. & Iscan, M. 1986. *The human skeleton in forensic medicine*, Charles C Thomas, Springfield, IL.
6. Chisum, WJ. & Turvey, BE. 2000. "Evidence dynamics: Locard's exchange principle & crime and reconstruction", *Journal of Behavioural Profiling*, Vol. 1, no. 1. https://bit.ly/1XDEIpF
7. İşcan, MY. 2005. "Forensic anthropology of sex and body size", *Forensic Science International*, Vol. 147, no. 2–3, pp. 107–112.
8. Edelman, G., Alberink, I. & Hoogeboom, B. 2010. "Comparison of the performance of two methods for height estimation", *Journal of Forensic Sciences*, Vol. 55, no. 2, pp. 358–365.
9. Özaslan, A., Iscan, MY., Özaslan, I., Tugcu, H. & Koç, S. 2003. "Estimation of stature from body parts", *Forensic Science International*, Vol. 132, no. 1, pp. 40–45.
10. Bidmos, M. 2006. "Adult stature reconstruction from the calcaneus of South Africans of European descent", *Journal of Clinical Forensic Medicine*, Vol. 13, no. 5, pp. 247–252.

11. Agnihotri, AK., Purwar, B., Googoolye, K., Agnihotri, S. & Jeebun, N. 2007. "Estimation of stature by foot length", *Journal of Forensic and Legal Medicine*, Vol. 14, no. 5, pp. 279–283.
12. Grivas, TB., Mihas, C., Arapaki, A. & Vasiliadis, E. 2008. "Correlation of foot length with height and weight in school age children", *Journal of Forensic and Legal Medicine*, Vol. 15, no. 2, pp. 89–95.
13. Berger, MM., Cayeux, M., Schaller, M., Soguel, L., Piazza, G. & Chioléro, RL. 2008. "Stature estimation using the knee height determination in critically ill patients", *E-SPEN, the European e-Journal of Clinical Nutrition and Metabolism*, Vol. 3, no. 2, pp. e84–e88.
14. Hauser, R., Smoliński, J. & Gos, T. 2005. "The estimation of stature on the basis of measurements of the femur", *Forensic Science International*, Vol. 147, no. 2–3, pp. 185–190.
15. Bidmos, MA. 2009. "Fragmentary femora: Evaluation of the accuracy of the direct and indirect methods in stature reconstruction", *Forensic Science International*, Vol. 192, no. 1–3, pp. 131.e1–131.e5.
16. Agnihotri, AK., Kachhwaha, S., Jowaheer, V. & Singh, AP. 2009. "Estimating stature from percutaneous length of tibia and ulna in Indo-Mauritian population", *Forensic Science International*, Vol. 187, no. 1–3, pp. 109.e1–109.e3.
17. Chibba, K. & Bidmos, MA. 2007. "Using tibia fragments from South Africans of European descent to estimate maximum tibia length and stature", *Forensic Science International*, Vol. 169, no. 2–3, pp. 145–151.
18. Bidmos, MA. 2008. "Metatarsals in the estimation of stature in South Africans", *Journal of Forensic and Legal Medicine*, Vol. 15, no. 8, pp. 505–509.
19. Cordeiro, C., Muñoz-Barús, JI., Wasterlain, S., Cunha, E. & Vieira, DN. 2009. "Predicting adult stature from metatarsal length in a Portuguese population", *Forensic Science International*, Vol. 193, no. 1–3, pp. 131.e1–131.e4.
20. Jasuja, OP., Harbhajan, S. & Anupama, K. 1997. "Estimation of stature from stride length while walking fast", *Forensic Science International*, Vol. 86, no. 3, pp. 181–186.
21. Kanchan, T., Krishan, K., ShyamSundar, S., Aparna, KR. & Jaiswal, S. 2012. "Analysis of footprint and its parts for stature estimation in Indian population", *The Foot*, Vol. 22, no. 3, pp. 175–180.
22. Mahakkanukrauh, P., Khanpetch, P., Prasitwattanseree, S., Vichairat, K. & Troy Case, D. 2011. "Stature estimation from long bone lengths in a Thai population", *Forensic Science International*, Vol. 210, no. 1–3, pp. 279. e1–279.e7.
23. Nachiket, S., Sujatha, N., Priya, R., Raveendranath, V., Rema, D. & Roopa, R. 2010. "Reliability of inter-anterior superior iliac spinous distance as compared to foot length for stature estimation in south Indians", *Journal of Forensic and Legal Medicine*, Vol. 17, no. 6, pp. 352–354.
24. Reel, S., Rouse, S., Vernon, W. & Doherty, P. 2012. "Estimation of stature from static and dynamic footprints", *Forensic Science International*, Vol. 219, no. 1–3, pp. 283.e1–283.e5.

25. Christensen, AM., et al. 2014. *Forensic anthropology, current methods and practice*, Information compiled from Chapter 11, Stature estimation, p. 292, Academic Press.
26. Kanchan, T., Krishan, K., Sharma, A. & Menezes, RG. 2010. "A study of correlation of hand and foot dimensions for personal identification in mass disasters", *Forensic Science International*, Vol. 199, no. 1–3, pp. 112. e1–112.e6.
27. Ozden, H., Balci, Y., Demirüstü, C., Turgut, A. & Ertugrul, M. 2005. "Stature and sex estimate using foot and shoe dimensions", *Forensic Science International*, Vol. 147, no. 2–3, pp. 181–184.
28. Ahmed, AA. 2013. "Estimation of stature using lower limb measurements in Sudanese Arabs", *Journal of Forensic and Legal Medicine*, Vol. 20, no. 5, pp. 483–488.
29. El-Meligy, MMS., Abdel-Hady, RH., Abdel-Maaboud, RM. & Mohamed, ZT. 2006. "Estimation of human body built in Egyptians", *Forensic Science International*, Vol. 159, no. 1, pp. 27–31.
30. Hasegawa, I., Uenishi, K., Fukunaga, T., Kimura, R. & Osawa, M. 2009. "Stature estimation formulae from radiographically determined limb bone length in a modern Japanese population", *Legal Medicine*, Vol. 11, no. 6, pp. 260–266.
31. Kahana, T., Lipstein, E. & Hiss, J. 1996. "Estimation of height in the Israeli population: A revision of the standard regression formulae", *Science & Justice*, Vol. 36, no. 2, pp. 81–84.
32. Kanchan, T., Krishan, K., Geriani, D. & Khan, I. 2013. "Estimation of stature from the width of static footprints-insight into an Indian model", *The Foot*, Vol. 23, pp. 136–139.
33. Karadag, B., Ozturk, AO., Sener, N. & Altuntas, Y. 2012. "Use of knee height for the estimation of stature in elderly Turkish people and their relationship with cardiometabolic risk factors", *Archives of Gerontology and Geriatrics*, Vol. 54, no. 1, pp. 82–89.
34. Klamklay, J., Sungkhapong, A., Yodpijit, N. & Patterson, PE. 2008. "Anthropometry of the southern Thai population", *International Journal of Industrial Ergonomics*, Vol. 38, no. 1, pp. 111–118.
35. Mohanty, NK. 1998. "Prediction of height from percutaneous tibial length amongst Oriya population", *Forensic Science International*, Vol. 98, no. 3, pp. 137–141.
36. Radoinova, D., Tenekedjiev, K. & Yordanov, Y. 2002. "Stature estimation from long bone lengths in Bulgarians", *HOMO - Journal of Comparative Human Biology*, Vol. 52, no. 3, pp. 221–232.
37. Krishan, K. 2008b. "Estimation of stature from footprint and foot outline dimensions in Gujjars of North India", *Forensic Science International*, Vol. 175, no. 2–3, pp. 93–101.
38. Sen, J. & Ghosh, S. 2008. "Estimation of stature from foot length and foot breadth among the Rajbanshi: An indigenous population of north Bengal", *Forensic Science International*, Vol. 181, no. 1–3, pp. 55.e1–55.e6.

228

39. Giles, E. & Vallandigham, PH. 1991. "Height estimation from foot and shoe-print length", *Journal of Forensic Sciences*, Vol. 36, no. 4, pp. 1134–1151.
40. Hens, SM., Konigsberg, LW. & Jungers, WL. 2000. "Estimating stature in fossil hominids: Which regression model and reference sample to use?", *Journal of Human Evolution*, Vol. 38, no. 6, pp. 767–784.
41. Roche, AF. & Davila, GH. 1972. "Late adolescent growth in stature", *Paediatrics*, Vol. 50, no. 6, pp. 874–880.
42. Friedlaender, JS., Costa, PT., Bosse, R., Ellis, E., Rhoads, JG. & Stoudt, HW. 1977. "Longitudinal physique changes among healthy veterans at Boston", *Human Biology*, Vol. 49, no. 4, pp. 541–558.
43. Krishan, K., Kanchan, T. & Sharma, A. 2012. "Multiplication factor versus regression analysis in stature estimation from hand and foot dimensions", *Journal of Forensic and Legal Medicine*, Vol. 19, no. 4, pp. 211–214.
44. Krishan, K. 2008a. "Establishing correlation of footprints with body weight-forensic aspects", *Forensic Science International*, Vol. 179, no. 1, pp. 63–69.
45. Krishan, K., Kanchan, T. & DiMaggio, JA. 2010. "A study of limb asymmetry and its effect on estimation of stature in forensic case work", *Forensic Science International*, Vol. 200, no. 1–3, pp. 181.e1–181.e5.
46. Krishan, K. & Sharma, A. 2007. "Estimation of stature from dimensions of hands and feet in a north Indian population", *Journal of Forensic and Legal Medicine*, Vol. 14, no. 6, pp. 327–332.
47. Woitek, U. 2003. "Height cycles in the 18th and 19th centuries", *Economics & Human Biology*, Vol. 1, no. 2, pp. 243–257.
48. Perkins, JM., Khan, KT., Smith, GD. & Subramanian, SV. 2011. "Patterns and trends of adult height in India in 2005–2006", *Economics & Human Biology*, Vol. 9, no. 2, pp. 184–193.
49. Pablos, A., Gómez-Olivencia, A., García-Pérez, A., Martínez, I., Lorenzo, C. & Arsuaga, JL. 2013. "From toe to head: Use of robust regression methods in stature estimation based on foot remains", *Forensic Science International*, Vol. 226, no. 1–3, pp. 299.e1–299.e7.
50. Forensic Science Regulator. 2017. Codes of Practice and Conduct. *For forensic science providers and practitioners in the Criminal Justice System*. Issue 4. October 2017. http://bit.ly/2ArhOFY [Accessed 21 February 2020].
51. Forensic Science Regulator. 2014. Guidance. Validation. FSR-G-201. Issue 1. http://bit.ly/2CsF2kO [Accessed 21 February 2020].
52. Forensic Science Regulator. 2016. Information: Legal Obligations. FSR-I-400. Issue 4. http://bit.ly/2CK5yY5 [Accessed 21 February 2020].
53. Alberink, I. & Bolck, A. 2008. "Obtaining confidence intervals and likelihood ratios for body height estimations in images", *Forensic Science International*, Vol. 177, no. 2–3, pp. 228–237.
54. Ramstrand, N., Ramstrand, S., Brolund, P., Norell, K. & Bergstrom, P. 2011. "Relative effects of posture and activity on human height estimation from surveillance footage", *Forensic Science International*, Vol. 212, pp. 27–31.
55. Edelman, G. & Alberink, I. 2009. "Comparison of body height estimation using bipeds or cylinders", *Forensic Science International*, Vol. 188, no. 1–3, pp. 64–67.

56. Photogrammetry definition. http://www.photogrammetry.com/ https://bit.ly/2xuGYJq [Accessed 21 February 2020].

57. Lynnerup, N. & Vedel, J. 2005. Person identification by gait analysis and photogrammetry. *Journal of Forensic Sciences*, Vol. 50, no. 1, pp. 112–118.

58. Larsen, PK., Hansen, L., Simonsen, EB. & Lynnerup, N. 2008. Variability of bodily measures of normally dressed people using PhotoModeler Pro 5. *Journal of Forensic Sciences*, Vol. 53, no. 6, pp. 1393–1399.

59. Liscio, Eugene. Photogrammetry in forensics introduction. *ai2-3D Forensics*. https://bit.ly/2RUYe3N [Accessed 21 February 2020].

60. Science Buddies & Scientific American. 2013. Stepping science: Estimating someone's height from their walk. *Scientific American*. https://bit.ly/2NvKQEQ [Accessed 21 February 2020].

61. Scoleri, T., Lucas, T. & Henneberg, M. 2014. "Effects of garments on photo-anthropometry of body parts: Application to stature estimation", *Forensic Science International*, Vol. 237, pp. 148.e1–148.e12.

62. Robinson, EM. 2010. *Crime scene photography*, second edition, Elsevier, Burlington.

63. Massimiliano, T., Doiron, T., Thompson, J., Jones, II, Ballou, S. & Neiman, J. 2013. *Dimensional review of scales for forensic photography*, NCJRS, USA.

64. Pawar, RM. & Pawar, MN. 2012. "Foot length - A functional parameter for assessment of height", *The Foot*, Vol. 22, no. 1, pp. 31–34.

65. Barker, SL. & Scheuer, JL. 1998. "Predictive value of human footprints in a forensic context", *Medicine, Science and the Law*, Vol. 38, no. 4, pp. 341–346.

66. Topinard, P. 1877. *Anthropology*, Chapman & Hall, London.

67. Kanchan, T., Menezes, RG., Moudgil, R., Kaur, R., Kotian, MS. & Garg, RK. 2008. "Stature estimation from foot dimensions", *Forensic Science International*, Vol. 179, no. 2–3, pp. 241.e1–241.e5.

68. Davies, C., Hackman, L. & Black, S. 2013. "The foot in forensic human identification - A review", *The Foot*, Vol. 24, no. 1, pp. 31–36.

69. Zeybek, G., Ergur, I. & Demiroglu, Z. 2008. "Stature and gender estimation using foot measurements", *Forensic Science International*, Vol. 181, no. 1–3, pp. 54. e1–54.e5.

70. Robbins, LM. 1985. *Footprints - collection, analysis and interpretation*, Charles C Thomas, Springfield, IL.

71. DiMaggio, JA. & Vernon, W. 2011. *Forensic Podiatry-Principles and Methods*, Humana Press/Springer.

72. Jasuja, OP. & Manjula. 1993. "Estimation of stature from footstep length", *Forensic Science International*, Vol. 61, no. 1, pp. 1–5.

73. Moorthy, T., Mostapa, A., Boominathan, R. & Raman, N. 2013. "Stature estimation from footprints measurements in Indian Tamils by regression analysis", *Egyptian Journal of Forensic Sciences*, Vol. 4, pp. 7–16.

74. Nor, F., Abdullah, N., Mustapa, A., Wen, L., Faisal, N. & Nazari, D. 2013. "Estimation of stature using lower limb dimensions in the Malaysian population", *Journal of Forensic and Legal Medicine*, Vol. 20, pp. 947–952.

75. Hemy, N., Flavel, A., Ishak, N. & Franklin, D. 2013. "Estimation of stature using anthropometry of feet and footprints in a western Australian population", *Journal of Forensic and Legal Medicine*, Vol. 20, pp. 435–441.

8

Photogrammetry

Contents

INTRODUCTION

Photogrammetry is defined as measuring by photography. As such, photogrammetry is a technique as old as photography itself. Photogrammetry is extensively used in surveying, mapping and architecture. More recently, photogrammetry has been utilised in forensic anthropology and may include measurement of unknown values by use of known values within single images.[1-3] Typically, the measurements focus on the estimation of height of a perpetrator or suspect.

There are two main photogrammetry procedures for such estimations (Figure 8.1 and Figure 8.2). The first of these (Figure 8.1) is referred to as projective geometry and uses so-called vanishing points of parallel lines and a reference height in the scene.[4]

Figure 8.1

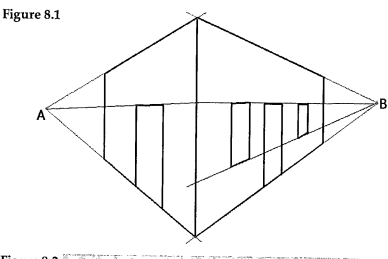

Figure 8.2

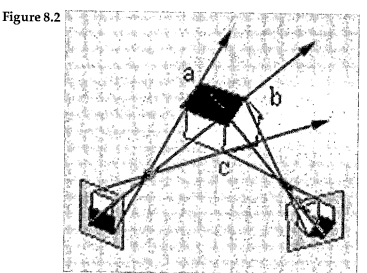

Figures 8.1 and 8.2 Illustrates the difference between photogrammetry methods using vanishing points (Figure 8.1) and 3D modelling (Figure 8.2). In the first method, parallel lines in the picture are localised, which will meet in 'vanishing points', and the internal parameters of the camera are calculated based on these points. In the 3D modelling method, a 3D model is created based on several photos taken from the crime scene.

The second (Figure 8.2) is based on 3D modelling, using photographs of the object taken from different sides and angles. Similar points on the different photographs are identified and a computer programme can then calculate the x-, y- and z-coordinates of the points, thus creating a virtual model of the object. If the camera which took the photographs of the object has been calibrated, then a true scale model can be made.[5] The latter method has been shown to produce more accurate estimations.[6]

Height and body composition, as well as other bodily measures, including neurology, matter in how a person ambulates. For example, obese individuals have a tendency to walk with a wider stance. Persons of a smaller stature would generally be expected walk with shorter and faster steps than taller individuals. Thus, some estimation of congruence between a perpetrator and a suspect in terms of bodily measurements can be useful when considering and comparing gait – a person's gait being the style or manner in which a person walks or runs. Photogrammetry may also yield derived measurements such as stride length and joint angles. An example is displayed in Figure 8.3, where the stride length and foot

Figure 8.3 Example of a comparison of stride length of the perpetrator at the crime scene (left subject and yellow feet marks) and the suspect (right subject and green feet marks) walking at the crime scene during a reconstruction.

233

progression angles of the perpetrator (seen on the left with yellow feet marks) and the suspect (green feet marks) could be compared. Both stride length and foot progression were found to be in concordance when taking into account the different gait directions.

PHOTOGRAMMETRY AND FORENSICS

A first step in photogrammetry is internal and external calibration of the CCTV cameras.

This is done by placing frames with targets on the locations (Figure 8.4). The frames are photographed with both the surveillance video cameras and a calibrated digital camera. Using the digital camera images (Figure 8.4, left pictures) and special software, the points position in a three-dimensional model are established (Figure 8.4, right picture) and subsequently imported as control points ('fiduciary points') to the surveillance video cameras. This allows determination of the internal parameters (internal calibration) and subsequent calculation of the exact placement of the surveillance cameras in the established 3D model (external calibration). The photogrammetry method described here has the advantage that there is no need to ascertain the position of the perpetrator in relation to a measuring device.

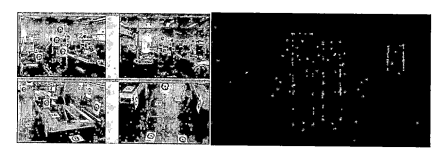

Figure 8.4 Frames with coded targets (all different from each other), which can be automatically recognised by photogrammetry software, and thus a 3D-model of the crime scene (right picture) can be created by the software if pictures are taken from different angles.

After calibration by fiduciary points, or preferably by a specifically marked calibration board or 'chess-board' (Figure 8.5), the photogramme-try analysis produces points in a three-dimensional space and an evalu-ation of the how good the fit is can be made directly by the software.

(*Note:* Utilising a calibration board allows for the assessment of the lens curvature and focal length, while fiduciary points only allow assessment of the latter.)

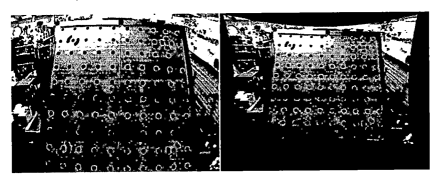

Figure 8.5 Calibration plate used to estimate the internal parameters of a camera such as lens curvature. Left picture shows the picture of the calibration plate of an uncalibrated surveillance camera. Notice especially the bottom lines of dots on the plate, and the sides of the plate appear curved due to the lens curvature of the surveillance camera. The picture on the right is an 'idealised' picture from the same camera after the internal parameters of the camera have been estimated and removed from the picture – now the calibration plate has its correct form. This then enables the measuring of body segment lengths, stature, etc. of a perpetrator in various locations and different kinds of stances by selecting relevant anatomical measuring points (Figure 8.6).

The selection of anatomical points occurs by choosing specific points on an image, such as the top of the head, eyes and shoulders. This selection is made by judging anatomical landmarks, clothing displacement and comparison with images just before and after the chosen photo. When focusing on the other images of the same situation, but from other cameras, the computer programme will indicate the epi-lines (the 'line of sight') from the first image, as well as a line connecting the two joints (Figure 8.7). When selecting the identical anatomical points in this image, it is immediately apparent whether these are in accordance and whether the points selected in the first image are suitable. Thus, the 3D coordinates are calculated not only by a simple averaging of the points chosen from two images, but reflect a dynamic process where the tightness of the intersections of the epi-lines is minimised.

Crime scenes vary in the type and amount of evidence presented. The ability to perform accurate and reliable photogrammetry measurements from images of a perpetrator can depend upon a number of

Figure 8.6 Measuring the height of relevant anatomical points above floor (shoulder, eye and top of the head) based on images from two cameras.

factors, including the cameras available. A physical or even virtual measuring screen can be placed near to where the perpetrator was standing. The perpetrator can then be measured against this screen, akin to seeing a person standing in front of a light source, and whose shadow is cast on a screen or wall behind him. Hence, the challenge is to place the virtual screen in the same position as the perpetrator, especially if the surveillance camera is mounted higher than the perpetrator (as illustrated in Figure 8.8).

In Figure 8.8, the diagram on the left shows a subject whose position has been estimated within an interval of 20 cm. The virtual screen is placed in the middle of this interval. Camera1 in the drawing is placed level with the head of the subject – it can be realised by following the line

Figure 8.7 Left image shows the placement of the point at the top of the height of the person based on the first camera. This camera is later seen as an epi-line in the other camera in the model (the horizontal black line touching the perpetrator's head seen in the image on the right).

of sight from the camera that the measured height of the subject will be the same regardless of the actual position of the subject. This is exemplified in the middle image in Figure 8.8 where the right shoulder height is measured to 140 cm. If the virtual screen is moved within the described interval of 20 cm, the measured height will not significantly alter. However, if the camera is placed like camera 2 (which is a common type of position for surveillance cameras), then a significant source of error is introduced as illustrated in the image on the right in Figure 8.8. In this example the shoulder height is measured to 148 cm, in the range of 145–151 cm (within the interval of 20 cm), and where the shoulder has been estimated to be located vertically above the ground. It has also been suggested to use an approach that locates and calculates the 3D position of points automatically based on a single 2D image.[7-10] However, these methods require the use of a biomechanical model combined with a number of control points on the body that have to be placed manually.

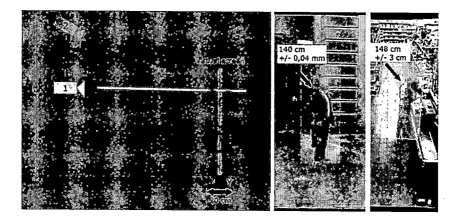

Figure 8.8 Visualisation of virtual screens and errors in a model with a virtual screen, where points that can be measured are only seen from a single camera. The middle picture illustrates a measurement and associated errors of the right shoulder height with a camera placed level with the subject (camera1 in the diagram). The image on the right depicts a measurement with camera 2 in the diagram. It can be seen that the possible error increases, the higher the camera is placed. (Modified figure, original by Jens Vedel.)

COMBINING PHOTOGRAMMETRY AND GAIT ANALYSIS

As forensic analysis, for the purposes of this context, mainly pertains to analysis and comparisons of perpetrators and suspects, the most suitable way to obtain comparable material from the suspect has to be considered. Ideally, the setting for performing the image capture should to some extent have resemblance to the crime scene. For example, if at the crime scene there was a step at the entrance to premises, which the suspect engaged in a distinct fashion, then filming the suspect engaging a somewhat likewise step would be obvious for one comparison exercise. If the crime scene images show a perpetrator walking along a corridor, either towards or away from the CCTV camera, then a comparative setting, for example, at a police station with a long corridor could be suitable. The conditions under which images are collected can vary and consideration needs to be given to this in the analysis and when carrying out comparisons. Ideally, if the captured images are to be used for gait analysis, it could be argued that the gait images captured should be performed in a way where the suspect is unaware they are being filmed to avoid them altering their gait. Of course, one recognises that it is reasonable to acknowledge that most people go about their daily activities without having at the forefront of

238

their minds that they may well be recorded on CCTV and particularly so in urbanised areas where there may be a greater number of cameras. If a person is conscious that they are being filmed, then they may alter their gait. With cameras that are perhaps not immediately obvious, this helps to ensure the gait is not 'changed'.[11]

The filming usually takes place with ordinary digital video (DV) cameras and carried out by forensic technicians, and the setting would have been discussed in advance (Figure 8.9). For instance, a policeman may be instructed to accompany the suspect but walking at a speed that matches the velocity of the perpetrator. It is known that the speed of gait can influence some of the features – in this study the relationship between the lower extremity joint angles during the gait cycle and gait speed were explored. The relationship was found to be non-uniform. Phases were found with both high and low concurrences between different gait speeds with highest concurrence in the middle of the stance phase of gait. (The stance phase is the weight-bearing phase where the foot is placed on the ground and the opposite leg is in swing phase.) In conclusion, endeavouring for the same gait speed for the perpetrator and the suspect was recommended.[12]

Figure 8.9 Example of covert video recording of a suspect from different angles using several cameras.

Conversely, if the recordings are used only for photogrammetric measurement, the recordings of the suspect are most easily performed overtly. Preferably, photogrammetry measurement of the suspect should be made with the suspect in the same stance/position as the perpetrator, or at identical instances in the gait cycle which also may give the opportunity to compare joint angles in the measured position. It is possible, to some degree, to distinguish between different subjects based on their lower extremity joint angles in a single position, especially in the middle of the stance phase.[13] Ideally, the suspect could be requested to stand and walk in the exact same locations as the perpetrator (Figure 8.10).

Figure 8.10 Reconstruction where the suspect (right) is instructed to walk the same path as the perpetrator (left) at the crime scene.

The situation as depicted in Figure 8.10 has the further benefit of being able to use the same recording equipment, and thus using the exact same photogrammetric model; so differences between different 3D models are eliminated. The suspect can then be filmed from the same angles, which also provides the advantage of measurable silhouettes, and not only single measurement points, can be compared of the perpetrator and suspect (Figure 8.11). However, overt recordings do require the willing participation of the suspect, which may not always be an option. This means that when planning and acquiring video footage of the suspect, the possible use for both gait analysis and photogrammetry measurements should also be taken into account by having possibilities for both overt and covert recordings.

While height could be just as easily acquired using a stadiometer, preferably the same measuring method (photogrammetry) should be used for comparing the perpetrator and the suspect.[14] At first glance, a stature measured by a stadiometer might seem as a 'gold standard'. However, it has been found that people almost automatically appear to straighten themselves when asked to stand against a stadiometer, meaning that results have shown better agreement between subsequent measuring of stature by photogrammetry

Figure 8.11 Perpetrator and suspect measured from the same angle in the same model based on pictures from the same camera following a reconstruction. Then measurable silhouettes can also be compared.

than between photogrammetry and a stadiometer. Of course, measuring the suspect by photogrammetry also makes it easier to measure other heights, such as floor to eye, floor to shoulder and floor to earlobe.

ASSESSING ERROR

Error is a measure of the estimated difference between the observed or calculated value of a quantity and its true value.[15] Photogrammetry measurements should be compared to physical measurements between fixed points at the crime scene. For example, the height of fixed counters, the width of doors, etc. to estimate the error. In a previous case,[5] for instance, the height of a desk (bolted to the floor and not moved between the incident and the analysis) was measured by photogrammetry (result: 89.3 cm) and compared to an actual physical measurement (result: 90.0 cm). The error was thus 7 mm, or less than 1% (Figure 8.12).

This serves as a control as well as an illustrative way to explain measurement error. It was found that the position of a clearly defined reference marker on the floor could be reproduced within 0.5 cm[14] and on par with another study.[4] If the internal parameters (inner calibration) of the surveillance cameras have been estimated with a 'chessboard' screen, the

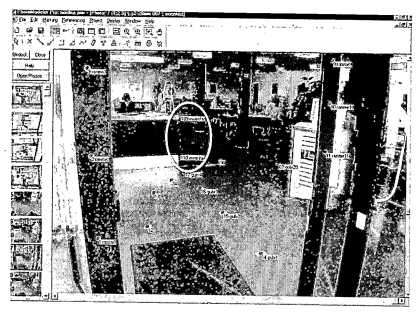

Figure 8.12 Assessing error – the difference between known and true value. The difference between the measured and actual height in this case was 7mm. (Figure by Jens Vedel.)

errors in the model will normally be in the range of 1–2 cm. If only the focal length is being calculated, the object of interest is placed far away from the camera, or the camera has very low resolution, then the error can be much higher. The error will be greater for 'bodily points' such as joint midpoints and midlines, due to masking from clothing and other items. Intra- and inter-observer tests of photogrammetry measurements of body segments seem to indicate that the error associated with clearly identifiable body points, such as the top of the head, eyes, earlobes or other selected reference points, is small (Figure 8.13).

When the body points are hidden or obscured by clothing, such as joint centre-points, the reproducibility generally decreases, especially in inter-observer analyses.[14] It was therefore proposed to use easily identifiable facial traits as measurement points, for example the eyes, which may also be seen through holes in a balaclava, or a prominent nose-tip as seen in profile. Also, it was suggested that location of the elbow joint and the joints of the lower extremities should be performed on images with flexed joints, if possible, to enhance reproducibility. Another challenge of measuring body points is that the body is not a rigid object like a table, for

242

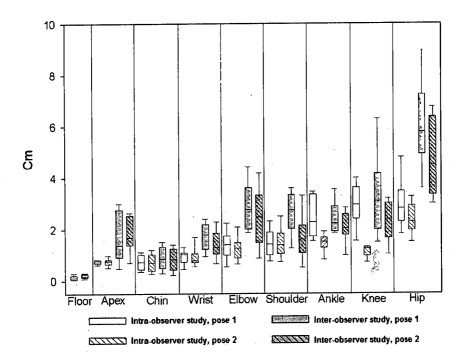

Figure 8.13 Box-plots showing the differences between two determinations of length. The horizontal line inside each box is the median of the data, that is the value of the observation in the middle after the observations have been ranked in order. There is the same amount of observations, which are higher and lower than the median (the observations are split into halves around the median). The upper and lower borders are the median of the upper and the lower halves of the data, respectively, so these borders represent the 'middle half' of the data – known as the data between the 25th and 75th percentile (or first and third quartile). The whiskers represent the 10th and 90th percentile of the data[14]

example, so it can be difficult to define what the true value is. A person can be more than 1 cm higher in the morning than in the evening due to decreasing thickness of the vertebrae discs during the day,[16] and different positions can have a big impact on measured height. It has been examined how much the eye height changed when the head was tilted in different ways.[17] The maximal vertical displacement was found to be around 5 cm. Experience with casework further indicates that shoulder height can change up to 10 cm if the arm is being elevated compared to a relaxed shoulder position with the arm hanging along the side of the body. An example of this can be seen in Figure 8.8, where the right shoulder height is compared between a suspect (middle picture) and the perpetrator (right picture). The perpetrator has a clearly elevated shoulder compared to the suspect, and it was concluded that the perpetrator and the suspect could have similar shoulder height if measured in the same position.

It can therefore be very difficult to compare photogrammetry derived height measurement of a perpetrator in a given position at a crime scene, where a suspect's height is measured without wearing shoes using a stadiometer in a straight position with the person's back against a wall. However, this can be performed in order to compare the height of a perpetrator to a given population, which can be useful information where an estimate is required on the quantity of subjects having that height. This estimation for the perpetrator in Figure 8.6 is shown in Table 8.1

Table 8.1 Estimation of the Stadiometer Height of the Perpetrator in Figure 8.6 without Shoes

	Minimum height (cm)	Maximum height (cm)	Comment
Measured height	173	173	This is a measurement based on two cameras, so there is no interval for the point as in Figure 8.7
Body point correction	−1	1	Clearly defined points such as the apex of the head can be estimated with an accuracy of ± 1 cm^{-14}
Position correction	3	6	Estimated correction for the head and in minor degree the upper body bend forward
Model correction	−1	1	Top of cashier's counter measured as control (Actual height 96 cm, measured height 96 ± 1 cm)
Correction for shoes	−2	−1	A pair of shoes typically adds 1–2 cm to the height
Estimated height interval	172	180	
% of male population within this interval		49%	

244

and compared to an anthropometry database.[18] As can be seen from that, every time a new correction is estimated, the final height interval gets larger. The height of the perpetrator in Figure 8.6 is just about the mean height in that database, giving a high percentage of possible subjects within this interval. The photogrammetry measurement would clearly have resulted in a better evidential value if the perpetrator had a more unusual height.

CASE EXAMPLES

Robbery

In this case it was possible to compare both the gait and photogramme-try measures of the perpetrator and the suspect. The suspect was first photographed in the police yard for the purpose of photogrammetry

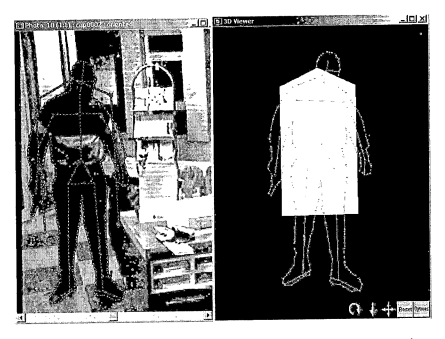

Figure 8.14 Photogrammetry measures of a perpetrator in a one camera situation against a virtual screen. (Figure by Jens Vedel.)

and afterwards he was covertly recorded for gait analysis when he left the police yard. The perpetrator was measured in a one camera situation against a virtual screen (Figure 8.14) and compared with measurements of the suspect in a similar position (Figure 8.15). All measures of the perpetrator and the suspect were within the same range when differences in, for example, head and shoulder position were taken into consideration.

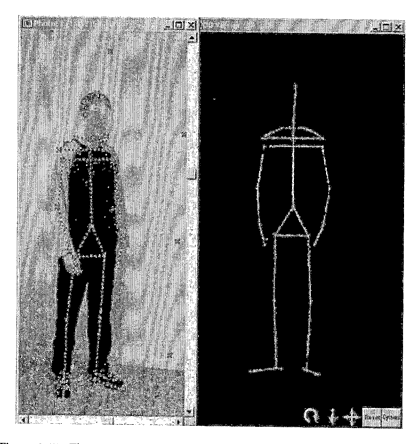

Figure 8.15 The suspect is recorded and measured in a similar position to the perpetrator seen in Figure 8.14. When taking into account the differences in positions, all measures were within the same range. (Figure by Jens Vedel.)

Several other similarities were found in the gait analysis, including (a) the degree of abduction of the feet in the stance phase and, most notably in this case, (b) inversion of the left ankle (Figure 8.16 and 8.17).

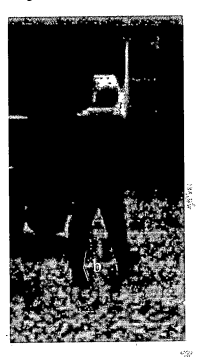

Figure 8.16 Gait analysis comparison of perpetrator (Figure 8.16) and suspect (Figure 8.17). A similar degree of abduction of the feet is observed and, most notably in this case, inversion of the left ankle (marked as b).

Figure 8.17 Gait analysis comparison of perpetrator (Figure 8.16) and suspect (Figure 8.17). A similar degree of abduction of the feet is observed and, most notably in this case, inversion of the left ankle (marked as b).

In conclusion, the analysis and comparison confirmed the presence of the same features of gait in the perpetrator and the suspect. There were also other forms of evidence deployed in the case. In the outcome of that matter, the suspect was found guilty of the robbery

Axe Throwing

In this case, a perpetrator was seen throwing an axe towards a policeman. The policeman stated that the axe passed just next to his ear. The perpetrator stated that this was not the case and that he had just meant to 'dump the axe'. The path of the axe throw is depicted in Figure 8.18, which displays the situation where the axe could be seen for the first time in the picture (illustrated with a red arrow). The perpetrator was placed outside the right boundary of the picture.

'0' depicts the position of the right foot of the policeman when the axe enters the scene. '1' illustrates the impact of the axe on the ground. After that, the axe jumped over a 30 cm pile of snow, landed at position '2' and slid to its final position '3'.

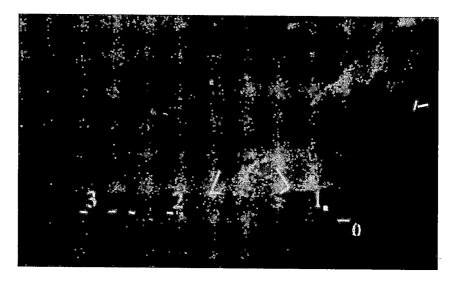

Figure 8.18   Path of the axe throw.

After a reconstruction was performed, it was concluded that the perpetrator must have used a large overhand throw to achieve this kind of path, lending support to the view that the axe was not simply dropped onto the ground. However, it could also be concluded that the axe has passed the policeman's hip instead of his ear. Furthermore, based on photogrammetry measurements of the crime scene, it was found that the perpetrator was positioned at around 2.0 metres from the policeman when throwing the axe and that the axe hit the ground approximately 2.20 metres from the right foot of the policeman. The perpetrator was subsequently found not guilty of attempted murder of the policeman.

REFERENCES

1. Thali MJ, Braun M, Wirth J, Vock P and Dirnhofer R. 2003. 3D surface and body documentation in forensic medicine: 3-D/CAD photogrammetry merged with 3D radiological scanning. *J Forensic Sci* 48 (6): 1356–1365.
2. Thali MJ, Braun M, Wirth J, Brueschweiler W and Dirnhofer R. 2003. Morphological imprint: determination of the injury-causing weapon from the wound morphology using forensic 3D/CAD-supported photogrammetry. *Forensic Sci Int* 132: 177–181.
3. Thali MJ, Braun M, Wirth J, Brueschweiler W and Dirnhofer R. 2000. Matching tire tracks on the head using forensic photogrammetry. *Forensic Sci Int* 113 (1–3): 281–287.
4. Criminisi A, Zisserman A, Van Gool LJ, Bramble SK, Compton D. 1998. New approach to obtain height measurements from video. Higgins, Kathleen. Investigation and Forensic Science Technologies. *Proc. SPIE, 3576, Investigation and Science Technologies,* (1999/02/04). doi: 10.1117/12.334540
5. Lynnerup N and Vedel J. 2005. Person identification by gait analysis and photogrammetry. *J Forensic Sci* 50: 112–118.
6. Edelman G, Alberink I and Hoogeboom B. 2010. Comparison of the performance of two methods for height estimation. *J Forensic Sci* 55 (2): 358–365.
7. Ambrosio J, Abrantes J and Lopes G. 2001. Spatial reconstruction of human motion by means of a single camera and a biomechanical model. *Hum Mov Sci* 20: 829–851.
8. Barrón C and Kakadiaris IA. 2003. On the improvement of anthropometry and pose estimation from a single uncalibrated image. *Mach Vis Appl* 14: 229–236.
9. Mori G and Malik J. 2006. Recovering 3D human body configurations using shape contexts. *IEEE Trans Pattern Anal Mach Intell* 28: 1052–1062.
10. Yang F and Yuan X. 2005. Human movement reconstruction from video shot by a single stationary camera. *Ann Biomed Eng* 33: 674–684.
11. Larsen PK, Simonsen EB and Lynnerup N. 2008. Gait analysis in forensic medicine. *J Forensic Sci* 53 (5): 1149–1153.
12. Yang SX, Larsen PK, Alkjaer T, Lynnerup N and Simonsen EB. 2014. Influence of velocity on variability in gait kinematics: implications for recognition in forensic science. *J Forensic Sci* 59 (5): 1242–1247.
13. Yang SX, Larsen PK, Alkjaer T, Simonsen EB and Lynnerup N. 2014. Variability and similarity of gait as evaluated by joint angles: implications for forensic gait analysis. *J Forensic Sci* 59 (2): 494–504.
14. Larsen PK, Hansen L, Simonsen EB and Lynnerup N. 2008. Variability of bodily measures of normally dressed people using PhotoModeler® Pro 5. *J Forensic Sci* 53 (6): 1393–1399.
15. Error. Oxford Dictionaries Online, Lexico. https://bit.ly/2YtYoBK [Accessed 03 July 2019].
16. Reilly T, Tyrrel A and Troup JDG. 1984. Orcadian variation in human stature. *Chronobiol Int* 1 (2): 121–126.

17. Yang SX, Larsen PK, Alkjaer T, Juul-Kristensen B, Simonsen EB and Lynnerup N. 2014. Height estimations based on eye movements throughout a gait cycle. *Forensic Sci Int* 236: 170–174.
18. Hansen K, Feveile H, Finsen L, Jensen C, Jensen A, Merkel J, Ekner D and Christensen H. 1998. *Kropsmål for danske arbejdstagere; Antropometriske mål på 467 danske arbejdstagere.* 48. Copenhagen (DK), The National Institute of Occupational Health.

9

Interpreting and Communicating Forensic Statistics

Contents

INTRODUCTION

In late 1999 at Chester Crown Court in the United Kingdom, Mrs Sally Clark, a lawyer, stood trial for the murder of her two baby sons. Mrs Clark's first son had died suddenly within a few weeks of his birth in 1996. After her second son died in a similar manner, she was arrested in 1998 and tried for the murder of both sons. She denied smothering her sons, 8-week-old Harry and 11-week-old Christopher, and said they must have died of 'cot death syndrome' (sudden infant death syndrome – SIDS). However, eminent paediatrician Professor Sir Roy Meadow, an expert called by the prosecution, estimated the likelihood of two siblings dying of 'cot death syndrome' as 1 in 73 million. At the trial he likened this probability to that of the chances of backing an 80/1 outsider in the Grand National four years running and winning each time – "the chance of it happening four years running we all know is extraordinarily unlikely. So it's the same with these deaths".[1] This statistical 'evidence' proved damming, and in November 1999 Mrs Clark was convicted of murder of her two baby sons and given two concurrent life prison sentences[2].

It was Professor Meadow's view that "one sudden infant death in a family is a tragedy, two is suspicious and three is murder unless proven otherwise".[3] For an affluent non-smoking family like the Clarks, he stated the probability of a single cot death as 1 in 8543; therefore, the probability of two cot deaths in the same family was around *1 in 73 million* (8543×8543). Since there are about 700,000 live births in the United Kingdom each year, it was argued that a double cot death would be expected to occur only once every hundred years (73 million/700,000 – see numerical conversion error below).

However, this presentation of the statistical evidence in this case was widely criticised. A news release from the Royal Statistical Society (RSS) pointed out that,

> This approach is, in general, statistically invalid. It would only be valid if SIDS cases arose independently within families, an assumption that would need to be justified empirically. Not only was no such empirical justification provided in the case, but there are very strong a priori reasons for supposing that the assumption will be false. There may well be unknown genetic or environmental factors that predispose families to SIDS, so that a second case within the family becomes much more likely.[4]

In other words, if one child in a family dies of SIDS, it may be more likely, not less likely, that a second might also succumb to SIDS.

The RSS's News Release went on to say that,

> Aside from its invalidity, figures such as the 1 in 73 million are very easily misinterpreted. Some press reports at the time stated that this was the chance that the deaths of Sally Clark's two children were accidental. This (mis-)interpretation is a serious error of logic known as the Prosecutor's Fallacy. The jury needs to weigh up two competing explanations for the babies' deaths: SIDS or murder. Two deaths by SIDS or two murders are each quite unlikely, but one has apparently happened in this case. What matters is the relative likelihood of the deaths under each explanation, not just how unlikely they are under one explanation (in this case SIDS, according to the evidence as presented).

Mrs Clark's case was appealed but the conviction was upheld at appeal in October 2000. When the case came in front of the Criminal Cases Review Commission in January 2003, the conviction was quashed.[5] At the second appeal it emerged that the a pathologist called by the prosecution at the original trial had failed to disclose microbiological reports that suggested one of Mrs Clark's sons had died of natural causes. Nevertheless, at the second appeal the Court recognised that statistics had played an important part in Mrs Clark's original conviction and criticised the presentation of the statistical evidence and the cited 1 in 73 million figure in particular –

> Quite what impact all this evidence will have had on the jury will never be known but we rather suspect that with the graphic reference by Professor Meadow to the chances of backing long odds winners of the Grand National year after year it may have had a major effect on their thinking notwithstanding the efforts of the trial judge to down play it.[1]

Full details of the deleterious effects of the miscarriage of justice had on the Clark family are described in the book, *'Stolen Innocence: The Sally Clark Story – A Mother's Fight for Justice,'*[6,7] and the presentation of the statistical evidence in that case has focused public attention on how statistical evidence is given by an expert witness. Also, *'Math on Trial'*[8] describes the Sally Clark case and others, where mathematical arguments were used.

Directly as a result of Sally Clark's case, the President of the Royal Statistical Society wrote to the Lord Chancellor about the Society's concerns over the misuse of statistics[9] and set up a Statistics and the Law Working Group with the aim of improving the understanding and use of statistics in the administration of justice. The Royal Statistical Society's intention was that this group would provide an interface for the RSS with the legal, scientific and justice communities. Under the auspices of the working group, four Practitioner Guides have been produced on aspects of statistical evidence and probabilistic reasoning.[10] These guides are intended to assist judges, lawyers, forensic scientists and other expert witnesses in coping with the statistical evidence in modern criminal litigation:

- Fundamentals of Probability and Statistical Evidence in Criminal Proceedings.[11]
- Assessing the Probative Value of DNA Evidence.[12]
- Logic of Forensic Proof: Inferential Reasoning in Criminal Evidence and Forensic Science.[13]
- Case Assessment and Interpretation of Expert Evidence.[14]

INTERPRETING AND COMMUNICATING STATISTICS FOR THE COURTS

Interpretation

Whilst expert witnesses are instructed by the prosecution of the defence, it is not the role of the expert to simply support one side or the other. As is repeatedly stated, the duty of an expert is to the court and not to those who instruct them or who are responsible for their fees. Experts are expected to be impartial and to help the courts to achieve their overriding purpose, which is administration of justice in civil, criminal and administrative matters in accordance with the rule of law. To do so, experts must be objective and give their opinion without bias on matters within their expertise. This duty overrides any obligation to the party from whom they received their instructions or by whom the expert is paid. This is true whether the expert is involved in providing reports for use in the criminal justice system[15,16] or in relation to matters in the civil justice system.[17,18] In the jurisdiction of England and Wales, the forensic science regulator also sets out guidance for expert witnesses giving evidence in the criminal justice system.[19-24]

It is therefore incumbent on the expert to consider their opinions, taking into account both the defence and the prosecution's views of events. In doing so the expert must make clear their understanding of the circumstances, and which aspects of the circumstances are relevant to them forming their opinion. In giving their evidence, the expert needs to consider the probability of the issue that they are addressing would have occurred if the prosecution's version of events were true, and the probability that the issue would have occurred if the defence's version of events were true. The ratio of these probabilities, the *likelihood ratio*, expresses relative likelihood of the issue occurring under the prosecution's and defence's version of events. This form of statistical reasoning has been used to evaluate evidence for many years and is underpinned by Bayes' theorem.[25,26]

Bayes' Theorem

It is important to recognise that a Bayesian approach should not be confused with the use of Bayes' theorem. A Bayesian approach does not necessarily involve the use of Bayes' theorem.

Bayes' theorem provides a logical rule for updating probability in the light of new evidence. A good example to illustrate how this works in practice is given by Robertson, Vignaux and Berger.[27] The authors describe a breath alcohol testing machine that has a false positive rate of 1 in 200 (0.5%) when the true concentration of alcohol in breath is just below the legal limit, and a 95 in 100 (95%) true positive rate if just above the legal limit. If you get a positive result, then the likelihood ratio for being over the limit is:

$$\frac{\text{Probability of positive if over the limit}}{\text{Probability of positive if not over the limit}} = \frac{95}{0.5} = 190$$

So the likelihood is that you are 190 times *more* likely to be over the limit if the breathalyser gives a positive test. Odds can be converted to a probability by using the equation:

$$\text{Probability} = \frac{\text{odds}}{\text{odds} + 1}$$

But Bayes' theorem requires the prior odds to be taken into account and the new (posterior) odds updated using the likelihood ratio:

$$\text{Prior odds} \times \text{likelihood ratio} \rightarrow \text{Posterior odds}$$

So if, for example, it is assumed that if the police stop a driver for a moving traffic offence, there is a 50:50 chance of them being over the limit before testing; then, if there is a positive reading, the odds of them being over the drink drive limit is 190 to 1:

$$\frac{1}{1} \times 190 = 190 (\text{probability } 99.5\%)$$

However, in reality the true prior odds is probably lower. For example, over Christmas 2013, in Dorset (UK) the police stopped 1472 drivers for whatever reason and breathalysed them, but only 103 went on to be charged with drink driving,[28] so the prior odds are 103:1472, approximately 1 in 14, figures are now:

$$\frac{103}{1472} \times 190 = 13.3 (\text{probability } 93\%)$$

Still a high probability but not as high as 99.5%!

The estimation of the prior odds brings a degree of subjectivity into Bayesian calculations and may be influenced by the database used.[29] Consequently, the use of the Bayesian approach to evaluating evidence is not without controversy, and a Court of Appeal judgment in England and Wales raised several issues relating to the evaluation of scientific evidence.[30] The judgement could be seen as a proscription of the use of this approach in evaluating scientific evidence, other than DNA evidence, and not surprisingly caused considerable concern among forensic scientists not only within the UK but also in other jurisdictions[31]. In response to the judgment a number of leading forensic scientists published a position paper as an editorial in *Science and Justice*.[32] The editorial summarised the logical principles of evidence interpretation that underpin forensic reasoning and opposed any movement away from the use of logical methods for evidence evaluation.

Statistics and Probability

These two terms are often taken together as they overlap but they are not interchangeable.

Statistics is about the collection and summary of data.
Probability is a measure of uncertainty on a scale of 0 to 1.

The RSS considers that there are seven key concepts that expert witnesses, forensic scientists and statisticians need to be familiar with to interpret and describe statistical data and probabilities.[11] These are:

1. Frequencies (absolute and relative)
2. Likelihood of the evidence

3. The likelihood ratio
4. Base rates for general issues (prior probabilities)
5. Posterior probabilities
6. Bayes' Theorem
7. Independence

These concepts are well described in the readily available RSS Practitioner Guide No.1 and will not be re-iterated here.

Communication

Experts need to be careful with their use of language when describing inferential conclusions. An opinion commonly expressed is that 'the evidence is consistent with ...'. It simply states that the proposition (hypothesis) is not excluded by the evidence but it says nothing about how probable it is that the proposition is true. In terms of match evidence, it gives no idea of the weight of evidence supporting the match or against the match. The use of 'consistent with ...' has also been criticised as not being impartial.[33]

Another commonly used construction seen in opinions is 'could have...' as in 'the person in the CCTV pictures *could have* been the defendant'. As with 'consistent with ...', no probability has been assigned and it gives the court no idea as to likelihood that it was or was not the defendant. A similarly vague opinion is 'cannot be excluded ...' as in 'the victim's blood *cannot be excluded* as the source of the stain on the accused shirt'. Again no evidence of the degree of association is given. It *cannot be excluded* that I will win the lottery with the ticket I bought earlier today but unfortunately the odds are still about 14 million to one against!

Likelihood Ratios – Strength of Evidence

The use of the Bayesian approach may be limited by the courts,[34] but where it is applicable, and can be used, the result can be communicated in a meaningful and understandable way by experts using the *likelihood ratio* as it expresses relative likelihood of the prosecution's and defence's version of events.

By the very nature of the use of the word 'ratio' then there must be two numbers for a likelihood ratio calculation to be able to be performed. Where mistakes can occur in using the term *likelihood ratio* is when there are no datasets for a *likelihood ratio* to be able to be calculated, yet the 'expert' includes the qualitative descriptors in terms of the strength of evidence and then refers to that as a 'likelihood ratio without using the numbers'. Such statements have no merit.

Where a qualitative descriptor scale alone is used to give some guide on the strength of evidence, but there are no datasets available, then the term *likelihood ratio* must *not* be used in conjunction, as to do so would be misleading and dangerous. Instead, a suitable qualitative descriptor scale should be described as that, and without reference to the term *likelihood ratio*. That then amounts to an expert's opinion and needs to be stated as such.

Evett and colleagues[33] proposed a very simple and easily understood vocabulary to describe the strength of evidence – *limited, moderate, moderately strong, strong* and *very strong*. The Association of Forensic Science Providers has revised these definitions and assigned a range of likelihood ratios to each description (see Table 9.1).[35]

Table 9.1 Scale of Support

Likelihood Ratio	Strength of Evidence
>1 to 10	Weak
>10 to 100	Moderate
>100 to 1000	Moderately strong
>1000 to 10,000	Strong
>10,000 to 1,000,000	Very strong
>1,000,000	Extremely strong

It is important to remember that when any comparisons are performed, including of gait analyses, such comparisons are for similarity and dissimilarity.

The descriptors 'limited', 'moderate', etc. can still be used to express the forensic practitioner's confidence, or opinion, as to the degree of similarity (or dissimilarity), but it is important to include the category of *None* when a qualitative descriptor scale alone is used to allow for when there is no positive likeness in comparison.

In *R v. Atkins and Atkins* [2009] EWCA Crim 1876,[36] a case concerning facial mapping evidence, Hughes LJ said at para 31:

> We conclude that where a photographic comparison expert gives evidence, properly based upon study and experience, of similarities and/ or dissimilarities between a questioned photograph and a known person (including a defendant) the expert is not disabled either by authority or principle from expressing his conclusion as to the significance of his findings, and that he may do so by use of conventional expressions, arranged

in a hierarchy, such as those used by the witness in this case and set out in paragraph 8 above. We think it preferable that the expressions should not be allocated numbers, as they were in the boxes used in the written report in this case, lest that run any small risk of leading the jury to think that they represent an established numerical, that is to say measurable, scale. The expressions ought to remain simply what they are, namely forms of words used. They need to be in an ascending order if they are to mean anything at all, and if a relatively firm opinion is to be contrasted with one which is not so firm. They are, however, expressions of subjective opinion, and this must be made clear to the jury charged with evaluating them.

MISINTERPRETATION OF STATISTICAL EVIDENCE – TRAPS FOR THE UNWARY

The Prosecutor's Fallacy

This is an easy mistake to make and is very commonly encountered.[37] It confuses two very subtly different probabilities: the probability that the accused is innocent given the match with a particular piece of evidence, and the probability that the accused is a match with a particular piece of evidence if they are innocent. The first probability is what should be of interest to the Court but more often than not it is the second that is usually reported. To illustrate the problem consider the case where a blood spot is analysed for DNA and matches the accused. The jury are told that in the general population 1 in 500,000 people have this match. They interpret this as a 1 in 500,000 chance that someone (anyone) other than the suspect left the stain, or a >99.99% chance that the accused is guilty. However, this is the chance of a random individual matching this sample, not the chance of their innocence. They should have interpreted the data as there is 1 in 500,000 that some (particular) person other than the suspect could leave a stain like the actual stain. So if the suspect population is 10 million, then there are 20 people who would match that blood sample; probability of the accused being innocent is actually 20/21, so the probability of guilt is 1–20/21 or <5%. That is, a less than 1 in 20 chance that they are guilty given this data alone.

The Defender's Fallacy or Underestimating the Value of the Probabilistic Evidence

This is the defence's counterpart to the prosecutor's fallacy. The jury are told that in the general population 1 in 500,000 people have a particular match which is shared with the defendant. The defence dismisses the evidence as having little value as in the UK over 120 people have that match. However, if the number of suspects has been narrowed to 10 million, then there are only 20 people who would match that sample and in any case, if there is any other evidence, it is unlikely that all 20 are equally likely to be guilty.

Source Probability Error

An item of clothing linking the defendant to the crime scene has a trace on it. When tested, a forensic scientist reports that 'The probability that the trace on the clothing came from someone other than the victim is 1 in 5 million. This suggests that the probability is 4,999,999/5,000,000 that the trace came from the victim'. But this is wrong, it is simply a random match probability. The scientist would have to know the size of the potential population that could have left the trace before a true probability could calculate that the trace came from the victim.

Numerical Conversion Error

If a particular characteristic occurs with a prevalence of only 1 in 1000, it is sometimes claimed that it would require 1000 individuals to be encountered before another person was found with the same characteristic. This is clearly wrong as the next person who was met could have the given characteristic.

False Positive Probability or Base-Rate Neglect

If you have tested positive for a terminal disease which has a prevalence of 1 in 10,000 and the test has 99% accuracy, what is the probability you have the disease? You might imagine that your days are surely numbered but actually your chance of having the terminal disease is less than 1% as the false positives will far outweigh the true positives (in 10,000 individuals 100 will test positive but only 1 person will have the disease). This is a counter-intuitive result that over 85% of people get wrong.[38]

Fallacious Inference of Certainty

It is tempting when the random match probability is very low, say 1 in 10,000 million, to assume that no one else on earth shares the same match and therefore a unique identification has been made. However, such a conclusion may be unwarranted as the assumptions underlying the random match probability could be unwarranted or simply due to analytical error, as in a recent UK case in which a man was wrongly accused of rape on the sole evidence of a DNA match.[39]

Erroneous Assumption of Independence

Although several aspects of the statistical evidence in the Sally Clark case were criticised, the major error was due to the assumption of independence made by Professor Sir Roy Meadow.[40] If you throw a six-sided dice, your chance of getting a three is one in six (1/6); if you throw again it is still a one in six chance of getting a three. The chance is not altered by what you threw before, each throw is independent. So, the chance of throwing a three followed by another three is $\frac{1}{6} \times \frac{1}{6}$, which is one in thirty-six. So, if you have a 1 in 8543 chance of having a cot death, then the probability of two cot deaths in the same family was around 1 in 73 million (8543 × 8543) but only if the events are independent. However, the original publication from which the initial 1 in 8543 was derived indicated that rather than being independent, the chance of having a cot death increased in families in which a child had already died in similar circumstances.[41] So, rather than being independent, the events were dependent – if you have one child who dies of SIDS, the odds of having a second child dying of SIDS is increased.

SUMMARY

This chapter is not aimed to be a comprehensive read on statistics as there is plenty of published material on the subject. Instead, this is designed to provide awareness on the significance of appropriate presentation and interpretation of such facts and figures to the courts and, crucially, the potential and very real consequences of when such material is misrepresented or misconstrued.

Whilst appreciating many practitioners have some familiarity with statistical methods, statistics is a specialised area. Experts need to stick to their area of expertise and not stray into other fields in which they are not appropriately qualified and thereby help in ensuring the best evidence is available.

When statistics and/or probability are being presented and interpreted in court, it is necessary to be sure that the data are representative and correctly describe the occurrence of interest. The statistics need to support the conclusions being drawn and to have examined the probabilities of both the defendant's and the prosecutor's versions of events. If a database has been used, then the data within needs to be accurate and the database needs to be chosen appropriately to match the situation or occurrence being considered.

Nobel Laureate Richard Feynman stated, 'it is scientific only to say what is more likely and what is less likely, and not to be proving all the time the possible and impossible'.[42] Or put another way, 'science cannot tell us what is or what is not, only what is more or less likely based on the information we have'.[43]

Finally, in the environment of the court, experts need to be careful in their use of language and not to allow themselves to be drawn into making statements beyond their area of expertise.

REFERENCES

1. EWCA. 2003. *R v Clark* [2003] EWCA Crim 1020 (11 April 2003) [Online]. http://bit.ly/2krl3hX [Accessed 28 June 2019].
2. British Broadcasting Corporation (BBC). 1999. *Mother Given Life for Baby Murders* [Online]. http://bbc.in/2Blp9NT [Accessed 28 June 2019].
3. Meadow, R. (ed.). 1993. *The ABC of Child Abuse*. London: BMJ Publications.
4. Royal Statistical Society. 2001. *RSS Statement Regarding Statistical Issues in the Sally Clark Case, October 23rd 2001* [Online]. http://bit.ly/2k5Va5j [Accessed 28 June 2019].
5. Schneps, L. & Colmez, C. 2013. *Math on Trial*. p19. New York, NY: Basic Books (Perseus Books Group).
6. Barraclough, K. 2004. Stolen innocence: A mother's fight for justice-the story of Sally Clark. *British Medical Journal (BMJ)*, 329, 177.
7. Batt, J. 2005. *Stolen Innocence: The Sally Clark Story - A Mother's Fight for Justice*. London, UK: Ebury Press.
8. Schneps, L. & Colmez, C. 2013. *Math on Trial*. Introduction, px. New York, NY: Basic Books (Perseus Books Group).
9. Royal Statistical Society. 2002. Letter from the President to the Lord Chancellor regarding the use of statistical evidence in court cases. http://bit.ly/2Bymtiw [Accessed 21 February 2020].
10. ROYAL STATISTICAL SOCIETY. 2015. Statistics and the law - Practitioner guides. https://bit.ly/1zIUtkd [Accessed 21 February 2020].
11. Aitken, C., Roberts, P. & Jackson, G. 2010. The Fundamentals of Probability and Statistical Evidence in Criminal Proceedings. *Statistics and the Law: Royal Statistical Society Practitioner Guide 1*. https://bit.ly/2Jeg3qx [Accessed 21 February 2020].

12. Puch-Solis, R., Roberts, P., Pope, S. & Aitken, C. 2012. Assessing the Probative Value of DNA Evidence. *Statistics and the Law: Royal Statistical Society Practitioner Guide* 2. https://bit.ly/2XzoC8l [Accessed 21 February 2020].

13. Roberts, P. & Aitken, C. 2014. The Logic of Forensic Proof: Inferential Reasoning in Criminal Evidence. *Statistics and the Law: Royal Statistical Society Practitioner Guide* 3. https://bit.ly/302jCXU [Accessed 21 February 2020].

14. Jackson, G., Aitken, C. & Roberts, P. 2015. Case Assessment and Interpretation of Expert Evidence. *Statistics and the Law: Royal Statistical Society Practitioner Guide* 4. https://bit.ly/2UkZu0E [Accessed 21 February 2020].

15. Criminal Procedure Rules. Practice Directions. April 2019. https://bit.ly/2KNAIoM [Accessed 21 February 2020].

16. Criminal Procedure Rules. October 2015 as amended April 2018 and April 2019. Part 19: Expert Evidence. https://bit.ly/2AGjkL7 [Accessed 21 February 2020].

17. Civil Procedure Rules. Part 35 - Experts and Assessors. http://bit.ly/1tDEIKz [Accessed 21 February 2020].

18. Civil Procedure Rules. Practice direction 35 - Experts and Assessors. This practice direction supplements CPR. Part 35. http://bit.ly/2daQCF7 [Accessed 21 February 2020].

19. Forensic Science Regulator. 2014. Forensic Science Providers. Guidance: Validation. FSR-G-201. http://bit.ly/2CsF2kO [Accessed 21 February 2020].

20. Forensic Science Regulator. 2016. Information: Legal Obligations. FSR-I-400. Issue 4. P [Accessed 21 February 2020].

21. Forensic Science Regulator. 2017. Forensic science providers: Codes of Practice and Conduct. Issue 4. October 2017. http://bit.ly/2ArhOFY [Accessed 21 February 2020].

22. Forensic Science Regulator. 2017. Guidance on the content of reports issued by expert witnesses in the Criminal Justice System in England and Wales. FSR-G-200. Issue 1. Archived 14 February 2019. http://bit.ly/2Bujqnq [Accessed 21 February 2020].

23. Forensic Science Regulator. 2019. Guidance on the content of reports issued by expert witnesses in the Criminal Justice System in England and Wales. FSR-G-200. Issue 2. Archived 17 April 2019. https://bit.ly/2xna1P4 [Accessed 21 February 2020].

24. Forensic Science Regulator. 2019. Guidance on the content of reports issued by expert witnesses in the Criminal Justice System in England and Wales. FSR-G-200. Issue 3. https://bit.ly/323JrbO [Accessed 21 February 2020].

25. Finkelstein, M. O. & Fairley, W. B. 1970. A Bayesian approach to identification evidence. *Harvard Law Review*, 83, 489–517.

26. Mcgrayne, S. B. 2012. *The Theory that Would Not Die: How Bayes' Rule Cracked the Enigma Code, Hunted Down Russian Submarines, & Emerged Triumphant from Two Centuries of Controversy.* New Haven, CT: Yale University Press.

27. Robertson, B., Vignaux, G. A. & Berger, C. E. H. 2016. *Interpreting Evidence: Evaluating Forensic Science in the Court Room.* John Wiley & Sons Ltd.

28. DORSET POLICE. 2014. *Drink Drivers Targeted in Christmas Campaign* [Online]. http://bit.ly/2ziXwpc [Accessed 12 March 2020].
29. Champod, C., Evett, I. W. & Jackson, G. 2004. Establishing the most appropriate databases for addressing source level propositions. *Science & Justice*, 44, 153–164.
30. EWCA. 2010. *R v T* [2003] EWCA Crim 2439 (26 October 2010) [Online]. http://bit.ly/1OpEuu8 [Accessed 12 March 2020].
31. Berger, C. E., Buckleton, J., Champod, C., Evett, I. W. & Jackson, G. 2011. Evidence evaluation: A response to the court of appeal judgment in R v T. *Science & Justice*, 51, 43–49.
32. EDITORIAL. 2011. Expressing evaluative opinions: A position statement. *Science & Justice*, 51, 1–2.
33. Evett, I. W., Jackson, G., Lambert, J. A. & Mccrossan, S. 2000. The impact of the principles of evidence interpretation on the structure and content of statements. *Science & Justice*, 40, 233–239.
34. Fenton, N. & Neil, M. 2012. On limiting the use of Bayes in presenting forensic evidence. http://bit.ly/2CMSXDp [Accessed 12 March 2020].
35. Association of Forensic Science. 2009. Standards for the formulation of evaluative forensic science expert opinion. *Science & Justice*, 49, 161–164.
36. *R v Atkins and Atkins* [2009] EWCA Crim 1876.
37. Evett, I. W. 1995. Avoiding the transposed conditional. *Science & Justice*, 35, 127–131.
38. Barbey, A. K. & Sloman, S. A. 2007. Base-rate respect: From ecological rationality to dual processes. *Behavioral and Brain Sciences*, 30, 241–254.
39. Forensic Science Regulator. 2012. Report into the circumstances of a complaint received from the greater Manchester Police on 7 March 2012 regarding DNA evidence. LGC forensics. http://bit.ly/2yLQRQS [Accessed 12 March 2020].
40. Nobles, R. & Schiff, D. 2007. Misleading statistics within criminal trials. *Medicine, Science and the Law*, 47, 7–10.
41. Fleming, P., Blair, P., Bacon, C. & Berry, P. 2000. *Sudden Unexpected Death in Infancy. The CESDI SUDI Studies 1993–1996*. London: The Stationary Office.
42. Feynman, R. 1965. *The Character of Physical Law*. Cambridge, MA: MIT Press.
43. Vosk, T. & Emery, A. F. 2015. *Forensic Metrology – Scientific Measurement and Inference for Lawyers, Judges, and Criminalists*. Boca Raton, FL: CRC Press.

FURTHER READING

Forensic Metrology – Scientific Measurement and Inference for Lawyers, Judges, and Criminalists. VOSK T, Emery A.F. 2015. CRC Press.
A practical introduction to medical statistics. SCALLY AJ. The Obstetrician and Gynaecologist. 2014;16:121–8.

Math on Trial. 2013. SCHNEPS L, COLMEZ C. 2013. Basic Books (Perseus Books Group).

Interpreting Evidence: Evaluating Forensic Science in the Court Room. ROBERTSON, B., VIGNAUX, G. A., BERGER, C. E. H. 2016. John Wiley & Sons Ltd.

Judging under Uncertainty, An Institutional Theory of Legal Interpretation. VERMEULE A. 2006. Harvard University Press, Cambridge, MA.

10

Reports and Report Writing

Contents

INTRODUCTION

The expert's report is a key part of the evidence that an expert provides and presents at court. Hence, time and care must be taken to ensure a report is properly prepared on the subject matter, as per the instructions the expert receives within the expert's area of expertise and in keeping with the court procedure rules and according to the jurisdiction. The expert needs to remember the audience of such a report is manifold and therefore the layout and content needs to be designed in such a way that it makes for clear reading and avoids the use of overly technical language wherever possible. Depending upon the matter in hand, an expert's report is likely to be read not only by another expert in the same field, but also by lawyers, counsel, judges, other medical and forensic disciplines, and insurance industry experts and read out in court to juries and others. Therefore, knowledge and training in report writing for use in the legal arena are significant in being able to accomplish that task, which is a somewhat different skill, for example, to that of writing a specialist article for publication in an area of expertise where there perhaps exists a more specific or narrower area of readership.

On matters in the criminal courts, experts should expect that each report they prepare will result in that being part of the material at trial, whether for the prosecution or for the defence and upon which they will be expected to give oral evidence. For matters in the criminal courts in England and Wales, expert's reports need to be compliant with the Criminal Procedure Rules[1,2]; for matters in the Civil Courts, it is the Civil Procedure Rules[3,4] that apply. Other jurisdictions may vary in their specific requirements. The expert needs to be aware of these insofar as they relate to the expert's area of expertise and practice, including the expert's duties and responsibilities. Generally, there are not huge differences in the requirements of experts in the civil justice system and the criminal justice system of England and Wales of the UK. In relation to the criminal justice system for England and Wales of the UK, the office of the forensic science regulator (FSR) has also published guidance documents for expert witnesses.[5-7] The FSR document 'Expert Report Guidance'[8-10] provides useful advice. Experts should read the Guidance.

The Academy of Medical Royal Colleges (UK) has published guidance for healthcare professionals who act as expert witnesses and endorsed by other healthcare professional organisations. The key undertakings include that practitioners are now expected to undertake specific training for being an expert witness.[11,12] Other organisations are also providing documents in relation to expert witnesses and may need to be considered where appropriate and relevant to do so. The Royal College of Surgeons in England has also issued guidance.

In the civil justice system of England and Wales (UK), for example in matters such as personal injury or clinical negligence, a report is often the expert's only contribution into the resolution or determination of a civil dispute. Few claims go to trial and in those that do, experts (especially single joint experts – that is where one expert is jointly instructed by both parties) may or may not be called to give oral evidence. It therefore remains important that expert's reports are well crafted, properly compiled and comply with the appropriate instructions, court rules and any court directions in the case at the time. Of course, in the cases where the matter does go to a hearing at court, then experts are called to give oral evidence, including cross-examination on their report.

THE PURPOSE OF EXPERTS' REPORTS

A report is written by an expert to help the parties in the preparation and settlement of the case and/or to help the court to arrive at a decision. The report is for people who are not experts in the specialist field, and whether instructed by one side or the other, that being the claimant or defendant in civil justice system; the prosecution or defence in the criminal justice system; or by the court itself, a report must address the issues in the case on which the expert has been instructed and contain the facts which the expert has relied upon to reach their opinion.[13] It should be a reasoned analysis of the evidence based upon the expert's knowledge, skill and experience in their specialist field.

The expert may be:

a) providing a preliminary advisory report – that is a report to be used by the instructing party to decide if the case is worth pursuing, or defending;

b) preparing a report 'pre-action' to assist the parties in valuing or settling the case, or to prepare the formal court documents (statements of case). This type of report, perhaps updated, may be disclosed to the other party and the court at a later stage;

c) writing a report that is to be disclosed to both parties during the proceedings and which may be used to settle the case or at trial. This is usually the type of a report that will be requested of an expert.

269

Note: A preliminary advisory report may be privileged from disclosure in the civil justice system of England and Wales, but the expert may not be immune from a claim for damages if the expert is shown to have been negligent in its preparation. In fact, since the case of *Jones v Kaney* [2011] UKSC 13,[14] expert witnesses are liable for inexpert evidence for both breach of contract and negligence.

Where an expert provides advice to a party, and the same expert is then retained to provide a report for the court, it is probably prudent for the expert to set out the position in the report, in case of later queries with regard to his or her independence. However, this could prompt the other party to ask for the disclosure of the original instructions and is unclear whether these remain privileged.

In a report for disclosure to the other party and to the court, the expert has a particular duty to remain independent and to express an objective opinion, but only doing so *on issues that are within their area of expertise and which are part of the dispute before the court.* Courts want expert witnesses to cover the strengths and weaknesses of a party's (or both parties') case, and to provide honest unbiased opinions based upon a full appraisal of all the facts and issues relevant to their evidence; not just a partial view based upon what one party wants the court to hear. The expert should ensure that the instructions they receive are clear and if not then the expert should seek written clarification from those who wish to instruct the expert. For example, if an expert receives an instruction that only says, 'prepare a report', this would need further clarification and which should be provided in writing to the expert.

If, when preparing a report, the expert feels strongly that a particular matter is essential to their opinion, it is the expert's duty to include this in the report or to withdraw from acting in the litigation. Where a range of opinion may exist, the expert witness should include these in their report for the court, and to state the reasons for supporting their opinion. It is not acceptable to set out different views in a separate letter to the instructing party (referred to as a 'side letter' – see later section on Draft reports, side letters, screening reports and requested changes to reports), at least not once litigation is under way. In the event that an expert feels the need to receive advice or directions from the court, the expert may contact the court directly but usually only after having attempted to have such queries addressed by their instructing party. In the main, it is unusual for experts to need to contact the courts for advice or directions, although there may be occasions when this is necessary, for example, when the expert has not been provided with all the records or material despite requests to do so.

In the civil justice system, the case of *BA plc v Spencer and others (trustees of the pensions scheme)* [2015],[15] the judge noted that CPR 35.1 states that expert evidence is to be restricted to that 'reasonably required' to resolve the proceedings. Also, that the correct approach was to consider whether the expert evidence was necessary in the sense that a decision could not be made without it. If necessary, then the evidence must be admitted. If the expert evidence is not essential to the determination of the matter but is provided to assist the court to understand some technical issue, then a balance has to be struck and the proportionality of the evidence assessed. The court must take into account several factors, including the value of the claim, the effect of a judgement on the parties, who is to pay for the expert evidence and any possible delay, particularly if the trial date becomes threatened. The original Deputy Master's wholesale rejection of any expert evidence was found flawed and was set aside. The judge's view was that the expert evidence would be necessary to resolve a number of issues and would also be of assistance to the court in understanding several points. When considering proportionality, the judge noted a number of favourable factors, including a large sum of money was at stake, that without expert evidence the hands of the trial judge could be tied and that the cost of the expert evidence would be borne by *BA* in any event. The judge also thought that the expert evidence would not broaden the range of issues, result in lengthy reports or delay the trial. The judgement is worth reading if there is any question of excluding expert evidence. Although this was a civil claim, it is likely similar considerations would apply in criminal matters. Admissibility of expert evidence is also considered in Chapter 11.

CONTENTS OF EXPERT'S REPORTS

In *R v B (T)* [2006] *(ante)*,[16] the Court of Appeal set out what should be contained within any expert's report.

(1) Details of the expert's academic and professional qualifications, experience and accreditation relevant to the opinions expressed in the report and the range and extent of the expertise and any limitations upon the expertise.

(2) A statement setting out the substance of all the instructions received (written or oral), questions upon which an opinion is sought, the materials provided and considered, and the documents, statements, evidence, information or assumptions which

271

are material to the opinions expressed or upon which those opinions are based.

(3) Information relating to who has carried out measurements, examinations, tests etc. and the methodology used, and whether or not such measurements etc. were carried out under the expert's supervision.

(4) Where there is a range of opinion in the matters dealt with in the report, a summary of the range of opinion and the reasons for the opinion is given. In this connection any material facts or matters which detract from the expert's opinions and any points which should fairly be made against any opinions expressed should be set out.

(5) Relevant extracts of literature or any other material which might assist the court.

(6) A statement to the effect that the expert has complied with his/her duty to the court to provide independent assistance by way of objective unbiased opinion in relation to matters within his or her expertise and an acknowledgment that the expert will inform all parties and where appropriate the court in the event that his/her opinion changes on any material issues.

(7) Where on an exchange of experts' reports matters arise which require a further or supplemental report, the above guidelines should, of course, be complied with.

Guidelines regarding the provision of expert reports were also given by the Court of Appeal in England and Wales in *R. v Reed and Reed, R. v Garmson* [2010] 1 Cr App R 23,[17] where it was stated, inter alia, that:

(1) It is particularly important to ensure that, where there is a range of opinion on a subject, the report
  i) summarises the range of opinion, and
  ii) give reasons for the expert's own opinion; and if the expert is not able to give his opinion without qualification, states the qualification. Furthermore, where propositions are to be advanced as part of an evaluative opinion, each proposition should be spelt out with precision.

(2) It will then normally be necessary for the judge to direct the experts to
  a) discuss the expert issues in the proceedings; and
  b) prepare a statement for the court of the matters on which they agree and disagree, giving their reasons.

(3) The experts should be able to set out in that joint statement, in clear terms, for use at the trial, the basic science that is agreed, insofar as it is not contained in one of the reports. The experts must then identify with precision what is in dispute.

(4) If the order as to the provision of the joint statement is not observed and in the absence of a good reason, then the trial judge should consider carefully whether to exercise the power to refuse permission to the party whose expert is in default to call that expert to give evidence. In many cases the judge may well exercise that power. A failure to find time for a meeting because of commitments to other matters (a common problem with many experts as was evident in this appeal) is not to be treated as a good reason.

Expert's reports need to be compliant with the relevant Court Procedure Rules. As mentioned earlier, for the Criminal Courts (in England and Wales), these are the Criminal Procedure Rules. For the Civil Courts (in England and Wales), these are the Civil Procedure Rules. Other jurisdictions may vary.

Amendments to the Court Rules

Amendments can and do occur to the court rules over time and which are often published online. Experts are expected to keep up to date with any relevant amendments and in line with their duties and responsibilities.

CRIMINAL PROCEDURE RULES

Expert Evidence – The Rules

Part 19 of the Criminal Procedure Rules relates to Expert Evidence [also see the Practice Direction]:

Rule 19.1. When this part applies.
This part applies when a party wants to admit expert evidence
Rule 19.2. Expert's duty to the court.
Rule 19.3. Introduction of expert evidence.
Rule 19.4. Content of expert's report.
Rule 19.5. Expert to be informed of service of report.
Rule 19.6. Pre-hearing discussion of expert evidence.

Rule 19.7. Court's power to direct that evidence is to be given by a single joint expert.
Rule 19.8. Instructions to a single joint expert.

Expert Evidence – The Practice Direction

The Practice Direction V of the Criminal Procedure Rules for England and Wales, also refers to:

19A. Expert Evidence.
19B. Statements of Understanding and Declarations of Truth in Expert Reports.
19C. Pre-Hearing Discussion of Expert Evidence.

CIVIL PROCEDURE RULES

The Civil Procedure Rules and Practice Direction therein set out the detailed requirements for experts' reports. These include the requirement in reports of a statement that the expert understands their duty to the court and has complied with that duty and that the report contains the 'statement of truth'. The expert's report must state the substance of all material instructions, whether written and oral, on the basis of which the report was written.

There is a general Civil Procedure Rules (CPR) requirement for a report to be in writing (typed). The court requires experts to prepare a written report for use in evidence by one or more parties, and to assist the court in deciding the dispute unless it directs otherwise. In cases allocated to what are referred to as the 'small claims' or 'fast tracks', and whenever a single joint expert is instructed, expert evidence by a written report/s alone is the norm. However, this does not mean that the expert will not be called to give oral evidence at court.

The Civil Procedure Rules (CPR) that relates to Experts is Part 35 – Experts and Assessors [also see the Practice Direction 35 – Experts & Assessors]:

- *Duty to restrict expert evidence – Rule 35.1*
- *Interpretation and definitions – Rule 35.2*
- *Experts overriding duty to the court – Rule 35.3*
- *Court's power to restrict expert evidence – Rule 35.4*

- *General requirement for expert evidence to be given in a written report – Rule 35.5*
- *Written questions to experts – Rule 35.6*
- *Court's power to direct that evidence is to be given by a single joint expert – Rule 35.7*
- *Instructions to a single joint expert – Rule 35.8*
- *Power of court to direct a party to provide information – Rule 35.9*
- *Contents of report – Rule 35.10*
- *Use by one party of expert's report disclosed by another – Rule 35.11*
- *Discussions between experts – Rule 35.12*
- *Consequence of failure to disclose expert's report – Rule 35.13*
- *Expert's right to ask for court directions – Rule 35.14*
- *Assessors – Rule 35.15*

Practice Direction 35 – Experts and Assessors

This practice direction supplements CPR Part 35.

Part 35 is intended to limit the use of oral expert evidence to that which is reasonably required:

• *Introduction.*	*Para 1*
• *Expert Evidence – General Requirements.*	*Para 2.1*
• *Form and Content of an Expert's Report.*	*Para 3.1*
• *Information.*	*Para 4*
• *Instructions.*	*Para 5*
• *Questions to Experts.*	*Para 6.1*
• *Single Joint Expert.*	*Para 7*
• *Orders.*	*Para 8*
• *Discussions between Experts.*	*Para 9.1*
• *Assessors.*	*Para 10.1*
• *Concurrent Expert Evidence.*	*Para 11.1*

The expert's report must contain a statement that the expert –

(a) *understands their duty to the court, and has complied with that duty; and*
(b) *is aware of the requirements of Part 35, this practice direction and the Guidance for the Instruction of Experts in Civil Claims 2014.*

Statement of truth

An expert's report must be verified by a statement of truth in the following form:

> I confirm that I have made clear which facts and matters referred to in this report are within my own knowledge and which are not. Those that are within my own knowledge I confirm to be true. The opinions I have expressed represent my true and complete professional opinions on the matters to which they refer.

Part 22 of the Civil Procedure Rules deals with statements of truth. Rule 32.14 sets out the consequences of verifying a document containing a false statement without an honest belief in its truth.

Note: The court procedure rules are subject to periodic updates. These may or may not include amendments to statements. Experts and others should ensure they remain aware of the same where relevant.

The Case of 'The Ikarian Reefer'

In one of the leading pre-civil procedure rules cases on experts' reports, *National Justice Compania Naviera SA v Prudential Assurance Co Ltd ('The Ikarian Reefer')* [1993][18] 2 Lloyd's Rep 68, Cresswell LJ gave the following general guidance on the contents of experts' reports. In 2003, this was summarised and included in the Part 35 Practice Direction:

- The expert's paramount duty is to the court and this overrides any obligation to the person from whom the expert has received instructions.
- The report should be the independent product of the expert, uninfluenced by the pressures of litigation.
- An expert should assist the court by providing objective and unbiased opinion on matters within his expertise, and should not assume the role of the advocate.
- An expert should consider all material facts, including those which might detract from his opinion.
- An expert should make it clear when an issue falls outside his expertise and when he is not able to reach a definite opinion.
- If an expert changes his view on any material matter after producing his report, he should communicate this to the parties and the court without delay.

As we have seen earlier, the form and content of an expert's court report is dealt with in the Practice Direction of the civil procedure rules in some detail and experts should make sure they have the current requirements at the time. Some of the basic requirements are:

- An expert's report should be addressed to the court and not to the party from whom the expert has received his instructions.
- An expert's report must:
  (1) Give details of the expert's qualifications;
  (2) Give details of any literature or other material which the expert has relied on when preparing the report;
  (3) Contain a statement setting out the substance of all facts and instructions given to the expert which are material to the opinions expressed in the report or upon which those opinions are based;
  (4) Make clear which of the facts stated in the report are within the expert's own knowledge;
  (5) Say who carried out any examination, measurement, test or experiment which the expert has used for the report, give the qualifications of that person, and say whether or not the test or experiment has been carried out under the expert's supervision;
  (6) Where there is a range of opinion on the matters dealt within the report – summarise the range of opinion; and give reasons for their own opinion;
  (7) Contain a summary of the conclusions reached;
  (8) If the expert is not able to give their opinion without qualification, state the qualification; and
  (9) Contain a statement that the expert –
    a) understands their duty to the court, and has complied with that duty;
    and
    b) is aware of the requirements of Part 35, this practice direction and the Guidance for the Instruction of Experts in Civil Claims 2014.

The expert's report must include the statement of truth.

SUMMARISING INSTRUCTIONS

It is important that this is done carefully, or the letter from the instructing party is appended to the report, to avoid the risk of the court ordering the

277

disclosure of the actual instructions, including documents sent with them, although the decision of the Court of Appeal in *Lucas v Barking, Havering & Redbridge Hospitals NHS Trust*[19] somewhat reduces the risk of this.

THE RANGE OF OPINION

Where a range of opinion exists, experts should provide the range of opinion within their expertise on a particular issue in dispute, to enable the court to understand the full spectrum of professional views and not just the opinion of one or two experts. Judges do not want 'opposing' experts to adopt extreme positions on paper, each at opposite ends of a spectrum, and then agree under cross-examination that the most likely position is between the two extremes. Where there is a range of opinion, this is particularly important in a single joint expert report where the expert is instructed by both parties.

REFERENCE TO MATERIALS AND LITERATURE

An expert is required to give details of any literature or other material or experiments upon which he or she has relied in the preparation of their report. The reason for this is to enable other experts, and others involved in the proceedings, to read the same material and consider its relevance, if necessary raising written questions on it, or placing it on the agenda for the experts' discussion. It also displays transparency on what material has been provided to the expert to be considered in the preparation of their report.

EXPERT'S FAILURE TO COMPLY WITH THE COURT RULES ON REPORTS

Courts are unimpressed with experts who do not appear to be familiar with the rules. In the case of *Stevens v Gullis* [2000] 1 AER 527,[20] an unqualified design expert prepared his report late, did not include a summary of his instructions, failed to date the report or add a statement of truth, did not relate it to the pleadings or refer to any of the exchanged witness statements, failed to comply with a court order requiring him to rectify the deficiencies of his report and failed to sign a statement following an experts' discussion. One month before trial, the court (upheld by the Court of Appeal) made an order barring the expert from giving evidence on the grounds that he did not understand his duty to the court. The judge said:

> It is essential in a complicated case such as this that the court should have a competent expert dealing with the matters which are in issue

between the defendant and third party. Mr [X], not having apparently understood his duty to the court and not having set out in his report that he understands it, is in my view a person whose evidence I should not encourage in the administration of justice.

Thimmaya v Lancashire NHS Foundation Trust[21] *v Jamil* [2020], in the UK. This highly unusual clinical negligence case related to a consultant spinal surgeon acting as an expert witness, and serves to illustrate the importance of experts understanding their duties to the court and the potential consequences when an expert fails in those duties. Experts can expect to be challenged over their expertise where they have limited personal experience of matters on which they are providing an opinion. Where an expert has medical hindrance including mental health and cognitive difficulties which affect their ability to work, then they should take appropriate action, including notifying solicitors and ceasing to act.

STYLE, PRESENTATION AND STRUCTURE OF REPORTS

Model Report Formats

When attending expert witness courses, suggested model formats for reports are part of the training. These courses train experts in how to construct a court-compliant report. Expert witness organisations, and expert witness sections of some professional bodies have produced model forms of reports to assist experts, lawyers, counsel and the courts.

An expert may be very proficient in their field and have carefully analysed the facts of a case, but the impact of his or her evidence will be greatly weakened if the report is set out poorly. Badly organised reports irritate lawyers and judges; you can take steps to reduce the likelihood of this.

Suggestions on Presentation

- Clear headings and subheadings are useful for signposting, e.g. in the summary of the facts, the opinion and conclusion.
- Include a contents page also, with reference to page numbers and/or paragraph numbers.
- Page numbers and paragraph numbers are required, especially for longer reports, e.g. 1.1, 1.2, etc.; using a new number for each of the points in the next chapter, e.g. 2.1, 2.2, etc.
- Short sentences and paragraphs improve readability.

- Headers, or suitable reference, on each page are helpful to identify the expert by name and the date of the report.
- A front sheet can provide the essential details (see section on 'The Front Page/Cover Sheet of the Report').
- A synopsis might be included to help the reader to understand what the case is about, especially if the report is long – twenty or more pages.
- The report should differentiate between 'facts' that are in the expert's own knowledge and those that they have obtained 'second-hand'.
- There must be a clear conclusion.
- A chronology can help the reader, particularly in complex cases.
- Reports should be written (typed) preferably with double spacing, and in the first person; be signed by the expert personally; contain the necessary declarations and statements of truth (see earlier) and be dated the day the expert signs the report out.
- The report should make clear if anyone else has carried out tests or worked on parts of the report.
- A glossary of technical terms might be placed in the appendix if there are many such terms, or the terms should be explained in the body of the report if they are relatively few.
- Graphics, photographs, diagrams or models where appropriate will help the solicitor; the client and the judge understand the case.
- Reports when printed should be printed on A4 good quality paper, with good size margins around the edges to leave room for the reader to make notes. Double spacing is easier to read than single.

Structure of Reports

Reports should be clearly and logically structured, with the structure well signposted. *Fact and Opinion need to be kept separate.*

Ensure that you have identified the issues to be addressed in your report and that they are within your area of expertise.

If there are detailed calculations or investigations, they might be included in an appendix to avoid the detail obscuring the key points.

The length of a report may vary depending on the circumstances and proportionality, but judges have been known to criticise excessive length of reports. Nevertheless, whenever the amount of material the expert needs to inspect and consider when preparing their report is sizeable, then in such circumstances a more lengthy report can be unavoidable for completeness.

The Front Page/Cover Sheet of the Report

This is essential for identification purposes of the report and should include:

- The status of the report. Sometimes it will be necessary to provide follow-up reports, so do ensure the reports are numbered and dated accordingly. Address the report to the court and when ready send to those who have instructed you.
- The case title and case reference.
- The parties, and by whom the expert is instructed.
- The instructing party's solicitor's details.
- The expert's full name and contact details.
- Date the report when signed.

The Main Part of the Report

1. *The Introduction*

    This section might include:

    The expert's qualifications
    This should not give too much detail but relate the author's expertise to the case, to indicate to the court his competence to act as an expert witness in relation to the specific issues. The expert's CV might be included in an appendix.
    The identity of any other person who has assisted with the preparation of the report should be given, and whether the author accepts responsibility for their work.

    Summary of the case
    This should give a short synopsis of what the case is about.

    Summary of conclusions
    This should set out in brief the expert's opinions and conclusions and the answers to any specific questions raised in the instructions.

2. *The Issues to be Addressed*

    This section should set out clearly the summary of the expert's instructions (written and oral) and the issues or questions that the report addresses. One solution is to annex to the report the solicitor's letter(s) of instruction.

281

The documents that the expert has examined and relied upon should be listed, and the details of other sources of evidence given. This can be included as part of the introduction in the report, or if there is a particularly long list, it could be provided in an appendix.

3. *The Investigation of the Facts*

This section should address the facts. In a complicated case, a chronology can be helpful and can be placed in an appendix. Experts should identify separately:
   a) 'facts' the expert has observed for himself or herself, e.g. from examining the claimant or the site;
   b) 'facts' that are versions of events the expert was told by the client or by others, identifying the source;
   c) 'facts' that the expert has been asked to assume are correct, again identifying the instruction.

The expert must include all material facts, including those which might detract from his opinion.

In a report that deals with very technical issues, it can be helpful for the expert to summarise the technical background. All technical terms should be explained (and, if necessary, cross-referenced to a glossary in an appendix). Alternatively, technical terms can be defined as they arise in the report to help those reading the report as they go along. The avoidance of technical language in expert's reports is to be recommended where possible, whilst acknowledging that may not always be able to be achieved where the use of some technical language is necessary.

It may also be necessary in this section for the expert to refer to the opinions of others, including other experts, which the expert has considered in forming their opinion, and whether one agrees or disagrees. If that is necessary, and as part of your instructions, then ensure your opinion is couched in suitable terms and that these are not personal about another expert. Experts can and do have different opinions. Remember, it is *not* the expert's role to act as an advocate or the judge!

• Examinations

A description of any examinations and tests, as well as the dates they were carried out and by whom, should be given next. The detail may be put into an appendix.

• Research and References

Where appropriate, details of any research carried out should be given, and full references should be provided for any literature or works of reference consulted and relied upon. Copies of these papers should appear in an appendix if not too long.

4. *The Opinion and Conclusions*

In this section, the expert should present their opinion clearly and unambiguously. It is the most important part of the report. The way this is done will vary with the type of report and specialism. The expert should set out each of the issues, then link these issues to the facts and give reasoned argument derived from, and cross-referenced to, the evidence.

If there is a range of professional opinion on an issue, this should be set out and the expert should explain where their opinion sits within the spectrum, with reasons.

The expert should qualify their opinion if they could not reach a clear conclusion because of insufficient information.

Experts should *not*:
a) comment on matters outside their instructions, unless they feel very strongly that this is essential to the case;
b) comment on matters outside their expertise. When a matter, or item within a matter, is outside an expert's area of expertise, then the expert should make that clear.
c) try to do the judge's job. For example, in a negligence dispute, the judge decides if someone has been negligent, not the expert. The expert should only say whether or not, in their opinion, the professional's conduct or treatment provided fell below a reasonable standard of care as would be expected of someone practicing in the field at the same time. Similarly, in criminal cases, do not be led into passing opinion, if asked, on whether you think the defendant is guilty or not guilty. Normally, the judge would be expected to intervene should such an inappropriate question be put to an expert.

5. *Appendices*

These might include:
• The expert's resume/curriculum vitae including experience and qualifications set out in date order (attaching a marketing brochure is not the way to do this).

- The letter(s) of instruction.
- The list of documents examined.
- Results of investigations and tests or calculations.
- List of reference material referred to and possibly copies of that material.
- Chronology of events.
- Glossary of technical terms in alphabetical order.

DRAFT REPORTS, 'SIDE' LETTERS, SCREENING REPORTS AND REQUESTED CHANGES TO REPORTS

It may be that an expert is invited to prepare a report in draft, to enable the instructing lawyer and client to check the report for compliance with the instructions, the court procedure rules and any court directions, for factual accuracy, consistency and completeness and for clarity of presentation. However, this understandably can make experts feel uncomfortable in that if they provide a draft and then when having considered all the material may change their opinion. *This is a highly risky approach for the expert!*

Sometimes the expert can be requested to provide what is known as a 'Screening report'. The purpose of a screening report is to identify the issues that may arise and assist the instructing solicitors to understand the strengths and weaknesses of a case. The expert and solicitor should agree on the timescale for the completion of the screening report and make sure the expert has all the relevant papers available so far. The screening report may include indications of further investigations needed before a full report is written and other experts that may be needed if matters are outside their field of expertise. The expert and solicitor may need to talk during the report writing stage. It should be headed with words such as: 'Screening Report – Disclosable only to (X) the law firm instructing and (Y) the client'. For the avoidance of any misunderstanding, it could be useful to state on the front page of the screening report: 'this screening report is not compliant with the civil/criminal procedure rules', for in the event that report is later submitted as evidence.

An expert must not be asked to set out their comments on, for example, the weaknesses of the case in a separate 'side' letter (a common practice pre-CPR), as this would be in conflict with the expert's duty to provide their complete and true opinion to the court.

It is perfectly acceptable under the relevant court procedure rules to ask for amendments to an expert's report before disclosure, if:

1. The facts are not accurate.
2. New facts or evidence have come to light since the instructions were sent to the expert.
3. The report does not comply with the CPR formalities; the expert has commented on issues outside his expertise; or the expert has commented too definitively on matters which are for the judge to decide.
4. The expert has not annexed relevant material.
5. The report could be presented in a clearer way.

Experts must *not* be asked to amend their report in a way which distorts the expert's true opinion on key issues in the report.

REFERENCES

1. Criminal Procedure Rules. October 2015 as amended April 2018 and April 2019. Part 19. Expert Evidence. https://bit.ly/2AGjkL7 [Accessed: 21 February 2020].
2. Criminal Procedure Rules. Practice directions. April 2019. https://bit.ly/2KNAIoM [Accessed: 21 February 2020].
3. Civil Procedure Rules. Part 35 - Experts and assessors. http://bit.ly/1tDEIKz [Accessed: 21 February 2020].
4. Civil Procedure Rules. Practice direction 35 - Experts and Assessors. This practice direction supplements CPR part 35. http://bit.ly/2daQCF7 [Accessed: 21 February 2020].
5. Forensic Science Regulator. 2016. Information. Legal obligations. FSR-I-400. Issue 4. http://bit.ly/2CK5yY5 [Accessed: 21 February 2020].
6. Forensic Science Regulator. 2017. Codes of Practice and Conduct. *for forensic science providers and practitioners in the Criminal Justice System*. Issue 4. February 2017. http://bit.ly/2Arh0FY [Accessed: 21 February 2020].
7. Forensic Science Regulator. 2014. Guidance. Validation. FSR-G-201. Issue 1. http://bit.ly/2CsF2kO [Accessed: 21 February 2020].
8. Forensic Science Regulator. 2017. Guidance on the content of reports issued by expert witnesses in the Criminal Justice System in England and Wales. FSR-G-200. Issue 1. Archived 14 February 2019. http://bit.ly/2Bujqnq [Accessed: 21 February 2020].

9. Forensic Science Regulator. 2019. Guidance on the content of reports issued by expert witnesses in the Criminal Justice System in England and Wales. FSR-G-200. Issue 2. Archived 17 April 2019. https://bit.ly/2xna1P4 [Accessed: 21 February 2020].

10. Forensic Science Regulator. 2019. Guidance on the content of reports issued by expert witnesses in the Criminal Justice System in England and Wales. FSR-G-200. Issue 3. https://bit.ly/323JrbO [Accessed: 21 February 2020].

11. Academy of Medical Royal Colleges. 2019. Acting as an expert or professional witness. Guidance for healthcare professionals. https://bit.ly/38KzbIm [Accessed: 21 February 2020].

12. Bond Solon Wilmington Professional. 2019. Acting as an Expert Witness - New Guidance for Healthcare Professionals. https://bit.ly/2NvnrmI [Accessed: 21 February 2020].

13. Bond C; Solon M; Harper P; Davies G. 2007. *The Expert Witness - A Practical Guide*. Third edition. Shaw and Sons: London, UK.

14. *Jones v Kaney* [2011] UKSC 13.

15. *BA plc v Spencer and others (trustees of the pensions scheme)* [2015] EWHC 2477 (Ch), [2015] All ER (D) 101 (Aug).

16. *R v B* (T) [2006] (*ante*) EWCA 2 Cr App R 3.

17. *R. v. Reed and Reed, R. v. Garmson* [2010] EWCA 1 Cr App R 23.

18. *National Justice Compania Naviera SA v Prudential Assurance Co Ltd ("The Ikarian Reefer")* [1993] 2 Lloyd's Rep 68. Cresswell J.

19. *Lucas v Barking*, Havering & Redbridge Hospitals NHS Trust [2003] EWCA Civ 1102.

20. *Stevens v Gullis* [2000] 1 AER 527.

21. *Thimmaya v Lancashire NHS Foundation Trust v Jamil* [2020]. Hearing date 30 January 2020. Manchester County Court, UK. https://bit.ly/2QhD1Se [Accessed: 15 March 2020].

11

Expert Evidence in Court

Contents

THE LEGAL SYSTEMS

Any trial involves the determination of issues by an impartial body, be that a judge, a panel of judges or a jury.

The focus of this chapter will be on those jurisdictions deriving their rules and structures from that of the English common law. That is to say, from the law as developed through the tradition of legal proceedings that was refined in the various courts of England from the Middle Ages up to the last century. Those rules were not necessarily written down or codified, but acknowledged in reported decisions on cases, and taken to be binding precedents by courts deciding similar points later on.

Alongside those rules and concepts that the courts gradually evolved and recognised themselves were added particular specific laws and statutes passed by parliament. Although those statutes took precedence over the courts' rules, those laws had to be analysed and interpreted to fit various factual situations by the courts over time, and those interpretations themselves have been taken to form binding precedents. The common law system therefore consists of two main sources of law: *statute* – those laws passed by the legislature, and *case law* – the body of previous decisions and principles derived by the judiciary over time.

Following the historic expansion of British influence throughout the world, many territories adopted the English legal system. As those countries gained their independence, they naturally passed their own laws, but much of the principles embodied in the history of the *case law* remained, and remain the same. For that reason, courts in the United Kingdom, Ireland, United States of America, India, Australia, New Zealand, Canada and parts of the Caribbean are essentially more alike than they are different.

A particular feature of the English common law system that has spread through parts of the world is the *adversarial* process – that is the concept of two sides coming before a court as their version of events is in dispute and arguing before an impartial tribunal, whether that be a judge alone deciding issues of law and fact, or with a judge deciding issues of law, and a jury deciding issues of fact. The court has to find out what has occurred.

In the adversarial process the court does not carry out its own investigation, but decides the case based on the evidence presented to it by each side.

The court considers evidence of *fact* and evidence of *opinion*.

Facts are what someone heard, saw or did. Evidence of opinion is given by *expert witnesses*, where the opinion given is an independent view of the facts which is provided in order to assist the court in helping to understand what the matter is about. Witnesses are normally questioned by the advocates for each side, with few questions, save for matters of clarification, coming from the court itself.

Courts in the adversarial process normally consist of either a judge and jury or a judge or judge(s) sitting alone. Crown Court trials consist of a professional judge deciding matters of law and a jury of 12 randomly selected men and women deciding matters of fact by deliberating on their verdict, guilty or not guilty. Most trials in the USA are conducted with juries. An example of a court in the adversarial system which has judges alone deciding matters of fact and law are the Magistrates' Courts in England and Wales, where either a legally qualified judge or a group of three or so non-legally qualified regular volunteer judges will decide all matters. Appellate courts such as Courts of Appeal or Supreme Courts, as they are concerned with matters of law, only have judges.

The adversarial process is to be distinguished from the *inquisitorial* process used in the majority of European countries, where the court acts as an 'inquisitor', inquiring into the facts, carrying out an investigation, gathering evidence and examining witnesses. In the inquisitorial process, advocates act more as protectors of each side's legal rights from the actions of the court. In the adversarial process, advocates act more as competitors in an arena before an impartial referee.

This overview will concentrate on the adversarial process and use specific examples from the English legal system. It is hoped, however, that some of the fundamental principles will be of universal application, given that an expert's duty is to the court.

WHEN IS EXPERT EVIDENCE ALLOWED?

For several centuries experts have given assistance to the courts.[1] Where specialised or technical knowledge was required, experts participated on juries and later the Middle Ages experts began to testify as witnesses, becoming a more ordinary occurrence later in the eighteenth century.[2,3]

The South Australia Supreme Court in *R. v Bonython* (1984) 38 S.A.S.R. 45[4] held that there were two questions that had to be answered in the affirmative before evidence of the opinion of an 'expert' could be admitted:

Before admitting the opinion of a witness into evidence as expert testimony, the judge must consider and decide two questions. The first is whether the subject matter of the opinion falls within the class of subjects upon which expert testimony is permissible. This first question may be divided into two parts:

(a) whether the subject matter of the opinion is such that a person without instruction or experience in the area of knowledge or human experience would be able to form a sound judgment on the matter without the assistance of witnesses possessing special knowledge or experience in the area, and

(b) whether the subject matter of the opinion forms part of a body of knowledge or experience which is sufficiently organized or recognized to be accepted as a reliable body of knowledge or experience, a special acquaintance with which by the witness would render his opinion of assistance to the court.

The second question is whether the witness has acquired by study or experience sufficient knowledge of the subject to render his opinion of value in resolving the issues before the court.

The Court of Appeal in *R. v Luttrell* [2004],[5] approving the principle in *Bonython*, held that:

For expert evidence to be admissible, two conditions must be satisfied: first, that study or experience will give a witness's opinion an authority which the opinion of one not so qualified will lack; and secondly the witness must be so qualified to express the opinion.

As Kay LJ put it in *R v Bernard V* [2003] EWCA Crim 3917,[6] at para 29, expert evidence is admissible when it is necessary:

to inform the jury of experience of a scientific and medical kind of which they might be unaware, which they ought to take into account when they assess the evidence in the case in order to decide whether they can be sure about the reliability of a particular witness.

That principle was reaffirmed by the Court of Appeal in *H (Stephen) v The Queen* [2014] EWCA Crim 1555,[7] at paras 43 and 44, where Sir Brian Leveson P observed:

43. [...T]here is real concern about the use of unreliable or inappropriate expert evidence. As a result, Part 33 of the Criminal Procedure Rules has been revised (with effect from 1 October 2014) and a new Practice Direction is to be published which will incorporate the reliability factors recommended by the Law Commission for the admission of expert evidence. The Advocacy Training Council, also, is in the course of preparing a 'tool kit' for advocates to use when considering expert evidence

and its admissibility, itself based upon the recommendations in the Law Commission Report.

44. When these changes occur, a new and more rigorous approach on the part of advocates and the courts to the handling of expert evidence must be adopted. That should avoid misunderstandings about what is (and what is not) appropriately included in an expert's report and so either avoid, or at least render far more straightforward, submissions on admissibility such as those made in this case. In particular, as we have emphasised, comment based only on analysis of the evidence which effectively usurps the task of the jury is to be avoided: the task of the expert is only to provide assistance of the kind which Kay LJ articulated set out in [*R v. Bernard V*].

R v Calland [2017] EWCA Crim 2308 also considers when an expert is required.

The **weight** to be attached to the opinion must of course be assessed by the tribunal of fact, see for example *R v Robb* [1991] 93 Cr App R161,[8] 165, and *R v Darragher* [2002] EWCA Crim 1903, [2003] 1 Cr App R 12[9] para 23.

It is not part of the law of England and Wales that the expert in question should be able to evaluate their findings by reference to a database of random selection, such as to allow for statistical probabilities to be arrived at.

The English Court of Appeal in *R v Otway* [2011] EWCA Crim 3,[10] when upholding the safety of the use of expert podiatry evidence in a murder case, stated that: 'The proposition that evidence of a comparison cannot be admitted if its evaluation is expressed in terms [of] subjective experience is simply wrong in law'. The Court went on to say the following:

> We accept the submission made that in a comparison exercise based upon facial mapping or walking gait, it is a necessary condition of admissibility that the witness is able to demonstrate to the court the features of comparison upon which his opinion is formed. Since the comparison is visual, an inability by the witness to explain and demonstrate the features upon which his opinion is formed not only places in doubt the existence of the science or technique claimed; it undermines the foundation or reliability required. ... However, each such application must be considered on its own merits.

R v Atkins and Atkins [2009] EWCA Crim 1876,[11] a case concerning facial mapping evidence, Hughes LJ at para 31:

> We conclude that where a photographic comparison expert gives evidence, properly based upon study and experience, of similarities and/ or dissimilarities between a questioned photograph and a known person (including a defendant) the expert is not disabled either by authority or

291

principle from expressing his conclusion as to the significance if his findings, and that he may do so by use of conventional expressions, arranged in a hierarchy, such as those used by the witness in this case and set out in paragraph 8 above. We think it preferable that the expressions should not be allocated numbers, as they were in the boxes used in the written report in this case, lest that run any small risk of leading the jury to think that they represent an established numerical, that is to say measurable scale. The expressions ought to remain simply what they are, namely forms of words used. They need to be in an ascending order if they are to mean anything at all, and if a relatively firm opinion is to be contrasted with one which, is not so firm. They are, however, expressions of subjective opinion, and this must be made clear to the jury charged with evaluating them.

R v Senior [2009] Court of Appeal,[12] Royal Courts of Justice, London. The appellant was seeking leave to appeal to have gait biomechanics CCTV evidence included, having not done so at trial. Gait biomechanics evidence had not been submitted by the prosecution or defence at trial. Forensic gait analysis evidence was submitted to the Court of Appeal from experts instructed by the prosecution and for the defence. The Court of Appeal found that the defence expert's evidence would not have affected the jury's decision and outcome. The Court of Appeal held that gait biomechanics is 'not novel science'. Leave to appeal was not granted and the conviction upheld by the Court of Appeal.

Mearns v Smedvig Ltd [1999] SC 243[13] underlined the importance of establishing the reliability of the relevant body of knowledge relied on by the expert, where such a body of knowledge is outside a recognised forensic science discipline. In that case, Lord Eassie stated:

> A party seeking to lead a witness with purported knowledge or experience out with generally recognised fields would need to set up by investigation and evidence not only the qualifications and expertise of the individual skilled witness, but the methodology and validity of that field of knowledge or science.

R v Dlugosz & Others [2013] *EWCA Crim* 2,[14] the Court of Appeal also observed (at para 11):

> It is essential to recall the principle which is applicable, namely in determining the issue of admissibility, the court must be satisfied that there is a sufficiently reliable scientific basis for the evidence to be admitted. If there is then the court leaves the opposing views to be tested before the jury.

R. v Hashi [2012], *reported as R v Ferdinand and others* [2014] EWCA Crim 1243,[15] the Court of Appeal considered the admissibility of gait evidence in a murder trial and upheld the safety of conviction and admissibility of the forensic podiatrist evidence. The necessary scrutiny required in that case included, for example:

1. Establishing the necessary expertise and experience of the expert (including *current* clinical practice) in analysing (in this case) 'features' of gait, that is any abnormality in the position of body parts in the walking cycle and 'flow pattern', that is any product of the walking cycle, such as its speed or length of stride.
2. Ascertaining whether the quality of the images and variation of CCTV camera angles (the 'benchmark' material) permitted any meaningful analysis to be made.
3. Having decided that the images permitted analysis, the undertaking of careful analysis in order to identify any features or patterns that were repeated.
4. Having identified patterns and features in the benchmark material examination of the footage of the suspect in order to make a further comparison.
5. Conducting a review of findings frame-by-frame and selected still images from the CCTV recordings to illustrate those findings to the court, in order for the jury to form their own view of the evidence.
6. A full review of all that material by another expert appointed by the opposing side.
7. Cross-examination by counsel for the opposing side in order to test those images.

Criminal Practice Directions for England and Wales.*19A.1*:

> Expert opinion evidence is admissible in criminal proceedings at common law if, in summary, (i) it is relevant to a matter in issue in the proceedings; (ii) it is needed to provide the court with information likely to be outside the court's own knowledge and experience; and (iii) the witness is competent to give that opinion.[16]

Civil Procedure Rule (CPR) 35.1 for England and Wales ('Duty to restrict expert evidence') provides: 'Expert evidence shall be restricted to that which is reasonably required to resolve the proceedings'. This rule is also considered in the case of *BA plc v Spencer and others* [2015] EWHC 2477 (Ch).[17]

It will be important also, in a jury trial, that the judge adequately and accurately summarises the expert evidence to the jury. The Court of Appeal held in *R v Lunkulu and others* [2015] EWCA 1350.[18] that the trial judge in that case had acted properly in:

(a) rehearsing the evidence of the forensic gait analysis at 'considerable length',
(b) summarising the anomalies of gait that were present in the two samples (of the suspect in the CCTV footage and defendant) and
(c) providing a balanced and fair summary – all of which ensured that the jury weighed the evidence appropriately.

The principles in the case of *R v Bonython* were agreed to give relevant guidance on the admissibility of expert evidence in Scotland by the Supreme Court of the UK in *Kennedy v Cordia (Services) LLP* [2016] UKSC 6[19] (judgement given on 10 February 2016). Lady Hale stated that (paras 40–41),

> Experts can and often do give evidence of fact as well as opinion evidence. A skilled witness, like any non-expert witness, can give evidence of what he or she has observed if it is relevant to a fact in issue [...]. Unlike other witnesses, a skilled witness may also give evidence based on his or her knowledge and experience of a subject matter, drawing on the work of others, such as the findings of published research or the pooled knowledge of a team of people with whom he or she works. Such evidence also gives rise to threshold questions of admissibility, and the special rules that govern the admissibility of expert opinion evidence also cover such expert evidence of fact.

The Supreme Court of the UK in *Kennedy v Cordia (Services) LLP* set out the four considerations in determining the admissibility of expert evidence, normally termed 'skilled evidence' in Scottish law:

(1) Whether the proposed skilled evidence will assist the court in its task. With regards to opinion evidence, the threshold for admissibility will be one of necessity; however, the test for admissibility of expert evidence of fact will not be as strict necessity, as this may deprive the court of the benefit of an expert who is able to collate and present to the court efficiently the knowledge of others in that field of expertise.
(2) Whether the witness has the necessary knowledge and experience. An expert witness must demonstrate to the court that he/she has relevant knowledge and experience to give either factual evidence which is not exclusively based on personal observation or opinion evidence. Where such knowledge and experience are established, the expert may draw on the general body of knowledge and understanding of the relevant expertise.

(3) Whether the witness is impartial in his or her presentation and assessment of the evidence. The requirement of independence and impartiality is one of admissibility rather than merely the weight of the evidence.
(4) Whether there is a reliable body of knowledge or experience to underpin the expert's evidence. Where the subject matter of the proposed expert evidence is not within a widely recognised scientific discipline or body of knowledge, the party seeking to rely on the evidence will need to evidence not only the qualifications and expertise of the witness, but the methodology and validity of that field of knowledge or science.

The Supreme Court of the UK in *Kennedy v Cordia (ante)* also quoted approvingly the observations of the Supreme Court of South Africa (Appellate Division) in *Coopers (South Africa) (Pty) Ltd v Deutsche Gesellschaft für Schädlingsbekämpfung mbH* [1976] (3) SA 352,[20] when dealing with the admissibility of expert evidence. In that case Wessells JA stated that:

> [A]n expert's opinion represents his reasoned conclusion based on certain facts or data, which are either common cause, or established by his own evidence or that of some other competent witness. Except possibly where it is not controverted, an expert's bald statement of his opinion is not of any real assistance. Proper evaluation of the opinion can only be undertaken if the process of reasoning which led to the conclusion, including the premises from which the reasoning proceeds, are disclosed by the expert.

The case of *Kennedy v Cordia (Services) LLP* also underlines the importance of impartiality and independence of experts. This consideration is also reaffirmed in the Canadian jurisdiction by the Supreme Court of Canada, in the matter of *White Burgess Langille Inman v Abbott and Haliburton Co* [2015] SCC 23.[21] While the UK Supreme Court emphasised the continuing centrality of the Ikarian Reefer principles, it went on to stress the duty imposed on lawyers to ensure that experts are fully informed of the nature and scope of their duties, and particularly their duty to the Court.[22] The observations of the UK Supreme Court regarding Scottish law are also likely to have influence on how the Courts in England and Wales approach the issue.

In the Canadian jurisdiction, in the case of *R. v Mohan* [1994] 2 S.C.R. 9,[23] it was stated that, 'the evidence must be given by a witness who is shown to have acquired special or peculiar knowledge through study or experience in respect of the matters on which he or she undertakes to testify'. In *R. v*

Mohan at p. 20, Sopinka J identified the following criteria for the admissibility of expert opinion evidence:

1) Relevance;
2) Necessity in assisting the trier of fact;
3) The absence of any exclusionary rule; and
4) A properly qualified expert.

The scope of expert evidence must be appropriately limited to make sure that the proposed opinion does not go directly to the ultimate issue in the case and thus present the jury with a ready-made inference of guilt. Constraining expert opinion evidence in this fashion responds to the concern identified in *R. v Mohan*. Sopinka J stated:

> Expert evidence, to be necessary, must likely be outside the experience and knowledge of a judge or jury and must be assessed in light of its potential to distort the fact-finding process. Necessity should not be judged by too strict a standard. The possibility that evidence will overwhelm the jury and distract them from their task can often be offset by proper instructions. Experts, however, must not be permitted to usurp the functions of the trier of fact causing a trial to degenerate to a contest of experts.

R. v Aitken [2009]. The evidence of the podiatrist (gait analysis) was tested by voir dire and deemed relevant and admissible, before being admitted into the trial. This was the first known occasion of forensic gait analysis expert opinion evidence being led before the Canadian courts. No gait analysis expert evidence was presented on behalf of the defence. On appeal, *R. v Aitken* [2012] BCCA 134,[24] counsel for the appellant submitted arguments to various material and objections on a range of evidence at trial, including the gait analysis evidence and other procedures (para 22). The appeal was dismissed unanimously by the Court of Appeal, stating in its conclusion (para 104), 'the judge was very careful in this trial' and 'to repeatedly caution the jury to try the case on the facts and to avoid prejudice'. In 2013, the Supreme Court of Canada denied leave to appeal from the Court of Appeal judgement.[25]

At the High Court of Justice of England and Wales (EWHC) in 2014, in *EWHC 3590 (QB)*, Warby J found that the court's duty under CPR 35.1 to restrict expert evidence to that which is reasonably required to resolve proceedings did not, in his view, impose a test of absolute necessity. Instead, a judgement should be made in each and every case before the evidence is heard and evaluated. He concluded that, 'evidence which it is credibly said could conclusively determine the single most important issue in the case meets the criterion in the rule'.[26,27]

British Airways plc v Spencer & Others [2015] *EWHC 2477 (Ch)*[28] also illustrates how the courts should exercise its discretion to admit or exclude expert evidence. Recognising that evidence can be helpful even if it is not determinative of an issue, Warren J acknowledged the findings in *EWHC 3590 (QB)*, that the requirement for the evidence to be 'reasonably required to resolve the proceedings' does not impose a test of 'absolute necessity'. The court considered that it was, instead, necessary to exercise discretionary judgement in each case.[29]

EXP v Barker [2017] EWCA Civ 63,[30] a clinical negligence case, illustrates the significance of expert witnesses to be fully aware of their duties and responsibilities, including being completely impartial and independent, and emphasises the need to disclose any relevant connection between the parties to avoid potential conflicts of interest. Such responsibilities are applicable to expert witnesses and those from whom they receive their instructions and who rely upon their evidence. Irwin LJ, at paragraph 51 of the judgement, stated:

> Our adversarial system depends heavily on the independence of expert witnesses, on the primacy of their duty to the Court over any other loyalty or obligation, and on the rigour with which experts make known any associations or loyalties which might give rise to a conflict. Dr [X] failed to do so here, despite an express direction to that effect. Indeed, the omission of mention of papers co-authored with Dr [Y] points in the opposite direction.

In the case of *Toth v Jarman* [2006] EWCA Civ 1028[31] the Court of Appeal also gave guidance regarding expert evidence and potential conflicts of interest.

It is worthy of general note that experts and others must not usurp nor be seen to usurp the decisions of the courts, including where there is a 'Ban on Publication' as occurs in some cases. Where breaches occur carries the real and serious risk of being in contempt of court and consequences. Something that all, including 'commentators' (academic or otherwise), need to bear in the forefront of their minds and not be drawn into making unwarranted or potentially libellous statements, irrespective of any vested interests where they exist.

Frye Test

In the United States of America, the *Frye test* or 'general acceptance test' has been, and in certain circumstances still is, used to determine the admissibility of scientific evidence. That test provides that expert opinion based on a scientific technique is admissible only where the technique is generally accepted as reliable in the relevant scientific community. It comes from *Frye v United States*, 293 F. 1013 (D.C. Cir. 1923),[32] a case discussing the admissibility of polygraph test as evidence. The Court in *Frye* held that expert testimony must be based on scientific methods that are sufficiently established and accepted. The court observed:

> Just when a scientific principle or discovery crosses the line between the experimental and demonstrable stages is difficult to define. Somewhere in this twilight zone the evidential force of the principle must be recognized, and while the courts will go a long way in admitting experimental testimony deduced from a well-recognized scientific principle or discovery, the thing from which the deduction is made must be sufficiently established to have gained general acceptance in the particular field in which it belongs.

Daubert

In *Daubert v Merrell Dow Pharmaceuticals* 509 U.S. 579 (1993),[33] The Supreme Court of the United States held that the Federal Rules of Evidence superseded *Frye* as the standard for admissibility of expert evidence in federal courts. Other decisions by the United States Supreme Court and following *Daubert* have refined the legal principle and further clarified the position and the admissibility of expert testimony, which includes *General Electric Co. v Joiner*[34] (1997) and *Kumho Tire Co. v Carmichael*[35] (1999). This is known as the *Daubert trilogy* and relates to three cases in the United Stated Supreme Court that articulated the *Daubert* standard. In the year 2000, Rule 702 was amended with the Daubert trilogy in mind and again in 2011 to give further clarity.

The amended rule 702 and 703 of the Federal Rules of Evidence reads as follows:

- **Rule 702. Testimony by Expert Witnesses**
  A witness who is qualified as an expert by knowledge, skill, experience, training, or education may testify in the form of an opinion or otherwise if:
  (a) *the expert's scientific, technical, or other specialized knowledge will help the trier of fact to understand the evidence or to determine a fact in issue;*
  (b) *the testimony is based on sufficient facts or data;*
  (c) *the testimony is the product of reliable principles and methods; and*
  (d) *the expert has reliably applied the principles and methods to the facts of the case.*

- **Rule 703. Bases of an Expert's Opinion Testimony**
  An expert may base an opinion on facts or data in the case that the expert has been made aware of or personally observed. If experts in the particular field

> *would reasonably rely on those kinds of facts or data in forming an opinion on the subject, they need not be admissible for the opinion to be admitted. But if the facts or data would otherwise be inadmissible, the proponent of the opinion may disclose them to the jury only if their probative value in helping the jury evaluate the opinion substantially outweighs their prejudicial effect.*

Some individual states in the USA, however, still adhere to the *Frye* standard. The *Daubert* standard was explicitly stated by the Supreme Court of the UK to be consistent with the approach of Scottish law to *skilled evidence* of fact in *Kennedy v Cordia (ante)*.

Botehlo v Bycura (Ct. App. 1984).[36] To qualify as an expert witness in a case involving allegations of malpractice against a podiatrist, a witness must have knowledge of the standard of care in podiatric practice.

Bellamy v Payne (S.C. Ct. App. 1991).[37] Illustrates the authority of refusal as an abiding feature of law in the United States of America (USA), where judges refuse to admit expert evidence when the qualifications are not sufficient nor relevant. In this matter, an orthopaedic surgeon was held not to be qualified as an expert witness in a case of professional negligence involving podiatry because the proposed witness failed to demonstrate to the satisfaction of the trial court his familiarity with the diagnostic, surgical and treatment procedures employed by podiatrists.

Voir dire

It may be necessary to call expert evidence on what is referred to as a *voir dire*, that is to say, a preliminary oral examination of the expert's evidence, not in front of a jury, in order to assess and to test the admissibility of their evidence prior to the introduction of the evidence before the ultimate finders of fact. The trial judge(s) are the 'gatekeepers' and decide whether evidence is admissible.

THE ROLE AND DUTY OF THE EXPERT

What, in any legal system, is the role of the expert witness?

Expert witnesses are individuals with qualifications and experience which enable them to give opinions on the facts of cases within their specialist field. The role of the expert is to help the court to understand technical matters in the case and assist in advising on the case within their area of expertise.

The evidence of experts is in two forms: a written report(s) and oral evidence given in the witness box in court.[38]

Experts may be involved at many different stages, both before and during any trial. There are of course different types of courts and different types of trial, which may also affect the precise task of the expert witness. However, throughout the adversarial process, one concept is paramount: the duty of the expert to assist the court. *An expert's duty is to the court.* 'This duty overrides any obligation to the person from whom the expert receives instructions or by whom the expert is paid'. As per the Criminal Procedure Rules for England and Wales.[39]

It is important that experts are familiar with the relevant criminal procedure and civil procedure rules, or their equivalent, according to the requirements of the jurisdiction. Experts also need to ensure they keep up to date with amendments to such rules. For the criminal courts, an expert's duty to the court is specified in 19.2 of the Criminal Procedure Rules; Expert evidence.

The whole defining function of an expert is that they have specialist knowledge and skills unavailable to the normal person. Cases are decided by in the main, by non-experts. The purpose of a jury, for example, is that they are comprised of people without particular skills or knowledge. When, therefore, special skills and knowledge are said by one or both sides in a case to be required to determine a particular relevant issue, the judge or jury will frequently need the assistance of an expert witness.

In the *adversarial* legal system, the expert would normally be instructed by one or other of the parties and rarely by the Court. It might therefore be thought that the expert owed a duty only to the party instructing them and paying for their services. The adversarial system, however, is at pains to prevent the risk of an expert seeking wrongly to use their privileged position as the possessor of special skills and knowledge to the advantage of the party instructing them, by say withholding vital information or a dissenting opinion.

In the *inquisitorial* legal system, the expert might normally be appointed and instructed by the court or by investigators on behalf of the court. As such, the duty of that expert is to assist the court rather than any particular party. The responsibilities of the expert to keep the court informed of any material that may assist one party or undermine the expert's findings, and to retain material so that another expert can replicate any assessment, will inevitably remain the same.

The expert's overriding duty to the court has far-reaching ramifications for experts. This means, of course, that experts must be scrupulously honest. It means they must not mislead the court in any way; and if they come to a conclusion to the detriment of the case for the party instructing them, they must say so regardless of the consequences for the instructing party.

As has been already stated, the duty of an expert is to the Court and not to those from whom the expert receives their instructions, as set out in the Criminal Procedure Rules for England and Wales. (Rules apply according to the jurisdiction.)

Expert's obligations and boundaries of expertise are also considered in *R v Pabon* [2018] EWCA Crim 420.

Of course, as an expert *witness* and not just an expert, one must seek at all times to explain matters in a way that is comprehensible by the non-experts deciding the case and not seek to confuse or obfuscate with technical language and concepts. The job of the witness is to tell their story so that others may hear it, understand it and use it to decide the issues in the case. That does not change just because the witness is an expert.

In *R. v Harris and others* [2006] 1 Cr App R 5[40] the Court of Appeal of England and Wales set out the duties of an expert. They are:

(1) *Expert evidence presented to the court should be and seen to be the independent product of the expert uninfluenced as to form or content by the exigencies of litigation.*

(2) *An expert witness should provide independent assistance to the court by way of objective unbiased opinion in relation to matters within his expertise. An expert witness in the High Court should never assume the role of advocate.*

(3) *An expert witness should state the facts or assumptions on which his opinion is based. He should not omit to consider material facts which detract from his concluded opinions.*

(4) *An expert should make it clear when a particular question or issue falls outside his expertise.*

(5) *If an expert's opinion is not properly researched because he considers that insufficient data is available then this must be stated with an indication that the opinion is no more than a provisional one.*

(6) *If after exchange of reports, an expert witness changes his view on material matters, such change of view should be communicated to the other side without delay and when appropriate to the court.*

In *R v B (T)* [2006] 2 Cr App R 3,[41] the Court of Appeal of England and Wales said that, in relation to the duties outlined in *R v Harris*,

> We emphasise that these duties are owed to the court and override any obligation to the person from whom the expert has received instructions or by whom the expert is paid. It is hardly necessary to say that experts should maintain professional objectivity and impartiality at all times.

REPORTS

In *R v B (T)* [2006] *(ante)*,[42] the Court of Appeal set out what should be contained within any expert's report. Guidelines regarding the provision of experts' reports were also given by the Court of Appeal in England and Wales in *R. v Reed and Reed, R. v Garmson* [2009] EWCA Crim 2698 [2010] 1 Cr. App. R. 23; [2010] Crim L.R. 716.[43]

The content of an expert's report for use in criminal courts is as per the Criminal Procedure Rules[44] and the Criminal Practice Direction.[45] Where expert evidence is being given on matters in the civil courts (e.g., medico-legal matters, such as personal injury, clinical negligence and other areas) in the jurisdiction of England and Wales, the Civil Procedure Rules (CPR).[46] and Civil Procedure Rules Practice Direction[47] apply. Other jurisdictions may vary.

Amendments can, and do, occur to the court rules and these are often published online. Experts are expected to keep up to date with any relevant amendments in line with their duties and responsibilities.

In the criminal justice system of England and Wales in the UK, the forensic science regulator has also provided various information documents[48-51] and of course these would be expected to be further added to and updated over time Experts should read the documents and other related publications.[52-56]

Note: It must be remembered that expert's reports in the jurisdiction of England and Wales are required to contain a Statement of Truth and an Expert's Declaration, as required by the civil and criminal procedure rules. Experts need to ensure they are up to date with any amendments and to check the specific requirements and of jurisdictions accordingly. (Also see Chapter 10).

ORAL EVIDENCE

Often, the provision of an expert's report will not result in the expert having to give oral evidence at court. If the contents of the report are accepted by the parties, or deemed irrelevant or inadmissible, then funds will not be expended in asking the expert to come to court. However, if either side, or the judge, challenges the accuracy of the findings, or wishes to ask questions of clarification or to elicit further information not in the report, then the expert will have to provide a further report or give evidence 'live' before the fact-finding tribunal, whether that be a judge, or by a judge and jury.

Evidence is normally given 'under oath' or 'affirmation'. That is done at the start of their evidence. The witness takes a formal oath which is a promise on the Bible or other holy book to tell 'the truth, the whole truth, and nothing but the truth' or similar wording. Or, the witness can choose to take an affirmation which is a promise to tell the truth not based on a holy book. The expert witness should decide before going to court; it is entirely up to the expert which they choose to do. Most jurisdictions have specific and very serious criminal offences relating to those who deliberately tell lies or mislead when giving evidence under oath or affirmation, often referred to as the crime of perjury.

Examination in Chief

In the adversarial system, there are two methods of eliciting evidence. The first is what is referred to as 'Examination in Chief'. This consists of questions asked by the advocate for the party calling the expert. Those questions must, in the common law system, consist of 'open' questions', that is to say that where matters are disputed, the advocate is not allowed to suggest answers. For example: 'What is your occupation?' 'Did you see anything of note on the video footage?' 'What conclusion did you draw, if any?' (It may be that, when dealing with elements of the evidence that are not contentious, an advocate is allowed to ask leading questions to save time.) Furthermore, advocates conducting 'examination in chief' are not normally allowed to impeach the credibility, credentials or conclusions of their own witnesses. That is to say, they cannot suggest to the court that their witness is lying or unqualified. If that was the advocate's view, then the witness should not have been called in the first place.

Cross-examination

The other method of eliciting evidence is *'cross-examination'* and is conducted by the advocate for the other side. Advocates, when cross-examining witnesses, are allowed to suggest answers, called 'leading questions', or to suggest that witnesses are wrong, mistaken, lying or unqualified, provided that they have reasonable grounds to do so. The art of cross-examination is not simply to put to a witness, 'You are lying, aren't you?' or 'You are wrong, aren't you?' but rather to build up to a point where that comment can be later made to the jury. A good cross-examination might work by suggesting a series of propositions that the witness does agree with, and demonstrating any fallacies of the witnesses reasoning or logic

303

or by pointing out the steps the witness mistakenly took or mistakenly did not take.

Both methods are not vehicles for comment by advocates about the evidence. Comment should be reserved for closing speeches. Both *Examination in Chief* and *Cross-examination* are designed to elicit *facts* from witnesses.

Re-examination

Following cross-examination by the opposing party or parties, the advocate calling the witness is normally allowed to *re-examine* their witness. They still may not ask leading questions of the witness, and may only ask about matters which have arisen in cross-examination and require clarification.

Some Further Points

- The trial judge or tribunal may ask, at any time during proceedings, whatever relevant questions they wish of the witness.
- When giving evidence, it is normally the rule in the jurisdiction of England and Wales that, in any breaks, the witness is *not* allowed to discuss the case or their evidence with anyone, including their own lawyers. This is mainly to prevent any appearance of 'coaching'. Permission may be given by the court on occasion to allow discussion on certain topics if required.
- When a witness does not understand a question put to them, they should request for the question to be rephrased, or explained in another way. Similarly, if there is a point that in the view of the witness is important to the proper understanding of the issues, or relevant to the decision of the court, then the witness should draw it to the attention of the court, consistent with their duty to act in the interests of justice.

UNUSED MATERIAL

When providing expert evidence whether by means of a written report or oral evidence, the expert will have to retain all notes and other material generated by their investigation, including the results of any tests that were inconclusive or did not support the expert's eventual conclusion. The expert must then disclose the existence of their notes to the party calling them, and make them available for that party's legal team to review and, as appropriate, disclose them to the other side. It may be necessary to keep a list of those notes to be provided to the instructing party, which would then be kept up to date as the case progresses.

The other side may well also wish to inspect any material not capable of being copied. This is so that the other party or parties to the proceedings can attempt to:

(a) replicate the expert's findings, or
(b) utilise any material that casts doubt on the accuracy or reliability of the expert's opinion.

The England and Wales Court of Appeal in *R. v Ward*, 96 Cr App R 1[57] stated that:

> there was a clear obligation on an expert witness to disclose evidence of any tests or experiments which he had carried out or had knowledge of which tended to cast doubt on an opinion he was expressing and to bring the records of any such tests or experiments to the notice of the solicitors instructing him so that they might be disclosed to the other party.

The requirement to commence keeping records begins at the time the expert receives instructions and continues for the whole of the time they are involved.

If there is any doubt as to when involvement begins, then recording should start. Records should be kept of all the work carried out and any findings made. This should include (this list is not exhaustive):

- The collection and transfer of items received for examination.
- Notes of any examinations that take place and of any changes made to examined items.
- Notes of any one who assisted in the work, along with details of precisely what they are and what they did.
- Notes of any instructions and correspondence relating to the case received and sent.
- Notes of any conferences with clients and conversations with other experts (including any points of agreement and disagreement).
- Initial drafts of findings; and any witness accounts or explanations received.

Useful further guidance within the English and Welsh legal context on the disclosure obligations of expert witnesses can be found in the free booklet produced by the UK Crown Prosecution Service entitled, 'Guidance Booklet for Experts. Disclosure: Expert Evidence, Case Management and Unused Material'.[58]

GIVING EVIDENCE IN COURT

There are four very self-explanatory and basic principles that those giving evidence in court may wish to bear in mind.

Prepare

If all the parties accept an expert's opinion then the expert is very unlikely to be asked to attend court, as the report can be read or summarised to the court as an agreed document. The very fact that an expert has been asked to attend court normally means that there is some aspect of what the expert does or does not say that is disputed.

Preparation therefore starts with the initial witness statement, also known in this context as an expert's report. It should be accurate, carefully drawn up and full. When a witness attends at court to give evidence, they should arrive there early, having re-read their statement(s). They should normally bring with them any relevant materials that were used to create the statement (e.g. original notes). Those notes should have been retained since the original examinations/tests in which they were created (see above).

If an expert witness has other relevant information or if an error is discovered or has something else to add, then it is the expert's duty to bring it to the attention of the advocate as soon as possible.

Experts will normally have meetings with the advocates and lawyers for the party instructing them long before going to court, which are extremely helpful for clarifying the issues and the way in which the evidence will be presented.

Appearance Matters

Any court hearing is a formal event, and a professional witness such as an expert should treat it accordingly. Although the appearance of professionalism is merely an appearance, it helps to inspire confidence in the fact-finding tribunal. Experts should dress appropriately. Patronising or sarcastic responses to questions posed by those non-experts do not normally generate positive responses from the courts or tribunals, no matter how much they may be merited. Politeness is always to be encouraged. Questions of relevancy are for the judge, not the expert witness, to determine. The expert witness should attempt to answer every question put to them. Should there be no clear answer to a question posed, or if the expert does not understand a question put to them, then the expert should say so. If a question is irrelevant, then that is perhaps a matter for instructing counsel or the judge/s to address, and not the expert witness.

It is important to remain calm and unhurried. Cross-examination is designed to test, in some cases very robustly, evidence that can be at times wholly determinative of a highly contested issue. As such the process can be very demanding. Criticism can be trenchant if mistakes have been made or appear to have been made. The evidence of any expert is important, and sufficient time should be made available to hear it, and understand it. Although nerves are common, they can cause doubts about a witness's confidence in their own material.

An expert witness (unlike a lay witness) will be expected to use appropriate formal language and correct modes of address. Sir/Madam is normally considered acceptable when dealing with advocates. The judge may well have a specific title to be used (e.g. 'Your Honour' or 'My Lord'). Clarification as to the correct terms should be sought before the start of any evidence.

Keep It Simple

The easier a concept or fact is to explain, the more likely it is to be understood and accepted. Unnecessarily complex or technical language is a barrier to comprehension, not an aid to it. Any exaggeration or guesswork will be exposed by a competent advocate and will leave the evidence looking less credible.

During the hearing (trial), it is important to use one's brain and listen very carefully to what has been said, to the question that has been asked and process it properly before answering. If a witness is not clear about something, then they should not be afraid to ask for explanation, clarification or simply for the question to be rephrased.

Overly long and complex answers are likely not to be understood by the tribunal, particularly a jury. Short but accurate answers are to be preferred over long, unfocused speeches. If a point is complex, then of course it will have to be made at the appropriate length. However, a note will often be taken of the evidence by the lawyers and judges. As such, it is often desirable to break up a long answer into smaller pieces, pausing to ensure that the first section has been recorded and understood before moving onto the next.

Clarity

When giving evidence, it should be remembered that it is the judge and/or the jury who are the finders of fact. It is therefore the judge/jury that most need to hear and understand any expert evidence, and that they are

307

also (unlike the lawyers) potentially hearing it for the first time. As such, answers should be addressed not to the advocate asking the question, but to the person who most need to hear the answer – the judge/jury. This will not only aid clarity, but because the witness will then be looking at the relevant person, it can also assist the witness in assessing whether their evidence is being properly understood.

When giving evidence in court, the witness should direct their answers across court to the jury box, and not to the advocate asking the questions. Mumbling or inaudibility will soon cause a court/tribunal to 'switch off' and diminish the impact of the evidence. A polite, confident, manner will not only ensure that evidence is properly heard, but provoke a positive reaction in the court/tribunal as well. Remember not to appear 'overconfident' as that can be interpreted in other ways!

An inflexible or dogmatic approach can actually undermine the credibility of a witness much more than making careful concessions when appropriate to do so. If an expert agrees with a proposition being put to them, or realises that a mistake has been made, then it is part of the duty of an expert to say so.

Note: The Academy of Medical Royal Colleges in the UK published guidance for healthcare professionals who act as expert witnesses and endorsed by other organisations. Key undertakings include that practitioners are now expected to undertake specific training for being an expert witness.[59]

The following diagram shows a sample layout of a criminal court.

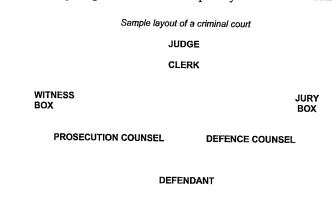

Sample layout of a criminal court

JUDGE

CLERK

WITNESS BOX   **JURY BOX**

PROSECUTION COUNSEL   **DEFENCE COUNSEL**

DEFENDANT

PUBLIC GALLERY   **PUBLIC GALLERY**

Figure 11.1 displays a traditional style courtroom. Figure 11.2 shows a more modern style courtroom.

Figure 11.1 Traditional courtroom.*

Figure 11.2 More modern courtroom.**

* Figure 11.1 Traditional courtroom. Attributed to fayerollison. https://commons.wikime-dia.org/wiki/File:Victorian_Civil_Courtroom,_National_Justice_Museum,_June_2010.jpg. Creative Commons Attribution-Share Alike 3.0 Unported license.
** Figure 11.2 Modern Courtroom. Attributed to Rock Li. https://commons.wikimedia.org/wiki/File:HK_HighCourt_Court1_in.JPG. Creative Commons Attribution-Share Alike 3.0 Unported license.

Expert Evidence – The Rules

Part 19 of the Criminal Procedure Rules[60] relates to Expert Evidence [also see the Practice Direction].

- *Rule 19.1. When this part applies.*
    This part applies when a party wants to admit expert evidence.
- *Rule 19.2. Expert's duty to the court.*
- *Rule 19.3. Introduction of expert evidence.*
- *Rule 19.4. Content of expert's report.*
- *Rule 19.5. Expert to be informed of service of report.*
- *Rule 19.6. Pre-hearing discussion of expert evidence.*
- *Rule 19.7. Court's power to direct that evidence is to be given by a single joint expert.*
- *Rule 19.8. Instructions to a single joint expert.*

EXPERT EVIDENCE – THE PRACTICE DIRECTION

The Practice Direction of the Criminal Procedure Rules[61] for England and Wales also refers to:

- *19A. Expert Evidence.*
- *19B. Statements of Understanding and Declarations of Truth in Expert Reports.*
- *19C. Pre-Hearing Discussion of Expert Evidence.*

As indicated earlier, experts need to be up to date on amendments to the rules and practice directions, insofar as they relate to the expert's duties and responsibilities.

Additional Points

- It can be useful for experts to maintain a list of cases in which they have provided initial opinions, full reports and have given oral expert evidence at court. It is also helpful to have an index where requests were rejected by the expert on the basis of not being able to provide any meaningful evidential product (report), which is usually when material (video imagery) is not suitable for the purpose of forensic gait analysis.
- To date, forensic gait analysis evidence deemed relevant and admissible by the courts over time has in the main been submitted

by expert podiatrists and podiatric surgeons; some other areas have also participated.

- In relation to the process of human identification, forensic gait analysis has received deployment evidentially and for investigative purposes. The first evidential use of forensic gait analysis as admissible expert evidence in criminal law was in 2000.[62] As an investigative tool, forensic gait analysis had notable utility in 2007[63] and in 2009.[64]
- The use of gait analysis in the civil justice systems, for example, as part of the medical evidence on matters such as personal injury claims, clinical negligence and tribunals etc., pre-dates the use of 'forensic gait analysis' as a tool in the context of human identification.

REFERENCES

1. *Buckley v Rice-Thomas* (1554) 1 Plowd 118, 124.
2. *Fokes v Chadd* (1782) Douglas' King's Bench Reports, 3, 157.
3. Hand, L. 1901. Historical and practical considerations regarding expert testimony. *Harvard Law Review*, 15, 40–58.
4. *R v Bonython* [1984] 38 S.A.S.R. South Australia Supreme Court.
5. *R v Luttrell* [2004] EWCA Crim 1344.
6. *R v Bernard V* [2003] EWCA Crim 3917, at para 29.
7. *H (Stephen) v The Queen* [2014] EWCA Crim 1555, para 43 & 44.
8. *R v Robb* [1991] 93 Cr App R161,165.
9. *R v Darragher* [2002] EWCA Crim 1903, [2003] 1 Cr App R 12 para.23.
10. *R v Otway* [2011] EWCA Crim 3.
11. *R v Atkins and Atkins* [2009] EWCA Crim 1876.
12. *R v Senior* [2009]. 10 November 2009. Court of Appeal, Royal Courts of Justice, London.
13. *Mearns v Smedvig Ltd* [1999] SC 243.
14. *R v Dlugosz and Others* [2013] EWCA Crim 2.
15. *R v Hashi and Others* [2014] EWCA Crim 1243.
16. Criminal practice directions. April 2019. CrimPR Part 19: Expert evidence CPD V Evidence 19A: EXPERT EVIDENCE.19A.1.
17. *BA plc v Spencer and Others* [2015] EWHC 2477 (Ch), [2015] All ER (D) 101 (Aug).
18. *R v Lunkulu and Others* [2015] EWCA 1350.
19. *Kennedy v Cordia (Services) Ltd* [2016] UKSC 6 (paras 40-41).

20. Supreme Court of South Africa (Appellate Division) in *Coopers (South Africa) (Pty) Ltd v Deutsche Gesellschaft für Schädlingsbekämpfung mbH* [1976] (3) SA 352.
21. *White Burgess Langille Inman v Abbott and Haliburton Co* [2015] SCC 23.
22. Sorabji, J. 2017. Editorial note. *Expert Witness Institute Newsletter*, Spring 2017, pp5.
23. *R. v. Mohan*, [1994] 2 S.C.R. 9.
24. *R. v. Aitken*, [2012] BCCA 134.
25. *R. v. Aitken*, [2013] SCC 35071.
26. *EWHC 3590 (QB)*.
27. Your Witness. 2015. Court's discretion to admit expert evidence. *Newsletter of the UK Register of Expert Witnesses*. Issue 82, December 2015, pp4. J S Publications.
28. *British Airways plc -v- Spencer & Others* [2015] EWHC 2477 (Ch).
29. Your Witness. 2015. Court's discretion to admit expert evidence. *Newsletter of the UK Register of Expert Witnesses*. Issue 82, December 2015, pp5. J S Publications.
30. *EXP v Barker* [2017] EWCA Civ 63.
31. *Toth v Jarman* [2006] EWCA Civ 1028.
32. *Frye v. United States*, 293 F. 1013 (D.C. Cir. 1923).
33. *Daubert v. Merrell Dow Pharmaceuticals*, 509 U.S. 579 (1993), Supreme Court of the United States.
34. *General Electric Co. v. Joiner*, 522 U.S. 136,118 S. Ct. 512,139 L. Ed. 2d 508 (1997).
35. *Kumho Tire Co. v. Carmichael*, 526 U.S. 137,119 S. Ct. 1167, 143 L. Ed. 2d 238 (1999).
36. *Botehlo v. Bycura*, 282 SC. 578, 320 SE. (2d) 59 (Ct. App. 1984).
37. *Bellamy v. Payne*, 403 SE 326 (S.C. Ct. App. 1991).
38. Bond, C; Solon, M; Harper, P; Davies, G. 2007. *The Expert Witness - A Practical Guide*. Third edition. Shaw and Sons: London, UK.
39. Criminal Procedure Rules. October 2015 as amended April 2018 and April 2019. Part 19. Expert Evidence. Rule 19.2. https://bit.ly/2AGjkL7 [Accessed 20 February 2020].
40. *R v Harris and Others* [2006] EWCA1 Cr App R 5.
41. *R v B (T)* [2006] EWCA 2 Cr App R 3.
42. *R v B (T)* [2006] *(ante)* EWCA 2 Cr App R 3.
43. *R. v. Reed and Reed, R. v. Garmson* [2009] EWCA Crim 2698; [2010] 1 Cr. App. R. 23; [2010] Crim L.R. 716.
44. Criminal Procedure Rules. October 2015 as amended April 2018 and April 2019. Part 19. Expert Evidence. https://bit.ly/2AGjkL7 [Accessed 20 February 2020].
45. Criminal Procedure Rules. Practice Directions. April 2019. https://bit.ly/2KNAIoM [Accessed 20 February 2020].
46. Civil Procedure Rules. Part 35 - Experts and Assessors. http://bit.ly/1tDEIKz [Accessed 20 February 2020].
47. Civil Procedure Rules. Practice Direction 35 – Experts and Assessors. This practice direction supplements CPR part 35. http://bit.ly/2daQCF7 [Accessed 20 February 2020].

48. Forensic Science Regulator. 2016. Information: Legal obligations. FSR-I-400. Issue 4. http://bit.ly/2CK5yY5 [Accessed 20 February 2020].
49. Forensic Science Regulator. 2014. Guidance. Validation. FSR-G-201. Issue 1. http://bit.ly/2CsF2kO [Accessed 20 February 2020].
50. Forensic Science Regulator. 2017. Codes of practice and conduct. for forensic science providers and practitioners in the Criminal Justice System. Issue 4. October 2017. http://bit.ly/2ArhOFY [Accessed 20 February 2020].
51. Forensic Science Regulator. 2019. Guidance on the content of reports issued by expert witnesses in the Criminal Justice System in England and Wales. FSR-G-200. Issue 3. https://bit.ly/323JrbO [Accessed 20 February 2020].
52. Hirson, A 2018. *Death knell to UK Forensic Science*. Expert Witness Institute Newsletter Summer 2018, pp8–9.
53. Burrow, G, Kelly, HD; Francis, B. 2018.Written evidence (FRS0092). Submission to House of Lords Science and Technology Committee Inquiry into Forensic Science. 27 September 2018.
54. Hak, JW(Q.C.). Evaluation of the Forensic Science Regulator's recommendations regarding image comparison evidence. *Forensic Science International: Synergy* 1 (2019) 294–297. https://doi.org/10.1016/j.fsisyn.2019.07.005.
55. Tully, G, Stockdale, M 2019. Commentary on: Hak. Evaluation of the Forensic Science Regulator's recommendations regarding image comparison evidence. *Forensic Science International: Synergy* 2019; 1(1) 298–301. https://doi.org/10.1016/j.fsisyn.2019.09.006
56. Hak, JW(Q.C.). Response to "Commentary on: Hak. Evaluation of the forensic science regulator's recommendations regarding image comparison evidence. *Forensic Science International: Synergy* 1 (2019) 302. https://doi.org/10.1016/j.fsisyn.2019.10.001
57. *R v Ward*, EWCA 96 Cr App R 1.
58. Crown Prosecution Service (UK). Guidance for Experts on Disclosure, Unused Material and Case Management. Updated 30/9/19. *Legal Guidance.* https://bit.ly/2XtIB9K [Accessed 20 February 2020].
59. Academy of Medical Royal Colleges. May 2019. Acting as an expert or professional witness. Guidance for healthcare professionals. https://bit.ly/38KzbIm [Accessed 20 February 2020].
60. Criminal Procedure Rules. October 2015 as amended April 2018 and April 2019. Part 19. Expert evidence. https://bit.ly/2AGjkL7 [Accessed 20 February 2020].
61. Criminal Procedure Rules. Practice directions. April 2019. Part 19: Expert evidence, CPD V evidence 19A, 19B and19C. https://bit.ly/2KNAIoM [Accessed 20 February 2020].
62. *R v Saunders* [2000]. Old Bailey, Central Criminal Court, London.
63. *R v Ahmed* [2007]. Investigation by City of London Police, London.
64. Investigation by Metropolitan Police Service, *Op.Minstead* [2009] London, in the matter of *R v Grant* [2011]. Case also known as *'The Night Stalker'*.

12

The Expert in Court – The Expert's Perspective

Contents

PREPARING FOR COURT

The preparation for a trial does not start a few days or even a few weeks before the trial – that begins as soon as you, the expert, receive instructions, and every telephone call, letter or note should be thought of in that context.[1]

You should have already completed courses and training as an expert witness, not only in report writing but also in cross-examination and courtroom skills and their relevance to experts. Expert witness training is invaluable and should not be underestimated as to its importance. In the UK in 2019, the Academy of Medical Royal Colleges published guidance for healthcare professionals who act as expert witnesses,[2] and is endorsed by many other healthcare professional organisations. The key undertakings include that practitioners are now expected to undertake specific training for being an expert witness[3].

Providing expert evidence and giving evidence in court can make considerable demands of the unsuspecting expert. Knowledge of law and procedure are also needed insofar as they relate to experts' duties and responsibilities as per the criminal procedure rules[4,5] and the civil procedure rules,[6,7] in the jurisdiction of England and Wales. These documents received periodic updates, and it is essential the expert ensures they are acquainted accordingly. Also, there are information documents from the office of the forensic science regulator for England and Wales, which sets out some guidance for expert witnesses in the criminal justice system in those nations.[8-13] Generally raising the standard of practise in any area, including forensic practise, is to be welcomed. The type of approach matters in attempting to achieve this.[14-18] Whilst the role and duty of an expert may not be expected to vary considerably in different legal systems, these are according to each jurisdiction. If you are unsure or not familiar with the requirements of a particular area or jurisdiction, then check at the outset when initially receiving instructions as that can help avoid misunderstanding or embarrassment.

So, you have completed and submitted your report. Now you and your report are ready to be examined in court. There is nothing unusual about this and is standard practise in the legal system. If you have not already been made aware of when the trial date is likely to occur, then enquire when submitting your report. At that time it may not be known on precisely what day/s you will be needed at court, but those instructing you should be able to give you some idea of when you are likely to be required to attend, if needed, and so you can plan your schedule accordingly. Having late cancellations to patient's appointments, meetings or other professional engagements is not ideal, so ensure those instructing you are well aware of the need to provide you with at least reasonable notice in advance of when your attendance will be required to give your evidence.

Some weeks or months have elapsed and you have heard nothing as to the date on which you are due to give evidence at court. Then, the party instructing you returns with the dates on which you are needed to attend. You may have also received a witness summons notifying you in writing of the dates on which you are to give your oral evidence at court. Do bear in mind that the actual timetable of when evidence is given may change once the trial gets underway, with some aspects proceeding more quickly than others, so the actual time or dates on when you are due to give your evidence could alter. You need to be ready for this nearer to the time, so do check beforehand.

This can all be somewhat disruptive to the expert's schedule, who may need to rearrange patients, clinics, theatre sessions, attendance at conferences, other professional commitments or important pre-arranged engagements. It is therefore relevant to emphasise this to the court, normally via those who have instructed you, and for you to provide dates of your unavailability at the earliest opportunity, well in advance. It is helpful to be given as much notice as possible to enable forward planning in making yourself available to attend court. Should you need a minimum period of notice, then it is also helpful to make that known in writing in advance via those instructing you, so the court can allow for that to be accommodated wherever possible. The court's timetable or events during proceedings can change in the order of who gives evidence and when, resulting in a delay to when you are required to give your evidence, so do be aware of this and try to make provision for such situations as far as is reasonably possible. Politely reminding the court that the longer you are there, the more time and expense is likely to be incurred can be a useful motivator to help reduce the amount of time you are kept waiting to give your evidence at court.

As the time period between when you prepared your report to when you are required to give your oral evidence at court can often be many weeks or months apart, you will need to refresh your memory on your report and familiarise yourself with all of its contents and any video material before attending court. Do not leave this until the night before! Good preparation is always helpful. Appearing unfamiliar with the content of your report is not to be recommended.

Remember that counsel, whether representing the prosecution or the defence, is there to represent their client. In the criminal justice system, for the prosecution that will be law enforcement agencies; and for the defence it will be representing the accused. Presentation of the evidence by the expert is an important area when considering that will affect how useful your evidence is to the court proceedings. Keep in mind that as an expert witness your duty is to the court and not to those who have instructed you in the matter, nor to those who pay your invoice! The presentation of the evidence at court takes into account all that you have done in preparing your report. Often the report will have taken several days to fully prepare to be ready and depending on the amount of material you have been requested to examine.

As a reminder, each piece of material received for examination needs to have been referred too. Even if the material was not suitable for analysis, you must acknowledge that either in your report or your contemporaneous notes. The contemporaneous notes need to be available of what you did with each piece of material, with times, dates and the location of where you performed all the work carried out. These form part of the expert's evidence, and although they may not be part of the actual report, they remain material which can be requested to be disclosed and be asked questions upon at court. Untidy contemporaneous notes may be challenging for the court to follow, so give advance consideration to this when making your contemporaneous notes. If there are differences in what appears in the report and your contemporaneous notes, then you can expect to be asked to explain any such differences in the reported findings. In *R v Smith* (2011) EWCA Crim 1296,[19] the court were concerned about the lack of contemporaneous notes of an examination stating, 'no competent forensic scientist in other areas of forensic science these days would conduct an examination without keeping detailed notes of his examination and the reasons for his conclusions'. It is therefore vital that all notes whether written or recorded should be preserved as they form part of the evidence that can be required at court. Ensure you take your report, your notes and any material remaining in your possession relating to the preparation of the report when you attend court. The *chain of custody* of the material you have examined needs to be maintained. Therefore, ensure that you make contemporaneous notes and keep a record of from whom you receive and return any material along with the times and dates.

In some cases before giving your evidence in a trial, you may be required to firstly give your evidence at a preliminary examination in court, or pretrial hearing, as it is also referred too. This is known as a *voir dire*,[20] or 'true say', which in this context is a preliminary examination of a(n) (expert) witness by the judge or counsel; that is an investigation into the truth or admissibility of evidence, held during a trial. The expert should approach this in the same way as they would do so for giving evidence in the trial. The aim of the *voir dire* is to test whether the evidence is suitable to be put before the jury. In such situations you will normally be required to present your evidence in court before the trial judge and counsel and in the absence of the jury. It is the decision of the trial judge as to whether the evidence is deemed admissible – that which is relevant and suitable to be put before a jury.

AT COURT

Ensure your attire is appropriate and that you are smartly dressed, clean and tidy and wearing suitable and clean footwear. Remember the court is a formal environment. Make sure you feel comfortable. For example, an overly tight neck collar is not only uncomfortable being worn all day, it will also not assist your clarity of speech.

On the day you attend court, ensure you arrive early and that your point of contact is promptly informed of your arrival and this has been registered. You may need to obtain forms in order to reclaim expenses, if this has not already been arranged, as well as for appearance fees for making yourself available at court. These would be subject to your Terms of Business, which you should have arranged to be signed before commencing any work and prior to accepting instructions at the outset. That should be done with each and every case. If not, you may find that you are only remunerated for a lesser amount than you expect. So, make sure you have your administration clearly sorted out early. Receipts for reasonable expenses also need to be retained so these can be submitted.

When you have made the court aware of your arrival, you will be directed to the court number that is hearing the matter in which you are giving evidence. Counsel may wish to go through some points with you in relation to your report for clarification prior to your giving evidence. You will be advised as to when your evidence is likely to be needed and informed as to whether to be available in the waiting area or to sit near counsel in the courtroom, as counsel may wish for you to hear the expert for the other side and advise counsel on points in the expert's report and testimony. Bear in mind your expert evidence is likely to be a part of a number of different pieces of evidence and other areas of expertise.

The decision become involved in casework will mean that in addition to the possession of appropriate qualifications and the acquisition of knowledge, understanding and experience in the area of expertise, there will also be a need for a real aptitude in the subject area. For example, when carrying out forensic gait analysis, those who do not have a good understanding and practise of clinical gait analysis in the diagnosis and management of patient's conditions are likely to be disadvantaged. Alongside your report you will have been expected to include your curriculum vitae (CV)/resume and this would be expected to be visited in questions to you at court from counsel as part of confirming your area of expertise. Ensuring your CV/resume is regularly updated is obviously useful. Your CV could need updating since you provided your report some months beforehand, so do make sure an up-to-date version of that, including any more recent and relevant achievements, are included and sent to those instructing you nearer to the time before you attend court. Do ensure you attend to that before attending court and is not realised when you arrive in the witness box! If for one reason or another you have not had the opportunity to send your updated CV/resume to the instructing party beforehand, then take copies of an updated version with you when attending court and pass that to those instructing you. They can then ensure that it is made available for counsel for the prosecution, the defence and the trial judge and, of course, a copy for yourself.

IN THE WITNESS BOX

Now you are in the witness box. Ensure you are standing comfortably with your feet turned towards the judge and jury and turn your body to face counsel. This should help to direct your answers to the judge and jury. It may be that you are invited to be seated whilst giving your evidence, and as you find preferable. When considering the choice of standing or being seated when carrying out tasks, it could be useful to bear in mind the work of Rosenbaum et al., who showed that participants' dual tasking performance is swifter when standing compared to when seated.[21] This built on the earlier work of Stroop, which revealed function is diminished when carrying out two tasks simultaneously.[22] Other studies have shown that walking augments cerebral blood flow and counterbalances sitting.[23,24] The relevance here, for example, is perhaps when the forensic gait analysis expert is requested to view and examine CCTV and other video footage in court and respond to questions on the observations, which are often uninterrupted periods and extend for quite some time. Counsel and advocates are usually standing when addressing the court and putting their questions and suggestions to the expert.

- **Examination in Chief**

At the commencement of the expert giving oral evidence in the witness box, you will normally be referred to your report at the relevant point in the court file/bundle. In any event, ensure that you have your notes and a copy of your report/s with you. As mentioned earlier, it is normal for counsel to ask details of the expert's qualifications and experience and counsel will have read this from your CV/resume that you provided with your report.

Your testimony will start by answering questions put to you by counsel representing those who instructed you. This is known as *Examination in Chief.* Counsel cannot ask you 'leading questions' – that is a question that suggests the answer. You must be asked to volunteer the information in your report. Counsel will then probably ask you questions on what you have reported usually (but not always), in the order in which you have laid out the material in your report. Avoid the use of technical language wherever you can – both in the report and when giving oral evidence. Should it be necessary to use a technical word/s, explain the meaning of these in non-technical language, which helps the court to grasp what you mean. It maybe natural for you to use terminology specific to your area of expertise, but those around you will not necessarily have that knowledge; and if the court cannot make sense of what you are saying, then that can affect the value of your evidence. If at any stage in proceedings you do not understand a question, then simply say so, which can then be couched in other terms that you understand.

The trial judge may also ask questions of you at any time. In understanding the expert's role it is useful to comprehend how the judge approaches the evidence of an expert witness. This is summarised in *Loveday v Renton*,[25]

> This involves an examination of the reasons given for his opinions and the extent to which they are supported by the evidence. The judge also has to decide what weight to attach to a witness's opinion by examining the internal consistency and logic of his evidence. The care with which he has considered the subject and presented his evidence; his precision and accuracy of thought as demonstrated by his answers; how he responds to searching and informed cross-examination, and in particular the extent to which a witness faces up to and accepts the logic of a proposition put in cross-examination or is prepared to concede points that are seen to be correct; the extent to which a witness has conceived an opinion and is reluctant to re-examine it in the light of later evidence, or demonstrates a flexibility of mind which may involve changing or modifying opinions previously held; whether or not a witness is biased or lacks independence.

It must be clearly understood by all experts that the trial judge will probably have formed a preliminary impression of the expert's capabilities even before oral testimony begins. In that sense, the relationship between the expert's report and the oral evidence at trial is extremely close. Impressive reports lead to impressive testimony.[26]

When you are in the middle of giving your evidence and there is a rest or break in court proceedings, whether for lunch or other reasons, including overnight when you may be required to return on subsequent days, you remain on oath and must *not* discuss any aspects of your evidence or the case with anyone else, including those who have instructed you, your family or friends. Normally the trial judge will remind you of your duty and responsibility on this at the time.

* **Cross-examination**

When questions are finished from counsel for those instructing you, then counsel for the other side will have questions for you. This is known as *cross-examination* and may be more demanding by the way in which counsel approaches you with questions.

Expert witnesses must be aware that counsel in cross-examination will attempt to affect the credibility of the expert and that of the expert's evidence. Such challenges are a normal part of the adversarial legal process. Remember to remain polite at all times and do not be drawn into an argument whilst equally recognising that you may have to stand your ground with a different opinion to the one which counsel may present to you in cross-examination. The presentation of your evidence matters as does your ability to retain composure during cross-examination. An expert may come under pressure from counsel to modify or change their opinion in order to help their side win the case. If there is no reason to deviate from your report, then do not do so. Also, be aware that there could well be points that it is correct to agree on. But should your replies be contrary to what is in your report, you will need to explain any differences. Be clear with your answers. Do not *um* or *er* in your replies. Take your time and do not be rushed. Mispronouncing the expert's name or occupation; using sarcasm or seemingly patronising remarks; interrupting the expert mid-sentence; repeating earlier questions in the hope you will change your answer; questions that ask you to give a *Yes or No* answer when such an answer alone is not suitable; multiple questions delivered in the same sentence and the use of hypothetical questions, these are all techniques to try and put you off your stride.

Do not be lured into performing an examination there and then of any 'new' material that 'suddenly appears' and that you have not been made aware of nor had the opportunity to fully inspect and consider beforehand. You would need time to think about any new material, which may or may not affect your opinion. Examining such material in the courtroom in that way is simply the wrong environment and is under adverse conditions. Should you be put in such a position, then bring it to the court's attention. Such considerations are also why expert witness training is necessary in order to help prepare you for such situations and how to deal with them, if or when they arise.

It is worth the expert bearing in mind the words of Lord Wilberforce in, *Whitehouse v Jordan*,[27]

> It is necessary that expert evidence presented to the court should be, and should be seen to be, the independent product of the expert, uninfluenced as to form or content by the exigences of litigation. To the extent that it is not, the evidence is likely to be not only incorrect but self-defeating.

If you are presented with a question to which you do not know the answer, then simply state that you do not know the answer. In the 'pressure cooker' environment of the witness box, it can be tempting to sometimes feel that counsel in cross-examination is trying to trick you – and they may well be! Always take your time in listening to the question put to you, pause for a moment to gather your thoughts before answering and then reply in clear voice. Keep your replies concise and do not waffle. Do not rush your answers and do not allow counsel to hurry you. If you need to refer to or read the relevant part of your report again before replying, then ask permission to do so from counsel or the judge. Again, take your time when considering what you are going to say before delivering your answer.

Whilst it is helpful to remain calm when giving your evidence, remember to defend your position where appropriate and do so in a professional manner. Do not stray outside your area of expertise or knowledge. As per the summary in the case of *The Ikarian Reefer*,[28] 'an expert witness should make it clear when a particular question or issue falls outside his expertise'. If you are presented with such a situation which risks you going outside your area of expertise, then say so. To comment on matters outside your area of expertise affects the credibility of your evidence and not in an enhancing way. Do not give way if pressed by further attempts to try and persuade you to digress outside your area of expertise, no matter how helpful you may feel you wish to be. In the rare event that you may believe the way in which questions are put to you are rude, unnecessary or out or order, then seek the view of the trial judge, if they have not already intervened.

Should it appear that a particular line of questioning put to you is becoming overly or needlessly repetitive, then state that you have already answered that question a number of times and there is nothing further you can add. If the line of questioning persists in an unbalanced way, then counsel or the judge would normally be expected to step in. If not, then as before cordially ask the judge for direction. If you are asked in the witness box to comment on another expert's opinion on the evidence, then perhaps respectfully direct counsel to ask that expert, and not you. It was not you who wrote their report. There may be nothing wrong in agreeing or disagreeing with another expert's opinion, but make sure you have considered that before entering the witness box. Normally, proceedings in court are conducted in a cordial and respectful manner to all; it may not perhaps always be perceived that way, especially when an expert is under 'heavy-duty' cross-examination in the witness box. Defend yourself in a professional manner as needs be in the exchanges. Remember not to be drawn into arguments or conjecture and do not rise to the bait!

- **Re-examination**

When cross-examination is completed, you may be re-examined by counsel again for those instructing you. This is known as *re-examination*. This is to allow for any points that may have arisen in cross-examination to be addressed and which counsel wishes to revisit.

On completion of your giving evidence, the trial judge will release you from your duties and you will no longer be on oath. Remember, your expert evidence is usually one part of a number of different elements to a case. It is the sum total of all the evidence presented to the court upon which the jury/court arrives at its decision. Your role in giving expert evidence is in your area of expertise and not in others.

APPEAL

Following the verdict, which may well be days or weeks after you have completed giving your evidence, there may in some cases be an appeal against the court's decision. If an appeal is allowed, then the case will go before the Court of Appeal in the jurisdiction. The appeal may be on one or more areas and not necessarily about your evidence. An appeal will normally be heard by a small group of judges. In some cases, an expert witness may be required to attend the Court of Appeal to give oral evidence and on other occasions may be requested to only submit written material, or not be required to attend at all as is often the case. Should you be needed, you will be notified. If a party remains dissatisfied with the outcome, then it may be that the matter is considered by the Supreme Court, the most senior court in a jurisdiction.

SUMMARY

Your ability to perform well in court will be dependent upon a number of factors, and the feedback on your performance in court is useful. In any event, all experts should have appropriate training and experience and ensure they maintain an up-to-date curriculum vitae/resume giving details of training, experience and qualifications.

In addition to their regulatory bodies in law, healthcare and medical practitioners may have memberships of professional organisations with whom they are affiliated in relation to their clinical or forensic practice, or who provide their professional indemnity insurance for expert witness work. A regulatory body and membership organisation perform different roles. Indemnity insurance for clinical work may be separate to the indemnity insurance needed for expert witness work, so check. The need for expert witnesses to have indemnity insurance is a must. This follows the decision in *Jones v Kaney*[29] [2011] of the Supreme Court, which overturned the Court of Appeal's ruling in *Stanton v Callaghan*,[30] thereby removing expert witness immunity from suit.

It is understood and accepted that expert opinion evidence varies and that experts can and do naturally have differences of opinion. However, when such experts' opinions on a matter are very opposing in their views, then reasons for that should be explored as it is helpful for the experts and courts to narrow the issues wherever they can. Joint statements can be provided by experts when instructed to do so, to help with such matters. Experts are there to help the court on matters in which a person would not ordinarily be expected to possess knowledge on. Remember that as an expert you are not there to take sides or to 'judge' the matter in question. Eyre and Alexander,[31] address matters in their extensive text and experts should not attempt to act as advocates.

Although jurisdictions may have different legal systems, it is a necessary practice for an expert witness to always maintain objectivity, impartiality and a balanced approach on matters which they are instructed. There is an expectation the forensic expert will be ethical when conducting their duties and responsibilities. The culture of surgery, for example, is an area fervently steeped in ethics, and surgeons can regularly face and resolve ethical predicaments, which may simply be part of the usual daily routine.[32] The examination of evidential material, the provision of reports, presenting opinions at court, dealing with the relevant personnel, investigators, counsel, lawyers, plaintiffs, defendants, judges and juries are all significant considerations for the dutiful and responsible expert.[33]

SOME FURTHER POINTS TO CONSIDER

- No matter how experienced you may feel you are, no one is infallible. Whilst being confident in answering questions in your subject area of expertise is helpful, do not display an 'overconfident' manner as that may be misinterpreted.
- Counsel are masters of language, but as an expert you are the one who should have greater knowledge about your subject area. That is why you are regarded as an expert in your area.
- Giving oral evidence in court is a particular skill which can be learnt. As with many areas, some will naturally be more suited to doing so than others, and with experience one gains a greater understanding and becomes a better practitioner. Remember, some cases will be more difficult than others. Just because one case appeared to go relatively smoothly when giving your evidence, it does not follow the next one will be the same. Preparation is always important.
- Being able to explain your subject in a straightforward and uncomplicated way greatly assists the court in understanding your expert evidence. Consider those listening to your evidence in the courtroom – it is not the same as speaking at a professional conference where your peers understand the technical terminology.
- Your evidence will not be the only evidence that the court hears. It is important not to concern yourself with other areas and to stick only to your role and your instructions. Remember, your duty and responsibility is to the court, to help understand your evidence and your area of expertise.

REFERENCES

1. Bond, C; Solon, M; Harper, P; Davies, G. 2007. *The Expert Witness - A Practical Guide*. Third edition. Shaw and Sons: London, UK.
2. Academy of Medical Royal Colleges. 2019. Acting as an expert or professional witness. Guidance for healthcare professionals. https://bit.ly/38KzbIm [Accessed 20 February 2020].
3. Bond Solon Wilmington Professional. 2019. Acting as an Expert Witness - New Guidance for Healthcare Professionals. https://bit.ly/2Nvnrml [Accessed 20 February 2020].
4. Criminal Procedure Rules. October 2015 as amended April 2018 and April 2019. Part 19. Expert Evidence. https://bit.ly/2AGjkL7 [Accessed 20 February 2020].

5. Criminal Procedure Rules. Criminal Practice Directions. April 2019. https://bit.ly/2KNAIoM [Accessed 20 February 2020].
6. Civil Procedure Rules. Part 35 - Experts and Assessors. http://bit.ly/1tDEIKz [Accessed 20 February 2020].
7. Civil Procedure Rules. Practice Direction 35 - Experts and Assessors. This practice direction supplements CPR part 35. http://bit.ly/2daQCF7 [Accessed 20 February 2020].
8. Forensic Science Regulator. 2016. Information. Legal obligations. FSR-I-400. Issue 4. http://bit.ly/2CK5yY5 [Accessed 20 February 2020].
9. Forensic Science Regulator. 2017. Codes of practice and conduct. *For forensic science providers and practitioners in the Criminal Justice System*. Issue 4. October 2017. http://bit.ly/2Arh0FY [Accessed 20 February 2020].
10. Forensic Science Regulator. 2014. Guidance. Validation. FSR-G-201. Issue 1. http://bit.ly/2CsF2kO [Accessed 20 February 2020].
11. Forensic Science Regulator. 2017. Guidance on the content of reports issued by expert witnesses in the Criminal Justice System in England and Wales. FSR-G-200. Issue 1. [Archived 14 February 2019]. http://bit.ly/2Bujqnq [Accessed 20 February 2020].
12. Forensic Science Regulator. 2019. Guidance on the content of reports issued by expert witnesses in the Criminal Justice System in England and Wales. FSR-G-200. Issue 2. [Archived 17 April 2019]. https://bit.ly/2xna1P4 [Accessed 20 February 2020].
13. Forensic Science Regulator. 2019. Guidance on the content of reports issued by expert witnesses in the Criminal Justice System in England and Wales. FSR-G-200. Issue 3. https://bit.ly/323JrbO [Accessed 20 February 2020].
14. Hirson, A. 2018. *Death knell to UK Forensic Science*. Expert Witness Institute Newsletter Summer 2018, pp8–9.
15. Burrow, G; Kelly, HD; Francis, B. 2018. Written evidence (FRS0092). Submission to House of Lords Science and Technology Committee Inquiry into Forensic Science. 27 September 2018.
16. Hak, JW (Q.C.). Evaluation of the Forensic Science Regulator's recommendations regarding image comparison evidence. *Forensic Science International: Synergy* 1, (2019), 294–297. https://doi.org/10.1016/j.fsisyn.2019.07.005
17. Tully, G; Stockdale, M. Commentary on: Hak. Evaluation of the Forensic Science Regulator's recommendations regarding image comparison evidence. *Forensic Science International: Synergy*, 1(1), (2019), 298–301. https://doi.org/10.1016/j.fsisyn.2019.09.006
18. Hak, JW (Q.C.) Response to "Commentary on: Hak. Evaluation of the forensic science regulator's recommendations regarding image comparison evidence. *Forensic Science International: Synergy*, 1(1), (2019), 302. https://doi.org/10.1016/j.fsisyn.2019.10.001
19. *R v Smith* (2011) EWCA Crim 1296.
20. Voir dire. Oxford dictionaries online. Lexico. https://bit.ly/2xqcRmg [Accessed 20 February 2020].

21. Rosenbaum, D; Mama, Y; Algom, D. 2017. Stand by your stroop: Standing up enhances selective attention and cognitive control. *Psychological Science*, 28 (12), 1864–1867. doi:10.1177/0956797617721270.
22. Stroop, JR. 1935. Studies of interference in serial verbal reactions. *Journal of Experimental Psychology*, 18 (6), 643–662. doi:10.1037/h0054651.
23. Carter, SE; Draijer, R; Holder, SM; Brown, L; Thijssen, DHJ; Hopkins, ND. 2018. Regular walking breaks prevent the decline in cerebral blood flow associated with prolonged sitting. *Journal of Applied Physiology*, 125 (3), 790–798. doi: 10.1152/japplphysiol.00310.2018.
24. Climie, RE; Wheeler, MJ; Grace, M; Lambert EA; Cohen, N; Owen, N; Kingwell, BA; Dunstan, DW; Green, DJ. 2018. Simple intermittent resistance activity mitigates the detrimental effect of prolonged unbroken sitting on arterial function in overweight and obese adults. *Journal of Applied Physiology*, 125 (6), 1787–1794. doi: 10.1152/japplphysiol.00544.2018.
25. Stuart Smith LJ., in *Loveday v Renton* [1990] 1 Med LR 177at 125.
26. Blom-Cooper, L. (Q.C.). 2006. *Experts in the Civil Courts. Expert Witness Institute.* p.101. Oxford University Press.
27. Lord Wilberforce in *Whitehouse v Jordan* [1981] 1 WLR 246 at p256.
28. Cresswell, J. in *The Ikarian Reefer* [1993] 2 Lloyds Rep 68.
29. *Jones v Kaney* [2011] UKSC13.
30. *Stanton v Callaghan* [2000] QB 75 EWCA.
31. Eyre, G, Alexander, L *Writing Medical Legal Reports in Civil Claims - An Essential Guide*, 2015. Second edition. Professional Solutions Publications, London, UK.
32. Sade, RM. (Ed.). 2015. *The Ethics of Surgery – Conflicts and Controversies*. New York: Oxford University Press.
33. Bowen, TR. 2017. *Ethics and the Practice of Forensic Science*. Second edition. Boca Raton, FL: CRC Press/Taylor & Francis Group.

INDEX